CHAS THE EiGHTiES

THE ULTiMaTe NORTH AMERiCAN MoViE-LoCaTioN RoaDTRiP

Spencer Austin

KNOW! THE SCORE

TO ALL THE AUSTINS AND GREENS – THE
NANS, GRANDADS, AUNTS, UNCLES, COUSINS,
MUM AND DAD – ALL OF WHOM
HELPED MAKE MY EIGHTIES WORTH
WRITING ABOUT.

SORRY ABOUT THE SWEARING ...

For exclusive video clips, bonus chapters and more information, visit:

www.chasingthe80s.co.uk

You can also find the *Chasing the Eighties* soundtrack on
iTunes as an iMix.

© Spencer Austin. 2008

Know The Score Books Limited

118 Alcester Road, Studley, Warwickshire, B80 7NT

Tel: 01527 454482   Fax: 01527 452183

info@knowthescorebooks.com

www.knowthescorebooks.com

A CIP catalogue record is available for this book from the British Library

ISBN: 978-1-84818-951-5

Printed and bound in Great Britain by Cromwell Press, Trowbridge, Wiltshire

Contents

Disclaimer

Please note a very few
names in this book
have been changed to
avoid embarrassment.

Introduction

Early 21st century. London.

My past was *constantly* on the telly.

You know, those clip shows with appallingly contrived comments from alleged celebrities (or at least someone who once shagged someone who once appeared in *The Bill*) reading their oh so insightful and clever and witty comments off a bit of cardboard (that the researcher wrote) about why *The Dukes of Hazzard* changed the world we live in. Don't get me wrong, the Dukes did change the world, forever, but I didn't need that Kate Thornton to tell me so.

Those shows taunted us with the past, wafted the scent of the good old days under our hooters then snatched it all away at the end of the hour; dumping us back in an unaffectionate present. One minute: *Bod* was back on the screen – strutting surreally up and down a pastel colour background; the Belfast *Why Don't You?* gang once again battled through their impenetrable accents to show us how to make disgusting peppermint creams and there went Erik Estrada, epitomising cool on a bike, chest hair jetting out of his gaping shirt with ridiculously uncontrollable manliness. The next minute: some bloke with a poncey hairdo called Vernon Kay jolted us back to the present, pouring pints of "I'm mad I am" down the lens ... and it was 2004 again. I felt teased by it. I wanted to stay in 1985, wearing leg warmers.

It made nostalgia this addictive mix of ecstasy and pain, a glorious ache of longing for a past *so* smoothed over that it probably bore no resemblance to what *actually* happened. Nostalgia was my unscratchable itch: one of those prickly ones, on that unreachable part of the back or up the arse crack when you're in a job interview and bound by etiquette not to claw at it. I just couldn't get enough.

I was about to mount the plinth with "30 Years Old" painted on: and although I loved them more than cheese itself, it was probably time to grow up and leave Rubik, his silly cube, Daisy Duke and *Teen Wolf* where they belonged ... in the past. But those sickly clip shows weren't helping; they just moulded the yearning into a gizzard-strangling desire for more. I needed more than just clips. I needed *ultimate nostalgia. Extreme nostalgia.* And if I could get one last massive hit, maybe it would cure nostalgia, satisfy it before it took over my present and destroyed my future (and, as Doc Emmett Brown would claim: the entire space–time continuum).

And so born was my journey. My gargantuan, ridiculous epic and probably foolish expedition to the USA and Canada – one last marvellous jaunt into the wonderland of the eighties, and then it had to be time to start looking forward, grow up, get on with it.

Why the 1980s, above all the other decades I've survived? For people my age, the Eighties were a time when parental dependence meant not a care in the world; when people cheered as the main feature started at the cinema; when TV was a fantasy land we all wanted to visit. I would have gladly been locked in a cage and had buckets of water lashed into my face by, of all people, Chris Tarrant. I didn't sit at home wondering where my next pay-cheque was going to come from – my biggest worry was that Sherbet Fountains might tip the 10p mark or that Tucker would leave *Grange Hill.* God forbid.

I don't want to downplay the nineties, but for me they were a time of zits and part-time jobs for a pound an hour. And the seventies were just too distant a memory – being wheeled into an operating theatre to be circumcised is my most vivid recollection of that decade. It *had* to be the eighties. Not a touch of acne or penis mutilation in sight. They were *my heyday,* and I missed them.

I wanted to find the places where my eighties were made. I wanted to sit where Harry and Sally sat, to feel like J.R. at Southfork Ranch and to have a chat with Johnny Five (because he *is* alive you know). My pilgrimage to the locations from famous eighties movies and TV shows was to be a celebration of the past in the present.

Though I'm no psychologist, I had a theory. If you'd given my brain a verbal trigger of *The Goonies* – for example – *before* this trip, I'd recall the times I sat watching the film in the eighties: with a can of Quatro and the Peanut Marathon. But *after* the trip, I'd expect to recall not only the film, the

Quatro and Peanut Marathon, but also the time in 2004 that I went to the house in Oregan where they filmed it and did my own version of Chunk's "truffle shuffle". By updating my recollections of the *The Goonies,* I would have bypassed the sad bit of nostalgia that makes you feel like you've lost something, and made it all a part of my past *and* present. I would *beat* nostalgia at its own game. I would scratch the unscratchable itch. I would achieve the ultimate nostalgia buzz, an unassailable eighties high. At least that was the idea.

Three months was the estimated time of this operation: Three months off work, three thousand pounds, a car, a Tom and a Luke. This job needed a team; it was too big a mission. An American might say I needed an emotional support network: I'd probably say I wanted to take my mates. Unsurprisingly, all three of us were single boys, all on that unstoppable juggernaut towards thirty.

Tom Thostrup is a nervous, wiry, Essex-based worrier, a Cambridge educated brainy boy who probably operates better in a theoretical world than the real one. Tom dithers and stutters and I generally get annoyed with him, but actually, he hasn't got a bad bone in his body. Apart from his knee, which is fucked. Importantly, he's an eighties obsessive, but perhaps not with quite the same objectives as me. You see, although these movies are universal in their appeal, everyone has their own nostalgic pulse; their own personal passions and memories. Tom's aim on this trip was to get photos, to be able to say he'd done it, to extend and *prolong* his eighties life. Although my aim was also to celebrate those times, ultimately I wanted to draw a line under my nostalgia. Overall though, our paths crossed at the simple fact that we *love* this stuff and *needed more.*

Luke Dolan didn't join us until Chicago – a couple of weeks into the trip. Even though I've known Luke even longer than Tom (ten years), the pair had only met once before the trip. But it wouldn't have mattered if we'd been three utter strangers – we had a very common language binding us. Luke is from Wimbledon; he's tall, thin and has a very silly sense of humour. What a card. What a laugh. Oh, the voices and impressions. Luke and I descend into sheer stupidity when we're together, utter nonsense. This annoys Tom. Luke unashamedly came on this tour for the sheer fuck-off-ness of it, the near-wee excitement of getting so close to the coolest films ever.

And then there's me. I think too much. I grew up in Walthamstow and it's still there in my accent and all over my sleeve. I've worked in the lunatic

TV industry – along with Tom and Luke – for ten years and as a Producer (on entertainment and comedy shows), have had to deal with the dreary *me me me, what about me* egos; the talentless politicians who squirm their way into high positions and revel in telling you what to do without *ever* looking you in the eye; the agents who can maintain a constant cocaine-shout grimace for up to 48 hours and the channel commissioners who are permanently petrified that their contract will be terminated because only six people watched *Celebrity Toilet Eating* and they'll have to cash in the Lexus. And the blame, for most stuff, always falls down to the *producer*. And that's me. Whatever I do, I'm to blame. I'm sorry about *Celebrity Toilet Eating*. But if I do well, out pop all those same people to claim their glory and my God how well they did, *despite me*. Lose-lose. This is not glamour, folks, not these days, it's a sordid *I want more than you* bunfight, and in 2004, I'd had it up to my gizzards. Fact was, I didn't want to be the person you needed to be to go far in that world, and I needed to get away. So there I was, ten years after falling into an industry I didn't mean to fall into, wondering how I was suddenly twenty-nine, disillusioned and spending more time thinking about the glorious past than the stupendous possibilities lurking in the present or future.

So, "Bollocks, why not now?" we said let's go and do it, let's go and have the nostalgia experience of a lifetime.

With Luke intent on riding the crest of our research wave, Tom and I bothered the Internet, bought books, phoned blokes and harassed agents, trying to unearth the bones of our 1980s. There were turned stones strewn everywhere. Tom did a lion-share of the research; his diligent brain and robotic attention to detail combed the scalp of every extra, tea-maker and Fifteenth Assistant Director still alive (he even called some of the dead ones, who were furious). No money was offered to anyone – we didn't have any – our subjects would all be goodwill participants who found enthusiasm for our project through our passion.

Our itinerary took two months to assemble and comprised visits to locations and cast from universally nostalgic movies and TV shows, as well as some slightly more personal hankerings that tickled our individual wiggle muscles. We even planned to shoot the thing as a documentary, so our evidence couldn't be scoffed at. "You met Hightower from *Police Academy*? Yeah, right..." We could just hear them all down The Dog and Duck.

Another layer of nostalgia inadvertently (but maybe subconsciously) loaded into this trip involved a Greyhound Bus tour of the States I'd been on seven years previously. Out of pure coincidence, our itinerary matched the route of my previous tour at various points. My concern about this collision of nostalgic paths regarded an ex-girlfriend. Well, not just *an* ex-girlfriend, *the* ex-girlfriend.

Elle and I were brought together in a bizarre situation by of all unlikely cupids, Jeremy Beadle, who was drunk as a skunk at the after-show drinks for the long-forgotten second series of *Beadle's Hotshots*, and actually introduced her as his agent's PA and a "slag", and that was good enough for me. She wasn't though, and after three months and the mindless whirlwind of meeting the person you think you're going to spend the rest of your life with, we both threw our jobs on the floor and jumped on a Greyhound Bus for the tour of our dreams. That was in 1997, and after that, the *dream* lasted three years, until the accumulation of two only-children living together in a cramped bedroom and the wear and tear of maintaining a relationship while going through those many early-twenties changes proved too much for us to continue. It needed to end; there was too much life out there to live before we got ourselves into something this intense. It was one of the most painful things I've ever been through, but at the time, it seemed to be for the best.

I didn't realise until five years later that all my subsequent romantic disasters related back to the fact that I'd never quite let go of Elle, and it preoccupied me for a couple of years following that. I'd never thought that we wouldn't get back together, someday. Until, that is, one day close to the departure of this trip, she told me it could *never* happen. Up until then, I wasn't aware that I had that much of a heart to break, but there I was, sitting in the toilets of the Trocadero in London, sobbing my guts out after meeting her for a drink (for the first and only time in five years; a 'catch up', a friendly quick pint – from her point of view anyway) and being told the news I had never faced up to, even after being apart for all that time. It was gone. Finally gone. She had someone else.

The nostalgia involved in visiting places Elle and I had been to, in the throws of young love, was a different one to that provoked by movies and decades. This *really* hurt. I mean physically, like having a cricket bat wrapped round your nads ... and it needed addressing just as much. Although really, I didn't have much of a clue as to how I would do that.

So, our journey was penned to begin in Toronto, head left then down, then right, then south, north and west back to Toronto. The details will unfold, but it was a drive worth around twenty thousand miles, twenty-five interviews, a hundred and fifty movie and TV locations, blood, sweat and Corey Haim.

We were serious, this was to be one final Eighties celebration to knock your block off. Goodbye Kate Thornton. Goodbye Elle. Goodbye past. Fuck off Guttenberg.

CHAPTER ONE SOUNDTRACK:

Back in Time

Huwie Lewis and The News (1985)

Whatever Happened to Corey Haim?

The Thrills (2004)

Chapter One

Fags for Corey

London to Toronto

Two months of research, planning and stonewashing of jeans to prepare for this journey. Two months to get the blood pumping through that nostalgia muscle and now I'm ready to shelve dignity and don the sleeveless denim jacket and headband once more. Not the deely boppers though – that would be appalling.

Well, *I'm* ready. But Tom is on the M25. I don't care if he has taken great pains getting his eighties costume ready, it's no good on the piddling M25. As if my journey on the tube hasn't been enough to get my wild up. At Walthamstow Central – scene of some of my *favourite* muggings – I put a ten-pound note in the ticket machine and it gets stuck. No one around. I have a backpack bigger and heavier than one of Obelix's obelisks, and have to trudge to the other side of the station to be told in a Molvanian accent by the Station Supervisor that the ticket machine is something that he can't supervise. *Oh no no, don't try me, Putin. Don't you dare.* I supervise him that he ought to start supervising it before my hair flies off and stinking horror pus spouts out the top of my head. He concedes that this would be unsightly, disturbing, and dangerous if unsupervised, but still doesn't open up the pissing ticket robot. He could open it next week, but next week I'll be in 1984.

I need to leave the country.

I eventually wedge myself and the obelisk into a seat and get to the airport, where I look around at the mishmash of people with expectations larger than their budgets. People on mobile phones, brandishing all their love to people they admit it to once a year from the airport before they get on a plane they think they might die in. All of them are far too excited about the hotel they'll end up complaining bitterly about (because of the noise or the food or the noisy food or the noisy kids or the distance to the beach or the weather in the room and the Germans). Six months of waiting (of brewing dreams of sunny perfection) for two weeks of possible rain and drunken fumbles with *her* from Hull in Magaluf. Is this any way to carry on? We have to wait months and months to go somewhere we *actually* want to be; only to find out we probably don't want to be there either.

I definitely need to leave the country.

Tom appears: flustered, conspicuous. What in God's name does he look like? Pork-pie hat and stonewashed jeans and *that* red leather jacket. *That* red leather jacket is going to annoy me.

This plane journey is a unique one for me. When we touch down, as far as I'm concerned, I'm in my own past; I lift the lid on memory *and get in*. This plane is a time machine and my, how time machines have developed since the DeLorean. But just like any other plane, this one gives me a bulging gutful of trapped wind and tomato juice. Planes hate guts.

The time machine drops us in a chilly, grey Toronto. Tom attracts undue attention at immigration with his profuse blithering and bizarre outfit. As I sail past the officials without so much as a furrowed brow furrowing at me, Tom is on the verge of being chucked disdainfully back on a plane and told by burly Canadians with moustaches to go sell crazy elsewhere. Two cartons of Marlboro cigarettes seem to cause the problem: Tom panics about customs' limits and decides to throw one of them across the line of immigration beasts to me on the other side. This is perceived as somewhat suspicious; probably a diplomatic incident. Idiotic at best.

"It's OK," quivers Tom at the scowling man guarding the border of the country he loves, "they're for Corey Haim."

"Corey who?"

Despite the dicksplashedness we get through and collect our hire car: a great big swish looking animal they call an Alero Oldsmobile. It's shiny and long and goes, that's all I understand. I don't get cars. It'll be our home for three months and I'm sure will be returned to this very car park in a much less healthy condition, having been slung around every corner of North America like the bitch it is and sweated in by three smelly boys sometimes wearing dirty pants.

Tom negotiates the Highway 427 with a little more decorum and less blither than his attempts to enter the country; he's been brave enough to accept the first driving leg because my top lip quivered at the thought of all that *other side of the road* stuff. We head straight for one of Toronto's many little pockets. It's only possible to *amble* a car through the cramped hippy hub of Kensington Market: an area of downtown that I guess you might twin with Camden in London. Funky ethnic shops, vintage clothing stores (full of musty old tat), chilled-out cafés: all soaked in a warm, anything-goes, dress-like-a-prat atmosphere. A Chilean cafe takes its place along the street from a Hungarian and Thai fusion restaurant called The Hungary Thai – eclectic is the feel and the fact. The shops are all scrunched up together and there's an air of urban decay that's more quaint and endearing than threatening; things are old and shabby but have been painted bright colours to cover the cracks, a bit like Nan. And then up away from the majority of the bustle is the College Hostel, where we're staying. Cheap as chips.

In the room, we celebrate discovering a telephone – not sure I've ever done that – so we can use it for our first piece of digging. A few weeks ago, back in England, Tom managed to get hold of Corey Haim's home telephone number from the Screen Actors Guild. Astonishingly, he got through to the artist contact section and they bunged us his mum's number in Toronto without even a hint of stalker-alert. Until then, I hadn't realised that Corey Haim was one of those famous American actors who's actually Canadian.

Corey's movie career seemed to have spanned only the mid to late eighties and a bit of the nineties, with films like *Lost Boys* and *License to Drive*, then he fell away from public consciousness pretty sharply. I'm *still* bitter that my first girlfriend loved him more than me and had posters of him all over her room. *I hate you Haim, you powder-puff ponce... Look at you, with that smug smile she thinks is soooo cute. Well let me tell you, with your silly dangly earring, just you stay up there on that poster because if you come sniffing round my bird, I'll show you what a Lost Boy is...* First base is a tough proposition in a girl's bedroom with Haim bearing down on you from all angles. Trust me.

Corey Ian Haim was born in Toronto in 1971 and seems as famous these days for his reported plight at the hands of iffy medication as for his 1980s acting career. He began in commercials at the age of ten and it all ended up with rumours of his death flying clumsily around the Internet for a number of years – speculation that Tom can now refute on the basis of first hand experience. At twenty-six years old, he filed for bankruptcy: Corey Haim is a true example of a young man being chewed up, sucked dry and spat out by the Hollywood fame machine. I wonder if my first girlfriend fancies him *now*, all bloated and bankrupt.

Now, there have been times during our pre-production when I've thought that Tom and I may be on the verge of being completely obsessed geeks: the type of greasy-haired, wispy-tashed losers that I'm desperate for neither of us to be. So I was a tad concerned that calling Corey Haim at home might be teetering between an eighties enthusiast and a bonkers mental loony obsessive geek-nerd the third. Tom was chosen to call Corey Haim, because he's good at the disarming English gentleman; whereas I would have nervously slung something so cockney at him he might have thought I was singing a punk song.

Tom told me afterwards that Corey had been very friendly and quite happy to talk about his films and the *other* Corey, Corey Feldman (who he referred to as 'The Feldog'). They chatted briefly before Tom went in for the kill and asked for an interview, or at least half a lager at a neutral location. Corey wasn't sure, but felt that a donation of some cigarettes might help swing the deal. Refusing to entirely commit, he insisted that we call him again when we got to Toronto (with cigarettes).

Now we've arrived in Toronto, it's time to call Corey again to see if we can get to see him and deliver the cigarettes. What a bizarre and tragic predicament: we need to get some fags to *poor old* Corey Haim. *Not so smug now, Haim, she wouldn't want you now. Oh boo-hoo.* So at the hostel, Tom's voice is all flaked and warbly with nerves as he speaks to this Hollywood has-been who's clearly reluctant to get involved in our sentimental folly. And I can't really blame him; he must get all this crap every single day of his Haimy life.

"Hi, is this Corey?"

Corey replies, but I am helplessly too far out of earshot to catch what he says.

"Hi, this is Tom, from England. I spoke to you a few weeks ago," he continues, with that sloped pitch at the end of the sentence that makes it sound more like a question. I hate that. I blame *Neighbours*.

"How are *you* doing?"

More sure now, Corey must remember him. We're in.

"I'm not too bad, erm, I'm just calling because myself and, erm, Spencer have arrived in Toronto and erm, I just wanted to give you a call and, erm, see you if you were OK to hook up some time briefly?"

Hook up. Like it. Smooth. Leave off with the "erms" though Tom, you sound like a Fiat Panda at an MOT fail. I've no idea what Corey replies with, but Tom's frown grows and it doesn't seem good.

"Oh no, it can be whenever, I mean, we're here until the first. And ... erm ... we'd thought about taking in a Blue Jays game and erm, whatever's convenient really."

Come on, Tom, he's not going to come to a four hour sports event with us. We'll be lucky to get a nod in the street. If I sat next to him for four hours, I would definitely have to have it out with him over my first girlfriend. Man to man. Tom looks at me puzzled and shocked.

"Erm ... next week, erm..."

Uh-oh, he's not far away from hyperventilating. Breathe Tom, breathe. You're just having a Haimxiety attack, it's fine, just breathe.

"...is Monday, is that erm...? After one o'clock on Tuesday. Erm... is there any chance? ... Erm ... I think Tuesday I think that was when we were actually scheduled to go into the US. Is there any ... any chance of doing it on Monday? Or..."

Blimey Tom, now you're politely standing *him* down. Tom's eyeballs are wide and I think he might blood clot right in front of me.

"OK, OK, great. Brilliant. Well, I'll give you a shout then. Bye."

Down goes the phone.

"Tuesday after two. He's got a lot of shit going on this week. But he did say Tuesday after two. Fingers crossed. Fingers crossed he'll come round. Tuesday after two."

You know what? Whatever. He lost me on "hello". I know we're a couple of weird eighties fans who want to come and stare at him all shakily, but we bought you some fags, you ungrateful deadbeat bird-stealing vampire chump.

Ambling away from the College Hostel, we inadvertently stumble upon our first movie location. *Yes yes yes, it's here, fandabbydozy, crush a bloody grape, get in son*, the hairs on the back of my neck rise, statically charged and mane-like. I practically have a "Hoxton Fin" on my neck. I grin with the gappy goof of an eight year old with missing milk teeth and no-one says a word because they're used to head-nutters round here. We stand in the middle of a riot scene. Well, not right at this moment, I haven't really got the riot gene, but had we been here twenty years ago, we would have seen characters from *Police Academy* being chased by a massive angry mob – all clad in denim and bandannas, pulling the "angry-smirk": a facial expression – half attempted rage, half embarrassed grin – that only unconvincing extras can perform...

POLICE ACADEMY (1984) (Movie)

Director: Hugh Wilson

Writers: Neal Israel, Pat Proft, Hugh Wilson

Producer: Paul Maslansky

Cast: Steve Guttenberg (Cadet Carey Machoney), GW Bailey (Lt Thaddeus Harris), Bubba Smith (Cadet Moses Hightower), George Gaynes (Comdnt Eric Lassard), Andrew Rubin (Cadet George Martin), Donovan Scott (Cadet Leslie Barbara), Leslie Easterbrook (Cadet Debbie Callahan), Michael Winslow (Cadet Larvelle Jones), Marion Ramsey (Cadet Laverne Hooks), George Robertson (Chief Henry Hurst), David Graf (Cadet Eugene Tackleberry), Kim Cattrall (Cadet Thompson)

Notes:

The *Police Academy* dynasty began in 1984, and at the time of writing *Police Academy 8*, *another* bloody sequel, is possibly in the making. The first film is the story of a disparate bunch of bad eggs, desperate souls and hopeless losers coming together for the "good" of the community; becoming bumbling but well-meaning police officer trainees ... with *hilarious consequences.*

The original star of the series, Steve Guttenberg, bailed out after only four films, despite *Police Academy* previously having been perceived as *his* platform (although it's rumoured that Michael Keaton, Tom Hanks and Judge Reinhold had been among Maslansky's original choices to play Mahoney).

I remember watching the first movie *every* night after school for three weeks and although the films seemed to have lost the public's respect as the sequels stacked, and the fact that watching the films as a (sort of) grown-up makes you wonder quite what you found so hilarious as a kid, most people still seem to look back at the original two or three corny debacles with great affection.

I still want a "bun in the oven" T-shirt like Mahoney had. (Yes, that's a birthday gift hint).

So, in the film, you see a street corner during the riot scene (actually on Kensington Avenue) where the angry-smirking mob emerges. We found the corner by chance; the big give-away is a sign up on the side of the building saying "Nuts", which is still there, old and weather-beaten now. I leap into *silly-sodsville* and imagine the film crew taking over Kensington Market for the day. I see the fake Latino love-god George Martin (Andrew Rubin) walking down the street holding a stolen television for an oriental lady he's hitting on. There he is.

I am there.

In my head I now see this scene from behind the camera, in 1984. I feel a part of it, like I'm involved in the film. The shops are all boarded up, the streets are desolate and dangerous, full of graffiti and fear. Round they come, pulling the smirk, *pan left mate, that's it, aaaaaand cut. Thanks everyone, that's a wrap. Same time tomorrow please.* I wake up to reality, the riot street colours itself back into the swarming scene of today: I'm standing in the middle of a bustling market with a dry gaping gob, looking ever so simple as all sorts of people bundle past – all pierced and tattooed. It's different now.

Here is a piece of nostalgia translated into something that now maps in my mind to an event existing in the present. I feel my brain synapsing away like those clicky things that light a gas stove, as semantic links are updated and nostalgia is enhanced, upgraded into an ongoing pleasure rather than a distant loss. This theory is going to work, I think.

We go into "Nuts" – a store that sells, unsurprisingly, nuts. But they've also got a coffee shop section, and I ask the guy at the counter if he was around when *Police Academy* was filmed. A pleasant enough chap with a moustache he shouldn't bother with and one of those faces that suggests he's either not happy with life or he's got some of the store's nuts jammed up his arse. I feel like apologising to him, for everything, on behalf of the world. Perhaps he needs a cuddle. He hands over my Mocha Latte Lite and says that he remembers the filming. I sense a story and get a bit light-headed. This is all so new, yet old, it's confusing.

"Do you remember anything particular about the filming?"...Expecting a delicious anecdote about Steve Guttenberg ordering a Cappuccino and then spilling it all over Kim Cattrall and then me and Kim start kissing. Or something. Not sure how I made it in there.

"Nope. It was just a whole bunch of people chasing after each other all day," he mumbles, with the tone of someone that's just lost *everything* in a poker game (and is still pissed off that he's got half a pound of walnuts up his jacksie). I shouldn't be surprised, really, I am asking about a very short scene shot a long time ago.

He tells us that all those tough-looking punks that chased the *Police Academy* bunch around the streets were the *real* local punks of Kensington Market. He says that the scene where the mob surrounded the car and Corporal Jones (the human sound effect, Michael Winslow) made them scatter with a machine gun noise over the Tannoy was shot right outside his shop and he'd been inside watching it happen. Throughout, his face remains on the edge of suicide – clearly the honour of witnessing 1980s movie history in the making had not boosted his serotonin levels in the least. Maybe life just couldn't get any better after that.

Police Academy portrayed Toronto as a dangerous, tough and poor place. Maybe it was back then. It seems to be a trait of movies in the 1980s that cities were shown to be hubs of chaos and crime, that things were going wrong out there; it wasn't working. Without a single shot of the pride of Toronto, the CN tower – a needle-like building surely stolen from *George and the Jetsons* – it would seem the film-makers had no intention of setting the film up as *being* in Toronto. Maybe they wanted us to think we were anywhere: just any or every piece of urban chaos. Twenty years on, anyhow, Kensington Market is a much nicer place than it looks in the film, and Toronto certainly doesn't have the sort of tension *Police Academy* portrayed.

–––––––––

Tom drives us onto Lakeshore Drive, where he hopes to find the studios at which *Police Academy* was filmed. I think this endeavour is a tad futile, as we have already established from the local film commission that the studios have been knocked down and condos are being constructed in their place. "This endeavour is a tad futile," I say, accordingly. But Tom is desperate to cling to anything he can find that suggests Mahoney had stood on any spot nearby.

We drive around aimlessly for a while, snapping at each other irritably like a Cannon and Ball routine, until a grubby garbage lady by the lakeshore tells us that the flowered circle and Academy buildings featured at the beginning of the film (when the recruits first turn up to report in for duty) *might* still exist. This partially exciting news gets Tom's voice breathy like a sex line, while I remain reserved and instinctively treat information given by a lady holding a bin as potentially dubious. A short drive around the corner and we are in Humber College. Red brick buildings in the near distance start triggering flashes of scenes, and the sound of the *Police Academy* music begins teasing itself in my mind. One swift turn around a corner and there it is – something that bears at least a structural resemblance to The Academy. Yup, that's it, The Academy.

Scaffold and pick-up trucks and dust and broken brick make the recognition process a little more cluttered, but there's no denying it. Everything is still here: the circle (now without flowers on it) and the main building, looking all serious and institutional. This sort of place makes my brain smell school dinners, *I can smell boiled cabbage and Spam*. I can see the window to Commandant Lassard's office and want so badly for all the characters to be milling around in their uniforms: Mahoney winding up Harris and Hooks tottering along in high heels.

George R. Robertson played the measly but consistent role of Commissioner Hurst in six of the seven *Police Academy* films, and I arranged to meet up with the old boy through sweet-talking his agent and subsequent email contact with George himself. George is probably best known for a classic line in the first film, where he tells a sucky Carl Copeland (Scott Thompson) to "Get away from me you asshole." From outside Lusard's office, I call George to let him know where we are. *"Be straight there,"* he says, bless him, what a lovely chap, what a gent.

When George draws up at the Academy in his car, it's the first time he's been here since making *Police Academy 3* in 1986. White hair sits atop his bonce like a pile of whitest snow, and this large, well-dressed smiley man grips a tight, friendly handshake – establishing himself as both businesslike and avuncular. You instantly trust him. He's genuinely pleased to have driven thirty miles from Mississauga to meet two geeks dressed like mannequins from a Sue Ryder closing down sale.

George sits with us on the edge of the Academy flower circle wearing his genuine *Police Academy* crew cap (which he is considering flogging on ebay) and we ask about the building we're sitting in front of.

"Well this was it, this was the beginning. It was Paul Maslansky's idea originally, you know. He was doing a movie in San Francisco and saw some police academy students in the street trying to direct traffic. Everything was screwed up and he thought what a great idea it would be for a movie. They came up here to Toronto for the usual reasons – it's a lot less expensive, we've got an incredible pool of talent up here ... and we work very cheap. Canadian actors, very cheap. Don't tell any Canadian actors I said that. But it all happened here, and this used to be the Lakeshore Psychiatric Hospital."

"At the time of filming?" asks Tom.

"No, it had been closed down by then. In their wisdom, the Government decided that the people who belonged in here didn't belong in here any more so they turned them all out on the street and left it empty."

We ask George about the extent of his role in the *Police Academy* movies. Although regular, his appearances were minuscule and it must have been proper crappy for him each time the script that spanked the doormat had very few highlighted scenes.

"I was in the first six, yes, I was Chief in the first and by the time we got to six I was the Commissioner."

"You did well," says Tom.

"Oh, an incredible career!"

"How many years?"

"Six years. The first movie was supposed to be the only one I was in. But in fact after we shot the first scene in the office up here [points to Lusard's office], they wrote a whole bunch of new scenes. I was supposed to be prominent in the second one, but the director was fired three days before I got there. So all the new stuff that we were going to improvise never got done. I had a very specific place in the films. The films were really about the cadets and George Gaynes [Lusard]. I was lamenting that point one day to Paul Maslansky, and he said, 'Come on, you're the glue that holds this series together'. And in a funny way, I think what he meant was that there had to be one serious guy, always, who was so dumb he didn't know he was dumb. And that was my role. I guess number six was my biggest role. I went to *see* number seven, the one in Moscow where they shelled the parliament buildings, but as a viewer it was a disaster. The two halves of the story never came together.The first movie cost $4.5 million and it grossed eighty domestic, I mean we *saved* Warner Brothers. And we kind of set a new comedic style for the eighties. But then we went to the world too often."

"There was a lot of crazy stuff in the films ... was it like that on set?" we quiz, hoping for hysterical tales of pranks with custard pies in hats or Guttenberg playing chess in a bra.

"Not really. Nothing out of the ordinary. Everybody took it all very seriously, and I happen to believe that is the only way you can do comedy that works: to be serious about it. Otherwise you're doing camp, and we were definitely not doing camp." Well, apart from the Blue Oyster Bar bits – it doesn't get much camper than that.

"Did you make particular friends with anyone? Did you stay in touch with any of the others?"

"Not really. But every year for the three years we were here, everyone would come to our house for Thanksgiving. We had elk one year instead of turkey. We had buffalo, and something else, beaver maybe." Beaver? "We'd have this big feast, but now they all live in LA I used to talk to George Gaynes, and really George was the heart of the series in my view."

Michael Winslow's portrayal of Jones (the man who makes the incessant silly noises like the machine guns or *Space Invaders* or the funny footsteps) makes me whine with irritation, crawl into the dog's bed, curl up in a foetal ball and whimper at how I hate his inclusion in such a classic film. I know many won't agree, he's pretty popular after all, but I personally think he simply shouldn't have been there. Mind you, if I could reproduce his noises, it would have given me a surprising cache to increase my popularity at school from zero and I might be more forgiving, but no, I can't even do an impression of myself let alone a comedy squelching boot. So in short, I don't like him and I'm determined that we wheedle something to that effect out of George, just to give me piece of mind that maybe I'm right: he should never have been there.

"Michael Winslow – was he always doing the voices on set?" I probe gently, testing the waters.

"On set, off set, in his sleep. Michael Winslow *does voices*."

"Did that annoy you?" Come on George...

"Just a teeny bit, yes, it did, to be honest." Yes!! "Michael's a terrific guy, but yes, he did. However, whenever we made a new movie, the first person they'd send over to France or Italy to promote was Michael. They loved him; they thought he was the greatest thing. But it is kind of limited..." Brilliant. Vindicated. A bit.

Being in his seventies, George is prone to long stories that end up somewhere seven miles of fascinating. I hate being seven miles away, but old men are entitled to witter a little. We mention his role in one episode of the Canadian kids' TV show *The Littlest Hobo*, a fact I am excited to ask about. *Shit almighty I loved that rancid old mutt, here boy, here boy, solve the murder boy. Please don't go boy, stay boy. Oh, balls to you boy. Maybe tomorrow you'll want to settle down.* But this leads to an endless tale of a friend of his who appeared in *Lassie* once, so we ditch the Hobo – just like he did to some poor sod every week. However, back on track, one story he tells us about the *Police Academy* building has me feeling a little edgy about being here.

"Down in the basement are the prison cells for the criminally insane, while they're on their way to wherever they put criminally insane people. There's a room down there that the paint man on the movie was using to store all his paints in. The sets were behind time, I think it was *Police Academy 3*, and so he decided he would spend all night here. And about three o'clock in the morning, he went down into the paint room and noticed that there were two cans of paint slopped on the floor. They'd fallen off the shelf. So he thought that was kinda strange. He cleared it up, had a cot brought in to hold the paints and locked the door. It's a really spooky place down there, I mean, all the memories of ... whatever. Anyway, he woke up in the middle of the night and the paint cans were flying *all over* the room. And he freaked! [laughing] He fled! Never to be seen again. It scared the hell out of most of the people on the set the next day."

Finally, we ask George if he looks back on his life and career with a smile ... hoping he doesn't think we mean he's about to expire.

"Quite honestly, at this point in my life... When I started out in New York all those years ago, I wanted to be a star. But what I really am is a working actor. It's been a marvellous life and I've had a lot of fun, and *Police Academy* was a major part of it." As George struggles back to his feet, almost toppling unceremoniously onto the ex-flowered circle (that would be an ugly, regrettable end to an interview and an old man's hip), he straightens his back, extends to a dignified height and mutters the words that send us away gleaming.

"Get away from me you assholes." And we do. Get away. Like assholes.

On the way back, Tom tries to call Corey Haim again. Voicemail. For the third time. This pursuit is becoming tongue-bitingly excruciating. Even if we do meet him now, I'm determined not to like him, or myself for this shamelessly undignified pursuit.

It's night, and considering the way we look, the dark is the best light to go looking for The Silver Dollar Room: the bar used in *Police Academy* as The Blue Oyster Bar; a gay hangout for leather-clad moustachioed brutes with a penchant for each other, ballroom dancing and not smiling much. The exterior of the place – on Toronto's Spadina Street – is unmistakable, and forces me to start humming the Blue Oyster theme: that jazzy horn section piece that simply screams to be ballroomed to. It's a gag that runs right through each and every one of the three hundred or so *Police Academy* films.

So here it is: we want to do it right, we intend to film ourselves wearing fake bikers' tashes and leather caps, so that we can say we've *done* the Blue Oyster *thing*. This seemed a good idea from the safety of four beers in a pub in Soho before we left England, but a little daunting when we arrive at the bar in costume, desperate to tell everyone walking past that we're not really gay. *Look at the state of us*. I don't make a good gay, I'm neither masculine and brutish nor feminine and pretty enough to cut the gay thing. I just look like a cellophane IT man at the Christmas fancy dress party.

We enquire sheepishly within about getting some shots of us ballroom dancing inside the bar. I can't believe I'm asking this. *Ballroom. Dancing. Leathers. Tash.* There remains an irrational concern that the regular clientele might want to ravish us, as happened in the film to Blankes and Copeland. I'm not up for that at all. However, our fears of sodomy, it turns out, are entirely misplaced. Some sort of Sunday daytime rave has been occurring, is still occurring, quite fiercely and suddenly we're shepherded into this crevice of a lounge decked out in dinge and corners you can't see, surrounded by hundreds of zombies – off their mash and vibrating vaguely to house music that apparently has been playing like this all day at Concorde sound thresholds. And it's not even a gay club.

It's dark, with occasional eye-wincing neon sparks. Writhing sweat-soaked bodies and heavy smoke are pierced by laser beams, and mass confusion reigns – all, apparently, for pleasure. We're offered substances by men with eyes that couldn't blink if Rusty Lee dangled off their lids. It's a dreadful nightmare starring three hundred *Big Brother* applicants. Just as the music begins to give me the whiplash and its juddering has successfully cured me of cellulite, a fat clammy man with a pointless ponytail and an arrogant doorman's demeanour informs us that actually, the interior of The Blue Oyster Bar was filmed at a *real* gay bar elsewhere in town and even that isn't there any more. *Relief? Disappointment? Not sure.*

This is our first taste of finding out that an exterior shot in a movie doesn't necessarily mean that the interior shots were taken at the same place and that turning up there in costume may be rash and perhaps socially unacceptable. I mean I sort of knew that, a TV producer should. But thank Christ for that, I really didn't fancy doing ballroom in front of these chemical-blooded monsters. As any good journalist should always dream of claiming: *we made our excuses and left.*

We get back and try good old Corey again.

Voicemail.

What a cunt.

CHAPTER TWO SOUNDTRACK:

Too *Shy*

Kajagoogoo (1983)

Wake me up before you Go Go?

Wham (1984)

Chapter Two

Kiss Me, Steph

Toronto

Our stomachs bulging full of polystyrene street hot dogs and deceptively heavy Lite beer from last night and our heads still jetlagged through to next week Thursday, we jump in the Oldsmobile and go location hunting around Toronto. We successfully negotiate Lakeshore Drive East, head down Lakeshore Drive West and edge the fresh bright blue glinting Lake Ontario in search of the real Degrassi Junior High.

DEGRASSI JUNIOR HIGH (1987–1991) (TV)

Created by: Kit Hood and Linda Schuyler
Awards: Won a Primetime Emmy
Cast: Nicole Stoffman (Stephanie Kaye), Pat Mastroianni (Joey Jeremiah), Stacie Mistysyn (Caitlin Ryan), Siluck Saysanasy (Yick Yu), Duncan Waugh (Arthur Kobalewscuy), Amanda Stepto (Spike)

Notes:
Degrassi Junior High followed on from an earlier series called *The Kids of Degrassi Street,* and was the brainchild of Linda Schuyler and Kit Hood, two local producers – at that time man and wife – in the Leslieville area of East End Toronto. *Junior High* was a drama that began in 1987 and followed the school lives of grade seven (up to grade nine) kids based in the area around the *real* Degrassi Street in Toronto.

In England, *Degrassi Junior High* played on BBC One until its edgy tackling of teen problems, such as clumsy pregnancy, resulted in complaints

---

and the show being shoved back to BBC Two at a later time, nearer Janet Street Porter's *DEF II* area of programming. The show spotlighted a different character's acnefied plight each week, though there was always space in every episode for cocky Italian-American mouthpiece Joey Jeremiah (Pat Mastroianni), and his sharp talking, pork pie hat-donning antics. I always remembered him for one line. 'Steph, you're so flat the walls are jealous'. Classic Joey Jeremiah. I did in fact try to contact Pat from back in England, through his website *patmeup.com,* but I didn't manage to get "Patted up" in the least. He never replied.

I felt naughty watching this show, it always toed the moral line and *Jeepers O'Reilly* did I want to be a student at DeGrassi. I wouldn't have lasted five minutes though, Joey was a real piece of work.

We'd discovered back home that the school building they used is actually The Vincent Massey School. It's not a Junior High either; it's now a language school for immigrants. The building – on tranquil Daisy Avenue – is exactly as Joey Jeremiah left it. An institutional-looking gaff with a real sense of "don't fuck with me, I'm the school" about it. Everything looks the same – the austere, grandiose doors, the long rectangle windows, the worn student-trodden lawn out front. At the top of the stairs by the entrance, just in nose-range of that institutional bleachy smell, there are holes in the wall where the "Degrassi Junior High" sign had been screwed on while they were filming. I walk up and down the stairs wearing my headband and sleeveless denim jacket, feeling just as (un)cool as those dudes in the show. Oddly, I can't stop looking at the holes made for the *Degrassi sign:* I'm drawn to them, they're actual physical evidence that the show was filmed in this spot. Back then, watching the show, I would never have guessed that a few years later I'd have my finger in a hole made for that sign. And why would I? *Dressed like Mark Knopfler. Fingers in holes in the walls of a school. Come and rescue me Mother.*

At this point, it all gets a bit too much; shivers of awe rampage down my spine, and I just sit on the stairs trying to comprehend the level at which I have visited my own past. I almost weep a tear for times gone by (and specifically for something as odd as a hole in a brick wall), but then realise

I'm a bloke and it's just not necessary or acceptable. I deem myself a big tart and sheepishly continue with slight quiver-lip, which Tom doesn't notice.

I start thinking about how school was a shit-scary place for me. I wasn't tough or a weakling, exceptional or stupid, just quite good at football and left pretty much alone by most people (apart from Lester Peterkin, who punched me a lot). But sitting here at this school for the first time, it reminds me of when I moved schools at eight years old. *The trauma, the finding new friends, knowing where to sit, what to do at lunchtime, terrifying, scarifying new kids, big kids.* I had nosebleeds every single day, three times a day at least, never knew why, just did. Touch my nose and off it went, *drip drop, nurse says pinch the top, teacher says pinch the bottom, he says head forward, she says head back ... gurgle, gurgle, I'm swallowing blood...* So maybe that's why I found a quiet solace in film and TV in the eighties. East London schools weren't easy, but the warmth and safety of a DeLorean was a delicious respite.

Meanwhile, as I sit here in this quiet, bird-chirpy little cul-de-sac, away with my thoughts, borderline weeping, the occasional language student eyes me curiously. Tom pulls me away (the first time I've ever had to be pulled away from a school) and I go back to the hostel like an exhausted medium who's had his power sapped by the demons.

Jetlag is real, it's here, and it can pay a visit at four in the morning. Youth hostels aren't fun at four in the morning, they're creaky and ominous. I cough and make short sharp noises in the hope Tom might wake up and talk to me, but instead he just gurgles away, doubtless trapped in a dream featuring himself and Scrappy Doo, solving a mystery. In the absence of company I sit and write some questions to ask one of my first TV loves, Nicole Stoffman. Nicole played the frankly slutty Stephanie Kaye in *Degrassi Junior High*, and later today we're meeting up with her. Gulp.

After some research back in England – including tracking a website that invites people to report sightings of ex-*Degrassi* actors (Nicole was spotted in the street in Toronto, which wasn't all that helpful in me finding her) – I managed to track her down through a network of cool jazz dudes on the lively Toronto music scene. I emailed websites belonging to local jazz bands and gained the information that Nicole jacked acting in after *Degrassi* and got into singing 1930s French jazz. Obviously. It's the natural progression. Often thought of it myself.

One of the jazz nutters I emailed happens to live next door to her and generously emailed me her contact details without a hint of suspicion. I could be, and am, *anyone*. But anyway, I sent Nicole an email, being very careful to write cleverly, wittily and just a bit flirtily. I told her that Stephanie was my favourite teenage slapper when I was fourteen and that it would be great if she could meet us and help bring *Degrassi* out of my eighties and into my present. I also intended to try it on with her a bit. Why not? I would never have stood a chance with someone like her back then – I wasn't cool enough – but now I can lie better.

Nicole's response came within minutes. Stephanie Kaye emailed me!

> *FROM: Nicole Stoffman*
> *TO: Spencer Austin*
> *SUBJECT: RE: UK Docco*
> *Hello Spencer,*
> *Yes, there is only one Nicole Stoffman! I'd love to meet up with you, and it just so happens that my vintage French Jazz Band, Le Jazz Boheme, will be performing at the Distillery Jazz Festival on Wednesday May 26th. The Distillery is a cobblestone district in Toronto (North America's largest collection of Victorian Industrial architecture in one spot, according to the plaque at the entrance) and the perfect setting for our interview before or after the gig, I think.*
> *Yes, I created Stephanie Kaye. All thirty-something (or twenty-something for that matter) available men who still have a crush on me from the UK with good jaw lines should send their photo and a brief synopsis of their passions in life to this email (or perhaps another email that I should set up for that purpose...?)*
> *À la prochaine,*
> *Nicole.*

Stephanie Kaye emailed me! Not only that, but she was single and wanted a man with a jaw! I have a jaw! A working one! *Oh, Steph/Nicole, at last; together at last.* I replied immediately. My mind ran riot with what "À la prochaine" might mean: "I love you my darling" or "you are handsome and impressive" or "you're the simply remarkable" or "I really fancy a lasagne". Who knew, and I didn't bother to find out because it was sure to be not as good as I'd allowed myself to imagine.

> FROM: Spencer Austin
> TO: Nicole Stoffman
> SUBJECT: RE: RE: UK Docco
> Hi Nicole,
> Thanks so much for getting back to me. Well, I'm one of those available twenty-somethings (thirty looming, ominously) with a bit of jaw line still traceable... So sorry if when we meet I go a colour somewhere in the region of aubergine.
> The jazz festival sounds cool – look forward to making more arrangements closer to the time
> Bashfully,
> Spencer.

I mildly flirted with Stephanie Kaye! As I flapped around light-headedly, Nicole replied immediately.

> FROM: Nicole Stoffman
> TO: Spencer Austin
> SUBJECT: RE: RE: RE: UK Docco
> Dear Bashful,
> Sounds great. I look forward to speaking with you again closer to the date.
> Nicole.

Stephanie Kaye emailed me! Again! And my more optimistic side forced me to believe she was flirting. Stephanie Kaye flirted with me! "Dear Bashful" ...oh, come on, she *so* wanted me.

Back at the hostel, still in the middle of the night (when I do *all* my overthinking), I start to wonder if maybe this is where I go wrong. It all seemed so fairytale: *Had a crush on her when she was on TV in the eighties and we meet up twenty years later and fall in love instantly, like wildebeest drawn by the magnetic inevitability of animal desire.* But you just can't go through life constantly looking for that sort of Mills and Boon impossible dream, and I think that's maybe what I've been doing. *Met Elle when we were young, but broke up in heartbreaking melodrama... But we get back together ten years later, oh the poetry, oh the delightful fate of it all, like wildebeest, drawn by the magnetic... Oh, you get the picture.* Life just doesn't work like that. My head knows it, but my heart's a bloody idiot. Maybe I need a reality pill, all this romance and nostalgia, all this make believe and legend.

My emails with Nicole leading up to today became a little more brief and practical, and I feel that our "relationship" has been on the wane. I decide I have to win her back, and the only way to do that is by going to a sports bar for a few beers before meeting up with her. A couple of pints of flirt-juice will do the trick. A couple, that's all, not four (or five).

I drink four (or five) pints and become *delightfully saucy.* Like Sid James.

We go to meet Nicole at The Distillery Jazz Festival on the west side of downtown Toronto. Just like Nicole promised, The Distillery *is* an old bunch of buildings that have been preserved beautifully. Cobble stones and red brick and big chimneys and big lumps of metallic mechanical relics and hordes and hordes of geeky jazz enthusiasts. The jazz fraternity seems to have a certain uniform that almost necessarily includes goatee beard, silly pork pie hat and dapper waistcoat with a pattern lifted directly from a Victorian chaise longue.

I find whom I suspect must be Nicole waiting for me at the entrance: a tiny elfin lady with short blonde hair, curled flat to her head in heavily gelled shapes – a style I'm more used to seeing worn by young black girls in East London. *There she is, Nicole, Steph, Nicole, Steph, oh God, oh Bloody Mary Julian Clary, relax, but what if she looks disappointed, what if she looks at my big fat face and laughs?* She has a guitar case strapped to her back that's larger than her own entirety. I introduce myself, and suddenly ... I'm spending time with Stephanie Kaye. It's hard to imagine that this tiny attractive woman in her early thirties who oozes class, self-assurance and hair product was the gawky under-dressed teenage girl I'd watched and palpitated over fifteen years ago.

I'm nervous, jumpy, pulsating like a slimy bullfrog and probably come across as a potential, if not practising, serial killer. I shakily introduce her to Tom and the painful pleasantries lead to us all wondering if we should just get the hell on with it.

We sit in the thoroughfare among the bustling heave of "musos" and tape the interview. It goes on for twenty minutes and I have a great time being cheeky and covertly half drunk. I begin the interview blushed and bashful, scared, but some of it forced – to cover up the true extent of my real fear.

"Pull yourself together, Spencer," she scorns. I love it.

I tell Nicole that I watched a tape of *Degrassi Junior High* recently and in retrospect, some of Stephanie's outfits were a bit near the knuckle for a fourteen-year-old girl.

"Tell me about Stephanie Kaye, because she was a bit of a tart, wasn't she?" I begin cheaply.

"You say that as if it's a *bad* thing," she giggles, demonically. "I don't know, *you* tell *me* about Stephanie Kaye."

"Well, to be honest, watching it now, you think, well, was it over the top? I mean, it was all hanging out." The beer squeezes honesty out of me like a ripe blackhead in a sauna.

"Have you seen what fourteen year olds are doing now? Have you heard of rainbow parties?" she diverts.

"No, what's that?"

"That is a party where a bunch of girls get together and put on different colour lipstick and go round giving head to different guys. And the idea is..."

"Nicole!" I'm shocked, and mildly titillated.

"The idea is that each guy wants to have a rainbow on his ... on ... his ... member. That's what a rainbow party is. That's what the little kids are up to. Relative to that? I think Stephanie Kaye's was a relatively innocent time." And to think that *Degrassi* caused outrage back then.

Nicole is my sort of girl. She's brainy and candid and comfortable with her sexuality. I am also very comfortable with her sexuality. We speak more about *Degrassi Junior High*, although she seems not to have too many memories of the show and cares little for those. I ask her again about Stephanie Kaye.

"Come on, tell me about the character." I demand. Nicole hesitates and looks to the sky.

"Erm .... erm ..." Bloody hell, she's turning into Tom "Erm Machine" Thostrup.

"Were you off your widget on drink and drugs, is that why you can't remember?"

"It's too much of an open question, I can't, I can't ... erm ... the character I guess was something that was developed in tandem with the writers, I think. I think the show was definitely a collaboration with the cast. So I guess the question would be 'what did *I* bring to Stephanie Kaye'?"

"Boobs, that's what you brought," I reply petulantly. I didn't mean to; it just came out. Now, if I knew her a little better, I might consider requesting that she gets over herself. Maybe she's over-egging the artistic triumph that she seems to maybe consider was Stephanie Kaye. As far as I can see, she was a young girl acting as a young girl – it was hardly *Nil by Mouth*.

However, Nicole wins me round again by suddenly pulling out a bag containing her *Degrassi Junior High* crew jacket (with her name sewn onto it). I manage to put the jacket on, just, and spontaneously begin singing the theme tune to the show with more passion than ever.

> *Wake up in the morning,*
> *feeling shy and lonely,*
> *gee, I gotta go to school.*

I encourage her to join me, though in 1930s French Jazz style. It seems appropriate. We're rocking now. Well, she rocks. My voice is more of a grizzle. Hers is like a pound of honey trickling down a water park flume; it's full of sexy, and suddenly ... Stephanie Kaye becomes a part of my now. Very now.

Then, a skimpy top comes out of her bag that turns out to be the very top she wore in the first episode of *Degrassi Junior High*. This can't get any better. The episode was called "Kiss Me, Steph", and after re-enacting a scene with her (I play her boring, minging friend Voula), I make sure that I do indeed *kiss Steph*. Three times. Once on the left cheek, then – on her request – once more on either side. That's three. I think for a second about stealing one on the lips (after the mild confusion of clashing noses), but the waft of a North American lawsuit is again too strong to risk. I manage to persuade her to put the old top on.

And there she is, Steph, circa 1987.

"Do you still hear from the other cast members?" I attempt to continue, not at all unperturbed by the top.

"No."

Not even from Voula [Nicki Kemeny]? She wasn't as fit as you"

"Wasn't as fit? What does that mean? Physically fit? Because I am rather well developed." Ooh, get her.

"Are you? Let's have the bicep out, come on." Out it comes. Can't believe it. It's huge, relatively.

"It's all the distance swimming."

"Really?"

"And it's the guitar playing too, and now I'm getting chilly." Coat goes back on. "I'm the artiste, and I *cannot* get a chill."

"Oh, come on. If you leave that off, I'll take my top off." I immediately regret that promise.

"Really?"

"No."

"Come on, Spencer, let's go!" She claps her hands demandingly. "It's the art of improv, you can't say no. You're blocking." And so ensues two minutes of Stephanie Kaye trying to persuade me to take my top off. I haven't envisaged this. I'm sure she doesn't really want my flab spewing out, 'but it's still made me go all unnecessary' *I haven't bloody envisaged this, I can't take my top off, spotty back, no muscles, no tan, beer gut, can't do it, can't do it, don't blush, please don't blush.* I blush, but manage to keep my top on and peel the conversation back on to her with some semi-jealous ramble about Joey Jeremiah.

"There was a lot of on-screen tension between you and Joey Jeremiah, played by Pat Mastroianni. What happened when the camera stopped? Was there a bit of, you know...?"

"Mmmmmm, you'd have to ask Pat that."

"You didn't?!" I'm outraged. Truly.

"What?"

"With Pat." How could she do this to me?

"No, no there was no romance, no onset romance." She starts chewing her lip nervously like Bill Clinton during Monica-gate.

"With anyone else?"

"No, we were young, thirteen, fourteen – that was *before* rainbow parties!"

"That's when boys are most virile." I conject really clumsily, not even believing what I'm saying, just trying to keep the conversation on sex.

"No, I disagree with that," she says with a glint I imagine is for me. It's not, but I imagine it anyway.

"So was there *any* scandal?"

"No, but there was one time when I really wanted to buy pot from Cathy Keenan [who played Liz O'Rourke] and she sold me basil. I never forgave her. I smoked it and then realised it was basil. But I don't smoke ever now. I actually don't. But I was trying back then and she sold me basil, which is probably one of the reasons I don't."

"Do you get recognised in the street as Steph or yourself these days?"

"More and more as a performer, or as a tap dancer."

"*Tap dancer*? Anything you *can't* do?"

"Errr, bake a cherry pie, or make my own tofu, or salt, or tread butter."

"Make your own salt?"

"Yes, some people make their own salt."

"What do they do, sweat and then let it dry and scrape the salt off?" I joke.

"Yes."

What? This is getting too weird, it's time I adjourn this circus of words. We say thank you and hug, careful to make it not too clingy, and as she walks away she levels an accusation that makes me think.

"You're a decadist, Spencer, that's what you are. You organise culture into decades as if they're something that actually exist."

Maybe she's right, but I'm not sure if I'm concerned by that. Should I be? Kilograms don't *actually* exist, but they're still a valid way of measuring how fat I am. How else should we group years, or indeed time itself? Furlongs? Calories? How else could we collectively remember our past without becoming confused? For a couple of minutes she puts our entire tour at risk, but I decide to override the doubt. I think maybe Nicole takes herself a little seriously. But the nostalgia is making me fancy her still... I can't help it.

We stick around at the festival to watch her band: Nicole up there, warbling away in French with that huge guitar covering most of her body so that she looks like a head stuck on top of a double bass. Another beer and I start thinking about how weird it is to be here, watching her, that girl from *Degrassi Junior High* (or at least her head), singing 1930s French jazz. I just couldn't have predicted anything of the sort back when I watched the show at home in the eighties.

On the way home, Tom's still wearing his pork pie hat and, as we walk through Kensington Market, a man sticks his head out of a second floor window and shrieks, "Hey! It's Joey Jeremiah!" I consider standing under the window and explaining to him that we've in fact just been with Joey's love interest Stephanie Kaye and she had her crew jacket and *that* top and ... but decide it's too tall a story to throw up to a random man hanging out of a window who's probably drunk, stoned or mental.

Nicole has grown into a talented, passionate woman who clearly loves what she does. You can't help but be impressed by her, and I am to the extent that I get back to the hostel and email her immediately, with drunk sausage fingers fumbling all over the keyboard like a clumsy lover, thanking her for the evening and hinting that I might like to kiss Steph properly...

> FROM: Spencer Austin
> TO: Nicole Stoffman
> SUBJECT: Wow
> > Madam Stoffman,
> > You should know that I fancy Nicole much more than I ever fancied Steph. We're in Vegas in a month or so... Meet me there and let's get married.
> > Adoringly (and yet still bashfully),
> > Spencer.

The next morning, a reply is sitting plum in my inbox, all bold and full of promise.

> FROM: Nicole Stoffman
> TO: Spencer Austin
> SUBJECT: RE: Wow
>
> Monsieur Spencer,
>
> Thank you for your wonderful email.
> How long are you in town for? I'm performing tonight at John's on Baldwin Street (that's south of the College between McCaul and Beverly). We start around 9:30 or 10pm.
> All the best,
> Nicole.

"All the best?" All the pissing best? Is that what you say to someone who's eyeing you romantically with nostalgic fancy? Well, yes it is, if you're not interested. Maybe. Anyway, I'm going to see her again! After dinner, I sit and watch TV for a while before we head out to see Nicole. Something twinges guiltily in the area of Elle, but I can't sit here thinking about bygones that want to stay bygones, can I?

Disaster strikes. And I don't even find out until the morning.

The disaster is jetlag. I inadvertently blow Nicole out in favour of the land of shitting cocking nod. Maybe it's over between us. Before I even got permission to begin even a little bit.

Meanwhile, Tom tries to call soggy old Corey Haim *one more time*, and leaves a message asking him to call my mobile.

No call.

Corey Haim has snubbed us. Officially. He's on the list. Oh yes, Corey Haim is on my list.

The next day is spent wandering around Toronto like true sandal-wearing tourists, skipping up the CN Tower for a glorious vista across the haze of Lake Ontario on one side and the sprawl of Toronto's skyscrapers jumbled together with old churches and urban scruff on the other. The grids of streets criss-cross each other and stretch off in all directions as far as you can squint. I nearly throw up on the glass floor, it's not natural being up there.

We catch a ferry out to Toronto Island: a tiny haven away from the city where people roller blade, cycle and bathe on the beach. The short distance across the lake offers a view of the city that scrunches all the skyscrapers up together with the CN Tower and the Skydome sitting in front like they're posing for a team photo.

Two years ago, I was on holiday in Toronto – sans nostalgia – and had been walking around the harbour area when this scraggy old boy on a bike stopped and asked me for some money, saying he was trying to cycle to Vancouver. He was filthy, stank of must and had the knotted calf muscles of someone who'd been cycling non-stop since the sixties. Impressed by the extent of his mission and the speed at which he spoke and spat, I gave him a couple of dollars. He went on to ask me if I knew his friend in Newcastle, who apparently had calf muscles like a Lou Ferigno bicep. I said I did, just to round the conversation off politely.

Anyway, later that day (still two years ago), I got this same boat across to the island and walking around, I spotted him again. It indicated to me that if he really *was* on his way to Vancouver, he'd made a big mistake getting stuck on an island. The old sod had conned me and couldn't stop laughing (and spitting) whenever he cycled past. That was my first meeting with "Bicycle Pete".

Two years on, and I walk around Toronto Island telling Tom about Pete, wondering if I'll see him again. Low and behold, as soon as we get across to the Island, there he is – seemingly *still* trying to work out how to cycle to Vancouver. I ask him whether he remembers meeting me two years ago, and he says yes. Of course I don't believe him; there must have been a million other mugs since then. But then he asks me if I managed to get a job, something I had told him I was going back to England to do.

Either it's a massive guess, or this grubby fast-talking mad old bugger, with white bits in the corner of his mouth and spittle flinging out every time he says "fuckin", *actually* remembers me. Out of reluctant respect, and because he's shaking my hand and won't let go, I give him another two dollars.

Back at the hostel, an email arrives from Nicole.

> FROM: Nicole Stoffman
> TO: Spencer Austin
> SUBJECT: Hi
> Hello Spencer,
> I hope you are enjoying your stay in Toronto. FYI, I'll be performing at Brassai restaurant on King, west of Spadina on Tuesday from 7-10pm. If I don't see you, best of luck with the film.
> Nicole.

Now, I know I'm trying desperately to read something into this (which probably isn't there), but could this be one more chance? *'FYI'* isn't *'really want to see you'*, but I'll take it all the same. I'll take all I can get.

The whole evening I debate internally over which novelty T-shirt to wear, which *French-jazz-friendly* body spray to smother myself in and whether I'll be cool and confident or energetic and ridiculous.

But then it happens.

Jetlag tricks me again. I am escorted off to nod again, like a criminal being taken from the dock back to the slammer. *Oh, Nicole, I messed up, didn't I?*

Fucking *bloody* nod.

CHAPTER THREE SOUNDTRACK:

Leaving Wallbrook/ *On the* Road

Hans Zimmer (1988)

Don't You Want Me

Human League (1981)

Chapter Three

Rain Nun

Toronto to Cincinnati

With the Oldsmobile packed up to its gullets in rucksacks, camera gear, 1980s paraphernalia and fags for Corey (which we'll keep, *just in case* we get back in touch with the old sod at the end of the trip in Toronto), we hatch the garage door open at the hostel and trundle out into the misty 5am streets of Toronto. We're eager to get this road trip actually *on the road*.

At Niagara Falls there's a *lot* of water being dropped over a ledge. Niagara is a desperately quaint place that even after all these hundreds of years of having that amazing waterfall?!, doesn't suit having thousands of visitors all at once. There's a vague attempt to drag people away from the falls: a little road full of fast food and waxwork museums featuring models of Elvis that look more like Shane Ritchie. Its tacky attractions go some way in spreading the masses out a bit, but I want Niagara Falls to myself and frankly, everyone else is getting on my tits. This *is* a location visit of sorts – Superman saved a kid here. It's such a *generic* location, however, that we have trouble getting really excited from that perspective.

So onwards we go. We nervously glide over the Rainbow Bridge, not even glancing across to the Falls one last time; chewing our lips and perspiring ... as the US border approaches like the gates to a holy land. I've already heard of TV people being turned away from the States, amid these times of paranoia over terrorism and, it would seem, bad television programmes being made in the country. This puts us under intense suspicion of trying to smuggle our shoddy programme-making skills over the border. I make *Entertainment and Comedy* shows you see, the scabby Chav of the industry, the hateful cousin of those trying to make worthy *films* about Chad or orphans or some brilliant new medical disorder they *of course* aren't exploiting to get attention and ultimately make money from. Still, America doesn't like inviting my side of the *"family"* in, and if they think we might come and try to knock out a quick reality show while on our holidays, they'll defend their borders like we're Mexicans.

Tom is the most nervous person I've met: even in situations that require very little of him, he manages to "umm" and "errr" his jittery way through, making even buying a pound of grapes seem a torrid ordeal. Just imagine him in a sex shop. I've noticed that he sleeps frightened too. So when the bulky looking cop at immigration singles him out, I don't fancy our chances. This could end up being a strictly Canadian 1980s tour. I half expect Tom to politely admit to some murder or terror outrage or that he's Lord Lucan.

Things look even graver when the fat pissy cop hauls me outside and savages every bag we have, discovering Tom's wad of papers relating to interviews and other bits of business we intend to carry out but have thus far failed to mention. Tom had assured me he purged his luggage of evidence. "It's all gone," he told me. Apart from, as it turns out, all of it. My frown becomes so heavy it nearly collapses onto my nose. I feel like we've stashed terror plans and have just been caught. So, back into the offices Tom is dragged. I grab him aside briefly to whisper a stern but constructive comment, something in the region of, "This is your fucking fault, don't you fuck it up you fucker." I'm not sure this helps. I'm an only child; I'm not the best at team-talks.

After about an hour of what must have been like a special edition of *Mastermind* devoted to Tom's knowledge of our trip, his own diary and whether or not his religious beliefs contravene law, he emerges looking like he's had the Rodney King treatment. It didn't get physical, you understand, it just looks like it. But seemingly, he comes out of it with tickets to the USA. We've started...and so we will finish. We high-five and I forgive myself for the sweary moment I had.

And so eventually into the US we wobble: through and out the bottom end of Buffalo and down the edge, but without a view of Lake Erie on Interstate Highway 90. Speeding is a dreadful and impossible temptation to resist, roaring along like Southend wideboys – *let's 'ave It you slaaaags,* and we begin to realise that these Interstate Highways aren't going to be much fun. *Too much time, stop thinking about Elle, she's gone, try Nicole, no no no, just don't think, just shhhh, leave out the thinking.* We face up to the painful reality that we may have to rely on a hundred radio stations all playing sound-alike adult-oriented rock dirge to keep us bemused. There's nothing to look at or talk about on these roads; they're merely carriageways of surrendered time, Bon Jovi and niggly arguments about ownership of crisps.

We storm through to Mansfield, Ohio, for a brief stop-off at a movie location that regrettably doesn't date from the eighties, but from 1994. Although we feel guilty for momentarily betraying the purpose of our trip, there is no resisting a visit to the Ohio State Reformatory – or to you and I, Shawshank. Come on, you'd do it, wouldn't you? It's Shawshank.

The Shawshank Redemption, starring Tim Robbins and Morgan Freeman, is the story of a man convicted of a murder he didn't commit. I suspect the Frank Darabont directed *Shawshank* is right up there with standards such as *Goodfellas*: in virtually everyone's top ten favourite films, but remarkably without an Oscar.

The old prison resides next to its replacement, the Richmond Penitentiary (which from the roof of the old building you can see is teeming with naughty bad men walking about in blue). It's a sorry yet proud building being protected by a small bunch of locals who adore it so much they dedicate their lives to saving it from inevitable destruction. It closed down finally in 1990, having hosted *the terrible people* since 1896. Since closure, it's been left empty and damp, a bit like Russ Abbott.

As soon as we step under the building's shadow, I feel its presence of authority and foreboding watching me. I feel all told off and guilty. It stands like a rich old man who's fallen from grace: dressed in a dirty old suit, but with a demeanour that fits his old life. We step inside and find the cell blocks: five floors of tiny cells covered in iron bars that are lit only sparsely by the sun barging through narrow windows covered in grubby muck. The silence almost echoes into itself, with only the odd flap of a pigeon wing to confirm we're not paused in time. It's an utter mess, but so so spectacular and striking that one can't begrudge the elements taking their toll. Flaky paint is the theme of the place (apart from the bits makers of the film *Airforce One* repainted in 1996 to serve their purposes), great dangling shreds of it. The cells are tiny, filthy, with graffiti all around, horrible wire beds and walls staring you out like they own you. Even the weakest of imaginations can go racing off to an alternate reality where *you are* the criminal. *I am doing time for Grand*

Larceny (I didn't do it, I don't even know what it is), and while not happy about being in the slammer, am enjoying a rampant affair with Kelly Brook, who surprised everyone by turning down a job on EastEnders to take the job as Chief Warden at Shawshank.

Unlike Tim Robbins, we don't have to crawl through three miles of tunnel dug out with cutlery to eventually emerge in a ditch almost drowned in turd just to get away from *Shawshank,* but we do have to run to the car because it's raining. We escape quickly, still consumed with the guilt of a non-eighties excursion. We speed through grumpy storms in Columbus, to reach a dingy motel in Cincinnati with time enough to do some really good sitting down and wishing that we'd booked a cell at the prison instead.

Our single day in Cincinnati has to be a flash bang wallop affair to fit in all our scheduled escapades. This is where our strangle-tight schedule really kicks in and we realise that at some point over the next three months we might start feeling the pace and end up at a small place called "the brink". But for now, with infantile enthusiasm intact, we go for early morning coffee at Pompilio's Bar in Newport, which sits on the Kentucky edge of the Ohio River.

Pompilio's is where Tom Cruise (as Charlie Babbit) took Dustin Hoffman (as Raymond Babbit) for breakfast in the film *Rain Man.* Most people will remember this scene as being the one where toothpicks are dropped on the floor and Raymond is able to use his autistic "talent" to count them, super-fast. Toothpicks being dropped on the floor seem a slender claim to fame, but one that the owners of *Pompilio's* cling to passionately.

RAIN MAN (1988) (FILM)

Director: Barry Levinson
Writers: Barry Morrow, Ronald Bass
Producers: Peter Guber, Jon Peters
Awards: 4 Oscars (Best Actor – Dustin Hoffman, Best Picture, Best Director, Best Writing, Original Screenplay and 4 other Oscar nominations). Another 13 wins and 19 nominations
Cast: Dustin Hoffman (Raymond Babbitt), Tom Cruise (Charlie Babbitt), Valeria Golino (Susanna), Gerald R. Molen (Dr Bruner)

Notes:
Rain Man was reported to be Princess Diana's favourite film. Oh, the honour. Barry Levinson had originally intended for Raymond to be happy but dim, but after Jack Nicholson and Robert DeNiro turned down the role, Dustin Hoffman came on board and managed to persuade him that autism would be the way to go. In fact, it's reported that Dustin had wanted Bill Murray to play Charlie, and just to spin the *Rain Man* casting story into an even thicker web, Randy and Dennis Quaid were originally down to play both lead roles. I wonder if Diana, Queen of Hearts, would have approved.

Newport is white-trashville: mullets and missing teeth and the distinct ming of whisky breath being herred across on the same lung of air as a friendly "Good Morning." It does seem friendly and relatively happy, however.

Tom has already phoned and arranged with the manager to visit the bar so that we can pay homage and film some bits and pieces of us inside. We arrive to find a big fat hairy man sitting at the bar: seemingly the owner and seemingly not bothered if we wander around the place doing whatever we fancy, even though it hasn't even opened for business yet. That suits us fine.

Pompilio's oozes old-fashioned charm; with a spectacular dark wood bar in the front half that dates back to the 19th century and carries the scars of a million drowned sorrows. The bar is lit mainly by sunlight streaming miserly through leaded windows, with the occasional puff of cigarette smoke getting caught in the beams to create the lazy haze that only seems to hang in bars. The tired mosaic floor tiles bear scrape-marks from the heels of generations of overworked waitresses... It feels like this gaff hasn't changed since Buddy Holly et al.

The back half – the diner section – is like something straight out of *Happy Days* (or even *Rain Man*). The tables and chairs and leather-padded booths sit in *exactly* the same positions and at the same angles as when Cruise and Hoffman filmed in 1988. The shiny silver telephone from which Charlie Babbit calls *Wallbrook* (Raymond's institution) is still here... In fact, everything is so intact that it's like walking around the actual set.

There are Rain Man posters, signed photos, souvenirs and memorabilia hanging off any hook and sitting on any ledge available. They'd have *Rain*

Man DVDs hanging round the waitresses' necks if it didn't contravene union regulations. On one wall, there's a huge 3D cushion sculpture that, despite being vile, interestingly depicts various parts of the movie and has the *actual* toothpicks they used in the film glued to it. If Pompilio's is the church of *Rain Man*, then this ugly piece of quilt art is the altar. It's sweet that someone's gone to the bother, but it's no oil painting. It's quilt art.

As we film ourselves flouncing around doing really bad *Raymonds and much uglier Charlies*, T.J. – the porky chef with a bonce bigger than a football – eyeballs us from behind his two-foot forehead. When the camera stops rolling, he admits without any external evidence of emotion that he's incredibly jealous of our mission. If he really does find our antics amusing, he hasn't let his face know. But it's nice that he felt moved to climb over his machismo and show some admiration towards us. You get the sense it doesn't happen much.

After Pompilio's, we pull up to St. Anne's Convent, which was used in 1988 as Wallbrook – the institution where at which Dustin Hoffman's character lives in *Rain Man* (and which Tom Cruise telephoned from Pompilio's). It's as impressive a building to the naked eye as director Barry Levinson endeavoured to portray it on screen. Beautifully kept gardens occasionally drag your gaze away from the main building, as the wooded pathway used in the famous poster for *Rain Man* trickles you into the arms of the convent's main entrance.

We stand in the spot where Charlie Babbit's open-topped car was parked in the film, gaping with awe at the stairs winding up to Wallbrook's immense wooden main door. The other-worldly haven we're asked to believe Raymond lives in is actually as secluded and tranquil as it appears in the film. The clouds are sparse yet fast-moving, casting occasional dappled shadows through the trees, then fading slowly as the next wisp of cloud blocks the sun's beams. The only noise breaking the silence in this spot of Kentucky paradise is that of a middle-aged man racing up and down on a lawn mower – skidding on the corners like he might once have done on a Vespa in his youth.

The building is like a big wide stately home, with big windows not too ornately framed, but brimming with grandeur; certainly a gaff to be taken seriously. I tiptoe up to the entrance like a cowardly cockney lion approaching Oz, not sure what lurks behind. Surely someone of my standing should be going through the tradesman's entrance. The door creaks open slowly and two broad-grinning nuns greet us with vigorous, almost violent kindness. Sister Lyn is clearly the boss: a tall angular woman with lips that purse oddly when she speaks. Sister Emerita is dumpier and throws her Boston drawl back and forth without much let-up. Both are lovely ladies, so welcoming ... but so absolutely exhausting. I feel we might be the only male visitors so far this century.

Until now, I've never ever met a real-life nun and can't resist the obvious gag in telling them that I might "make a habit of it". Ha ha. Ha. The ladies are polite enough to laugh as if they've never heard the habit pun before, and then I try to make sense of how my brain allowed that to pass my lips. Subsequent introductory pleasantries are exchanged, along with a few God-bless-yous, and then we're dragged from one wing to the next, back out through one, into the other, back out and then in again – being spoken at from both sides in stereo-nun at relentless pace. Sister Emerita was around at the time of filming and harbours incredibly vivid memories of the whole affair. I suspect she also has something of an unholy lust for Dustin Hoffman, with whom she admits to sharing *several* platonic cuddles, but maybe that's in my own deviant brain. Her *Rain Man* photo album includes a topless picture of Dustin, which I think appears a little more dog-eared than the rest of the photos. I wonder.

The sisters take us to all the places used in the film: the corridors, the TV room where Raymond formed his addiction to *Jeopardy*, the doctor's office they had a meeting in, and where the pond used to be. The film company actually dug the pond themselves, for a scene where Charlie and Raymond sat talking, but had to fill it back in at the nuns' request – because they didn't like the frogs or ducks it attracted. Sister Emerita says of the ducks that if they'd kept that noise up, "they'd have had to have gone up to the Heavenly Kingdom", the closest a nun could come to a death threat.

Sister Emerita is not at all shy in telling us how dour Tom Cruise had been and how wonderful Dustin Hoffman was – that is when he wasn't walking around the place as Raymond, trying to get into character. One morning, she says, Dustin was pottering around in full Raymond-mode.

"He absolutely terrified one of the nurses, like this..." She follows with an impression of Dustin's Raymond that reminds me of doing a Joey Deacon in the playground. It's the first time I've seen a nun imitate a person with learning difficulties. These nuns are shattering my previous image of how nuns are.

My favourite story Sister Emerita tells us is about how some of the older nuns kept dragging Dustin to see the chapel Dustin, a Jew, had reluctantly agreed but on the way back told Emerita, "I can *never* tell my mother."

She also feeds us some tittle-tattle about the on-set relationship between Cruise and his on-screen girlfriend Valeria Golino. Apparently, from the nun's vantage point high in the building (from which they'd gawp at the filming for hours), Valeria was seen forever hair-spraying and combing Tom Cruise's barnet. Curious behaviour from a co-star, but I guess you've got to believe a nun. I can't help thinking that this is probably the most honest Hollywood gossip you could possibly be privy to. Emerita also reminds us of Dustin Hoffman's acceptance speech when he won an Oscar for his portrayal of Raymond. He cryptically thanked "The lovely ladies on the hill". Not so cryptic now, he clearly meant all the energetic, life-loving nuns at St. Anne's.

The tour of the convent actually takes longer than the entire duration of the film itself, and afterwards Sister Lyn respectfully demands that we join the whole squad of nuns for lunch. Tom's eyes light up; he's so tight he'd swipe the food off a nun's plate if it means saving a dollar. I am a little more reluctant because Sister Emerita's incessant talking has sapped me of social energy and all I want to do is sleep it off in the car. But there's really no saying no in such situations.

It turns out that the saying "There's no such thing as a free lunch" is true, and it bites Tom right in the face. He's asked to stand up in front of a hall of nuns and talk to them about our trip. As he stands up, he looks grey, mortified, and stuffed full of free nun food. The ladies are utterly titillated by talk of our tour and Tom receives several rounds of giggles and semi-infectious bursts of applause that pitter patter back down into suppressed excitement.

We eventually tear ourselves away from the nuns of St. Anne's, having accumulated several phone numbers for "in case we get in any trouble". We've been made to feel thoroughly welcome on this trip to Raymond's institution.

From the Convent we head into downtown Cincinnati for a quick mooch around the sights. What we find though is a hollow city, closed and empty with just toothless dregs in dungarees wandering about like the day after the end of the world. It would seem that there's no life behind these skyscrapers after 5pm. Significantly though, this is the first place I recognise as somewhere Elle and I visited seven years ago. I stumble into streets that ring bells and spot bars we once sat in the windows of. It feels awful, difficult, vile. It's all so different now, but this is all the same.

Here we are, the two of us, at that bar by the big statue in the middle of the city bit. It's a sports bar, all Budweiser everywhere and pictures of famous sportsmen who probably don't drink it. We're in this big city alone, together; our dependence on each other far away from home magnified by the environment. It feels like the start of our life together; we're so sure this is it; every kiss feels like the only kiss ever, I'm so glad I found her. It's too early in the day but sod it, I'm having a beer, she's not, and we're talking about the pharmacy we were just in that had a pigeon stuck up on the nappy shelf, who would have thought it, a pigeon, in the nappies. Worth a beer to celebrate. I suddenly have a punched stomach and an elderly gentleman's life-weary wheeze. *It was here, we were here, together.* Flashes of our past whizz by, I hear her voice, remember every fleck in her blue eyes and feel her hand in mine. We'd hold hands everywhere. I try to snap out of it; this is madness, she's gone, it was seven years ago. It's so long ago, so much has happened, but I've got that nagging mistake chipping away at me, I shouldn't have let it go. I was just young and selfish, I wanted my twenties for myself, to travel, to play the field and she didn't really. She wanted me to be more committed than that stupid young me could handle ... but now? I'd lap it up. This conquering of the Elle nostalgia isn't as easy as going to Wallbrook, it's just a little closer to the heart.

With a lump the size of a Kinder Egg lodged in my throat, we drive back over the Roebling Suspension Bridge, which links Kentucky and Ohio and oddly hums as you cross over it (you can see Raymond humming along with it in *Rain Man*. We try the same and it *is* strangely satisfying: confirmed). We go back to Pompilio's, this time for some beer. We also think it might be cool just to hang out in the place and get beyond the *Rain Man* facade.

TJ the chef has loosened since the morning (with the aid of *much* beer), Joe the manager is off-duty and cracking open a bottle of fizzy red wine. TJ makes for us straight away, and I chat at his massive head and buzz cut about the details of our trip, while Tom makes friends with a regular sitting next to him at the bar: a woman in her forties or so, tucking way into the gin who ends up inviting us to stay at her home and, in as many words, help ourselves to her twelve-year-old daughter. Shocked? Yes, just a bit. I'm sure we've got this right. An astonishing offer that of course we politely decline (or, in truth, stare shocked and voiceless over for some moments). But talking to these people, I realise that there is a pulse underneath that *Rain Man* gimmick exterior; this place has soul, a community, and they're very quick to invite us in, despite the edges of that invite being slightly shady.

T.J. relaxes to the point of *also* inviting us to stay – on his boat with him and his wife (whom, he admits later, he would quite like to swap for an English girl).

"Boats are my thing," he slurs, as he pulls a gaudy anchor-shaped gold medallion from around his neck. I politely feign interest and then an argument between Tom's new friend and T.J. ensues over which home/ boat/ daughter we should go and stay with..

A lady behind the bar cooes over my accent and tells me how she's never been outside America, but once went to Santa Fe. Odd, I think, that a clearly intelligent girl hasn't had urges to travel at least a *bit*. Maybe that's small town America for you. People sit plopped at the bar in Pompilio's, haven't moved a muscle in years and have no intention to do so.

Kirstin grows on me more: her speeded up tape recorder voice and ginger curls and clear blue eyes through matronly glasses. *What am I doing?* I'm on the verge of shakily offering my business card to Peggy from *Hi-de-Hi*, to attempt to expand this fleeting meeting to a correspondence and then maybe ginger-haired kids.

Too many beers. Goodnight, God bless. Yes, I'll call you T.J., thanks lady-at-the-bar for the offer of your daughter. Thanks Joe, thanks Pompilio's for the memories.

CHAPTER FOUR SOUNDTRACK:

Oh Yeah

Yello (1987)

Twist and Shout

The Beatles (1963)

Chapter Four

Save Ferris!

Chicago and around

With beer chemicals still ganging up menacingly around the dank alley-ways of my brain, possibly making drastic challenges to my entire mental infrastructure, we pack our nonsense and head for the Interstate Highway; away from Cincinnati and up into Indiana. We zoom through lush green fields, bypass Indianapolis (with little of interest for eighties movie freaks), up into Illinois and across to Braidwood – a small, perfectly kept town that's like something out of the old computer arcade game *Paperboy*. It feels like the sort of place where an ill-kept front lawn can shatter a person's reputation among the local versions of *Stepford Wives,* who swan around in identical outfits that probably cover secret crotchless underwear and love eggs.

This is just the *start* of our two-chapter John Hughes *Chicago-athon.*

Braidwood sits close enough to (and far enough from) Chicago that a motel here can serve the city-*bound* and city-*fleeing* folk on their way through from either direction. Famously though, The Braidwood Inn served John Candy and Steve Martin as Del Griffith and Neal Page in the film *Planes, Trains and Automobiles.*

The Braidwood Inn (recently renamed The Sun Motel) is where, due to trouble with the planes, the pair of strangers had no option but to sleep in the same bed, resulting in them waking up to find John Candy's hand inadvertently wedged up Steve Martin's arse. "They're not pillows!" screamed Steve Martin; a line that most people remember from the film. "That's my arse!" would have been *my* immediate reaction, but then Steve Martin is a comedian and obviously there probably wasn't any genuine wedging *actually*

PLANES, TRAINS AND AUTOMOBILES (1987) (FILM)

Director: John Hughes
Writer: John Hughes
Producers: John Hughes, Neil Machlis, Michael Chinich, Bill Brown
Cast: Steve Martin (Neal Page), John Candy (Del Griffith)

Notes:
John Hughes scribed and directed *Planes, Trains and Automobiles* in 1987. By then, he'd already knocked out eight or so films and this seemed to have been a rare foray outside the gooey gristle of teen angst; into the world of the adult condition. Hughes uses loudmouthed Del Griffith (John Candy) as polar-opposite to reserved family man Neal Page (Steve Martin) to produce a sentimental tale exploring the comedy in how different human beings are ... while also tear-jerking us towards understanding how, at the end of the day, we all have the same hopes, fears and core aspirations.

Planes, Trains and Automobiles has a dream-team cast. The understated but angst-brimming observational *everyman* humour of Martin pairs brilliantly with the gob-open exhibitionism of Candy. And as a thirteen year old watching a pirate copy, it was the funniest thing I'd *ever* seen. *Ever.*

---

taking place. It's nonetheless a classic scene that attracts, apparently, around thirty-five movie location fans to the motel per year.

A small, amiable-looking Indian man with little English and very few front teeth greets us at reception. Despite the language gulf, he manages to convey that he only recently took over and that the motel has changed quite a bit since the film crew came – including alterations to the actual bedroom they used for filming.

I'm surprised in the first place that they shot interiors here at all. I'd assumed that a room so small must have been a set in a film studio, to allow room for the big movie cameras and John Candy's guttage. I've been really gearing myself up to have a go at Tom for bringing us to look at the dull exterior of a dull motel. But despite the drabness of an edge-of-city motel with the slight smell of damp and fags pumping continuously through the air-conditioning, this could be interesting. Even the stone-cladding outside remains as it did when the lead pair sat outside waiting for a ride and it's easy to imagine the crew being here.

After a little bit of semi-charming hustling, inane grinning and Tom's endearingly desperate (bordering on hysterical) pleas, the man agrees to show us the bedroom they used for the "they're not pillows" scene. We soon realise the man's reluctance has been because the bedroom in question is now *his living room*. Also, the front desk they approach in the film when they first arrive is now *his kitchen*. I feel a twang of guilt that we've bullied our way into this toothless man's life and brazenly filmed all over it.

It's even more fist-swallowingly awkward when Tom (who, bless him, hasn't always got the greatest ability to sense the incongruity of his actions, or the subsequent tension it can cause) wedges himself in the man's shower cubicle, wearing dirty shoes and a down-to-business face, telling the camera how Steve Martin had stood in the same spot twenty-odd years ago. The gentleman stands by, looking mildly raped. I have no luck in using the moment to conjure images of Steve Martin in my mind – I'm just harassed by non-commissioned mental snapshots of the little hotel owner soaping himself down, generously lathered in Summer Fruits Radox.

The bedroom itself is still recognisable, but we don't linger because there's really nothing spiritual to gain here. It is what it is. We quickly check back on a tape of the movie and see that the window is in the same place and by Jove, is the same shape. I ask the man, who has begun twitching erratically from our barbaric disruption, if he minds people coming round asking to see the room.

"Yes," he confirms succinctly and without a smidgen of doubt or aggression. It's just a "yes". We leave immediately, with apologies and smiles straining through the guilt and the shame. It feels like a burglary, this particular location hunt.

We arrive in downtown Chicago and take up residence at a hostel near Lincoln Park – a quiet, wealthy area that doesn't feel as though it ought to have a youth hostel plonked in the middle of it.

Chicago is a bully of a city. Everything hangs a shadow: a reminder of quite how tiny and silly I am. Buildings stand narrow and lofty: dark, gothic, historic and important. Chicago is grimy and chippy at the same time as being fresh and chirpy; while the people get on with being gruff and friendly. A city of contrasts. We park our car in the same lot (60 Randolph Street) that Ferris

Bueller and the gang parked at in *Ferris Bueller's Day Off* – checking the mileage on the clock before we leave, secretly hoping that the valet will take it for a cheeky spin, just like in the film.

FERRIS BUELLER'S DAY OFF (1986) (FILM)

Director: John Hughes
Writer: John Hughes
Producers: John Hughes, Michael Chinich, Tom Jacobson, Jane Vickerilla
Awards: Nominated for Golden Globe
Cast: Matthew Broderick (Ferris Bueller), Alan Ruck (Cameron Frye), Mia Sara (Sloane Peterson), Jeffrey Jones (Ed Rooney), Jennifer Grey (Jeanie Bueller), Cindy Pickett (Katie Bueller), Edie McClurg (Grace, the secretary), Charlie Sheen (boy in police station), Ben Stein (Economics teacher)

Notes:
Just one year before Del and Neal fisted each other at The Braidwood Inn, the prolific John Hughes mugged other locations around his beloved Chicago while directing *Ferris Bueller* – another of his self-penned screenplays.

Ferris, played by a cheeky young Matthew Broderick, was everything I wanted to be. He drank, he kissed girls and he constantly outsmarted and usurped the olds, the stiffs and anyone else trying to constrain his desire to go wild teeny-style. These were the eighties after all, and Ferris and I wanted a piece of that.

Of course, with Hughes being a responsible thirty-six year old, he couldn't let teenies leave the cinema thinking that Ferris et al. could steal cars and dance embarrassingly at street parades without *some* sort of moral penalty. Ferris' mate Cameron (the gawky Alan Ruck) wrecked his father's car, which led to that feisty soul-searching moment in his dad's garage where he and Ferris start to work out who they are and why everything they've done in the last hour and a half is wrong. With Hughes, unlike life, there's always a moral lesson to account for any wrongness he created along the way. But despite the eventual lesson, everyone knew back then that Ferris Bueller was the coolest kid in the history of the planet, and we all knew the moral conventions of movies were the must-add bit – to neutralise the letter-writing tendencies of eavesdropping parents – that we all ignored. We wanted to be badass like Ferris. End of.

Until 1997 – the year Elle and I visited Chicago – the Sears Tower was the tallest building in the world. The tower offers mighty views of the city jumble that piles up to the cold blue edge of Lake Michigan. It was built between 1970 and 1973 and stands at 1,454 feet tall, which if humanised, would equate to 256 Matthew Brodericks standing on top of himselves. Fact. I worked it out.

We jump aboard the elevator for an ear-popping journey one hundred and three floors up. At the top Tom and I lean on the glass with our foreheads pressed flat against it and look down – just as Ferris and friends did in the film at the beginning of their day of school-bunking insanity. Directly below me is death itself. I'd probably impact on that car park. I imagine one of the spaces has words written in that white car-park floor paint saying "Spencer's Squashed Body Here". Vertigo will do that sort of thing to you. Chicago busies itself as far as the eye can see, the tiny little cars pootling along and the people all milling with buildings seeming to all lean over each other, making the whole thing look an enormous mess. We're strange, us humans. Spread out, for crying out loud, just spread out! Vertigo and its best friend nausea nearly get the better of my nerves, and I swear never to play a building like the Sears Tower at its own game again. Especially when I have a pound and a half of cinnamon donut camped in my gut, drenched in sick juice and struggling for an exit. While collecting control of my stomach and its cinnamonny urges, I stare out towards Lake Michigan and spy a spot on the water's edge where all those years ago, in the most perfect 5am snow, I'd been before.

Elle and I are walking glove-in-glove under the misty winter silhouette of the Sears Tower and its Gotham-looking friends, which together form the foreboding Chicago skyline. The bitter wind chaps spitefully at our chops and there's just an eerie silence; created not only by the snow soaking up the few early morning noises, but by the moment itself. A moment of nowness, lying down, childishly making angels in the snow, freezing cold but not noticing, giggling like pillocks in that way where you can hardly catch your breath; completely caught in a timeless vacuum of just us. A few soluble seconds that soon just disperse among the many billions of others we spend so helplessly, carelessly without incident, and then completely forget. I suppose that's all nostalgia really is: a collection of moments, of instances, snapshots that hang as masterpieces on the walls of our memory. I'm sure just twenty minutes before that moment, Elle will have annoyed me in some way, or we will have bickered about something dreary like wet wipes. But of course you don't remember those bits. Depending on how it affects you, nostalgia is either generous enough or too cruel to allow you to see the faults in times gone by.

———————

TO: Spencer Austin
FROM: Edie McClurg
SUBJECT: Save Ferris!
   Hello. I just figured out how to read emails numbered past #20. You were in that group. You may contact me again when you get to town. Use this email address. I will start checking it more often.
   Edie McClurg.
   (little known but internationally [apparently] famous)

I'm excited about meeting Edie McClurg. You might not recognise the name, but everyone knows her for one particular line from *Ferris Bueller's Day Off*, in which she played Ed Rooney's secretary, Grace. It's a knockout line, a quote-in-the-pub corker that Edie has an immense talent for blurting out.

"What memories do you have of playing Grace in *Ferris Bueller*?" I ask, as we sit in a lovely lazy park while dogs bark, poo and run around excitedly. Edie looks perhaps even sprightlier than she did back in 1986; her trademark red perm has been updated into something a bit less grannyish and her grin beams intact youth through an older face – and that's possibly what makes her such an alluring on-screen presence. I suspect there's been a little bit of the compulsory Hollywood flab-tucking work done on that face, there's more definition there than the rounded cheeky face she sported in *Ferris*, but essentially she looks well, and friendly and wholesome and impossible to dislike.

"Well, let me see. Let's go all the way back to when we had to go in and read for the part. I decided that I would just do my mid-western character. I add a line, I said, 'Oh, he's very popular. There's the sportoes, the dweebies, the dickheads, the bloods, the jocks, the wastoids – they all adore him.' And then I added, 'They think he's a righteous dude.'" Shabang, shaboom, that's what Grace is about, and in truth that's basically what meeting Grace is all about for me. The "righteous dude" line has always been one of the funniest moments in eighties cinema for me. To hear an adult say something so "with it" was just hilarious and unexpected. Like Grandad saying "wicked".

"They still use that in the trailer for the ads on TV .... I get *nothing*. For being in the ad or coming up with the line. But that's life." Edie grins out a big metre-wide beamer.

"At any rate, they flew me from LA to Chicago to be in a "rain" scene. That's a safety scene that could be done inside, if their outside scenes weren't going well, like the parade and all of the stuff outside. So they always have to have that as a contingency in case of rain delay. They brought that whole desk set, in Rooney's office, and put it all together in Chicago. And so when all the weather was perfect, they were able to shoot outside, and I'd been there all week and didn't do anything but go to the museums and anywhere I wanted to go. Then I worked out in LA and we eventually did the scenes in a school in the San Fernando Valley. They flew the desks from Chicago and I said, 'Did this come from Chicago?' The guy said, "Yeah, it cost $10,000 to bring it over!' It was more than my entire salary for the movie. Why don't you just have the desk do the scene then? I'll just stand back and watch since it's making more money than I am. But since that time, cable and TV showings... I'm making more money than the desk."

"What was it like working with John Hughes?"

"Oh, it was great. He knew me when I did *Planes, Trains and Automobiles* with him. I was in a scene with Steve Martin at the car rental counter. The scene was written and it was just a "May I help you". But I decided I would be doing a transaction on the phone, just to make Steve wait a little bit longer, give him a little more heat, before he comes out with that scene with the expletives deleted. So we did the scene and then John leaned over and said, 'This time on the phone, just talk about Thanksgiving.' So I lay out this monologue and John says, 'How do you do that?' I said it's cannibalisation. Everything in that is about my family. The names are changed, but it's all there. He did cut out the Catholic references, because he's Protestant, he didn't understand how funny that was. But what I had said that's missing is 'We gotta keep Uncle Billy away from the bourbon and ginger, because he'll start arguing the virgin birth with Father Ed.'"

"Did you expect the success and cult status that *Ferris Bueller's* got now?"

"I did not expect the cult status. At the time I was pretty amazed at the storylines ... these kids were skipping school, borrowing the car, which could be construed as stealing ... and there were parents' organisations who really didn't care for the message that this was saying it's OK to skip school. The kids got it. They really got it. A lot of that end of the term thing, it's hot and it's nice out ... it's what they do, a ditch day."

"There you go kids, Edie says it's OK to ditch school!"

"I do not! [laughing] I'm highly educated, I have advanced degrees. I decided that I'm just going to live my life backward. I was very serious and studious and very "by the rules" when I was young and as I get older I just flout convention as much as I can and I enjoy myself dancing and larking about and having a good time." Maybe Edie takes more risks nowadays, but I don't get the sense that she really takes herself any less seriously. There seems to be a unifying factor that binds these actor-types: however *nice* they are, there's still a big bloated ego overriding everything they do and probably spoiling a lot of it for them with its demands.

"So how's work for you now?" I ask, wondering why I haven't seen her in much for years.

"You get rejected ninety-five per cent of the time. Could you stand that? I had early graduated success and then I kind of hit this plateau where I was recognised as a character, so that cuts me out of all the leads. Even when I was young. And right now, I'm in an in between spot where I'm not the young character actress and I'm not the old crone. So, I have to change people's minds when I audition." Grace has to audition? What's it coming to? By the frustration in her voice, I get a sense of what a struggling humping old bunfight it is out there. It's brutal. Even for the good ones.

"I've been around long enough that there's a taint of 'We know what it is she does and we don't want that' and I don't get many opportunities to show that there's a wider spectrum. And I get a lot of people saying, 'Well, why don't you just do what you're known for?' And I do get hired a lot by people who do want to see Grace or some permutation of her from *Ferris Bueller's Day Off*. But I don't think it's necessary for me to remain crystallised in someone else's idea because of something they saw when they were fifteen years old." I wonder whether I should feel a bit guilty for dragging her out to talk about Grace, *again;* for being part of that very brigade who've crystallised her into just one character. But then again, if she hadn't been

Grace, she may have been famous for something else and maybe we'd be here talking about that. Also, I'm here to worship her, and no performer can be annoyed by that, surely.

"So do you feel typecast as Grace?"

"Sure, but that's OK. It was a character I actually created when I was on radio in Kansas City Missouri in the early seventies. I did a satire of a Campbell's Soup commercial and it was given an award at this public radio conference. It was just me doing a character of a neighbour."

Edie seems more or less happy with her jobbing actor's life, although I feel a bit sad that this funny, talented woman has never moved on to carry films by herself. She waltzes off, waving energetically from her flashy car, all grins on her way to a drinks party. I think she likes this life.

And so further north we speed for an encore John Hughes tribute in Highland Park, another one of those leafy Illinois towns that are starting to look very familiar and similar.

My correspondence with the Roses began in England, when a couple of months before our departure I received a reply to my snail-mail begging letter regarding a visit to the house. I was surprised because I didn't think letters by post actually arrived any more. Frances Rose's handwriting looked like the muscles in her fingers had been replaced by elastic bands. It was obvious then that she's very old, but still very keen to host us.

Ben and Frances Rose own the home that was used as Cameron's house in *Ferris Bueller's Day Off*. This was where Cameron accidentally drove his dad's car through a huge window and off the stilted building into a ditch below.

On arrival, we discover that we haven't been quite prepared for how *old* Frances and Ben Rose are. They're so frail and delicate that I think I might have an arm off just shaking their hands. Frances does nearly all the talking and appears an intelligent, lucid woman who's simply had the pace knocked out of her by age. Ben is quieter and I get the sense that he doesn't always know exactly what's happening.

Just like so many of the locations we've visited, this house amazingly, looks no different to how it did in the film – right down to the same curtains.

St. Anne's Convent, KY. Tom and I walk the walk up that famous tree-lined walkway from *Rain Man*.

Tom, me, a highly dubious t-shirt and the late Paul Gleason, the teacher in *Breakfast Club*.

Tom and Jesse Ventura, former WWF wrestler, Governor of Minnesota and actor. Me loitering awkwardly in the background.

Me prancing around on the stage at First Avenue club, Minneapolis – where Prince's *Purple Rain* was shot. My costume is a *very* approximate pastiche.

Triple U Standing Butte Ranch, SD. Me approaching Kevin's Costner's house from *Dances With Wolves*. It got worse.

Tom embraces a replica K.I.T.T. from *Knight Rider* in Calgary.

Close Encounters...me with Devil's Tower on my head, WY.

Nelson, BC. The fire station from *Roxanne*. Note the fake rubber noses.

Even in transit, Tom lives in the eighties.

Anmore, BC. With Mario at *Roxanne*'s house.

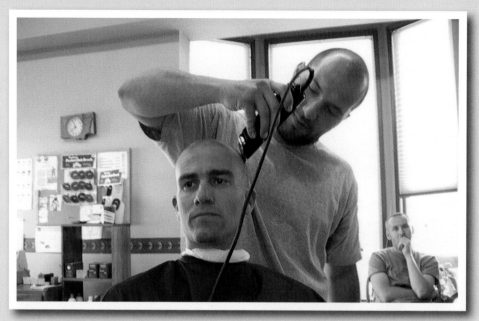

Tom has his hair removed in honour of *Officer and a Gentleman* at a barbershop in Port Townsend. I've had mine done already, and sit behind, devastated.

Port Townsend. The barracks from *Officer and a Gentleman*. Tom dresses me down in a most frightening fashion.

With Louis Gossett Jnr., Sergeant Foley from *Officer and a Gentleman*.
Not sure why I look so perturbed.

Astoria, OR. The Goonies house! Luke 'truffle shuffles' while I manhandle Tom's bike.

Burney, CA. The *Stand By Me* bridge. Scarier than it looks. Tom and I didn't actually jump.

Interviewing Jamison Newlander, who played vampire-hunter Alan Frogg in *Lost Boys.*

Twenty years seem to flash by so quickly for some. Somehow though, the people at this location visit are as interesting and touching as the place itself. Sometimes, we find that nostalgia isn't the only emotion that fires itself up.

The building, which has won some sort of prize or other for the architect, sits on iron stilts in the middle of a thick wood that appears secluded but is near enough to Beech Street to be given a number. It's barely visible from the road, and that's just how Ben and Franny say they like it. The Roses had the house built back in 1952 and then by 1974 had earned enough money from their careers as artists to form the dirty habit of buying vintage cars. This led them to create an outer building in which to keep their collection. It's this newer building – a posh Portakabin on legs – that was used as Cameron's gaff for most of the *Ferris Bueller* shoot. The main house was used only for Cameron's bedroom scene at the start of the film.

"You see, Chicago has a film board and they have a person that finds the locations," explains Franny. "They just drove by here. The original script doesn't have a car going through a window, the story goes that they bumped it into a tree or something. But when they saw this building, they changed the story a little bit and had the car going out the window."

"Was it just once that they drove it out the window?" Tom asks.

"Well, they could only do it once," Frances replies with a face that suggests she wouldn't have let them do it over and over.

"We were hiding under the building when they did it. When it hit the ground after breaking through the window, it didn't really have any damage, it just bounced around the bushes a bit. So they came down with hammers and flame torches and battered it up."

"We heard that the car was just a plastic shell, is that true?"

"Yes it was, it was amazing how real it looked."

I stand at the very position where the characters stood looking agog after the car had just smashed through the window. I suddenly feel like Ferris, as though I've had something to do with the car. The emotions flash through me. I peer down at where they kicked a little bit of glass over the edge and wonder to myself whether this can be classed as nostalgic masturbation. I especially like this location. It's not well trodden and the Roses have kept it all exactly as it was. I feel like I might be the only person who's stood right here in homage to that scene. Eventually, a waft of vertigo pulls me away from the (perfectly safe, not very high at all) window.

Ben and Franny were, of course, compensated for the use of their building, but that's not all they demanded, so Frances says. "They came to us and said that they'd like to use our home for part of a movie and we said no – we didn't want all that messing around here. So finally they said that they'd take the glass out and put in their own. I said wait a minute, while you're doing that, can you get someone to clean *all* the windows? We'd had lots of quotes on getting the windows cleaned, but nobody came back because of the stilts. They promised to wash the windows of the *whole* neighbourhood if we agreed to let them film here. So we said we're gonna do it, *just* to get the windows washed." There we have it; one of the classic scenes of eighties movies only exists the way it does because this woman wanted her windows cleaned.

As Frances regales her stock *Ferris* stories, Ben stands with a vacant grin, probably not hearing much of it.

"They wanted to plant lots of flowers around the house, but I didn't let them because we like it kinda natural. So they put plastic ones in and we still find them around the outside of the house, because they don't degrade! We said that we didn't want our names in the credits as a location because we didn't want people coming around."

"Like us?" I ask. It seems the birth of the Internet has ruined their anonymity.

"Like you. For a long time we just had people we knew who wanted to bring their grandchildren. Oh, and another story..." Frances is really on a roll now. "We said wait a minute, we have a son who's around Ferris' age and we'd like him to appear in the movie. They said yes. So, where is he in the movie? He's in the parade scene. One of thousands!"

"How often do you watch the movie?" I ask.

"Well, we can't help it, it's on TV so often. Once, we were on an overseas flight and they showed it on the in-flight TV. We'd gone on holiday to get away from home and there it is, following us!" They begin to warm to us and Ben drags out tens of photos of the cars they've recently sold for a bucketful at Christie's.

The building is half empty now (apart from some nude paintings, possibly of a younger Frances, and spaces where cars once sat), and we can tell that our visit has prompted their first laboured shuffle down the garden to the old car-house for some time.

Frances tells of the parties they had and all the activity that once surrounded their home, and I realise that they've visibly wound down their lives. They've sold the cars, packed everything else up in boxes and vacated their extra building. It's as if they're packing up ready to move out of this world and as it hits me, looking around their little vacated out-house, it chokes me up a little; I have a wave of humanity and compassion that doesn't often emerge within that concentrated selfish subjectivity of London life. Frances has just got out of hospital for age-related illnesses and Ben is slinging his hip round like his leg is a weight on the end of a string. They show us photos of their more active years and I realise that it must be sad for them to have to just let go of the lives they worked so hard to enjoy. Maybe they're *not* sad about it; maybe when you get that old you look forward to saying goodbye. It's too hard for me to tell from my twenty-nine years in, but to me they look tired and done with it all.

Before we leave, Ben and Franny request that we sign their guest book. I ask if the actors from the film had signed the book back in 1986 and am shocked when they say they've never checked. Nearly twenty years have passed and they don't know if these famous actors had signed their guest book. I become the first person to sign it since 2001, then finger back to entries in 1986 (in fact only ten pages back) and find Matthew Broderick's, Alan Ruck's and Mia Sara's signatures amongst the rest of the crew and John Hughes. And the Roses had never bothered to check if they'd signed it.

We say goodbye to Ben and Frances knowing that in not so many years, their stories about when the John Hughes bandwagon came to town and threw a car through their window will be buried with them. I feel honoured that we got a chance to meet these nice people, and hope that I get to pack my life up with someone too.

CHAPTER FIVE SOUNDTRACK:

(Don't You) Forget About Me

Simple Minds (1985)

Chapter Five

A Day in Shermerville

Chicago and around

With Luke finally arriving this afternoon, Tom and I decide to go on a delightful sunny drive around the outer rim of Chicago; maybe unconsciously honouring our last little outing as a couple. We intend to buzz around a few different movies before honing in on *The Breakfast Club*.

Hunting the suburbs for the houses used in some of our favourite films, we discover that there's always *someone*, on *every* street, out mowing his lawn and available to tell us where the hell we're going. That hazy, buzzy, somehow always slightly distant sound of lawn mowers always makes me think of lazy, dry summer days in Leyton. *Shaky singing "This Ole House" from tinny radios in concrete front gardens; ignore thirst because tap water is boring and warm and it's best to hold out for the cherryade with dinner to see who can get the best red cherryade tash; playing with water and being told off for pushing Donna Clark off her Chopper, even though she cheated at Computer Battleships. DEEEEeeeeeewwwwww ... kabachhhhhh. Direct hit. But you looked at my ships. Didn't. Did. Didn't. Did. Didn't. Did. You stink. No I don't, I'm skill, you're a fleabag. No, you're a derrbrain. So what, your dad's a Joey you spazmo...*

One house on Lincoln Avenue has pillars thicker than Stuart Pearce's Euro '96 thighs. It sits all pompous and snooty and was used as the home in *Home Alone*. There's no mistaking it. Especially in this middle-class suburban spread that's so often the target of John Hughes' attempts on our cinemas. An old man on the other side of the street (this street's on-duty *"mowing-the-lawn man"*, tells us that when the film was being shot, his son took loads of home video and cut a personal tape he called *The Making of Home Alone.*

HOME ALONE (1990) (FILM)

Director: Chris Columbus
Writer: John Hughes
Producers: Tarquin Gotch, Mark Levinson, Scott M. Rosenfelt
Awards: Nominated for 2 Oscars. 10 other wins and 3 nominations
Cast: Macauley Culkin (Kevin), Joe Pesci (Harry), Daniel Stern (Marv), John Heard (Peter), Roberts Blossom (Marley), Catherine O'Hara (Kate), John Candy (Gus Polinski)

Notes:
By the time *Home Alone* came along at the end of the eighties, John Hughes was well into the process of dropping the camera in favour of the pen. But even from behind his typewriter, Hughes' awesome power to create whole-family entertainment launched Macauley Culkin into the world as one of the biggest child stars since Zammo in *Grange Hill*. Well, maybe a bit bigger than Zammo.

Relieved that we're not invited in to watch three hours of seasickness spotted with occasional flecks of Macauley Culkin's feet on a handycam, we build up the courage to knock on the door of the *Home Alone* house: a door that certainly doesn't suggest a welcome with open arms sits grinning on the other side.

We expect a man with a monocle to call the police and have us sent to a workhouse, but what we get is a university-student girl wearing dirty white socks and a decent spread of acne. The surprise turns us into a couple of stuttering wallies, though we do manage to spit the words *"Home Alone"* at the poor girl, which prompts her to blurt memories of the film being shot at her house like a church recital. She was a young girl when her home was made into a film set for a few weeks and although she can't say that she *hung out* with Macauley Culkin (despite the fact that he used her bedroom as his classroom), she *did* hang out with Macauley's brother Kieran, who also appeared in the movie. She tells tales of Joe Pesci being very quiet and shy, and Daniel Stern teaching all the local kids how the special effects worked, and it all sounds like a festive community-spirited John Hughes jamboree.

We ask if she would mind answering a few questions on camera but she goes all hesitant and coy before disappearing for a few minutes to ask her dad. Then, out pokes this gargoyle with a glass eye (if it isn't actually a glass eye, it's a bloody good try), growling about having just taken an English documentary company to court over an interview he gave and wanting nothing more to do with us all. Fair enough, we don't want a piece of that. Interesting that he's written an entire nation off due to one iffy film crew though. He pops his funny little head back in and the girl embarrassedly continues with what feels like her matinee performance of stock anecdotes on her family home's claim to fame.

She tells us that after the film was released, cars would line up in the street right around the corner just to drive past and get photographs of the house. Once, a couple of tourists knocked at the door and asked what time the next tour would be. I can imagine all that palaver being a novelty for the first five minutes, but had it been my home, there may have been reports of tourists having their audacity violently smeared back over their stupid faces. Then I realise that *I'm* one of those liberty-taking anorak door-knockers and I should shut *my* stupid face. I'm furious with me.

And so from streets that give a peaceful yet painful reminder of the limits of my own wealth, we head back to the northern edge of Chicago, to the less desirable area of North Milwaukee Avenue. Here, among the scruff and decay, we find Chris's Billiards, where scenes featuring Tom Cruise and Paul Newman were shot for the film *Color of Money*.

COLOR OF MONEY (1986) (FILM)

Director: Martin Scorsese
Writers: Walter Tevis, Richard Price
Producers: Irving Axelrad, Barbara De Fina
Awards: 1 Oscar (Paul Newman – Best Actor), another 1 win and 5 nominations
Cast: Paul Newman (Fast Eddie Felson), Tom Cruise (Vincent Lauria), Mary Elizabeth Mastrantonio (Carmen), Helen Shaver (Janelle), John Turturro (Julian), Bill Cobbs (Orvis)

> **Notes:**
> Following the successes of *Raging Bull* and *King of Comedy*, Martin Scorsese left DeNiro alone for five minutes and pulled together a young Cruise with stalwart Newman to create a film about a talented young pool player (Cruise as Vincent) being taught the way of the hustler by a retired old legend (Newman as "Fast" Eddie). The whole exercise earned Newman an Oscar.

In a messy street where deadbeats and head-nutters talk to themselves but *never* each other, Chris's Billiards flies tired hoardings across its frontage, advertising an unprecedented forty-eight pool tables within. The musty stench of stale old men's trouser pockets greets us as we arrive, as do browned newspaper clippings and various aged photographic memorabilia on the wall, flagging up that if it was good enough for Cruise and Newman then you should get the hell up here too. The walk upstairs is like journeying from a world of colour into a sepia netherworld of broken men's dreams and flaky paint.

At the top of the stairs, a fat man called Eric twiddles his beard (I assume all day), although today he stops for five minutes to talk to us, until a newsflash appears on the television telling everyone that Ronald Reagan has just died. Another ingredient of my eighties has just been consigned to the trash folder. Oddly, I have flashbacks of the Reagan *Spitting Image* puppet. That show politicised my generation to such a single-handed extent that we were a nation whose eleven year olds knew the names of the entire cabinet and some of the foreign ones too. That would never happen today.

The place looks exactly as it did in the film: dark and dusty with a sense that men have wasted whole weeks trying to win money back to feed the kids without even noticing a single hour passing. The high chairs still sit where the film crew found and left them: dark wood seats that men only sit in when they're losing. The overall theme is dirt brown: both in the wood and the air, the men's teeth and the dust that cakes in corners.

Tom and I play a few games on the very table that Cruise and Newman played on in the film. Cruise's character was a real pool hotshot, but reading through what appears to be bloodstains on a newspaper clipping on the wall, I discover that apparently he was pretty ropey at it in real life. Newman, it claims, was a pretty passable player, and if Tom is Newman, then I'm Cruise. I flap a pool cue around like a bit of old rope and refuse to admit I'm *actually trying,* just to cover the shame. Tom slaughters me. *Don't hit Tom with the pool cue, Spencer. Don't hit Tom with the pool cue. Flashback to 1981. My tiny Pot Black snooker table all set up in the living room; Donna Clark is beating me, I can't stand it, and her brother Jason finds that just hilarious. Wallop, I clump him with the cue. WALLOP, he cracks me across the back, even harder, oh my God it stings, not fair, he's much older than me, tears and sick everywhere.* "It's your own fault," *Mum says.* I never was a good loser. But I manage not to hit Tom with the pool cue.

––––––––––

Loping along like a moist tornado of four-lettered self-deprecation, still livid about my pool performance, we get out to O'Hare airport to collect the third member of our nostalgia-hunting geek squad.

Luke Dolan has a memory of eighties films that makes me look like a pretender from another generation. He hasn't been involved in researching the tour though, he just wants to piggyback our hard work, but he *has* got a very good video camera and that seems like a decent trade. So here we are, us three eighties adventurers, the team complete. Us and the eighties versus the present. Back home we're not *best* friends, I might see either of them once every couple of months or so. But sitting in the car, with the slight awkwardness of Luke and Tom having only met once, I realise that in just under three months' time we will have shared a life-affirming, extraordinary journey together, and no matter how often we see each other afterwards, we'll always have this trip. Ironically, in a way, the same bonding thing happened to the characters at the movie location we're about to hit, even though they only spent a Saturday morning's detention together.

Luke's body believes it to be ten at night but straight away we drag him out: partly to get him in the mood and partly because our schedule demands we get moving on our Chicago locations. So with Luke looking flaky and floppy with not a tickle of what time zone or decade he's in, we get to Des Plaines and spend a fair wad of time looking for The Illinois State Police Station. It's here that scenes from *The Breakfast Club,* one of John Hughes' finest films, were shot.

THE BREAKFAST CLUB (1985) (FILM)

Director: John Hughes
Writer: John Hughes
Producers: John Hughes, Andrew Meyer, Michelle Manning, Gil Friesen, Ned Tanen
Cast: Emilio Estevez (Andrew "Andy" Clark), Anthony Michael Hall (Brian Ralph Johnson), Judd Nelson (John Bender), Molly Ringwald (Claire Standish), Ally Sheedy (Allison Reynolds), Paul Gleason (Principal Richard Vernon)

Notes:
Squidged in during a time when Hughes was writing and/or directing two movies a year, *The Breakfast Club* offered everyone still at school in 1985 a character to identify with. I was definitely some sort of bastard Molly Ringwald/Judd Nelson amalgam. In this film, Hughes threw us a huge mirror reflecting the geek, the gothy freak, the moody crim, the prom queen and the sporty meathead: then invited us to *be* one of them. How simple the world would be if *The Breakfast Club* was an accurate microcosm of society. Today, of course, he'd have to add an eleven-year-old gang member who carries a knife.

The nondescript, concretey outside of the building has a gaping entrance under which some stairs lead to glass doors. This is instantly recognisable as Shermer High School: the school where Emilio Estevez et al. began Saturday detention as a disparate bunch of brats and finished best of friends with worldly wisdom way beyond their years. Personally, I'd never have turned up for Saturday detention: missing *Tiswas* was *not* an option.

We slope guiltily up the entrance stairs. We have of course done nothing wrong, but I'm always concerned that "the rozzers" will find something to pin on me; I must be doing *something* wrong. We're met by strapping State Trooper Greg Rieves and fully expect not to be allowed a sniff at the building, let alone to *film* the inside of it. But nice as pie and thrilled to listen to our *adorable* accents, Greg agrees to drag us around the place filming whatever we like.

Greg's healthily moustachioed superior officer gives us a stern warning about not filming doors or anything that might lead to a breach of intelligence on how to get into the building. Which is odd, because I'm sure anyone could work out – without video footage – that *doors* are generally the way into any building. But Greg doesn't really care. He just stands by laughing with slight gent-breast wobble and encourages his colleagues to join in as we skid around the corners of the very same corridors the kids did in the film. They refuse. It feels strange and wrong to be skidding around in my socks at a state police headquarters, but it's an opportunity that mustn't be passed up. "Hey hey hey hey", sing Simple Minds in my mind, "ooh oooh oooh oooh". I'm smiley-nervous and just a bit self-conscious. When I'm self-conscious I get this weird thing where I feel like my head is ten times its real size and that everyone is looking at it. It's a large head anyway, but when I'm under pressure it's enormous, like Frank Sidebottom's. It was really hard as a kid joining a new football team with a head that felt like that size. *Come on, Spencer, they're all watching, all looking at your head, it's in the air, your ball, head it, shouldn't be a problem, how can you miss it with that thing breaking your neck every time you change direction?* You can't blame me for feeling a bit wallified; I'm skidding around, shoeless, in a state police station. I haven't felt this naughty since 1993, when I walked home from Walthamstow Central at midnight with my trousers down for a bet.

The shiny, hospital-esque corridors are pretty much all that's left (other than the exterior) to suggest that this was the building used in the film. Greg tells us that the place was *originally* built as a school, but only existed as one for a single year in 1981. Sudden migration – probably down to new employment opportunities elsewhere – led to kids being sent to other areas and the building lying dormant until the police took pity and moved in around 1994. With shoes back on, he takes us to the gym that featured in the movie (which looks like any old gym: basketball, tennis, gymnastics – all the equipment you'd expect), and Luke recreates *The Breakfast Club* dancing, from the scene that's basically a music video montage effort. It's Luke's debut contribution to the insanity of this quest, his initiation ceremony if you will. With jetlag troubling his limbs and affecting much of his motor neuron work, the dancing is hauntingly grotesque and makes me feel ever so slightly bilious. I wonder if having Luke come along might have been a mistake.

Greg narrows the embarrassment by getting us out of the gym as quickly as possible, leading us to a series of plain white, boxy rooms with flimsy walls that he reckons together once constituted the library area in the movie.

"These rooms are now where we work on a lot of cars; it's a mini lock-up area." *Oooh, a lock-up; cockneys love a lock-up.* "There was a lot of hype among the officers when we first moved in, but now?" He pulls a squashed up face as if to say that no one gives a button. "This is now a room where we do fingerprinting, and *this* is where we keep the cars." He's moving quicker now, perhaps itching to go and nick someone instead of indulging our flimsy nostalgic whim. Or maybe he can sense that we're really not convinced. I feign immense interest in what basically looks like a garage, and move on to the next room, which is *actually* a garage holding a horrific car wreck. Jesus mother of Jim, this is barely recognisable as a car. We all share a collective wince.

"Did they come out of that alive?" I ask, referring to the passengers of this squashed up ball of metallic nonsense.

"I'm not sure exactly what happened here, but it's under investigation. That's why it's in here, so we can find out what happened."

"I think it crashed, Greg."

"Oh yeah, absolutely, it definitely crashed." It's all gone a bit wrong. This isn't quite the nostalgia trip we envisaged. We've gone from gentle thoughts of cheesy eighties teenagers dancing camply in a library to an appalling motorway pile-up memento that really doesn't look hopeful for whoever was inside that car. Greg has seen it all before and giggles his way around the carnage as I gawp and ponder on the injuries it must have caused. I wanted teen angst based on zits and insecurity, not a crushed tin can splattered with what I convince myself are bits of tomato.

Disappointed and harrowed, I half-accuse Greg of changing the way the place looks and so destroying an important historical landmark. He laughs again, like Kris Akabusi in a comedy gas chamber, gun glinting remindingly on the side of his utility belt.

The next day we spout unleaded discharge out of the back of the motor, sprint a bit away from Chicago and stop off at Glenbrook North High School in Northbrook, where John Hughes shot scenes for two of his films *and* went to school himself as a youth. The school sits on *Shermer Street* and Northbrook was once called Shermerville, which explains why Hughes uses the name Shermer a lot as a sort of generic place name in his films.

Given the current climates of hysteria, we're a tad concerned about security at schools in the US. We have visions of our lurking around looking for movie locations being misconstrued as men with altogether more sinister intentions. A conviction for lurking near a school would not look good on either a CV or an email home to Mum. So, to keep it all above board, we wade through the spotty oiks (purposely not looking at any of them in case we get accused of harassment), go through the visitors' entrance and find exactly what we've found nearly everywhere else in Chicago burbsville: a warm and slightly jealous welcome. The two parents working a shift on the school reception are so impressed by the idea of our tour that the words "You're so cool" are followed quickly by visitor passes slapped on our breasts and excited shoves back out of the door to go and "do whatever you gotta do". The kids gawp at us like we've just jumped ship at Roswell and one pus-ridden gink with a gobful of train tracks dares come and ask us why we are here. As he grins the sun catches his braces and momentarily blinds me. For at least an hour after, the image of his gob is burned onto my retina whenever I blink.

The stairs that run up to the Debate and Art Society block at Glenbrook is the very spot where Ferris Bueller waited for his girlfriend, Sloan, to be allowed out on compassionate grounds after he'd faked her grandmother's death so they could cut loose and go mental-nuts in Chicago. Our homage to the film is to recreate this scene, although I think it ends up more like a pantomime version starring me as John Inman starring as Widow Twanky starring as Sloan. While I have to mince down the stairs as Sloan for the camera, Tom dresses up as Ferris. In the film Matthew Broderick as Ferris dresses in a grown-up mac and hat to give the impression he's Sloan's dad and looks uncannily like he did some twenty years later for his role as Inspector Gadget. At this point I notice that Tom always gets to play the cool guy wearing the hat or sunglasses and I play the idiot or the goon or the girl.

An argument regarding who plays who in our reconstructions of the famous scenes spills across to the school playing field, where a grandstand forms the background for the very last shot of *The Breakfast Club*. Here Judd

Nelson walked towards camera and punched the air (which Hughes froze; a classic eighties last-shot-of-the-movie device). Tom is yet again down to be the tough guy, but when he re-enacts the (you would think simple) scene, I'm so appalled at his camp little punch in the air and queer smile that I have to physically wrestle him for the fingerless leather glove and sunglasses so I can show him how to really *Judd it up*. It must cut a pathetic sight – two men fighting over a single black leather fingerless glove. What's happened to me?

Eventually, with the glove won, at least *my* swagger has a hint of masculinity about it. However, on looking back at the tape, I do look like I'd shit myself.

I wouldn't mess around with Paul Gleason. As he paces around waiting for Luke to set the camera up, smoking his face off, I wonder whether he's just as tough and *shoot-you-in-the-knees* no-nonsense as the characters he plays. He always seems to be the white-collar bastard, the snide cop or most relevant to us today, the nasty teacher. In *The Breakfast Club*, Gleason played Richard Vernon, the menacing headmaster that got everyone quivering; whose despot authority spurred the group to bond. So, we all sit down, the camera's rolling, and Paul awaits our questioning with a most serious face. He looks old. He's coughing all over the place and with his white hair and nineties style big round glasses; he looks like he's had way more than twenty years to age since the film was made.

"I guess you've been in so many classic movies that it's hard to know where to start. But what do you think has been your career highlight so far?"

"Well the best movie I was ever in was probably *Die Hard*. The best made. One of the first great modern action movies."

"Better than *Trading Places* or *The Breakfast Club*?"

"Well, *The Breakfast Club* I thought was kinda silly. But it was good because everyone could identify with each of the kids. Everyone knew someone like that or *was* like that. I mean even the teacher was somebody that they had known. But when they broke into song and dance and all that I thought it was kinda silly. Stupid. Plus they cut out a lot of my good moments and I didn't like that. All actors hate that when they cut them out.

I thought it just trivialised the movie because when we first rehearsed it I thought it was like a play. A nice small drama, you know. I have regrets about the way I played the part sometimes, I wished I'd been a little more tongue-in-cheek maybe, because I took it a little too seriously and allowed myself to go a little over the top with the anger. I would have liked, just in a couple of moments, to have been a little more controlled, had a little more control of myself. But I thought it was gonna be a nice little drama and it turned out to be a bit of a cult hit down the ages, because of the five kids I think." It's interesting hearing him criticise his own performance in the film. I get the sense Paul Gleason is a perfectionist, unflattered by the glamour of Hollywood and in it for the art, the craft.

"I heard that you had a moment staring at some girls in the swimming pool and they cut it out."

"Yeah, they cut it out..."

"At least you got to do it," Tom interjects over-excitedly. Perhaps not the moment to reveal your penchant for schoolgirls.

"Yeah," Paul continues, without making reference to Tom's little outburst. "'Cos the original janitor was Rick Moranis and then for some reason they had a parting of ways, I'm sure it was friendly. And they brought in another janitor, so all the stuff with Rick Moranis was cut. Universal didn't think much of the movie so they made John Hughes cut it down to ninety minutes. Then the movie took off and became popular, so the guy at Universal eventually got fired."

"You played Principal Vernon who was essentially *another* villain."

"Yeah, he was an antagonistic teacher, wasn't he."

"Were you a figure of authority to the kids off set?"

"Well not really. We were all fairly equal. I became very friendly with Michael Hall, I thought he was great in the movie; he was the best one in the movie for me. And I thought Molly Ringwald was very good. And Judd did a good job too."

"I heard that Judd Nelson was nearly fired by John Hughes."

"Well I might have been one of the people who said maybe give him another chance. John told me he was gonna fire him. Judd was very good in the rehearsals and then when it came time to shoot, I think he was very tense and was difficult for John in some way. But then he got loose and got more relaxed and I think was excellent for the part, so it ended up being a good thing. Originally, I was cast in the movie and I read with two actors, they had it narrowed down to Nicholas Cage and Judd Nelson and he chose Judd. I don't know what it was Judd did that pissed John off but he was kind of cantankerous. Judd would play the part in the hotel lobby and everything; he could turn it on and turn it off. He was kind of controversial. I think in real life, he's a pretty regular guy, but I think he wanted to be consistent and wanted to nail it."

"He would wind Molly Ringwald up, wouldn't he?"

"Yeah, maybe that was it. Maybe he was abusive to her, I don't remember. I'm glad he stayed with him though; it was good for Judd and good for the movie. Nick was good in the test; they were both good so it was like you could flip a coin."

I just can't imagine Nicholas Cage playing that part. I'm sure he'd have been OK, but the line up they ended up with is so set in movie stone that it's hard to imagine any other formula.

"Did you enjoy working with Murphy and Ackroyd in *Trading Places*?"

"Very much. Yeah, that was a good movie to make. They shot a lot of that in New York. Downtown. It was good for me, I was in the very first shot of the movie and the very last of the movie. It was a twelve-week job, so I got paid for every week. Eddie Murphy is very funny. Dan Ackroyd is very cerebral with his humour; Murphy's is more physical and instinctive. For example, Eddie Murphy was in the Jacuzzi and he ad-libbed a lot. He said that when we were kids and wanted a Jacuzzi we'd have to get in the bathtub and fart."

"Have you stayed in touch with any of the actors?"

"Not really. I see Michael Hall from time to time. And I saw Eddie Murphy from time to time after the film. I never saw Ackroyd. I've seen those kids. I've seen Molly, I worked with Molly again. I really didn't see much of Ally Sheedy, she sort of had an up-and-down career. I think she's worked, she did some excellent work in a couple of movies and in some other movies she wasn't so good."

"In *Die Hard*, again, you played another slightly unpleasant character in Deputy Police Chief Robinson..."

"Oh yeah, yeah, he *was* unpleasant. I think I overdid it in that movie. There were things I'd like to take back; I think I should have played it closer to the vest of being a cop. I fell into some traps there."

DIE HARD (1988) (FILM)

Director: John McTiernan
Writer: Roderick Thorp (novel), Steven E. de Souza (screenplay)
Producer: Charles Gordon
Awards: Nominated for 4 Oscars
Cast: Bruce Willis (Officer John McClane), Reginald VelJohnson (Sgt Al Powell), Bonnie Bedelia (Holly Gennero McClane), Alexander Godunov (Karl), Paul Gleason (Deputy Police Chief Dwayne T. Robinson), William Atherton (Richard Thornburg), De'Voreaux White (Argyle), Hart Bochner (Harry Ellis), Alan Rickman (Hans Gruber).

Notes:

I have limited memories of watching *Die Hard*. It was one of those end-of-term English lessons where we could do whatever we liked. So after Mrs Peterson realised that *Animal Farm wasn't* a George Orwell adaptation (and in fact something a lot more bestial), she allowed us to put on *Die Hard*. The reason my memories are limited is because Terry Coldwell – who later went on to become an incredibly unlikely pop star in the boy band East 17 – and a couple of other rowdies spent the entire film shouting, throwing things and re-enacting the most violent scenes of the film on the class weaklings.

Here he goes again, with that admirable professionalism that actually must be tough to pull off. I find it odd that people who do what is essentially *pretending* can take it and themselves so seriously.

"You were outside the building the whole time, did you see much action? Any scenes with Bruce Willis?"

"At the end of the movie, outside the building, when he came out and I came up to him. But we were all there every day. Bruce had a nice big dressing room trailer that he'd just bought. They paid him a lot of money for that. But it *made* a lot of money, it made a ton and it put him on the map too. As a movie actor."

"Did you know all those movies were going to be big hits?"

"Yeah, I thought *Trading Places* was going to turn out to be a good movie and I thought *Die Hard* would be very successful, although I didn't realise how successful because that director did a hell of a job with all the special effects. It was a great plot, a good story with all the hostages and stuff, it really worked well and the head villain was terrific – he was from England, Alan Rickman. They had a good cast in that: Bonnie Bedalia [Holly McClane], she's a lovely actress and Bruce did a great job. He brought a lot of humour to that part too, which he was very good at."

"As well as the movies, you've been in a lot of classic TV. *Friends, Seinfeld, The A-Team...* Were you always a villain?"

"Always. Always a villain. Did you get those in England?" Are you kidding? The A-Team are more popular than the Windsors. "One of those I did, the wrestler Hulk Hogan was in it. The Refrigerator, the footballer William Perry ... it was great, I played kind of a drunk whose son was getting in trouble and they rescued me and some guy was trying to kill me or something. In the other two I was a villain. Hulk Hogan was great. And Mr T I liked a lot. He's a short guy, and he kept saying..." Paul puts on a pretty ropey Mr T voice, '*People keep saying I'm short. I ain't short. When I stand on my money I ain't short*'. Peppard was an interesting fellow. I'd known him from the Actors' Studio, we were both members there. He was a kind of snobbish, aloof kind of guy. I used to get on to him a lot. He used to try to direct you a little bit and tell you how to do things and I used to say '*Hey, George, you play your part and I'll play mine.*' You had to put George in his place because he was kind of a prima donna."

"We've heard *The A-Team* wasn't a happy set."

"I don't think they *hated* it. I think they were pleased and grateful to have a hit show. But George would create a certain tension on the set, because he was sort of the boss. Those guys were great, Dwight Schultz was a talented actor, he did some great parts on that show. And Mr T., who knew? George was I'm sure happy to be on a hit show, even though he had to share some of the spotlight with the other fellows."

"So what's next for you, Paul?"

"I'm working on my backswing, I play a lot of golf."

Sadly, in 2006 Paul Gleason died of lung cancer. Maybe this was the last time he talked about his work in the eighties, who knows. But I do know there'll be a lot of casting agents who'll miss their reliable bad guy.

The HappyDays Theme Song

Truett Pratt and Jerry McClain (1977)

La Bamba

Los Lobos (1987)

Chapter Six

Frozen Custard and no time to bleed

Chicago to Minneapolis

Our guidebooks suggest that Milwaukee's juices are mainly made of beer, but all *we* have time for is *frozen custard...*

According to its sign out front, Leon's Frozen Custard is *world famous*. I'm not sure they're all talking about it in Beijing or Addis Ababa, but it's certainly well known in Milwaukee. Although we're way out of the centre, everyone we ask seems to know of it. However, no one seems to have been there for years and we get horrifically lost. We eventually reach Leon's after some accurate directions from a huge toothless black man with a twang I thought only existed as a joke in an Eddie Murphy film. Either it's a bit of tobacco he spits through the car window as he talks or the brown remnants of a once great tooth. Either way, it ends up wrapped in a wet wipe and remanded to the ashtray.

Legend has it that Leon's Frozen Custard is the diner that Arnold's in *Happy Days* was modelled on. Heyyyyyy, what a claim. Leon's is one of those metallic fifties style diners that blurts out mono rock and roll and somehow shows how innocent those times seem to have been. People weren't getting trolloped on gin cups and cocaine pipes, they were having frozen custard underscored by Fats Domino, and even though they may well have gone home to beat the crap out of the family ... at least it wasn't *in your face*, it was behind closed doors. Fair's fair.

HAPPY DAYS (1974–1984) (TV)

Creator: Garry Marshall
Awards: 2 Golden Globes, another 10 wins and 18 nominations
Cast: Henry Winkler (Arthur Fonzarelli), Tom Bosley (Howard Cunningham), Marion Ross (Marion Cunningham), Erin Moran (Joanie Cunningham), Ron Howard (Richie Cunningham), Anson Williams (Warren "Potsie" Weber), Don Most (Ralph Malph), Al Molinaro (Al Delvecchio), Scott Baio (Charles "Chachi" Arcola), Pat Morita (Matsuo "Arnold" Takahashi, Suzi Quatro (Lather Tuscadero).

Notes:

Happy Days wasn't *strictly* an eighties entity: Joanie wriggled around inside that opening titles' hula-hoop for ten years between 1974 and 1984. The reason this programme *must* feature on our tour is that for eighties children, The Fonz – whether in an episode shot in the seventies *or* eighties – was *the man.* Throw me ten Michael Jacksons and a Prince (not literally) – and they still wouldn't add up to one single Fonz.

Arthur Fonzarelli was like a third parent to me. If at any time I have ever acted in any way vaguely cool, it's down to The Fonz. Even now, I'll catch myself in the mirror at a bar, thumb in pocket with the rest of the hand casually dangling out. The Fonz made that look cool...although these days I look more like I'm trying to not-so-subtly touch myself. Even Shakin' Stevens does it better than me.

We meet with the owner of Leon's Frozen Custard – Ron Schneider (son of Leon), a middle-aged man with something funky going on with his eyes whereby they look in various directions simultaneously. He seems otherwise like a normal middle-aged gentleman. Ron is rushed, flustered and late – it must be a busy time of year for frozen custard – and greets us warmly like a celebrity granting fans a moment of precious time. I cut to the chase and ask him if it's true that Arnold's was based on his place.

"Well, we've been told that. No one has directly come out and said that. But one of the original writers of *Happy Days* was from the north side of town. We get associated with that probably because we've been around so long and it's much the same as it always was. But a few years ago some of the cast from *Happy Days* were here in Milwaukee for promotion and they ended up here. They came by."

"Did you get chatting to them?"

"A little bit. I talked to Tom Bosely [Mr Cunningham] and I had a picture taken with Marion Ross [Mrs Cunningham] and Scott Baio [Chachi]. He looked small on screen but he's a real big guy. He's got to be six feet two plus, a real big guy."

"So that's probably where a lot of the rumours on the Internet about Leon's being the inspiration came from?"

"The rumours were rampant long before that."

Our visit here does seem a tenuous slab of poppycock really, but sometimes myth turns out to be a more convenient way to explain things which might otherwise require thought. My stomach though is still intrigued to find out *what*, in the name of Mister Softee, frozen custard is all about. Asking Ron, however, stirs some sort of vehement custard-crazed beast from within, and he rattles out a history of the "famous" iced leisure product for around half an hour, insisting repeatedly that we try cones full of the stuff in various flavours to make the tour of his world a veritable 4D experience.

"So, frozen custard is a real Milwaukee tradition?"

"Sure it's a Milwaukee tradition, though it didn't originate in Milwaukee, it originated in Coney Island in 1919. It was a carnival treat and it's never outgrown that carnival atmosphere. My father was Leon and he started here in 1942. It's never changed. Unlike ice cream, it's made right here and sold fresh straight away. I assume you've had some?"

"No, let's try it!" I blurt rabidly, with no idea of the extent to which I was about to betray my own dear loyal gut.

"There's around sixty calories per ounce. You know, calories taste good."

"Do you eat a lot yourself?"

"Yeah, too much. How do you think I got to be this size?" It is quite tasty, no doubt. Like ice cream but creamier and more custardy, simple as that really. But rich, oh my days, it's so rich.

We come away green in the gullets with this cold egg and cream desert, not sure if we've chased something that was part of the eighties at all. All I seem to have chased is nausea, and I've nearly caught it. With my curiosity regarding those cones of pure cholesterol cured forever, we get in the car as Ron follows behind asking if we'd like to buy some machinery and start a Leon's franchise in England. I gurgle "no, thanks" through the emerging acid and yoke, and feel like we're escaping some sort of dessert-based horror movie. This is worse than the time Auntie Jo forced me to eat a whole Walls' Vienetta.

We continue on the Interstate 94 west, towards Minneapolis, as the custard seeps from my stomach to top up every pore on my face like an ice cube tray of pus just waiting for a nod from the "acne gene" to present itself as a faceful of blemishes.

We arrive in Minneapolis and check into a hotel for a delightful bout of insomnia. At 2am, Tom's retro eighties watch decides to spontaneously play a digital beepy tune. I think it may be "La Bamba". It's hard to tell; my face is so contorted through rage that my ears are partially squashed closed. But yes, on the fourth time around I decide it's definitely poxy "La Bamba".

"Turn ... the ... fucking ... thing ... off." I hiss through gritted teeth and all the spit available. Next, lightning illuminates us as negative images, and rain cracks at the windows like frozen broad beans thrown by an angry vegan. I consider quietly standing up and holding a werewolf pose until the next lightning flash, so the others would just get a glimpse of the most terrifying thing they've *ever* seen. But I'm too tired.

As if the night couldn't get any more hectic, in amongst the chaos of the storm, one of our neighbours starts making noise. This isn't your ordinary neighbour-noise. This is some sort of hysterical shrieking that gives me immediate visions of the worst bits of *The Exorcist* (or various ex-girlfriends after a night on the gin). A woman is screaming at the top of her voice and the only words that don't sound like part of a death-filled Latin incantation are "fuck", "shit" and the phrase "kick your ass" – all repeated in various orders but all with the same vile venom. It's like being caught up in an improv session featuring one of those *Monty Python* drag characters portraying Janet Street Porter. Given the lack of another voice returning obscenities, we decide that the woman is asleep and having quite a bad time in a nightmare. But not as bad as us, at least *she's* asleep.

Given the night's atrocities, our early start doesn't help me pick the best of moods out of the mood wardrobe. Nonetheless, we have an exciting trip up to the tiny lakeside town of Dellwood, directly north of St Paul.

We drive slowly, probably looking a little suspicious – as usual – past mansion after mansion on this exclusive-looking road out among the wild wood surrounded Minnesota lakes. We finally find the pad – distinguished, according to the directions, by its huge iron gates and train tracks running through the garden. Here we wait, as instructed by his personal assistant, to be collected by ex-WWF wrestling legend, movie star and former Governor of Minnesota ... Jesse Ventura.

He doesn't collect us though. After all that drum roll and lingual trumpet. We repeatedly ring on the bell and start to think that he saw us arriving on his security camera and didn't appreciate Luke accidentally driving over the bush at the front of his property. Or maybe it's Tom's stupid WWF headband or the sheer size of my head. Or maybe he just doesn't think we're as important as *we* do. Then, at the last minute, his wife drives up behind and tells us to follow her in. She tuts and huffs that Jesse hasn't heard the bell. She's quite fit. Suddenly, we are in the Ventura compound and feeling a little bit scared of being "clothes-lined", shot or just generally menaced. He's had all that time to stew over the bush and now we're on his premises and fair game as intruders. I hide my fear by humming the theme tune to *Grange Hill*. That usually works. A man comes wandering out of the garage with a strange platted beard and hair spilling out the sides of a baseball cap. He must be some odd-job man here to greet us, but I just want to cut the odd-job and get straight to the Jesse.

Thankfully we don't get a chance to talk down our noses at him before he reveals himself to actually be Jesse Ventura.

Jesse offers a towering welcome with a handshake that makes me feel like a toddler with M.S. After being told scornfully by his wife to do the interview in the living room rather than standing here in the driveway, Jesse invites us into his home. It's a plush affair no doubt – the living room window spans one side of the building and offers a widescreen vista across White Bear Lake. It's neat and tidy and quite obvious that the hell-raising wrestler and action movie hard-man didn't personally choose the pretty patterned upholstery or the delicate vases spilling blooming flowers. *She* probably did that.

Almost immediately he draws attention to his beard, which he needn't; I can't keep my eyes off the monstrosity. It's been platted into pigtail type things in three or four places and while he's keen to seek our opinion, I'm keener to avoid the subject. I *might* dare telling him that a balding man with a platted beard *could* be the wrong way to go, but I'm in his house and scared shitless of him. So I admire it most convincingly, even managing to tremblingly stroke my own chin to give the impression that it's something I can't believe I haven't considered yet. He tells us that he took a photograph of Johnny Depp, as per *Pirates of the Caribbean*, and asked for his beard to look just like Johnny's. It seems a strange thing for the former governor of a state to do. It's like John Major turning up at Lords with a Hoxton Fin. But I kind of admire his childish excitement about it, if not the end result. It really is a horrid piece of facial graffiti.

We quickly discover that although he's no longer the "Governor" of Minnesota, we're still to refer to him as 'Governor', out of respect. That's the way they do it here. I've already called him "Jesse" twice and "mate" once (when I thought he was the odd-job man), so that's disappointing for us both. I should have learned from the time I called Timmy Mallet "Tim". Mallet went ape-shit and said, "I don't like people who call me Tim. My name's Timmy." I should have learned.

Just to make me feel worse, Jesse continues, "If properly respectful, you call me Governor, because you are always the Governor, just not the current one. It's like if you're the Prime Minister of England, you know, Margaret Thatcher is always the Prime Minister." Yes, but Lady Thatcher had a little more trouble acknowledging that she was no longer the "current one" after she got booted out.

"You were also known as "The Body", did you give yourself that name?" Tom asks. "Fans did. It started when I came to the AWA [one of the original American wrestling organisations] and my whole routine with the posing. One day the fans just started calling me Jesse "The Body". I started off actually as Jesse "The Surfer" Ventura, because I had long blonde hair. But you just evolve, you know, and the fans themselves will help you evolve."

Evolving from a wrestler into a politician though is maybe further than you'd expect. I can't imagine Giant Haystacks making a point at Prime Minister's Questions. Only in America.

Throughout our meeting with "The Gov", he remains a serious and articulate machine who's clearly spent years talking *at* people, whether commentating on wrestling or debating politics (two genres of show-business Jesse considers to be very similar). Sitting in his Navy Seals T-shirt and cap, the Governor's service in the military is very much a defining aspect of his personality and it seems he tries to live by the Seals' mantra in everything he does.

"You don't ever talk about your Vietnam experiences..." Tom probes, open-endedly, hoping Jesse might start gazing into the middle distance with a single tear trickling down his cheek as he tell us horrors never before told.

"I just say I served honourably, just like any other soldier, sailor or airman. Many of our types of work are clandestine. We all had top-secret security clearances and my commanding officers always told us not to talk to anybody about anything. So I've held on to that position. I've taken abuse over it, people say you should talk about it, but no, not necessarily, that's between you and whatever."

Our *real* reason to meet Governor Ventura is to talk about how he figures in our memories of the eighties, and not really all that politics waffle. It's like going to visit your grandad – a few old war stories are worth the fiver pocket money at the end. It isn't long before we get talking about *Predator* and *The Running Man* – our pocket money treat.

"Obviously, you starred in *Predator* as a bit of an intense psycho soldier..."

PREDATOR (1987) (Movie)

Director: John McTiernan
Writers: Jim Thomas, John Thomas
Producers: Jim Thomas, Laurence Pereira
Awards: Nominated for an Oscar
Cast: Arnold Schwarzenegger (Dutch), Carl Weathers (Dillon), Elpidia Carillo (Anna), Bill Duke (Mac), Jesse Ventura (Blain), Sonny Landham (Billy), Richard Chaves (Poncho), R.G. Armstrong (General Phillips), Shane Black (Hawkins), Kevin Peter Hall (The Predator)

Notes:
This film made taking the dog for a walk up to Epping Forest a much more terrifying experience than it should have been. I constantly expected to turn a corner and find the dog hanging from a tree, all skinned. Forests were never the same again

---

"Not a psycho," Jesse jumps in swiftly and decisively, "not at all. I used to *do* that. From my time in the Seals, it's a case of you'd *better* be intense. It's life and death and it's not a game. You are on edge because it's the job you do. The intensity always has to be there."

"So you're bringing your real life experiences to the movie?"

"Yeah. That wasn't an easy role to play. But was it challenging? No. I just got back to what I used to do. In fact when we first got down there we went out every day with Schwarzenegger and I taught those guys how to patrol. For a week, we went out every morning for hours, because I wanted it to be real, as authentic as I could make it. But of course on the other side, I had to learn that you're not doing a documentary, so there's gonna be camera angles and shots that they wanna get that wouldn't necessarily be like that in reality. I was always complaining right away that we were patrolling too close. Bunched up like that, one shot would take the whole platoon out. They had to settle me down and say that we were shooting a film, we were not a real patrol here. But always remember, you're never a former Navy Seal. You *are* one. It stays with you until you die."

"Didn't Jean Claude Van Damme play the alien in *Predator* to start with?"

"He did, but he got fired. That was right before he got famous. But he did get fired, he's a wimp. All he did was complain how hot the suit was ... he'd whine and cry about it every day so they sent him home. And then he became a big star. But he did complain a lot. I like Jean Claude, he's a friend, but I think it was more a case that he realised they weren't going to see him, that he was going to be inside the suit and nobody would see his beautiful face. So I think that played a part. It was his first job."

"And then there was The *Running Man*..."

THE RUNNING MAN (1987) (Movie)

Director: Paul Michael Glaser
Writers: Stephen King (book), Steven E. de Souza (screenplay)
Producers: Rob Cohen, Keith Barish
Cast: Arnold Schwarzenegger (Ben Richards), Maria Conchita Alonso (Amber Mendez), Yaphet Kotto (William Laighlin), Jim Brown (Fireball), Jesse Ventura (Captain Freedom)

Notes:
This movie was perhaps an early warning that at some point in the future, TV's going to go too far. A game show to the death; *The Running Man* was set in 2017. Look at TV now, could it go that far in the next ten years? Don't count it out. The story that the film is loosely based on was written by Stephen King in just seventy-two hours. That's ridiculous.

"Oh yeah, Arnie said to me during *Predator* that there was this next film and that there was a part in it that would be perfect for me. And so it made it very easy to get the role, when the star of the film wants you. Definitely helps with the money negotiations."

"You were also in *Demolition Man* with Sylvester Stallone. How did he compare to working with the Arnie?"

"They were different people. This is just my opinion, but Arnold isn't bothered about people who are bigger than him. Sly *is* a little. I think that that's just something that I noticed. I ended up in a big fight scene with Stallone, where he had to shoot me to kill me, and they cut it out. Apparently his ego ... he didn't want to have to *shoot* me to kill me. You know, I guess I was too powerful. It got cut out and you don't even know what happened to my character. But that's Hollywood."

Apart from being friends, the weird comparison between Arnie and Jesse are that they're two muscle-bound caricatures who made it into political office.

"Does Arnie ever call you up and ask for some advice?"

"No. And I haven't offered any. You gotta remember that he's a Republican and I'm an Independent. So I still would be a bit reluctant."

"I know that Arnold can't run for President because he's a foreigner."

"They're trying to change that. They see Arnold as a star on the horizon, so now they've decided that maybe they can change the constitution. I opposed it."

"Would you take him on if he was running for President?"

"Well, if I was inclined to run then I'd have to."

"What are your political intentions at the moment?"

"Nothing. Right now I'm doing virtually nothing. Retirement. I just felt it was time to take a rest and take some time for *me*."

Then we get to talking about what I remember Jesse most for: wrestling. We manage to get his deep voice grumbling away at the foundations of the house by mentioning Hulk Hogan, with whom Jesse famously fell out with a few years ago.

"You used to be friends with Hogan and then things went a bit pear-shaped. Did you reconcile?"

"No. No. We've never spoken since. When he constantly goes on television and lies, I'm not gonna renew a relationship with him. It fell apart between Hogan and I when the whole steroid controversy happened way back in the eighties. He called Billy Graham a drug abuser. Billy was my hero. And he did that on *The Arsenio Hall Show* and he sat on there and told the public he never used steroids. And he was lying. And I didn't like the fact that he called Billy a drug abuser. That's the pot calling the kettle black. How does one do that? He's trying to say that what happened didn't happen. And both Vince [McMahon, Chairman of the wrestling organisation, WWE] and I have said publicly that 'yes, it did'. He denied what I wrote in my book, he went on national TV and denied that it happened and he's lying. Hulk Hogan used steroids and he lied and said he didn't. There used to be this joke thing where he would tell all the kids to take their vitamins and say their prayers, and the joke was that the guys would mumble 'Are they orals or injectibles?' Everyone was laughing and saying, 'Yeah, tell the kids truly what the vitamins are you're taking.' See, I was always honest about it. I took some steroids, I didn't take many, but I went public with it on posters in the public schools saying don't take 'em. They're not good for you. Don't use them. I didn't come under any scrutiny because I was honest from the start. Then you've got people like Hogan, who want to deceive the public, and he wants the public to believe that he got that big naturally? Plus I found that after I won Governor, Vince McMahon did a tribute to me that was very respectful. Hogan was at the time with WCW, and he came out and made a mockery of it. And me. And I watched that and saw the way the two organisations dealt with it. Vince treated it with respect and dignity. Hulk didn't like it because I now overshadowed him. *I'm* now the most famous wrestler in the world. He's not. And he has to live with that."

Suddenly, I get the sense that all the behind-the-scenes theatrics you see on wrestling programmes, where the wrestlers perform these painfully over-egged, ego-maniac tirades of diatribe down the lens, seem to have got caught up somewhere between an argument between two legendary wrestlers and the politics of an entire state.

"Do you think that hurts him?"

"Yeah. It hurts his ego, I guarantee you that." Jesse loves it. He's edging with smugness that he got to be Governor and Hulk got to be, allegedly, a liar.

"Never forget, a Navy Seal doesn't get mad, he gets even. Always remember that. And they can be very patient. Years can go by."

"Is there anyone you're waiting to get back at?"

"Oh sure, I have a list. Absolutely I have a list. I won't go any further than that, but I have a list." Oh shit. Jesse, we're so sorry about driving over the bush and not calling you Governor and for Tom's headband and my big head, *please* don't put me on the list.

"So behind the scenes, I think wrestling fans are quite intrigued to know how the wrestlers get on. After a fight, do you have a chat with your opponents?"

"Yes and no, depends on the individuals. There's naturally a common courtesy and respect, because the first thing you're taught in pro-wrestling is to respect your opponent's body as if it was your own. Because you're putting your life in that other person's hands and he is putting his life into yours. I mean when you lie on the mat and you see Randy Savage coming off the top rope with that elbow, if he misses by two inches, you're dead. He'd kill you, easily. *Easily.* There's a trust that has to take place. Nobody's out to get anyone's livelihood, we all know we earn livings, we all have families to take care of. There is some camaraderie to a certain point, naturally, but I wasn't that way very much. I was very independent. I didn't run with anyone particularly."

"A lot of wrestlers have died very young – Mr Perfect, Texas Tornado, British Bulldog and Rick Rude – why do you think that is?" Tom asks, knowing pretty much that drugs are often the fatal floor of these athletes.

"It's the life. The life is difficult. Many of them take different drugs to get through the life, be them recreational or steroids. At one point I wrestled sixty-three nights in a row. And when people see you on TV and you're two hundred and sixty pounds of muscle and you work to the point that you've dropped to two hundred and twenty... when you show up, they laugh at you. This isn't the guy I saw on TV. And so it kind of leads you to steroid use because it's the only thing that'll keep your weight up and keep you going. So it's the business itself that I think leads to the use of steroids. It's the abuse of the talent. Night in night out, you're required to perform.

"Do you think that's improved now?"

"Yeah. They get more time off now. They get more time between matches. I tried to unionise wrestling because I felt that we didn't have any benefits, no healthcare, no retirement. You know, wrestlers are not financial planners, many of them didn't have educations. I've watched wrestlers spend twenty-five, thirty years in the business and then retire and have nothing. And the business gives them nothing back but a pat on the back and a kick out the door."

"You played a bad guy in wrestling. Did you have any problems with angry fans?"

"Sure. You have to always be careful of them, because they get emotional. People often don't think clearly when their emotions have taken over. You're a bit of an antagonist by what you do, it's part of the job. You have to be prepared to protect yourself because they get carried away, or they drink too much. There was an older lady who took her fingernails all the way down my back. She was a wealthy woman, an elderly woman, but I had her arrested. I don't care whether she was beautiful, young, or whatever, if they've got nails and they carve you up with them... I don't get paid to have that happen to me."

"Most people my age know you for the commentating, but which did you prefer – the wrestling or the commentating?"

"Both. When I was at the peak of my career I enjoyed the wrestling, but as I got older and there were more injuries, I preferred being a commentator and not having to be body slammed any more."

"Do you ever watch wrestling now?"

"No."

"Never?"

"No. I see it for like five minutes over a five-month period. And that's just due to channel surfing. I don't work in it any more; I'm onto other things now."

Our ten-minute interview begins to slope toward the hour mark, and Jesse is still going just as focused and forthright as he began. Meanwhile, behind the camera, I start to flag and mist over into a foggy gaze out the window towards a paddling duck serenely floating around the lake, occasionally glancing over at Jesse to smile and nod inanely as if I'm still in the room. After a few minutes I pull my focus back to discover that the subject of conversation has moved around to underwear and why Jesse doesn't wear any. I stop grinning and nodding, because it occurs to me that I may come across as over-relishing the thought of Jesse's underwear stance.

'There's a practical reason and then there's a more fun reason too. The Seals are arrogant in many ways because they've earned the arrogance a little bit, if you want to call it that, and we don't view ourselves as the *regular*

Navy. And the regular Navy is very famous for wearing those boxer shorts, so for us to be different, we became famous for not wearing *any*. Now the practical end of that is because during the Vietnam era there was a lot of jungle warfare and a lot of river crossings. If you're out in the bush and you got to use the toilet, you're not afforded any luxury. You've got to do it in what you're wearing. For sanitary reasons, it's much better not to be confined with underwear. Also because underwear can chafe. And now, I do it with pride." Proud not to be wearing pants. How noble. I'm only ever proud of having no pants when I'm drunk.

As we walk out of the door, the stories continue spilling out of Jesse like a fountain of Jackanory: how he was bodyguard for the Rolling Stones in the late seventies and how he'd been the lead singer of a band that toured for a while – during which time he discovered that the music business is even more cut throat than the wrestling game (though not as violent, I suspect, as politics).

As we thank him in the driveway, Jesse says, "Well, you came all the way from England, I couldn't *not* see you."

Jesse's a polite, interesting man and more powerful and important than anyone we've asked for an interview and yet he's been more accommodating than any of them. We've been given less time of day by bit-part actors who consider themselves too big for our project, but let's not name names, like, for example, Guttenberg. Again though, with Jesse there's this sense of incredibly adamant self-worth that emanates from him; an all consuming feeling that his extremely confident, serious facade might be protecting something much more brittle underneath.

Luke drives us back over the bush he's already trounced on the way in, just to make sure, and speeds us to the highway, back through St Paul and out the other side to southwest Minneapolis.

CHAPTER SEVEN SOUNDTRACK:

Let's Go Crazy

Prince (1984)

Purple Rain

Prince (1984)

Chapter Seven

The Purple One

Minneapolis

M att Fink lives in a neighbourhood that oozes money but not a great deal of flamboyance. Sensible money. His home lines up among three thousand identical pads along River Oak Street, and it's clear that this man invested for his family and not in a lifestyle of drug-whoring showbiz indulgence. These square, simple gaffs are built for Minnesota winters, not parties with extravagant poets with beards and absinthe in pints. I found a website for "The Doctor" while back in England and sent a positively charming email to which he replied straight away. He seemed immediately happy for us to pop over to his family home to be generally soppy and worshippy.

While I was growing up, Matt was *Dr. Fink* – Prince's loyal keyboard player for thirteen years, spanning 1978 to 1991. In fact, he survived The Revolution and went on to be part of the New Power Generation. It all sounds a bit more important than pop bands; extra-terrestrials might go through Prince's discography and assume he had a hand in changing the entire world order over those years. Then again, maybe he did. But I'd be most interested in what they'd make of *Purple Rain*.

PURPLE RAIN (1984) (Movie)

Director: Albert Magnoli
Writer: William Blinn, Albert Magnoli
Producers: Robert Cavallo, Steven Fargnoli, Joseph Ruffalo.
Awards: Won 1 Oscar for Best Music, 3 other wins and 4 nominations.

Cast: Prince (The Kid), Apollonia Kotero (Apollonia), Morris Day (Morris), Jerome Benton (Jerome), Billy Sparks (Billy), Dez Dickerson (Dez), Wendy Melvoin (Wendy), Lisa Coleman (Lisa), Bobby Z (Bobby Z), Matt Fink (Doctor Fink), Mark Brown (Brown Mark)

Notes:
Let's face it, if it wasn't for the music, this movie would be a howling stink bomb. But all the hype surrounding Prince's explosion onto the world stage meant that this film flew at you album-first, begging you to forgive the acting and storyline because the music's so stonkingly good. Albums don't get much more eighties than this. I remember the whole of my school football team singing "Purple Rain" after winning a match, though I suspect it was our parents back in 1984 that really *got* the music.

We tread over dangerously-placed kiddie toys, positioned suspiciously like a scene from *Home Alone*, and make it down to Matt's basement, a no kid zone where his recording studio is wired up with so much equipment it's like walking into Darth Vader's bathroom. I barely recognise the man. He looks like someone's dad; in his forties and all daddified. Probably because he *is* someone's dad. A few extra chins swing where there was once the chiselled jaw of a nonchalant-looking keyboard wizard. Now Matt Fink looks generally disconcerted and bulgy.

So, we plonk ourselves down in Matt's world of wires and electronics and begin talking about his life and career. It's weird though; I've actually seen him play in concert twice and listened to songs like "Let's go Crazy" – on which he plays that beginning organ part – a thousand times and now I'm sitting in the bloke's house. But it just seems so difficult to relate this pudgy family man to the funky musician I've seen fingering the keyboard for the pleasure of millions.

"I was with Prince for twelve years," Matt confirms.

"And you were called Doctor Fink. Are you still known as Doctor Fink? How do we address you? The Doc? Or Matt? Or The Finkster? Or Finkatron?" I'm a little weary, after Governor-gate with Jesse Ventura.

"Yeah, I still go by the name. Depends on how you know me. Fans still call me Doctor Fink. People who come to the studio who don't know I was ever with Prince, which happens a lot, go with Matt. Or Mr Fink, if they want to." Matt shoots me a look as if to say the 'Mr' option is the one I should go for, before laughing and releasing me from the potentially awkward following half hour.

As I speak to Matt, or Mr Matt or Doctor Thingy, he looks at me as if he really can't believe I'm still interested in this stuff. He maintains this cautious eye of suspicion as he speaks, as though every word might be used against him. Maybe he thinks it's all a big wind-up. I also begin to wonder if my terribly inaccurate Prince outfit isn't putting him off just a little. It's certainly not helping *me* feel very comfortable. Under duress from Tom, I've reluctantly thrown on a frilly white shirt, purple velvet jacket with the price tag dangling off, dandy cuff and a wig that more resembles the mop-top hair of Ruud Gullit than Prince. It's a *very* approximate attempt at resembling the "Purple Man", and I'm not sure Matt understands that I *know* I don't look like Prince. Perhaps it's not even ironically funny, I just look stupid. Maybe that's why he's eyeing me like I could be slightly spastic or even an immediate physical threat. Nonetheless, he stumbles carefully into his account of 1978.

"I was with him from the beginning of his record deal with Warners in 1978. I was in the original group and worked with him up until December of 1990."

"That's a massive amount of time, especially for Prince, because he has a high turnover of musicians, doesn't he?"

"Yeah."

"How did you manage to cling on for so long?" Oops. I didn't mean this to sound insulting, as though he was in some way lucky to stay in the band, but it just came out that way, so I laugh nervously as though I'm just kidding. Which makes it sound even more sneery. I got that question all wrong.

"How did I manage to *cling on*?" he replies, a bit stunned that I dare insinuate, round his house, that he was *clinging*. "Well, he and I just clicked really well, got along really well for the most part and respected each other's musicianship. I probably would have stayed on longer, I know he wanted me to go back. But I was kind of wanting to branch off in some other ways and do something of my own. I was gonna get married and have kids and settle down and not be touring all the time. That's one of the main reasons really."

"Were you the longest serving band member?"

"Pretty close. One of the other keyboard players who came in after me, Morris Hayes, stayed around eleven years too."

"So how did you meet Prince in the first place?"

"It was through another friend of mine, Bobby Z. We both went to the same high school. One time he came to me while I was playing in another band and brought me Prince's demo tape to listen to. He took me out in his car and said, 'You've got to hear this, he's a young guy, like your age'. Prince and I are the same age, we were eighteen. I listened to it in the car and Bobby said that this guy played all the instruments *and* wrote *and* produced the whole thing. I was just shocked because *nobody* was doing that. Especially at such a young age. So I said 'Well, this guy's somebody I'd be interested in meeting. Is there any way I could meet him, or be involved with a group to support his record, if he gets a deal at some point?' And Bobby was like, 'Well, I'll let you know when the time comes.' So then, after he was signed, which was maybe six months later, he had to record a first album. At that time they had already chosen another keyboard player. But after a year of not much going on, the keyboard player, Ricky Peterson, had some other offers and didn't want to wait around for Prince. So he said 'Prince, I'm taking off, I'm going to LA, but I'm still interested in working with you.' But of course Prince didn't really want to wait around for him, so they put the feelers out for another keyboard player. That's when I contacted Bobby and said can I get an audition?"

"Did you go along in your doctor's outfit?"

"I wasn't The Doctor back then. That didn't come until early 1980. So it was 1978 when Prince decided to hire me. Then I would say around 1981, 1982, *Controversy* [Prince's third album], things started breaking. And then *1999*, which followed that, things were *really* breaking quite big for him, you know, that was a two to three million-selling record. That's when the idea for *Purple Rain* came along, which of course really put us in the spotlight."

"Where exactly did the doctor thing come from then? Was that you, or did Prince decide on it?"

"No, that was something I came up with. Originally I had taken on an image of a guy in a black and white striped jail outfit, back in 1979. Prince said he wanted me to come up with something a bit wacky. He liked the jail suit, but then the opportunity came to be a warm-up act for Rick James. During the first couple of shows for the Rick James tour we realised that Rick was coming out in a jail suit for one of the songs. Prince came to me and said that Rick was doing it, and did I have another idea? I just went, 'No, but I'll think about it.' He said, 'Alright, you think about it and get back to me...in about an hour.' So I threw three or four things at him and one of them was a doctor. He thought that was the best and said, OK, you're gonna become Doctor Fink.' He sent the wardrobe people out right away and got some scrub suits and a stethoscope. No scalpels though. I told them I needed all the stuff that a gynaecologist would need, in case, you know. But that's how it started."

"Do you ever still wear The Doctor's outfit?"

"Yeah, I did last December for a reunion."

"Was it the same one?"

"No, I can't wear the old one; I've gained too much weight."

The thought of being a part of Prince's world from the start and seeing it explode from the confines of the local Minneapolis scene into international fame is mind-blowing. I ask Matt what it was like to experience such immense success and I'm not sure whether he's bored by the question, bored of talking about the *Purple Rain* days or just so used to the idea that the words just flop out with the mundanity of reading out Mum's shopping list.

"It was a very big thing that catapulted him into worldwide fame, yeah. It was exciting, of course. I mean here we are; we're coming out of the Midwest of the United States. Minneapolis, not really a huge music town at the time. Of course you've got Bob Dylan though and several other groups that were bouncing around throughout the sixties and seventies. But he was one that really became as big as Bob Dylan, or bigger, so yeah it was really exciting for all of us to be a part of that and be in the spotlight and have all the fame and travelling and playing all over the planet."

"Now. The movie." Here I go. For some reason I don't trust my own tongue today, it's being a bitch. "I watched it the other day and I'm not quite sure it stands the test of time..." It seems I've got some sort of ridiculous agenda to give Doctor the arse ache. It really is one of those both-feet-in-gob days, but I don't mean it to come out that way, honest.

"You're telling me *Purple Rain* ... now you're not so sure about it?" Matt looks shocked and incensed and hurt and appropriately arse-achy. I've come round his house dressed like a prat, and now start telling him that the biggest year of his career and one of the most important rock movies in history doesn't stand the test of time. Fucking liberty. I'm a pillocking titting idiot.

"No, I mean..." Come on, Spencer, you stuttering prick, before it all kicks off "... in terms of a *movie*." I half rescue. And that's actually what I mean, that the movie is a poorly acted camp little effort with some really great music videos almost dragging the wafer-thin plot together.

"Oh, in terms of the plot and acting you mean? OK, I'll give you that. Maybe not the most polished piece of work, but still probably one of the better rock and roll films." I feel so guilty. Here I am, drinking his tap water, slagging off his film.

"It works really well as a series of music videos." I continue the rescue mission.

"Yeah, it's a great testament to Prince's talent."

"You had a few lines in it, didn't you?"

"Oh, I only really had one. Kind of a close-up, it had something to do with Wendy [Melvoin, another member of The Revolution]. I'm just trying to think what it was... Wendy and Lisa [Coleman, the other member of Wendy and Lisa] were having a bit of a disagreement with Prince. They were trying to get him to listen to their demo tape and he just said, 'Aah, leave me alone.' So they got upset and Prince looks over to me and says, 'What do you think?', like about them wanting to collaborate, and then I make a joke about Wendy's period or something." Nice.

"So what's your favourite record you made while with Prince?"

"Probably *Dirty Mind*. But other than that I'd say *Purple Rain* was a good one. *Sign 'o' the Times*, certainly. That's the top three." I try to base as many of my questions to Doctor Fink on his own experiences of the whole *Purple Rain* phenomenon, but the temptation to ask the utmost turgid of qquestions, 'What was Prince like?' is simply too tough to resist. I just have to steamroller in and come out with the question he *must* be sick of answering.

"So, we see all the eccentric stuff Prince does, with the name change [to an unpronounceable symbol], is that what he's *really* like?"

"No, there was a reason for the symbol thing that he did. At first, I was a little bit miffed by it because I didn't know what his reasoning was behind it. Later on he revealed that he was having a dispute with his record label, he was unhappy with Warners owning his masters. Prince felt that he had served them quite well, made them a lot of money and he wanted to be more independent and own his own masters."

"So what is he *like*?" I push.

"He is actually a very funny guy to be around. He's got a great sense of humour. He likes to joke around with everybody. But then he's got this serious music side, he's very dedicated to what he does and works very hard at it. We all played jokes on each other though. One time Prince came to rehearsal and one of the horn players had a plaid shirt on, and Prince didn't really care for the plaid shirt. He made a joke about the guy's shirt, so the next day we *all* wore plaid shirts to get back at him. Just to mess with him. And then later he did a video, where he's wearing a plaid shirt. He said, 'What the heck, if you can't beat them, join them. Because you know, in Minnesota, a lot of people wear the flannel shirts."

I've always been intrigued by the whole world of Prince and his high turnover of supporting musicians, so on being given an opportunity to talk to one of them about their experiences ... *of course,* my mind goes entirely blank. I stutter out similar question after similar question about where Morris Day is now and where Sheila E is now and where Apollonia is now and if he still speaks to Prince etc. etc. etc. blah blah blah SHUT UP, SPENCER. This is the hazard of being an enthusiast and an interviewer at the same time: the geeky fan side of me can't help but poke out like a baboon's multi-coloured arse. And right now my multi-coloured arse is flapping out all over Doctor Fink.

"In terms of the old Prince fraternity, all the musicians, who do you keep in touch with still? Are Wendy and Lisa still around?"

"Yeah, a little bit, you know. Last December we had a huge reunion with all the people who were involved in the eighties. Sheila E put it together to raise money for abused children. We all flew in, The Revolution, some of The Time, The Family, Madhouse, Patty Labelle, Chaka Khan, Appollonia...it was just a great time. The Revolution hadn't played together for seventeen years and we played stuff, without Prince. He wasn't there, didn't make it." He didn't make it? What a spoilsport.

A little guilty for bleeding Fink dry about the supporting role he played in my Eighties, I feel I have to edge in an uncomfortably prised question about what he does now, just so he doesn't think I wanted Prince juice only.

"So, what's happened to you since The Revolution?"

"Well, I stayed on for four years after *The Revolution* and became part of the NPG at that point. After that, I just started my own production company and started producing different projects for artists here in town. Did some work for a video game company, and lately, I've been working on several different projects. Still doing a little live work, but not much. I got together with a couple of former members of the band The Rembrandts, they did the theme tune for *Friends*. We worked together for a short time, but The Rembrandts are back together again now. I have a CD I released in 2001 and I sing on it."

Off camera, Matt relaxes a lot more. When we mention that our next stop is downtown Minneapolis and First Avenue – the club where the concert scenes in *Purple Rain* were shot – he jumps to life about the ghosts that are rumoured to be there. He asks if *we've* ever had any ghostly experiences (to which I mention that I once felt a draft) and then thrusts off on how his wife had an evil spirit hanging around her for years that they eventually had to get removed by a real-life Ghostbuster. His matter-of-a-fact account of how this *thing* caused trouble and how he'd had to chase it out of the room on a number of occasions was a curious add-on to what we thought we'd found out about this ex-rock star cum family man. I suppose his experience of life with Prince was such an out-of-the-ordinary way to go that having to chase a spirit out of the bedroom would be no more bizarre than the plaid shirts and *Purple Rain* and playing keyboards dressed as a doctor.

We shake hands and leave Fink-towers not *really* any the wiser about this bloke. Maybe I'm disappointed not to get the resounding slanderous quotes that Jesse Ventura spilled so voluntarily. Perhaps I wanted him to hate Prince and reveal the truth with a shocking exposé of violent pinching and hair-pulling or torturing of the drummer with a sawn-off ukulele. But in reality, we met a man who's actually moved on and consigned the pop star stuff to the past. If *I* could do that – consign the glory of yesterday to somewhere less rueful – we wouldn't be on this trip. He seems happy with his place in this world and is probably a good example of why our attempts to explode nostalgia are a worthwhile endeavour.

Heading north from the Fink, we start getting glimpses of the Minneapolis skyline we'd missed in the dark last night. It's one of those generic city views that could be *any* American city. Impressive-but-similar shiny tall buildings sprout rudely next to each other in big clumps that fill up with fast-walking workers wearing suits and clutching spill-proof coffee mugs ... all of them off their faces on caffeine and office politics.

Walking around downtown Minneapolis, we could be anywhere in America. I start itching to get out of these huge Starbucks-conquered grids and into the open country or at least somewhere more human. It feels like we've visited the same coffee shop, same bookshop and slept in the same motel room every day and night for sixteen days and even though we've only traipsed a quarter-width of the country, I feel like we need a change. The last thing you expect on a road trip encompassing such a huge continent is to get bogged down with the same old routine in a different place every day.

Before those thoughts take greater shape and start turning my mood into bastard mode, we head to the corner of 7th Street and 1st Avenue, where First Avenue sits ... the club used in the film *Purple Rain*.

I've been here before.

November 7th 1997. Six-thirty in the morning and snow is landing on our coats and soaking through the weave as other flakes serenely brush our faces. Elle and I have been travelling all night and are waiting a while before walking away from the Greyhound station; until the mild glow of emerging sunlight makes the desolate streets feel a little safer. Elle has no reason or desire to be in Minneapolis, but has generously indulged my pursuit of the essence of Prince's heritage. As we drag our backpacks around the corner, I spot the First Avenue club. There's a strange déjà vu feeling of the film and reality colliding.

The last memory I have of this moment is of the two of us holding hands, peering through a window into the club; into the darkness of the empty foyer as snow gently piled up on our shoulders, shoes, my jutting chin and anything else we had protruding. That moment, just looking through to the club, I loved her. For being here with me, for allowing herself to be dragged into this personal moment and sharing it with me. I immediately feel sick, like I'm cheating on Elle, like I'm knocking a hole through our memory, making a mockery of our visit, as if the first time wasn't adequate and now it's time to pave over it all.

Although reluctant, I keep quiet and go ahead with the nostalgia-removing operation. This *must* be the healthy thing to do. It must be, right? Or is this going to make me worse?

We walk through the door of First Avenue, and look for my contact, Steve McClellan, the manager of the place. He sits in the upstairs of the club: more than plump, unshaven and distinctly like a lifelong roadie. I can't smell anything, but suspect he has an odour. He looks like a vague whiff of yesterday's vodka and the day before's sweat.

Steve walks us across the dance floor, which back in 1984 was the scene of the film's atrocious bopping and rhythmic body-slinging. The very stage where Prince performed "Purple Rain", "Let's Go Crazy", "Darling Nikki", "When Doves Cry" and all that stuff looks small, black and plain, but hums with the aura of stale music history clinging on from way before Prince's efforts in 1984. It actually feels a little unpleasant, being in here. The faint smell of bleach smothering spilt sticky drinks and secret vomit corners. Crevices where groping, smoking and doping have kept sordid indulgences as lost moments never to be told of and mostly forgotten.

Steve seems reluctant to talk about Prince and the whole *Purple Rain* thing. He considers it a small and insignificant part of a much broader history of First Avenue. I find this irritating: not that the place has a proud history, but that he disregards our interest as the tip of a much fatter iceberg. Fair enough there's more, but it's the tip *we* want to talk about, not the fat.

"So you were here at the time of filming?"

"Yeah, I pretty much tried to ignore it. I didn't want to be an extra. I've never seen the movie. I've seen snippets. Maybe I've seen it in different parts, but I've never sat down and watched the whole thing."

"How often did Prince play here at First Avenue?"

"Just once or twice a year." Steve is much more interested in talking about The Ramones starting fires outside the dressing rooms and Metallica and U2 and other bands that played in their earlier days before making it massive.

I feel he's being a bit shitty just for effect: he knows that we're easily impressed by anything Prince, and to be so dismissive of the whole thing makes him think he looks cool and wantonly frank. So balls to him. I don my ridiculous Prince outfit once more and get on the stage as Luke films me. I do the splits and haul myself up unaided: just like Prince did. The only difference is that the whole operation takes me around four and a half minutes per move and I tweak a mystery muscle in my groin. I also hump the stage in the same way Prince did for "Darling Nikki" – all of this in front of an unimpressed punk band trying to do a sound check behind me for their performance later on. What. A. Tit. Even though I'm out of my depth and embarrassed in front of the smirking punk band, I feel honoured to stand in the same place as Prince and indeed all of the other famous musicians that have performed here.

Perhaps part of the presence I feel is a dead old lady that Steve reckons appears late at night when the place has closed.

"The little old lady sits down there by the bar. She's still waiting for her bus. That only happens when you're all alone here at about three in the morning when everyone else has gone." This'll be what Doctor Fink referred to earlier. The First Avenue building used to be a Greyhound station back in the thirties. Maybe she's just the remaining scraps of some moody acid Steve might have taken in 1986; maybe she's a real ghost.

After spending the odd pensive moment lurking around the doors Apollonia sneaked through in the movie and the stage door that Prince minced in and out of, we drive back out of the centre to our motel. I look back at First Avenue in the mirror and imagine Elle and me standing outside holding hands in the snow. A lump like a snowball with stones in clogs my throat. (And it's only now I realise that I never did look good in that coat. Should've got the black one.)

Back at the motel, I mention to the receptionist about last night's terrible kafuffle with all the screaming from the woman next door. The young receptionist says apologetically that, "We have a guest with a mild case of Tourette Syndrome." We point out that last night wasn't *mild*; last night was like being heckled at the gates of hell. We're offered another room, but say no, because in fact we're quietly looking forward to another bout, in the knowledge that no one is *actually* being bludgeoned to death.

While the abuse looks after itself, I lay face up thinking about what we've done today. I realise that if I ever come back to Minneapolis, I'll always think about the time I dressed up as Prince round Fink's and on the First Avenue stage ... not so much about Elle and I or when I watched the film in the eighties. Success, I think, for nostalgia has been replaced with something new. The edge has been taken off.

CHAPTER EIGHT SOUNDTRACK:

A Knightrider Christmas

Kitt The Amazing Car of Tomorrow (1983)

Chapter Eight

Dances with KITT

Minneapolis to Calgary

With the Tourette's lady still screeching at her imaginary demons, we leave and get the hell on the Highway 212, west out of Minneapolis and eventually across the state border into South Dakota. But before that we draw up outside Prince's house – – – the famous Paisley Park and try to peek past the security barriers hoping to see him prancing around somewhere inside with Apollonia and the gang. No such luck, it's just a big industrial-looking building that gives no clue that Purple Royalty resides within. A plain old winter-resistant prefabby type effort. So we say goodbye to all that *Purple Rain*-ness and move on.

Suddenly we're in the middle of a relentless nowhere, on a road that winds off into a samey distance that we consistently never seem to reach. So *this* is what they call The Prairies; a big sloping green and straw-coloured desolate wilderness. Out in the open at last. We reach Pierre, the capital of South Dakota: a small messy city, with little to draw people other than commerce and casinos. Having pronounced it the *French way* all day, I feel a right pranny at a service station when they tell me, witheringly, that it's actually pronounced "peer". But if that's the capital then there can't be much happening in South Dakota other than bison and betting and they can stick it *and* their pronunciation. I'm off to feel silly elsewhere.

We pass straight through, over the Missouri River and knock an hour off our watches in honour of the Mountain Time Zone. Route 1806 takes us to more remote an area than we've experienced thus far. Huge expanses of grassland fold into silky lumps as far as the horizon can be bothered to reveal; interrupted only by a dark blue lake sunk into the hills like an enormous pore. We imagine the horror of running out of fuel around here, and then try not to. As we get closer to the *Triple U Standing Butte Ranch (Butte pronounced "bewt"* like '*isn't that a 'bewt*'), wispy clouds begin turning sour dark, until a menacing blanket of moist black-grey smothers us and tucks itself in over the distance. A sign declaring that the ranch is just eight miles away has bull's skulls dangling off it. Not sure what they mean by that, but I decide it's threatening and have a quiet little worry.

Just as we reach the entrance to the ranch, the sky bursts its dirty guts all over us – hailstones the size of babies' fists smack the windscreen and the mud road of two miles to the ranch begins eating up the Oldsmobile's tyres as it argues its way in skids and apologies through the quagmire. Luke keeps losing his back end (the car's, not his own, for a change) and when fork-lightning pierces the hills around us, we start to wonder if we're in a bit of a pickle. Of all the places we've driven so far – the urban slums and chaotic city centres – this is the scariest. We're totally at the whim of nature and it's chucking its stuff all over us.

Eventually, Luke squelches us successfully to the ranch: dodging lightning like a game of *Space Invaders*, and we find the building that declares itself "The Gift Shop". I've already spoken to a woman on the phone about coming to the ranch to meet their buffalo and pay tribute to the place where a great deal of the film *Dances With Wolves* was shot in 1989.

DANCES WITH WOLVES (1989) (Movie)
Director: Kevin Costner
Writer: Michael Blake
Producers: Jake Eberts, Kevin Costner, Jim Wilson
Awards: Won 7 Oscars
Cast: Kevin Costner (Lt Dunbar), Mary McDonnell (Stands With A Fist), Graham Greene (Kicking Bird), Rodney A. Grant (Wind In His Hair)

Notes:
This movie was one of the few true old-fashioned epics to be made in the eighties. Blockbusters were more often full of machine gun-slinging and biceps. So when Costner came out with this one, it stuck out from the rest of the eighties' popcorn cinema as a beautifully shot old-style classic that we thought had all but become extinct. It seemed to open the door to the nineties and a more artistically considered era of film-making.

We enter the building, which appears to double as someone's home. Kaye, the lady I've spoken to, is on the blower and we stand dripping in her dark hallway as she discusses nothing in particular at leisure and length with a friend. Look at us. We're stood in a hallway in a ranch house in the middle of nowhere as a fierce electrical storm gets closer and closer and a woman slowly finishes her phone chat about bisen cakes or something. It's a ridiculous scenario. Eventually a teenage girl appears and shows us to the gift shop – an emporium of anything buffalo: buffalo hair, buffalo bones, buffalo beer mugs and buffalo jam. There's a pair of buffalo hooves turned into lamps and a mangy old cat smarms around with the odd snidey meow.

Dances With Wolves is vaguely credited on the odd T-shirt, but really, this place is all about the buffalo. They love those crazy buffalo. The girl tells us that the beasts can live up to forty years old and we immediately develop hopes that we might be able to interview one that was around when Costner and crew were here. Or at least get charged by one; I'll take all I can get.

But she bursts our bubble by subtly mentioning – like you would break the news of a death in the family – that, "We have our own slaughter house here, so they don't make it that old." beaming with a weird murderous pride afterwards. "We go out and shoot them on the pasture and then cut the throat and haul them on the hearse," she says through a demonic grin. They have a hearse for the buffalo; these people are mental.

The weather is just too treacherous for us to sludge out to meet buffalo that might be distant cousins of buffalo from the film. However, the girl does throw us a location-hunting lifeline.

"Oh and if you'd like, the actual buildings they used in the film are right down over there."

"You mean the out-post Costner stayed at?" I breathily return at the mere hint of a location, suddenly ignoring the bloody murder and imaginary threat all around me.

"Yeah, they used to be down by the river but we ran them up so, like, guests could look at them." Brilliant, a delightful unexpected trip to Fort Sedgwick.

On our way out to brave the elements, Kaye – the lady from the kitchen we dripped outside of for a while – has finished her marathon phone call and agrees to say a few things to us on camera. She owns the ranch and was around when the film crew took over for that brief while and had even met Costner, but all she has to say about the experience is that it had been "nice".

"We never realised it was going to be as big as it turned out to be. It was *nice.*" Whoopee. I want her to wax lyrical about how she humped Kevin Costner raw on the back of a bison, but there's just no juice here. No humping. It was just *nice.*

"He was real nice."

"What did you think of the film, Kaye?"

"*Real* nice." Christ on a bike.

"Goodbye, Kaye."

"Oh, nice." Yes.

By now the rain is coming down like Indians' Wild-West-movie arrows and we hope that we can get a "seen it, done it" view of the huts from the warmth and safety of the car. *That's* how bad it is out there. Unfortunately, they're obscured by barns and stuff, and our location-hunting duty sends us traipsing off down a muddy hill as Luke waits, brimming with cowardice, in the car.

The huts are really just empty wooden sheds that have the faint smell of buffalo poo. They're damp and dark and muddy and like I said, empty. With his everlasting exuberance for this sort of stuff, Tom shoves the camera in my hands and poses by the door to present his carefully worked-out piece to camera. Tom likes his pieces to camera, I think he sees himself as a sort of movie version of Tony Robinson (without the suspect earring).

"There are some interesting facts surrounding this film." Here we go. "Viggo Mortensen was originally down to play Kevin Costner's part. Costner's daughter was in the movie. Erm, there were two wolves, one of which had its legs painted white to match the other one. And also, erm, in one scene, Kevin Costner had to run from the wolf but had to keep throwing it meat because the wolf had just bitten the trainer. So I think maybe we should go now. Or maybe we should wait here." We're not going anywhere, Thomas. We're now actually a bit stuck in this bloody thing. The lightning is hitting the ground not far from the hut, the whole place is vibrating and the thunder is exploding in nerve-jumping cracks. This has gone beyond a bit of a silly adventure; we're *actually stranded*; we're *actually scared*. Properly scared, with that ominous *headmaster wants to see you in his office* feeling in the stomach. I can't work out if this is a great, glorious way to go, or a Darwin Awards' silly death candidate that would cast a shadow of idiotic shame over the Austin family for eternity. What a predicament.

After quivery consultations with each other, we decide to make an end-of-days dash for the car before the road becomes an impassable washed-out nightmare and we have to ask Kaye for a room for the night or an ambulance. That wouldn't be *nice*. The mud has doubled in depth even since we made it down the hill to the huts, and we have to run so that our feet don't start penetrating to a depth we can't get out of. Quicksand is the form of death best left to the worlds of Dick Dastardly and Scooby Doo than me, here, in my tracksuit bottoms.

We scramble slippingly back to the car, skating through the mud like Torville and Dean in a fetish club wet-room, weather-beaten and traumatised, to find Luke has been really worried that we might have actually been struck by lightning.

"Oh my God, I honestly thought I'd have to go and get someone to find you." Well thanks Luke, but that could easily have been *you* coming to find us, no? Despite his concern seeming to be genuine, as I sit shivering and twitching like a 'nam vet, I notice that the eighth track on his *Bugsy Malone* soundtrack CD is playing. He'd just pressed play when we left. Oh yes, poor Luke was *so* worried ... but not *so* worried that he couldn't sit here mouthing gaily along to seven tracks of full-blast Bugsy...

Hail and worrying depths of mud and bison shit hinder our desperate scramble out of the ranch: mud up to our tongues, we feel lucky to escape Costner country.

I decide that my native American name would be Mud In His Mouth.

An early start thrusts us – now dry – out into the deeper West towards Badlands National Park. Interstate Highway 90 not only offers swift carriage but also a plethora of opportunities to visit tacky tourist attractions, relentlessly advertised on signs lined up for miles all the way along the road; they're like a small child tapping you on the shoulder asking for sweets.

Among the choices of tired-looking tourist traps such as Petrified Gardens, Prairie Dog sanctuaries, rock garden shops and ghost towns is the 1880 Town. Although normally I'd handcuff myself to the car to avoid being dragged through such awfulness – we can't resist the promise of *Dances With Wolves'* movie props *and* a *real life* star from the film itself.

We pay our seven dollar entry and, Marty McFly-style, step back to 1880. It's basically a re-creation of a small cowboy town, with music piped through the whole thing to make it feel like you're an extra in *Bonanza*. The props from *Dances With Wolves* include a teepee and some arrows. Pretty unspectacular. But then we go outside to *actually meet* one of the stars of the film.

"What was your motivation in playing the role of Sisco?" I ask Buck, a shabby, ageing horse who was ridden by Kevin Costner throughout the film. Poor old Buck stands under a shelter watching us watching him, as Tom and I fire some of our best interview questions on the tour so far.

"So Buck, we haven't seen a lot of you since the film. What have you been up to? TV? Movies? Corporate videos?"

"Do you feel you've been typecast as a horse?"

"Did you have anything prepared for the audition to play Sisco?"

"I know you and Costner got on very well during the filming. Do you keep in touch? Meet up for drinks? The odd game of squash?" I know it seems a bit sad that we're standing here asking these questions to a horse, like buffoons, while Buck doesn't even credit us with a "no comment". We seem to be the only people to have wandered away from the "street" – and its kooky replica Wild West banks and hotels and post offices – to see this aged star, and it makes me feel a bit sorry for him. They don't keep Corey Haim chained up to a barn so the occasional tourist can come and stare. Although maybe they should.

–––––––––

As we near Badlands, the flat rugged South Dakota terrain starts showing signs of rocky peaks the guidebook tells us to expect. Indeed, once we enter the park, an immediate viewpoint offers a spectacular gaze across a valley smothered in ridges and spikes, all striped with various shades of red. Bizarre stripy columns sit up in this arid basin, as if sculpted by a child with a ball of mixed up Plasticine; some mind-boggling act of nature must have been in action to create something so intricate.

We head further into the park and take a gravel road that no one else seems inclined to. It winds its way for miles into the very heart of nothing:

Sage Creek Wilderness area, where the wagon riding scenes were shot for *Dances With Wolves*. This area doesn't have the spiky mounds that made the outer area of Badlands so impressive, but it does have an expansive prairie sky that seems to show clouds so far away they're probably raining on people in another state.

After skidding our way along the gravel road for what seems like several weeks, running over a snake and passing through crowds of bison that have heads bigger than me and a really bad attitude, we manage to find a route leading into the Black Hills area and onto Mount Rushmore. Seeing Mount Rushmore in the flesh (or the granite) is exactly the same as seeing it in pictures and on screen. So we don't bother with it so much. Beyond Mount Rushmore, we get to Deadwood, and steam northwest: out of South Dakota and into Wyoming. The Black Hills are replaced by great wide grassy expanses and the only thing to keep boredom at bay is the variety of road kill wildlife that gives us a closer look at deer, skunk, squirrel and funny-looking bird things with their brains and wings welded together by the tyres of several hundred cars.

The urge to start sculpting mashed potato into a tower shape with stripes down the side is upsettingly absent on our approach to the Devil's Tower National Monument – the odd shaped thing that Richard Dreyfuss and the rest of the alien-lovers become obsessed with in *Close Encounters of the Third Kind*.

CLOSE ENCOUNTERS OF THE THIRD KIND (1977) (Movie)

Director: Steven Spielberg
Writer: Steven Spielberg
Producers: Michael Phillips, Julia Phillips.
Awards: 1 Oscar (Best Cinematography)
Cast: Richard Dreyfuss (Roy Neary), Terrie Garr (Ronnie Neary), François Truffaut (Claude Lacombe), Melinda Dillon (Gillian Guiler), Bob Balaban (David Laughlin), Justin Dreyfuss (Toby Neary)

Notes:
Close Encounters was actually made in 1977, but the reason for its brief inclusion on our journey back to the eighties is that when I was a kid, the

film was just beginning to get shown on TV – thus making it very much a part of *my* 1980s. Also, the tune that the aliens contact earth with (you know, "dum dum dum dum dum dum") is the only song I can play on the piano. I will therefore ask you to indulge me on this one. This film made me really want to believe in UFOs.

I hadn't realised – until I'd started scavenging on the Internet – that the oddly shaped tower thing in the film *actually* exists. I suppose I must have imagined Steven Spielberg drawing it on a fag packet and giving it to a special effects man to create on a ZX81. But no, it's a 60-million-year-old slab of volcanic rock that has great religious significance to the indigenous population. Viewing the tower from a mile or so away, I just can't work out how this great obelisk came to sit in the fields of Wyoming. It's utterly out of place – all protruding, all naughty and incongruous.

I think about Spielberg sitting down to write a movie about aliens, and how he thought it definitely needed to include a scene featuring people sitting down to eat dinner and ending up manically sculpting Devil's Tower out of the mashed potato. Imagine the stage directions: 'CU ROY NEERY SCULPTING TOWER IN MASHED POTATO'.

We drive closer to the tower and get to the entrance. They want too many dollars for me to crack the wallet and wander through the wilderness just to touch its base, so I jump out to the souvenir shop and buy a mug with it on instead. That's a close enough encounter, right?

From that big rude-looking tower, we put the eighties away for the rest of the day and make progress north up to Great Falls, Montana. It's said that Montana has really big skies, which I've never really understood. Surely the sky is the same size wherever you are? It's the sky; look up and there it is, the sky, and the amount of it you see is simply dependent on what's in the way of your vision.

But when you get to Montana you instantly get it. The skies are so immense, bloody massive. It's like an Imax theatre version of a Walthamstow sky. The horizon circles you uninterrupted and it's actually quite hard to adjust your visual depth of field to cope with the magnitude of it without going boss-eyed.

We pass through towns where people wear cowboy hats without even a tinge of irony. There are people being driven around in horse-drawn wagons and cattle goaded down the main streets. I just can't help myself from screeching a "yee-haaa" when we drive down the main drag of Hulett, and am thrilled to get a tipped-hat response from the man on a horse. I bet he muttered "prat" under his breath though. But so did I, so let's leave it there. As we get further into Montana, snow-peaked mountains begin emerging in the distance, and finally we're on that middle-of-nowhere road again, winding off into a hazy distance that I'd imagined a road trip in the USA to be all about. We're the only buggers out here, the road is ours, and I feel an overwhelming sense of freedom.

Without getting even a faint whiff of what the hell's in Great Falls, apart from a cheap motel on the edge of it, we straggle out of our beds at 5.30am to get an early start off towards Glacier National Park. Overnight I manage to compensate my body with just one hour of sleep due to becoming annoyingly fixated on the sounds of Luke snoring, someone in the room next door snoring, and the toilet trickling slowly into itself. Insomnia is bad enough at home, but in a minging hotel room it's the very edge of insanity; a complete liberty.

Through the blear and bloodshot I see those white-tipped mountains we'd spotted on the road yesterday getting closer, and it looks as though something of a nightmare is in store for us atop them. Fat bruised clouds cloak the peaks and their smudged edges suggest it's raining rather fiercely. Whatever's happening up there, it looks irritable, and so am I. As the Oldsmobile drags us up the mountain, the temperature starts dropping dramatically and those distant clouds now surround us – all damp and clingy like an Internet bride. Pine trees seem to have stubbornly grown wherever there's anything near a foot of dirt, and winding around and up these mountains is like being transported in a spinning Tardis to the Swiss Alps. From summer at the entrance to the park, we've circled our way up to deep winter near the top. Huge piles of snow and ice cling to the sides of the rocks and the dewy spray of mountain rain becomes snow sprinkling through the fog. Usually you have to drive or fly many miles to see such a rapid change of weather, but we've got there in fifteen minutes, upwards on a coiled road. Tom and I even manage a brief snowball fight before the cold prevents rational speech.

Then we spot the bit of the mountains we'd come to see. The Going to the Sun Road is where Jack Nicholson's character, Jack Torrance, drove his car at the beginning of the film *The Shining* in 1980.

THE SHINING (1980) (Movie)

Director: Stanley Kubrick
Writers: Stephen King (book), Stanley Kubrick (screenplay)
Producer: Jan Harlan
Cast: Jack Nicholson (Jack Torrance), Shelley Duvall (Wendy Torrance), Danny Lloyd (Danny Torrance), Scatman Crothers (Dick Halloran)

Notes:
So I watched the film. Brilliant. "Here's Johnny" and all that madness, the first tracking shot in cinematic history and all that Kubrick excellence. And then as an adult I read the Stephen King novel. Swallow a Pritt Stick, what a bore. I couldn't believe that Kubrick had managed to pick such a great story out of the slowest read of my life. Two months it took me to get through that. It was like going to work. In short, I wouldn't recommend the read, just the watch.

The film shows this road (which going by the book, really ought to be somewhere in Colorado) in a wide shot as Jack drives around the corner and through a tunnel in a mountain. It's spectacular, hard to believe. How did they dig this road and tunnel out of this pointed rock? To see this spot first-hand is an even more exhilarating experience than the film could suggest. If anyone came off the road they would almost certainly be done for. It has entirely its own weather system up here and if Gandalf and a couple of hobbits turn the corner any moment it wouldn't be a big shock. Well, I say that, but I expect it would be a bit of a surprise.

We curl back out of what feels like being in one of those novelty snow globes, back down to June and proceed north towards the US–Canada border. A brief interrogation at the tiny crossing doesn't really slow us and we speed as fast as the law (and slightly beyond) allows, back into the land of the kilometre. Our journey continues north through Alberta to High River, seventy kilometres south of Calgary.

High River is a particularly buzzy bee in Tom's bonnet, and today he's wearing one of those persistent and finicky bonnets that I don't like people wearing. I'm knackered and want a motel bed so bad, but no, we have to go and look at a house that *might* have been used in *Superman 3*. We eventually find a house ... and none of us recognise it. At all. Which we all knew would be the case. It's just a house. Miles away. Despite that, Tom insists on going and knocking on the door to ask if it was used in the film.

This sparks a discussion/rant...

I think this movie-location hunting is all about the recognition: that moment when a one-dimensional image moves from reel to real. There's a certain buzz in the moment you see a location, where flashes of the movie scenes start going through your head – it's dizzying and emphatic and a true collision of your past and the now. What Tom's doing now is knocking on a house he doesn't recognise at all, to find out if it *might* be a location. And if it is, where's the satisfaction in that? It's merely a ticked box. That's not what this is all about – there's no buzz in that. I make a vow to myself to refuse to go out of our way to visit a location that no one is going to recognise – especially if I've got the raving grumps of a sleep-deprived two-headed beast.

And we still have no idea whether or not the bloody house was used in *Superman*.

––––––––––

After finally getting some sleep, a brief wander into the downtown area of Calgary leaves us feeling pretty much as most of the big cities in America and Canada have done so far. There's nothing exceptionally different about Calgary except it seems to have a sense of order about it that's best exhibited in the way they cross the road. I'm not sure if jaywalking is a crime punished with beatings and lashes with burning maple branches, but people seem to avoid wandering into the road unauthorised at all costs. At one point I stand at a crossing with fifteen people looking at a "Don't Walk" sign on the other side, as absolutely no traffic passes by. Not even a bicycle casts any doubt as to how safe it is to walk, but still a horde of people stand patiently waiting for that all-commanding autocrat, the green man. Tom – not known for patience in such situations – tuts and huffs until we get clearance: avoiding a death sentence for jaywalking only by my gripping the cuff of his jacket so tight he can't move.

In the evening, we drive out to Martindale, on the northeast edge of the city. A while ago, Tom made contact with Tony Bourne, one of the more active members of the *Knight Rider* website fan scene. Tony owns the *third* most accurate replica of *KITT in the world*, and he's agreed for us to visit the car (and him). Third most accurate seems a bit disappointing, if you're going to go to all that trouble of having the car, you'd *have* to be the number one to justify the effort and expense. But he seems proud enough to want to flash it out to the English.

In a quiet suburban block, family cars and people wagons sit outside identical rows of affordable-looking homes. But in between the wheelie bins and the Cheverolets sits a 1982 Pontiac Tranz Am that talks.

KNIGHT RIDER (1982–1986) (TV)

Creator: Glen A. Larson
Awards: Nomanated for a Primetime Emmy
Cast: David Hasselhoff (Michael Knight), Edward Mulhare (Devon Miles), Edward Basehart (Narrator), William Daniels (K.I.T.T.), Patricia McPherson (Bonnie Barstow)

Notes:
Hasselhoff's remarkable transformation from the second coolest man on television (The Fonz first, of course) to a bit of a culty joke astounds me. Michael Knight was *the man* and I was hooked immediately after watching the first feature-length pilot episode.

We arrive at Tony's house a little early, and he's not even in from work yet. His wife lets us in and then goes to another room to continue talking on the phone as their young daughter and ridiculous tiny dog, Peanut, keep us company. No normal holiday would find you sitting in a stranger's home like this, but here we are, suddenly part of Calgary suburbia, entertaining Peanut.

Tony finally arrives, podgy and squat with a cheeky *fuck you I'm not growing up* grin; he's dressed in full *Calgary Flames* uniform – the local ice hockey team that's just lost the Stanley Cup final. Tony tells us that money is tight and that he's waiting desperately for his pay-cheque and I wonder –

wildly judgmentally and suspiciously – what sort of man spends CA$17,000 (around £8,500) on the nostalgic frivolity of a KITT while his family wait for money for food. But it would seem that his wife and daughter are just as into the whole *Knight Rider* thing as he is.

"How did you get into all of this?"

"When *Knight Rider* came out I was around five. And it just blew my mind. I was like, wow. Every boy was into all sorts of stuff – *Transformers*, *He-man* and all that. But *Knight Rider* was the only thing for me. And I followed it all the way through. Then in 1997, I discovered the Internet and found that you could get a replica KITT. So from 1997 to 2002, I always wanted one, always wanted one, always wanted one." I think he always wanted one. Five years of wanting one. "My eldest brother had passed away; he died in 2000 of heart failure.

He'd been hospital-ridden since an accident in 1989. When he passed away there was an insurance settlement left to my father and my middle brother. My dad always said that 'when the settlement comes through I'll give you some money', and stuff like this. I said 'no no, I don't want any money', But if I see anything I want, just buy it for me. That's all I actually wanted. Then I stumbled across the phone number of the gentleman who owned the car and I spoke to him for about three hours about the car. He tells me the magic words towards the end of the conversation, 'I'm thinking about selling it'. So you know what's in right?" Uh-oh. "Dad's got this money now and I thought, I don't want the money, I just want the car. I got the guy down to CA$17,000, just on a handshake. So when the money He decided 'I'm not giving you a penny. You're getting nothing'. I thought oh, OK. Because I'd helped my father for several years before that. He'd injured himself at a job site, so I helped him out, paid his rent and I got nothing in return. So I told my brother and he said don't worry about it, just go and get the car. I said how can I do that? I haven't got the money. He said well, you do tomorrow in your bank account. He told me to go and bring our new buddy home. So I did." I don't know how to feel about this. A family torn apart after the death of a son, and all over a replica KITT. I mean there's dedication and there's dedication.

Keen to get him off this vehement track of family disintegration, we try and fail to persuade Tony to go and put his Michael Knight costume on, which is a big shame. So we go outside to properly meet KITT He presses buttons and lights come on, as does an introduction from KITT himself on the speakers, along with that trademark baseline. Everything on the dash lights up just like the car on telly and most of it is functional, except of course the eject button. It has detailed replication of *everything* including the number plates which, although authentic-looking, are illegal and have cost Tony a few dollars in fines from the cops that aren't fans of the TV show (the *fan* cops all let him off).

He drives us through town, attracting laughs and waves and people trying to beat KITT away at traffic lights (which isn't that hard, considering the motor's getting on a bit now), as the *Knight Rider* soundtrack plays off a CD. It's especially potent at night, the red pulsing light shifting from side to side, attracting all sorts of attention. I guess that light was a device to make the car into a character; something to suggest that KITT was alive, breathing, and it became enormously emblematic of the show.

"So this apparently is the only KITT replica in the whole of Canada. How many are there in the US?" Tom asks.

"Oh, tons. About a hundred. They come as a kit. Although the guy who did this one added his own stuff, but not very well."

"Is it exactly as KITT was?"

"Just some minor things are different. The TV screen is too small." I can tell by the slight lip-twitch that this small detail annoys him a little.

"The real KITT actually sits in Hollywood. There were thirty-two cars used in *Knight Rider*. Several of them were destroyed. Rumours are that there's only ten in existence left, out of thirty-two" Yes, and actually I know where a bit of one of them is – a TV friend filmed at Hasselhoff's pad a while back and The Hoff actually has a "show house" he uses *just* for interviews, he doesn't even live there. At one point, he went on the intercom and asked for his assistant to bring KITT down. The guy arrived, promptly, with the nose of KITT mounted on a plinth. That's where the remains of one KITT are.

"Hasselhoff was actually here in Calgary filming a while ago, but I never got to meet him." Tony says bitterly.

"My friend got to meet him," which I wasn't really impressed with, because my friend's a loser. He got to have beers with him while I'm sitting here with my thumb in my bum waiting to meet him and have photos with my car." Tony's descriptions of what's been done to the car and the painstaking accuracy of the specifications of all the buttons are a pain up the eardrum. I don't understand a word of it, I only just understand petrol, but it was worth enduring until 11pm just to get a ride in the car. Despite all the pleasantries and Tony's amazement at meeting his first real-life Englishmen, he still takes it upon himself to ask us to fill the beast up with petrol through our wallets, which we do obligingly: thankful to have been given the chance to ride in Canada's only KITT.

On reflection, I realise that this visit isn't really so much about the car itself. Sure, it's great to meet a replica and its likeable infantile owner, but actually, I'm more interested in what drives a man to sacrifice his family's money and bond for such a superfluous pursuit. And I suppose even deeper at the core of my curiosity is that there's something in Tony that's exactly what our journey is really all about. In the same way we've recklessly put our lives on hold at great expense to follow a nostalgic whim, Tony's indulgences are much the same symptom. Working out what it is that drives Tony would perhaps in some way hold a mirror up to us.

"When I first drove it, I was like, oh my God, twenty years later, I *got* KITT ... like, wow." He's so childlike and excitable. But listening to Tony, I realise that although he might not be a stupid man, I doubt he's really thought beyond the basic instinct of *wanting* that car. In the same way he *needs* to eat too many donuts, he *needed* that car. Like a kid *needs* sweets. Maybe something inside him said that he needed an element of comfort from his childhood, to help him through the agony of adulthood. And maybe that's at the core of all our nostalgic tendencies – salvaging solace by keeping times-gone-by alive and present. I can see why: there's no unpredictability with the past – it happened already, it can't go wrong, it's there on the plate perfectly cooked and ready to eat. The present and future? It's raw and who knows whether it'll be palatable.

I don't feel inclined to burst that bubble for Tony by addressing it like some spiteful cod-psychologist – especially as I'm hardly one to talk – maybe it's something he needs to work out for himself. Or maybe he'll continue long into his old age, wearing full ice hockey outfits and wide eyes, blissfully oblivious that he never quite grew up and that most of the child in him still resides somewhere in the eighties.

And *maybe* he'll be quite happy with himself, too.

CHAPTER NINE SOUNDTRACK:

Roxanne

The Police (1978)

It's a Long Road

Dan Hill (1982)

Chapter Nine

First Blood to Roxanne

Calgary to Vancouver

Calgary has barely shaken itself out of googoo land when we jump in the car with side-quiff bed heads and roll out westwards towards Banff. A massive day of transit: we sit strapped to the inside of the car watching the Rocky Mountains smile by, wrapped happily in their own world of cloud and snow – views of which never seem to translate on camera and are quite difficult to process even for the naked eye. The marathon nine-hour drive that takes us through Banff National Park is ridiculously serene: pine-smothered billowing hills with snowy summits poking out the top and vivid blue lakes reflecting the whole picture for double the glory. The whole thing is suspicious, like it's man-made to the specifications of tourist perfection. It stinks of Disney. Over the course of the journey we seem to have replaced the misery of Calgary's flopping drizzle with fresh blue mountain skies that from the car suggest blinding heat, but in reality is a little chilly round the willy. It's sensational, but I do wonder what you actually *do* here – unless you're some compass-licking, map-loving, yoghurt-knitting ourdoorsy-boresy who actually *knows* what a crampon is, all you can do is *look* at it. But that's alright, looking is good.

Eventually Highway 3 gets us into Nelson, a place people in Calgary said was worth a visit.. I'm instantly charmed by its main drag, Baker Street:

attractive girls with bare midriffs, tie-die and dreads, old hippies and sleepy locals cohabit in the shadow of steep pine-infested hills that all angle down towards the deep blue of Lake Kootenay. Nelson is small-town in all its unabashed, quaint, eccentric glory. This former silver-mining town is a stop-off point for travellers, transients and wandering souls who sit outside cafés for a few days or a few years, watching the town go about its lazy business.

We march through town at English rush-hour pace, checking ourselves every five minutes to slow down, remembering that for once there *is* no rush: the end of the road and plenty of daylight will still be there if we dawdle. Locals look at us funny – probably it's the big long fake rubber noses we've got strapped to our faces. Given the fact that the tourist information office gives out photocopied leaflets that take you on a walking tour around the locations used for the movie, it's clear that our traipse around the town where Steve Martin fell in love with Roxanne is a relatively well-trodden path.

ROXANNE (1987) (Movie)

Director: Fred Schepisi
Writers: Edmond Rostand (play), Steve Martin (screenplay)
Producers: Steve Martin, Daniel Melnick, Michael I. Rachmil
Awards: Nominated for a Golden Globe
Cast: Steve Martin (C.D. "Charlie" Bales), Daryl Hannah (Roxanne Kowalski), Rick Rossovich (Chris McConnell), Shelley Duvall (Dixie)

Notes:
Roxanne was based on the play *Cyrano de Bergerac*. No, not that thing with John Nettles in. Written in 1897 by Edmond Rostand and set in 1640, it was actually based on the life of the Cyrano de Bergerac, a brilliant poet and swordsman who finds himself in love with his own cousin, Roxane. Steve Martin's version in the 1980s didn't of course have Roxanne as a cousin, that would be a bit wrong.

It was 1986 when *Roxanne* came to town, and Nelson's hilly charm was so much a feature of the movie that the locals – those who are actually aware of it – are still proud of their brief international spotlight eighteen years later.

The tour first has us panting with whistley lungs up one of the steeper bastardy Nelson inclines. Director Fred Schepisi played carefully with the gradients to create interesting and other-worldly camera angles that shove reality slightly up itself and round the corner. We slide childishly down the stair rails that at the start of the film Steve Martin's bum was too sticky to get down. I can see why he didn't want to slide down that rail: it's rusty and smarts and is even worse if you get a nut caught underneath the thigh on the way down, as your pants work their way internally up towards the liver. At the bottom of the rail is where C.D. fought a couple of punks with tennis racquets and tight eighties shorts because they dared insult his long nose. Here, Tom and I use our long rubber noses to have a duel, an approximate homage which I lose when my nose springs back on its elastic for a reverse gouge painfully to the eye. Tom enjoys this victory spitefully and I make a note of that.

Out of respect and partly in silliness, we keep our fake rubber noses on *all day* and despite causing a ludicrously sweaty real nose underneath, and probably a gaggle of new blackheads, they spark quite a reaction from the locals. Remarkably – amid all the laughing – most people call us "Pinocchios" and come up with corny witticisms about lying; totally missing the Roxanne link. Here we are, expecting everyone to be flattered by our nostalgic tribute to their town, and very few of the bleeders get it at all.

On Baker Street the tour takes us to the bookstore where Chris – (Daryl Hannah's first Nelson conquest, played by Rick Rossovich) – buys a posh book for a friend who's embarrassed about being brainy. Roxanne sees him buying the book and assumes he's an intellectual, which seems to give her the horn and a misconception about his intelligence that feeds importantly into the plot.

So we storm the bookstore, now called Otter Books (hopefully not dealing exclusively with books about otters), Roger Cook style, with noses on, camcorder rolling, and ask for the same book – *Being and Nothingness* by Jean-Paul Sartre – just like Chris did. The lady behind the counter is surprised, shy, reluctant and frankly a bit shitty about it all. And it's difficult trying to deal with a mardy moo when you've got a fake nose on. It sort of compromises your stance.

"I'm *not* going on video camera," she stabs.

"But we were just wondering whether you have *Being and Nothingness* by Jean-Paul Sartre?" charms Tom, most Englishly. I stand by, having a little seethe about the miserableness.

"We don't," she smiles a little bit, at last.

"What?" I outrage. "You're *supposed* to have it, otherwise Roxanne won't fall in love with Chris and the whole plot will fall apart because C.D. won't get to charm her away from him. For Christ's sake woman." I'm not *really* having a go at her, it's all tongue in cheek, but there's perhaps a tinge of irritation on either side. She checks the computer system and it's definitely not on there.

"You know *why* you're supposed to have it, don't you?" She shakes her head with couldn't-care-less-ness.

"This bookshop was used in the film *Roxanne*. One of the lead characters comes in here and buys the book. That's probably why you haven't got it; *he* bought it eighteen years ago. Time to re-stock, don't you think?"

"Oh, really? I haven't seen the movie." With this bombshell I go all quiet and arch. I can deal with this harpy no longer. She doesn't even have *Mr Nosey* by Roger Hargreaves and doesn't find our mission in the least amusing or acceptable. A bit humiliated, angry and with silly rubber noses on, we storm back out.

"OK. We're going to storm out now," I iterate, just to make sure she knows we're leaving with the hump.

"Oh, OK."

Next stop, says the tourist board's photocopied tour leaflet, is a fair wander up one of the hills to the fire station where C.D. was Chief. We bowl through the front doors to find no one at home and finally resort to shouting "Fire!" up the fireman's pole to get some attention. Eventually, a squat young man named Scott comes down and works out that *Roxanne* – not *Pinocchio* – is our thing. At last, some purchase.

Amazingly for such a small place, the fire department gets about one call a day, none of which are cats or fat kids stuck up trees. Given that the station is reasonably busy, I wonder how filming *Roxanne* must have affected the running of the real fire department.

"During the filming, everything had to be moved down to the local school, all the trucks and everything. The main bay here was actually taken over by Steve Martin's motor-home. This was his dressing room. All of the inside stuff was actually filmed on set in Vancouver, they rebuilt the station over there. Steve Martin, as a sign of appreciation after he packed up and moved out, bought the fire-fighters a new TV and VCR. And the actors had a fundraiser here, where they all got up and did comedy routines ... apart from Steve Martin, who was under contract and couldn't." How odd, a contract that says you must only be funny in designated scenarios. It would appear that Nelson enjoyed hosting Steve and the movie. Another fireman emerges down the pole after a while. "It came at a great time for the city," he says. "We'd just lost one of our main industries and this made everyone start smiling again. It changed the whole ambience of the city. It was a really neat experience. I shook Steve Martin's hand," he says with an especially boastful tone at the end.

Unfortunately, due to insurance reasons we're denied the opportunity to slide down the pole – which is just as well because vertigo may have got me quivering like an old lady in a Moss Side alley, and anyway, the pole bits were filmed on a set in Vancouver, so it would have been a pointless and terrifying exercise. Double also, the slide down that rail earlier has left my left nut vulnerable.

Nelson feels just as the film portrayed it: lazy, friendly and slightly detached from reality. I'm pleased that this visit hasn't burst my bubbles – I really wanted to find *that place* in the movie, and we've found just that.

We pile onto Highway 3, westwards towards Hope, BC. Anyone we mentioned Hope to in Nelson was amazed that we're bothering to go there. One woman in a café referred to it as "Hope? It's a hole." The seven-hour journey through BC is a curly road indeed. We drive through miles and miles of beautiful mountains and pine forests on hills and get there in the early evening to find little else but rows and rows of motels. Like the woman said in Nelson, it *is* a bit of a hole, but only in the sense that it's like a hole in the mountains. A sort of scooped out crater. The mountains are ominous and interfering; never out of view; which makes the whole place a little enclosed, smothered. We go directly, of course, to the local liquor store to stock up on amber-coloured long-drive relief liquid. It always works. It's hot and dusty and there's no real breeze because the mountains provide a pretty impenetrable wind-shelter. Thirst rides my gob most aggressively. In the store, behind the counter, there's Toni. Hello, Toni. A brash lady in her early forties, who, it turns out, lived in the town when *First Blood* – the first *Rambo* movie – was filmed.

FIRST BLOOD (1982) (Movie)

Director: Ted Kotcheff
Writers: David Morell (novel), Michael Kozoll, William Sackheim, Sylvesterr Stallone (screenplay)
Producers: Andrew Vajna, Herb Nanas, Mario Kassar
Cast: Sylvester Stallone (John J. Rambo), Brian Dennehy (Sheriff Will Teasle), Richard Crenna (Samuel Trautman), Bill McKinney (Capt. Dave Kern)

Notes:
I thought *First Blood* was just a movie about Sylvester Stallone running around a small town gurning at everyone. An absurd vehicle for Stallone's ego: one man who only wanted something to eat takes on an entire police unit *and* army - creating an arch enemy in Brian Dennehy as the police chief. They develop an unfeasible hatred for each other over the space of *one* day. Sure, there might be more to it, maybe it's about how America (with Hope portraying the average American town, albeit in Canada) treats its Vietnam vets, but the plot itself just doesn't wash with me. But hey, people like it and Stallone undoubtedly takes his place in movie history as John Rambo: the man who grimaced a whole town's infrastructure into defeat.

Toni is a loud fake blonde who claims to know every one of the five thousand tight-knit inhabitants of Hope. You get the sense she probably does. Most of them seem to come into the liquor store as we're there and many chip in the odd grunt or nod as Toni tells her stories.

And so to the rancid Rambo meat of our conversation. We ask Toni what she remembers about when Rambo came to beat up their town for no particular reason.

"Sylvester Stallone, he had a stunt double that like did all his stunts and motorcycle stuff. We'd see a lot of him a lot of the time; he'd go out partying and everything. But Sylvester Stallone stayed behind closed doors with all the young girls." What? Shit. Is this *News of the World* stuff?

"He liked 'em young, he did. He had a girlfriend of mine, he actually *saw her*. After he left he would send her plane tickets to Hollywood. He would phone her up and send her tickets. And he was married at the time too, he had a wife. But my girlfriend would go down, see him for a couple weeks or whatever and then a couple months later, he would send her another ticket ... and away she'd go."

"How old was she?" Is really what we want to know.

"She was a year older than me and I would have been grade ten at the time. She would have been sixteen, seventeen."

"How old was he?"

"He would have been late thirties?" Hmmm, and what's the legal age in America? Hmmm. Of course, all this might not be true, but right here, right now, I don't really see why Toni would be lying. She's not bragging, she seems to think the whole business is quite OK.

"Is she still in the area?" I ask, hoping to meet her.

"No, she's in Vancouver. She's not doing very well right now. She got into a lot of hard luck; she got into drugs very bad. And that's actually what happened when he was seeing her, she started getting into it, she was quite young. And I guess he would notice each time she went down there she was getting a little worse and a little worse, so he had to finally break off all ties." Another lady walks in to buy some booze and Toni mentions it to her.

"I was telling these guys about Sylvester Stallone. The girls at lunchtime, hitting his trailer and coming back to school. There was about three or four he had little things with."

"Yes. Yes, yes, yes," the woman replies. This is all *so* iffy.

Toni continues, "I only knew of my girlfriend for sure, but some of the others, they may have just padded it up a bit to look good. I mean, you couldn't get near him, but if he liked you, no holes barred, right?" Hmmmmmmmmm.

Toni has a fair amount to say about Brian Denehy too, and I begin thinking how lucky that the first person we meet in Hope is an amazing squealer.

"Brian Dennehy, he was an awesome, awesome gentleman, very nice. He got to know a lot of the town's folk and stuff. We used to have a friend in a wheelchair and he doted on her. He was so good to her. He would take us for dinner and we hung out with him quite a bit actually. He was in love with my mother." Ah, so maybe it wasn't *all* selfless charity? Using the cripple to show some tart how kind he is.

"He wanted my mother to leave my father."

So, the *Rambo* tag-team of Stallone and Dennehy waltzed into town and brought to life the old *locking up wives and daughters* proverb, almost perfectly.

"He fell for her big time. It was unreal. He met her in the lounge one night, my mom worked in a lounge, she was a cocktail waitress, and that's where he hung out the whole time he was here. Every day he'd get there about five o'clock and stay until closing every night. My mom *almost* did go for dinner with him. *Almost*. She was very smitten. Because he was a very nice fellow. Big. Very nice big man."

"What did your dad think?"

"My dad was away at camp at the time. So he wasn't home. But my mom didn't do anything to cross the line. It was like a running joke, he was like, 'I'm going to take you to Hollywood.' And we were like, 'We're ready to go!'"

A little shell-shocked at being given so much juice without even having to resort to saucy exploitation of our "cute" English accents, we wander off with beer and immediately, inadvertently stumble upon and recognise the very corner where Rambo enters town and is accosted for the first time by Brain Dennehy, which kicks the whole debacle off. This is it; we're in Ramboland alright. After looking around the place – at the sign that introduces the entrance to the town (and is featured in the movie), the area where the blown-up petrol station stood and the bit where Rambo jumped over the railway lines on a motorbike – we feel that just like Nelson was *Roxanne* all-over, Hope *feels* very much the place John Rambo turned all nasty on.

Hope seems to have taught itself to tolerate invasion in the summer months – not least because it makes a packet out of visitors. It's a nice enough place, with its quaint-ish main road and wall-to-wall views of surrounding mountains that look like painted backgrounds from cheap TV shows, but I'm not really sure what else there is. Nice enough, that's all it seems to be.

Our last hope in Hope is the bridge that Rambo was driven to by Brian Dennehy at the beginning of the film. At last, something to really get the neck-hairs all fluffy and erect. This is where Rambo was tipped out of the car but turned around to walk stubbornly back into town, which gets right up the police chief's hooter. From there things turned into USA versus a single Italian-American ex-soldier with a face-ache. I decide to throw Tom out of the car, to replicate the scene. He's up for it to start with, because it's a homage and we want to film it. But when I drive off, I go quite a bit further along the road than we agreed – four minutes further, actually – and sit having a sandwich with Luke while Tom catches up in the baking midday sun.

Cruel? Well, I told you I'd made a note of the result of the fake nose duel that ended with my eye taking a rubber gouging. I'm like a Navy Seal, I always get even. If only Jesse Ventura could see me now.

Further along the same road we learn that while movie-location hunting can take you to the most *absurd* extremities of any place you've never imagined (or wanted to), sometimes it takes you to *amazing* places that you'd never have heard of otherwise and are damned thankful that the mission dragged you there. One such example is the Othello Tunnels – an area which was used for the scenes where Rambo flees into the forest and dangles off rocks while a policeman unbelievably not only manages to miss him with a gun from a close-range helicopter, but clumsily falls out of the thing to his death on big slab of stone.

As we walk along the bridges between the tunnels, we constantly proclaim that *here* is the place where Sly (or his stunt-bunny) hung off the rock. In fact, it's all so similar that it could be any bit along these steep rocks that tower just on the other side of a white water river gushing noisily like a badly tuned television. Looking up to the sun-hazy tops of the cliffs makes you feel like the whole jagged face, with bits of tree sprouting out horizontally, is going to tumble down on you. The tunnels are long and dank with pinpricks of light glowing at the ends, and big dribbles of cold water seem to have honed the skill of dripping accurately between your T-shirt and neck. It feels like this safely fenced off, brilliantly chiselled walkway through an exceptionally hectic piece of landscape should be dangerous, with its sharp rocks and heights and furiously gushing water all around us. It's definitely somewhere around here that Rambo came off the rock and broke his fall in some trees. It just feels right. Sly actually did that stunt himself and broke some ribs in the process. That'll learn him. Even though we haven't found the *exact* spot Rambo swung perilously from, we have found a hidden beauty spot that would otherwise have passed us by. So cheers to that.

––––––––––

We leave Rambo clinging up in the rocks and chug west two hours on Highway 1 to somewhere vaguely near Vancouver. Anmore is supposed to be a tiny but easy-to-find village just northwest of the city. Very well-to-do, apparently. However, it turns into our personal Holy Grail, and after driving in and out of Vancouver on pretty much the same silly road, tension in the car starts bubbling like a vat of hot piss.

We're now twenty days into the journey and there are all sorts of the tensions you get with cooped up sweaty men and the cross-purposes of our own personal nostalgia fetishes. Tom is still keen on the box-ticking of *any* location from *any* film – which is more to do with bragging rights on the return home, I think – while I just want that recognition buzz of that right here, right now moment. So now we're squabbling over whose apple that is and the wrong left turn and it's your turn to drive and it's my turn on the double bed and you owe me a dollar, fifty for that coffee and can you stop pissing in the shower.

And it's funny when you're on a long journey away from home. You take stock, you look over at yourself with the sort of objectivity that's impossible when you're back there, *living it*. I'm realising more and more that the Elle thing has caused grief in so much of the last few years: break-ups; the way I've approached relationships; expectations I have of girlfriends... Everything goes back to the fact that I never dealt with it, I never got closure, I never let go. And right now, I don't know how I can.

Several hours of introspection later, we *get* to Anmore: a quiet hilly area with an eclectic mix of house styles – some grand, some cute, some twee, but all worth a packet. As soon as we turn left into Sugar Mountain Way, a turret pokes out of the trees as if part of a fairytale, and there's no mistaking it: the house where Roxanne lived.

We nervously walk up onto the porch area and my brain starts replaying moments from the film: where Chris tries to pull Roxanne using C.D.'s script and where C.D. has a massive argument with Roxanne. It's just the same, and I once again feel like I've slipped back into the curious, quirky world of *Roxanne*.

Mario Piemonte is expecting us, but we've not actually spoken to him yet. Tom spoke on the phone to his wife, Lynne, and she loved the idea of our tour, so she invited us over to stay the night – despite the fact that she wouldn't be there and it would be just her husband. I'm a typical Englishman in this respect: I don't like to impose. I feel like I'm taking liberties if I have an extra biscuit at Mum's, let alone turn up turning up on the doorstep of a stranger expecting to be put up for the night. What if he's got the hump with his wife, all annoyed that she's been so bold and generous as to willy-nilly invite foreign stranger sweatbags around without actually being there herself.

Mario answers the door, all shuffly, short and stocky with very little neck to speak of. If I were him, I wouldn't claim it as a neck. His grey hair makes me want him to be the spitting image of Steve Martin, but he's more like Richard Dreyfuss in the latter stages of the Devil's Tower obsession. He's friendly but a little reserved and serious, and although it *seems* as though he's happy for us to be here, it's hard to tell. But then after very little messing around with formality or nicety, to my relief, he directs us straight to the garage where an entire fridge of Canadian beer sits chilling, *for us,* and instructs us that beer in this house operates on a self-service buffet system. Result. We're in. What a man. *Roxanne* and beer.

It turns out that Mario is a retired software whizz who started in the game when one computer filled an entire room and could calculate little more than a hypotenuse. After thirty years, a lot of hypotenusing, two grown-up kids and a happy marriage, he retired to spend more time with the dog while his wife continues lecturing (which is where she is now). Cut to very shortly after meeting Mario and the Canadian beer begins to gratefully seep treacherously into my blood and I manage to make lifetime friends with the dog, Lucky Piemonte. We make all sorts of promises to each other. Mario takes us on a tour of the *Roxanne* house and explains the story in as much detail as an IT man feels necessary, which is a *lot.*

The strangest part of this potted history is that the house had originally been built about four doors down the street, and after the filming, a Japanese couple had it moved up the road and built a basement flat underneath so that it stands six feet higher than it appears in the movie. It all seems such an enormous faff – I'm amazed anyone could be arsed to go to such lengths. Why not just buy a proper house? Was it the movie memorabilia aspect of it? Or was it that they were flogging the shell so cheaply that even with building it up and moving it, they'd still be saving a load of wonga? Who knows? Mario doesn't.

As we stand next to a wooden sign on the pathway that says "Welcome to Roxanne's House", we ask Mario why he's wearing a fire department T-shirt, and he explains that he's a part-time fireman. A bizarre coincidence, that a man bearing a minor resemblance to Steve Martin who lives in the house used in the film is also fireman, just like C.D. Back on the porch landing, he shows us an iron bar that's still attached to the underneath – jutting out so that Steve Martin's acrobatic stand-in could swing up to the roof to gain entry when Roxanne was locked out and all naked. Cracking. Through the front door, you're a straight walk through the hall to the kitchen where after C.D. lets her in, he helps himself and prepares them a meal in ten seconds flat. At this point, of course, she wasn't impressed in a romantic fashion because he clearly had a massive hooter and she didn't fancy it too much. The wooden counter he prepared the meal on is still there and the table sits in just the same place.

Upstairs we go into Roxanne's bedroom – where Chris attempted to seduce her. Bastard. I sit on the bed where Roxanne sat and think briefly about how much I fancy her. The perfect woman. Brainy and beautiful and romantic and clearly not that worried about looks, which suits me just fine.

All the while around the house, Mario barks non-stop facts at us as to the precise alterations that had to be made to make the house what it is today. He's a little nonplussed by our childish quoting of lines and general over-excitedness at being here, but does manage a wry smile as I present him with an honorary long rubber fake C.D. nose. Actually, it's my one and it's a bit grubby, so he doesn't go so far as to put it on, but he seems slightly pleased with it. He's definitely chuffed though when we give him a Nelson Fire Department T-shirt.

"The guys down at the station will love this," he spits through a rare giant grin that squashes his face into a happy little flesh ball.

Over the course of the evening, we've wheedled our way into Mario Piemonte's life and it feels like we're becoming friends. In between swigs of beer and fierce bouts of house measurements, I have to stop and think about where I am: a posh bit of Vancouver at the house of someone I've never met before. Not even spoken to. Nothing links us to him other than he lives in a house once used eighteen years ago for filming bits of a movie I like. The whole social set-up of the situation is *so* tenuous that somehow this peculiar circumstance makes our bond stronger: we're all so chuffed that random and exciting things like this in life can actually happen. If we can chase our past, we can chase our dreams; our random desires and possibly some sort of exciting future. The world is enormous and anything is possible.

Mario is nearly sixty and our age gap might be conspicuous if not for Kim – the lodger who takes up the basement. Kim is a thirty-four-year-old single mother and looks good. She has nice eyes and a cute laugh and I like that sort of thing. Maybe I just fancy everyone. All three of us trip over ourselves like awkward lusty giraffes to get chatting to her, unfortunately tripping over our own tongues too – partly down to the beer and partly to ineptitude.

"You know about bollocks don't you?" says Luke during that conversation you always have with North Americans about the words we use that they don't and vice versa. Kim knows about bollocks all right and very soon after, she disappears downstairs to bed, on her own, hopefully not offended or repulsed or both.

As midnight rolls closer and the patio becomes chilly, Mario rolls back the covers to a hot-tub, which I haven't spotted until the steaming bubbles are unsheathed. Splash bang wallop. We're having a barbecue, beer and hot-tub party at Roxanne's house. Hey, come on down! Yeah! And if we make it a true eighties party, a girl's going to get spontaneously topless within minutes. Unfortunately though, Kim's gone to bed so we have to make do with Mario's pert, grey-fluffy man boobs and my on-the-way cleavage.

––––––––––

I wake up with a fuzzy beer head and stinking of hot-tub chlorine (which makes a nice change from a random snog's cheap perfume and congealed chip fat on my chin).

Mario has prepared us a big breakfast – one of those real hangover carb-monsters – and breaks the news to us, as coffee starts wedging our eyelids open, that he wants us to stay another night. We've truly stormed our way into this man's world, and he likes it. It's like being on a stag weekend without spending a fortune on hotels and strippers and silly string. We tell him that we'd be honoured to stay another night, thank him an embarrassing number of times and jump in the car to hit downtown Vancouver for the day.

We arrive at a street of uniformly similar houses in the area of Katsilano, west of downtown. There now seem to be too many trees between the houses for anyone to spy on a house opposite, but that's what happened in the film *Stakeout*, and it all happened here.

STAKEOUT (1987) (Movie)

Director: John Badham
Writer: Jim Kouf
Producer: John Badham
Cast: Richard Dreyfuss (Det. Chris Lecce), Emilio Estevez (Det. Bill Reimers), Madeleine Stow (Maria McGuire), Aidan Quinn (Richard "Stick" Montgomery), Dan Lauria (Det. Phil Coldshank), Forest Whitaker (Det. Jack Pismo)

Notes:
There's an interesting piece of geek-trivia surrounding this film. During one of the scenes where Estevez and Dreyfuss are camped out in the house, through boredom they were ad-libbing a trivia quiz. Estevez asks the question, "What movie is the line 'We're gonna need a bigger boat' from? Dreyfuss didn't know the answer despite the fact that he had actually starred in the film (it was *Jaws* of course). Fact over, I thank you.

All that secret spying and the saucy snogging went on right here, in this very ordinary road in Vancouver. But in finding it, we ask some people in the street where exactly the house is. First we meet Thomas, a thin grey-haired man with enough about him to suggest he favoured the 1970s as a decade to the current one. He sits eating lunch on the steps of one of the houses and on asking, he doesn't have a clue which house it is. He's just working here as a painter. But as he sits eating a vile-looking homemade pasta concoction from a Tupperware container, he tells us that he was a cameraman on *First Blood* before quitting the industry to train in psychotherapy and work as a painter in the meantime.

Thomas isn't prepared to say an awful lot about the making of *Rambo* other than Sly and the director had been pains in the arse and hadn't got on with each other at all.

"It was a tough shoot. It rained. A lot. Temperamental people involved. Sometimes there'd be no production for a while because of tempers flaring. Stallone was temperamental. It's hard to say who was to blame, who was temperamental first. There was a temperamental director." I get the sense from him that the *Rambo* shoot was a bit *temperamental*. We leave him alone with his moody pasta and cross over the road.

Here we meet a sweaty middle-aged man arriving back at his house, which we've worked out is next door to the house from which Dreyfuss and Estevez spy on Madeline Stowe. He apologises for his sweat (which he suspects may smell) and tells us that he was around at the time the film was made.

"What was it like?" we ask, obviously.

"Pain in the ass. They take over the whole street, trailers everywhere. *Actually*, I'm *in* that business." Oh right. Whatever. We smudge over that shameless attempt to get us to ask what he does.

"Did you have much to do with the stars?"

"Well, it was *only* Dreyfuss and one of the Sheen boys, so..." This guy is as camp as a male Shirley Bassey impersonator singing songs from *The Wizard of Oz*, but Tom hasn't quite twigged that he might be a close friend of Dorothy. He's screaming. Howling. And when he tells Tom that no, he hadn't tried to spy on Madeline Stowe (just like Dreyfuss and Estevez had next door), Tom refuses to believe him and insists that he *must have*. I almost crawl back into the car with embarrassment as Tom attempts to prise the gayest man in the world out of an inverted closet, using the thought of Madeline Stowe, naked through a window, back in the eighties, as the lure.

"Actually, that would have been all shot in the studios and computer enhanced you see." Riiiight. "I did an episode of the *X Files*..." Here we go. "...and I was supposed to be stung to death by killer bees and it was all shot in a studio with five thousand bees. Don't ask." I didn't mate.

We say goodbye and shoot some video of us outside the door of the lookout house. Suddenly though, old X Files next door re-emerges and calls Tom over. Tom trots over innocently and is offered some free weed and PCP. Tom astonishingly makes a blithering excuse about having to fly a plane later on that day, something the guy seems to accept quite willingly. How curious. Afterwards we have to explain to Tom that the man *may* have been a homosexual, and the penny dropping on his face is so spectacular that it's like watching two different peoples' faces being morphed together.

Back at Chateaux Roxanne, beer and hot-tub and Kim and dinner are waiting for us, and I still can't believe we've been so generously invited to be a part of that.

I feel Mario's genuinely enjoyed having us around and I'm sad that this almost random encounter of kindness to strangers has to end. But, we have to move on, and that's that: something this trip is slowly teaching me.

CHAPTER TEN SOUNDTRACK:

Up Where We Belong

Jennifer Warnes and
Joe Cocker (1982)

Goonies 'R' Good Enough

Cyndi Lauper (1985)

Chapter Ten

An Officer and a Goonie

Anmore, British Columbia to Roseburg, Oregon

The journey south sees another exit from Canada and we again expect to be viciously interrogated right down to our toenails in trying to get back into the US. However, we're waved through with just a few vaguely concerned questions around the theme of "Do you have any fruit in the car?", and before we know it, we haven't even left our seats and are flying down Highway 5 towards Port Townsend with a bag of slightly bruised, apparently contraband plums hidden in the boot. Ha.

Coursing down the west coast, the backdrop of icy Evian-esque mountains that have been watching over us since Alberta remain scored onto the horizon. We coast-hug until running out of land, then we're shoved onto a ferry across the pleasantly choppy water to Port Townsend: a holiday town, for all the family. Oh, how quaint, how delicious. Buckets and spades and big novelty lollipops and the salty sniff of sea air.

The main drag is Water Street: a very relaxed affair with old Victorian style buildings making it feel like a desperately safe cross between Brighton and Florida. Here, big fat American holidaymakers – the types who have weeping sores on the backs of their knees – wander around chafing their inside-thighs, gawping at how quaint it all is before ducking into the pizza place to carefully maintain their morbid obesity. *Mustn't let the weight slip.*

We head *straight* for a barbershop with every intention of cranking machismo to positive and bolshily say what every man has always *wanted* to say but has probably never been stupid enough to *actually* say.

"Take it *aaaallllllll* off," I bark, or yelp, with last-minute indecision forcing a quivery fray at the end which tells the scissor-wielding man that I'm not as brave as my swagger suggests. The barber smiles limply (as though I might be the tenth twat today who thinks he's the *first* to bring such galling nuttiness through his doors). He attaches the *number one* clipper as though he's a hangman prepping a noose for my upper bonce, and ploughs through it slowly enough for it to feel dramatic. Piles of barnet flop off like it was attached by Pritt Stick. My face is a picture, something by Edvard Munch. Within helpless seconds ... I'm a bald man.

I'm a bald man with a big fat misshapen head like a bloated walnut. Like a Ferrero Rocher with the outer chocolate nibbled off. Like Sloth from *The Goonies*. Christ it's ugly. And translucent. I have the head of a corpse dragged out of the Thames after a month of bobbing around the sewage works. It's devastating.

Meanwhile, Tom has the same thing but asks for a Mr. T style cut along the way, just to see what it would look like. On discovering that he looks more like Ed the Duck than Mr. T, he promptly asks for the rest of it to come off. At least he *grins* and goes with it – I could hardly keep the tears back. So here we are, two bald men. And Luke, who for reasons approaching dignity, remains hairy, like a deeply masculine Debra Winger. I *hate* the new do, but it's all about devotion to the cause: our next stop is a former navy base called Fort Worden, where most of *An Officer and a Gentleman* was shot. If Richard Gere had to have his head shaved, then who are Tom and I to turn up with big hair intact?

AN OFFICER AND A GENTLEMAN (1982) (Movie)

Director: Taylor Hackford
Writer: Douglas Day Stewart
Producer: Martin Elfand
Awards: 2 Oscars (Louis Gossett Jnr – Best Supporting Actor, and for the theme song, "Up Where We Belong")

Cast: Richard Gere (Zack Mayo), Debra Winger (Paula Pokrifki), Louis Gossett Jnr (Sergeant Emil Foley), David Keith (Sid Worley), Robert Loggia (Byron Mayo)

Notes:
I get the feeling that I really shouldn't like this film as much as I do, because technically, it's for girls. But actually, it's got a bit of something for everyone. Louis Gossett Jnr injects most of the man-fodder into the film, especially with that classic "steers and queers" speech that pretty much won him the Oscar.

We drive out of downtown Port Townsend and up to the Fort Worden State Park, which in the movie, was known as '*Fort Ranier*'. The place actually closed as a naval base back in the 1950s but has been kept exactly the same – all austere and immaculate – and now attracts many visitors and groups, who hire the old barracks to stay for activity weekends and such. You know, father and son camp, band camp, camp camp.

At the beginning of the movie, we see Richard Gere riding a motorbike down the main path and across the front of the all white, wooden main buildings. As we do the same in the Oldsmobile, not quite as handsomely, we can see that everything looks the same, as was, and this is very believably the place in the film. The plane near the flagpole in the film isn't there – I suspect it was a prop used just for the film – but the flagpole is in the same place and the main buildings look just as impressive and institutional, to the extent that I feel as though I shouldn't really be here. However, instead of soldiers marching around smartly in the background, all we can see are fat children and their sunburnt dads playing sport badly.

We make our way up to the youth hostel, and check ourselves in for the night. I get a bit carried away with the imaginary feeling of conscription – accepting my pile of bedding sheets with the determined grimace of a new recruit who knows he's probably going to be shouted at in Oscar-winning fashion quite shortly.

There's already someone in our dorm when we walk in, another *new recruit*, unpacking his stuff meticulously. He's got wiry white hair, a bony, muscular face and must be in his fifties. He starts talking to us – all unprovoked – and is very keen that we know he was once in the Marines.

Well? I used to go to the Leyton Cub Scouts, but I don't feel the need to shove it down *his* throat. But OK, I think, respect to you. I did only make it to *Seconder* after all. But then during all the talk of Marines, he fiddles with his bag, carries on talking and edges into the bathroom with a pair of hair-straightening tongs. What? Really? Hair tongs? He looks all tough and mean, as though he may have seen some proper war and shooting action and that ... and then he goes and walks into the bathroom with *hair-straighteners*. Tom and Luke and I don't look at each other in the eye. If we catch each others' eyes, there'll be a giggle issue. And I don't want to upset a vain Marine; I could end up Brian Dennehy to this Rambo.

He says he's from San Diego and has been wandering to and from Alaska for years. That's quite a wander. But my God, he must have looked good. *Because he's worth it.* He's like a homeless version of Rambo with even less of a point and the hair of Siegfried from Siegfried & Roy. You can always trust youth hostels to introduce you to the world's wandering strange. After much combing of hair and folding of kit, we all agree to lights out on our first night as officers and gentlemen and hairdos. I lie back and start clambering towards the almighty nod ... all woozy and knackered and bald ... and the only thing that could possibly hamper a good night's sleep is an old-fashioned ringing telephone in the hallway and an old Marine kicking a hat stand over.

Doh!

The old fashioned telephone rings in the hallway and the old marine kicks over a hatstand.

Military style, we get up early and set ourselves the task of paying homage to all the *An Officer and a Gentleman* location stuff before 11am, because that's when we have a special meeting to attend. So, we decide to do it all chronologically, according to the film: beginning with a shot of me riding a motorbike down the entrance to the fort. Well, not a motorbike, it's actually just me crouching and running at the same time while making bike-like noises through my mouth that sound more like a constipated Donald Duck than a Harley Davidson. But you get the picture. Unfortunately, the campers' early morning game of baseball goes a bit slow and perturbed while I'm at it, as half the field pull that *what the fuck* face, and perhaps I'm to blame for a couple of *outs* that would otherwise would have been more carefully observed *ins*.

We walk across and stand by the flagpole out the front of the building, which features significantly in the movie – most memorably at the beginning when Louis Gosset Junior as Sergeant Foley warns the new recruits that to *eyeball* him would not be the best of ideas.

We re-create the scene, which basically means me standing by the flagpole, being shouted at by Tom, who sounds just as Sergeant Foley might have done with a few lungfuls of helium and a completely different script. Rather than the violently eloquent spiel Louis spat out, Tom unleashes a tirade of any swear word his memory can spew up, and I get the feeling that he's using the cloak of this re-creation to express some tension. With a little bit of post-traumatic *Tom-went-mad* awkwardness hanging in the air between us, we head up to Battery Puttnam, a corner of the base just by the sea that has a concrete platform where Gere was made to do press-ups as his friends sped by on a boat, flashing their bums. Tom stands over me as I heave my body like a stranded seal through as many as *eight or nine* almost perfect press-ups while he once again unleashes jabs of screeching diatribe that cuts a little close to the bone. Ginger this, poofter that ... it's all there.

After running up and down the steps more times than my blood pressure would prefer, and with my ragged frame about to collapse, we head down to the lighthouse on the beach, where we re-create a super-distinctive shot where Mayo – rifle lofted up in the air – runs around Foley in silhouette. It's a pretty emblematic shot of the film and has everything a montage shot would ever want. Of course, I fall over. I was about ready to do that before we started, so running in a circle in the sand really wasn't going to last very long. My knee cuts open quite badly, and through the smarting I secretly hope it bleeds a treat, in order that I'm elevated to some sort of location-hunting hero. There's *a lot of blood.* It's on the verge of being legitimately coined a *squirter.* The whole time I know that Tom's relishing putting me through the paces, as some sort of nostalgia-based revenge for all my ribbing and lack of patience and spitefulness. He's almost urging, willing the blood out of my knee. It's all coming back at me and I'm accepting the punishment in acknowledgment of my awfulness. But also it means the slate is clean and I can start again without guilt. He's had his day. Don't you eyeball me, Tom.

Having knackered and torn myself open within just an hour, we wander over to find block 204: the very place where the final scene in *An Officer and a Gentleman* takes place. Here, Foley presents Mayo with a commendation –

touchingly placing a shiny dollar coin in his pocket (apparently quite a tribute for naval types). Tom presents me with a shiny quarter for my efforts – a proportionate amount relative to my performance – and we hop away from that military life and back into society as civilians who would *never ever* survive in the services, not even the Catering Corp. They would eat me alive.

Back in downtown Port Townsend, just before our 11am meeting, we find the Tides Inn –   the hotel which had the same name when it appeared in the movie. It's here where scenes featuring Richard Gere and Debra Winger having naughtiness in a motel room were shot. The lady at reception is very receptive, as you'd hope, and is only too happy to allow us a look at the room; sending us off with the key and a fifteen-minute limit. Room 10 at Tides Inn has a piss-poor biro written sign outside proclaiming it to be "The *An Officer and a Gentleman* Suite". Inside, the smell of stale old sods, vague traces of bygone cigarettes and whisky shots rush at you. The room looks the same but tired - the pine wood panelling, the windows that overlook the ocean and the kitchen where Debra Winger cooked Gere breakfast the morning after a massive row. Among all the little details around the room, including photos from the relevant scenes in the film, I notice that for twenty-five cents you can make the bed vibrate, which is a nice feature that they dubiously call "Magic Fingers".. I wonder whether Winger, or maybe even Gere, shelled out on a bit of Magic Fingers. It's hard to imagine how a film crew and their cameras piled in here; this is a pretty small room.

Along at Room 12 is where Mayo finds his best friend hanging in the bathroom, and where Tom hides, with his belt around his neck, so that when I open the door I nearly shit and throw up all at once... Tom's not usually as devious as this, he really is getting the better of me on this leg of the journey. He's slaughtering me. What makes the whole hanging behind the door bit even more grim and disturbing is that Tom is topless, which he likes being. He's very proud of his torso and likes to get it out whenever he can, but I don't necessarily want to walk face-first into it, and I make that known in no uncertain terms.

It's 11am.

The restaurant is a lazy place where sun-botherers drench their thirst in beer and douse their hunger with seafood. We clack our way along the wooden floor and meet our breakfast date – a very thin and, it must be said, *old* looking Louis Gosset Junior. He's coming up for seventy now and has clearly lost a lot of the muscle he bulked up to play Sergeant Foley in *An Officer and a Gentleman*. We made contact with Louis back in the UK and for an Oscar winner, he was extremely amenable. That doesn't mean that you can just phone up old Louis and meet up for a breakfast, I think he just took a shine to our mission and happily agreed to meet us for a brunch-type scenario.

Wearing a Hawaiian shirt and dripping in gold, he's courteous and friendly right from the start. We begin with handshakes and brief introductions and then he tells us he has to go for a shit. Erm, OK. When he comes swaggering back, clearly relieved of his burden, it's high-fives all round, although Luke only manages to flap a limp wrist that misses twice before finally connecting with a dull slap that has all the enthusiasm missing. Louis doesn't want to start rolling on the interview until after breakfast, because he doesn't want a *spinach-in-tooth* or *egg-spit-at-lens* moment, so we have to make small talk and drink too much coffee while he hacks his way through a carb-tastic omelette. It's carb-heavy because he's been suffering with parasites in his blood, which explains his surprisingly bony appearance. The illness has been pretty bad, but he's just had the all clear and is going about eating as much food as possible to get the pounds back on.

Louis seems well known and well loved at the restaurant: constantly waving at waitresses and other customers, all of whom he has a cute one-liner or flirty tongue-in-cheek compliment for. So after he's shovelled the last bit of egg down his trap, concluding the whole weight-gaining exercise, we get on with talking about the film.

"We've read that up until the big 'Don't you eyeball me, boy' speech, you were actually a bit stand-offish to the co-stars, so that they'd be a bit frightened of you."

"Yeah, I wouldn't talk to them. I was staying about eight miles away from town. So, I would wake up in the morning, put on my army fatigues on, and I'd run eight plus miles to the set. And when I'd get therethey'd say, 'Hi, Louis,' and I'd say, 'Hey, I'm not Louis, I'm Sergeant Foley.' And they'd say, 'Oh yeah, right.' So they thought *this guy was nuts*, and that's how I got the reaction in the scene, they thought I was nuts. They thought, *he's out of his mind*, but after the movie and I got the Oscar, they said, 'We gotcha, we gotcha.'"

"Do you still remember all the lines from the flagpole scene?" I ask, hoping for a full on Oscar-winning recital.

"Almost. The thing I liked the most was, 'This education is worth a million dollars. But before you get to that job, you've got to get past me.' I liked that bit".

"We recreated the 'Don't you eyeball me' bit at the flagpole earlier."

"Oh, right. Well you know what the rest of that line was, right? Don't you eyeball me man. I'll rip your eyeballs out of your sockets and skull fuck you in the head." He's not actually got the wording quite right, but the sentiment is the same, and it *was* a long time ago.

"I've always wanted you to say that to me. Not actually *do it* to me, I mean, just say it, for nostalgia reasons." Louis laughs.

"I was watching *Full Metal Jacket* and some of the same lines are in that," he adds. It's true – the "steers and queers" bit is replicated and tweaked to suit a Texan rather than an Oklahoma fella, and the whole skull-sex situation was employed too.

"After those scenes, did you and Gere become friends?"

"A while ago, at the New York Film Institute, they spent a lot of money on a tribute to Richard Gere. I surprised him and turned up and he went to tears. He's quite a man. Richard Gere is one of the greatest actors in our business. Why? You have to push him, you push him you get the best performance in the world out of him. I like him a lot."

"Do *you* need pushing?"

"No. I'm a pusher. I do *like* to be pushed. I like Daniel Day Lewis, he works hard." Not sure what Day Lewis and his funny left foot have to do with the price of fish at this juncture. So we carry on with a little game – the sort that really crap interviewers on *The Big Breakfast* would have done.

"We always wonder how well the stars remember the behind-the-scenes crew on films. So, we've picked out three names from the *An Officer and a Gentleman* crew, and wonder if you can remember what they did..."

"Oh boy."

"Do you remember Gerald O'Dell?"

"The man I really remember mostly was Don Thorin. He was the DP." Louis is clearly uncomfortable at being tested like this. And I start wondering whether this is a very nice thing to do.

"Well actually Gerald O'Dell was the make-up artist."

"Oh really? He was the one that made me the best moustache. I can't do it myself. I've been trying my best to duplicate that moustache but I cannot. Thank you, Gerald."

"Do you remember Daniel Heffner?"

"I don't know."

"He was the Second AD. Now, I think this one might be a challenge. James Berkey...?"

"I know that name. Was he an operator?"

"No, he was a set decorator."

"Oh, well we would never have seen him."

"Oh. Well, he actually died the same year as the film was made."

"Oooh." That's enough of that. I feel like we've been a bit odd. I've clearly turned back into an early morning TV producer looking for an opportunity to show the celeb up. I didn't like being it then and it just feels grubby now. So I decide to snuggle up to his ego a little.

"You deservedly won the Oscar in 1982 for Best Supporting Actor. Was that your career highlight?"

"That's one, the other one was *Roots*. *Roots* was what got me here."

Indeed, *Roots* was an incredibly important TV series – made in 1977 – not just for really launching Louis (who played Fiddler), but for ripping open the issue of slavery. Using Alex Haley's story of Kunte, a boy who was stolen from his village, the series got the public talking openly about the issue for the first time. In terms of breaking ground and impacting on culture, *Roots* makes *An Officer and a Gentleman* look like an episode of *The Krankies*.

"You beat your co-star David Keith to the Oscar. Was he absolutely gutted?"

"Oh, no. David is a free soul. He's a talented man. He was kind of *pleasantly surprised*. I like him a lot."

"Do you have fond memories of the film?"

"Very much so. The food was delicious. You know the town was born I guess in the 1800s, because of the lumberjacks. And then the lumber market went down and the town was almost dead. And then during the Vietnam era, they had a mayor who was a jazz pianist. So it was a different population, you had the hippies. Because it's only ten minutes to the border, when they got drafted, they'd hop over to Canada to avoid it. The food was incredible; any little café would just fill up." Well, OK but what about the film?

"What was the camaraderie like on set? We've heard that Debra Winger and Richard Gere didn't really get on."

"Debra didn't have the best of times. Her and Richard ... but I don't really know because I wasn't there. But Richard was quite a gentleman."

"And an officer," I add. Hmmm, I'm sure he knows a bit more about that. I've read on the Internet that they despised each other – especially on the Winger to Gere side.

"Yes, and an officer. I don't know why they didn't film a sequel. I think the producers on an executive level didn't like each other. I don't know because I wasn't there." Blimey, he's like Arsene Wenger, the man who never saw it. "But there *should* have been *An Officer and a Gentleman 2*," he adds.

"Did you have to really buff up for the role?"

"Oh, yeah. Thank God, because the things I've had to buff up for have probably saved my life. Because with the parasites, my resistance was so strong. I had muscle memory."

"I heard that John Travolta and John Denver were both originally up for Richard Gere's role."

"Really? John Denver I would have eaten alive. You know *An Officer and a Gentleman* was *supposed* to be a throwaway project. It was the third picture on Richard Gere's contract. And *then* we were the biggest thing in show business."

"A couple of years after, *Top Gun* came out. They're quite similar, aren't they?"

"People say to me, 'How do you like Tom Cruise?' I say, 'I've never met him.' They say, 'How come you've never met him?' I say, 'Well, Tom Cruise was in a different film.' They get the two films confused. They're very close."

Our list of questions seems to take ill-prepared twists and bends as we change subjects in a flash.

"Didn't you write a song for Woodstock?"

"Well, yeah. I was out of work and I wrote a song. I wrote a few songs. I put on a hootenanny. A hootenanny is a thing where I was the MC and I put on acts all day and all night. Then I got a job in Hollywood as an actor in a series called *The Young Rebels*. It eventually failed as a series and I've got the gift of the gab, so I talked the landlord into letting me not pay the rent for around seven months. After that, he's packing the van up. The *same day* I got a residual cheque for $72,000 from the record company. Richie Havens had sung my song at Woodstock and then he put it in his album called *Mixed Bag*."

"And you later found yourself hanging out with the Beatles."

"Yup, I hung out with the Beatles. And Mick Jagger and those guys too. They didn't remember when I saw them again because I didn't have my head shaved, but then finally I said "Baghdad Gardens" and they got it. Baghdad Gardens was off the Abbey Road I guess, on the other side of Chelsea. Downstairs we used to sing together and have hashish, you know, and all that stuff. That was quite a period."

"How comes we haven't seen an album from *you*?"

"I had one album. But I'm a Gemini. And I'm the kind of Gemini who wants to devote all of their attention to one thing. If I split my attentions, no one thing gets the best of me."

And so along comes the bill and off leaps Louis and his freshly stretched gut. We take the tab, of course. It's been great to meet this nice, kind, popular gent and buy him some carbohydrates to feed his parasites.

Off we speed towards Oregon and the small town of Astoria. However, going through a hicky beach town called South Bend, Luke recklessly risks our lives and those of the locals by twatting the motor up to 35mph...in a 25mph zone! Unbelievable daredevilry. A flabby cop with a drawl and a lisp and great flapping chops that combined render him virtually unintelligible, pulls us over and seems so devastatingly appalled at our high-speed antics that he decides to slap a hundred-dollar fine on us before heading back to his carful of donuts and gone-off sweat. Our first brush with the law leaves me fuming that they bother pulling people for such slender a breach, and over the next hour I flick through my mental thesaurus for different ways to curse a fat ugly cop.

Keeping religiously to the speed limits, like scorned kids, allows us to enjoy views of the curling oceanside road all the way down finally into Oregon, which first says hello after the Astoria–Megler Bridge. Crossing the mouth of the Columbia River from Washington to Oregon, the big, spiky, gnarly bridge is the longest continuous truss in the world and looks like a Victorian roller coaster. We get talking about how so many eighties films seem to have a moment where someone slides or falls down something and screams

"NOOOOooooooooo" all the way down. So, going across the slopey and exceptionally long Astoria–Megler Bridge, we maintain our NOOOOooooooooos for a good few minutes as a tribute to that convention, until each other's voices become a bit much.

For the first time in a while, we're looking out to water that doesn't have land on the other side: this is sea and not lake. And on the other side of the bridge we find Astoria, one of the most prized legs of this journey...

The home of *The Goonies*.

THE GOONIES (1985) (Movie)

Director: Richard Donner
Writers: Steven Spielberg, Chris Columbus
Producers: Steven Spielberg, Frank Marshall, Kathleen Kennedy, Richard Donner, Harvey Bernhard.

Cast: Sean Astin (Mikey Walsh), Jeff Cohen (Lawrence "Chunk" Cohen), Josh Brolin (Brand Walsh), Corey Feldman (Clark "Mouth" Devereaux), Kerri Green (Andy Carmichael), Martha Plimpton (Stef Steinbrenner), Jonathan Ke Quan (Richard "Data"Wang), Jonathan Matuszak (Lotney "Sloth" Fratelli), Robert Davi (Jake Fratelli), Joe Pantoliano (Francis Fratelli), Anne Ramsey (Mama Fratelli), Lupe Ontiveros (Rosalita)

Notes:
Not only did everyone want to be a Goonie in the eighties, but everyone wants to be a Goonie *now*. Being a Goonie represents all that was crazy, cool and wild about the eighties, all the things we miss about it. The feeling that adventures can be born out of any situation. All through our trip, Tom has had comments from passers-by about his Goonies-themed T-shirts – it clearly strikes a chord with the nostalgia-sensitive and even those who are too young to have seen it the first time around. *The Goonies is* the Eighties.

Astoria wakes us with its thick-as-syrup baked summer air and we get ourselves out onto the streets with a spring in our step, skipping towards the Astoria Column: a viewpoint from which to look over the entire town. After a few minutes of near-vertical hill walking, our spring has sprung and my dry leathery tongue drags between my legs. My lungs are probably bleeding, or at least weeping some sort of noxious sputum. The view is worth it though, and we can see the Astoria Bridge in its spindly entirety: spanning all the way across to Washington State with its bizarre hump in the middle. The town looks small, insular, all packed up together among the hills. Then, to the right, we spot the place we all want to sprint over to...

Having gained our bearings from the height of the column, we make our way to not only the reason we're here in Astoria, but one of the main reasons we came on this trip in the first place...

Slap me twice and call me Margaret ... IT'S THE GOONIES' HOUSE!

Everyone knows what it looks like. *Everyone*. For some reason, it encapsulates the eighties: a houseful of crazy kids off their nut on sugary drinks and white bread, with a scatty, disorganised single mother who hates men. The Goonies' house is an example of an eighties movie family home that's chaotic and full of crap everywhere: displaying how fast living and single parenthood and the clawing capitalist desire to own as much as possible, as quickly as possible, results in domestic catastrophe. You can also see this boom-time chaos in Ally Sheedy's house in *Short Circuit*, Doc Emmett Brown's place in *Back To The Future* and Billy's house in *Gremlins*. Other films also played off the dysfunction created through the eighties capitalist revolution: Ferris Bueller's rebellion, the Breakfast Club bunch; all of them wanting to crack open the old family stereotype and become singular, free and independent, according to the Gordon Gekko fragmented society model of how we *should* want to be. Of course, at the time we didn't notice the commentary these films offered because we were so stuck inside it all.

As we approach the steep dirt track that veers off-road and up to the house, we notice that another house on the street, at the bottom, has fragile-looking home-made Goonies memorabilia for sale. We decide not to, thanks. We climb further up and run into the man living at the house next door to the Goonies House, who tells us that up to fifty people a day come up to catch a glimpse, and that's why people in the neighbourhood have seen an opportunity to take advantage through fashioning crude ornaments and uncollectibles. We still decide not to, thanks again.

And there it is. The house itself looks more or less as it did – the porch with its white decked walkway and the front door on the side being the most recognisable features. The whole thing sort of faces you corner-first. The white picket fencing that surrounded the house in the film is no longer there – the film people took it away – and we have to work quite hard to pinpoint the very spot where Chunk performed his famous "Truffle Shuffle". We coyly attempt our own version, but it really takes the class of gut that Jeff Cohen had going on when he played Chunk. Up come the shirts and what bellies we have are wobbled as a proud homage to Chunk's dance.

This is amazing. This is weird. You can visit places from films that you like, but this is movie legend, the heart of movie cool. The Truffle Shuffle is an iconic, emblematic beacon for eighties film and right now, I'm standing in the very spot that it happened. A world-famous moment occurred right here. Comprehending it is difficult, it's like the brain-befuddling idea that space is infinite or that Spurs will never win the Premiership. It feels like we've visited some sort of temple or shrine; there are wind chimes hanging all over the outside of the place and they're clanging away in the breeze as if to calm the moment into a sort of ethereal haven.

OK, it's hardly the spot where Kennedy was shot or the tomb of Lenin or Tiananmen Square. No, no, no.

It's more important than that.

When the movie first visits the Goonies' house, a big sweeping pan soaks up the Astoria skyline from its slightly lofty vantage point and hooks round to the house. Next door stands the house where Data lives in the movie. Now it looks run down (and probably owned by old people or rented out to students – either way, people who can't or won't care too much about its upkeep). The only emphatically recognisable part of that house is the top window that Data zip-wired out of across to the living-room window of the Goonies' house. It looks quite a way in real life; I wouldn't fancy it, I probably would have gone the old-fashioned knocking-on-the-door route.

We had the foresight while in downtown Astoria to get our hands on a very small child's bike. We didn't steal it; we bought it shadily in the dank basement of a second-hand bike shop for a measly two dollars. The price seems extraordinarily low, even for the ugly thing it is, and I begin wondering if it had something crucially wrong with it that could lead to a terrible accident on the Goonie hill. I don't say anything though, because Tom has staked claims on riding it and I'm thinking that a good accident might be great on camera – at least to send off to the *You've Been Framed Movie Location Hunting Special*, and at least to get one over on Tom.

We re-create the scene where Josh Brolin (as Brand) steals a bike from a little girl outside Data's house. Tom lifts me off the bike and I stomp around shouting "I want my bike back" just like she did (but with an extra twelve stone and the deathly burden of a mortgage etched on my face). Tom then takes off down the sloping dirt road, peddling manically on his dubious two-dollar bike. Dust and gravel spray and high-pitched wails trail off into the distance and we'll never know if Tom actually fell off at any point. The fracas has all the sound effects of a crash, but with the distance and dust cloud and a slight curve in the road, it's impossible to diagnose. Tom refuses to discuss the incident, which to my mind is an admission.

We take our final photos and glimpses and head away from the house, downtown to the cop shop, where the Sheriff of Astoria is expecting us.

We ask for John Raichl at the counter and are promptly introduced to an immense skittle with a face on. This man is so bottom heavy I doubt even a gravity failure would tip him upside down. He really is very, very fat down the bottom. He wears a smart suit undermined by dandruffed shoulders but seems pleased to see us and only too happy to take some time out to show us the County Jail building that Robert Davi as Jake Fratelli escaped from at the start of the movie. The jail building looks just the same as it did in the movie and even though the cells haven't housed criminals for many years, the old "County Jail" sign is still hammered into the concrete above the door.

The sheriff seems to enjoy faux threatening to arrest the staff we bump into and put them in jail, and whoever he says it to responds with comments that suggest he's thrown the same japey toothless threats at them yesterday and the day before. Maybe that's his *thing*, his joke. As we walk inside the County Jail, the sheriff fumbles cluelessly with the giant keys to the door, because it's been such a long time since they've been used. I like that. I feel like our tour of the jail is *very* exclusive.

"When were the last tourists shown around here?"

"Oh, I don't think we've opened it up for the public in three years or so." Yes! We rule. "When it was open for public viewing, people would like to play and get in the cells and close the door. We'd then get called over because they couldn't figure out the combination to get out."

We find the very cell that Jake Fratelli pretended to hang himself in before kneeing a cop in the gob and escaping out the front where his ugly old mum with a toupee was waiting in the car.

"The odour's less than pleasant," Sheriff points out. I already know. It's rancid. "But these were the cells they used. You could make do, but it's not where you want to spend your life."

"We were stopped for speeding yesterday, Luke was driving and he was going ten miles per hour over the limit. Would it be possible to put him in detention for a bit just to teach him a lesson?" Can't believe I'm shopping a fellow Goonie, but it amuses me to imagine. Although Luke's so narrow, he'd probably slip through the bars.

"Oh, ten miles per hour, that's probably just around ten days without food and water. We don't hang any more any more unless they're doing at least twenty miles an hour over." He's good at keeping a straight face, this sheriff.

We ask John if he was around at the time the movie was made.

"We were moved out during the filming. I started working here in 1976 and they'd just closed it down as a jail because it no longer met State code. But the control division worked out of here until 1980. But we didn't have much to do with it, they would pretty much have their own key and lock after they'd finished."

With that, we leave the sheriff to waddle off back to the *real* jail and further down the street we bump into a barman who Tom got talking to last night. The guy had told him that his fiancée used to live in the Goonies' house and it just so happens that she's standing next to him in the street. As we take our chance and interview her on the spot, I realise that I was eyeing her up just a few moments ago. She clearly didn't notice, or just thought I had a wandering glass eye or something. But it makes me feel a bit pervy, so Tom asks the questions while I sex pest behind the camera.

"So..." he says to Mindy, "you lived in the Goonies' house then?" and off she goes, it just spews out of her...

"Yeah, we got a lot of tourists from all over the world coming and knocking and they'd ask if they could tour the house or see the attic. But the attic was a set in Hollywood, there's not actually an attic up there. They also built the front gate part where Chunk does the Truffle Shuffle and ended up selling all that after the filming. I told people they could come onto the porch and I'd leave the windows open so they could look inside. People would even ask if they could take rocks from the driveway! My brother lived in Data's place next door and that was the same, he still had people coming over there. People from Hong Kong would come really, really early and knock on the door. That was kind of troublesome. We actually moved here from California after seeing the movie, because of the trees and the greenery. Four years later we ended up getting the Goonies' house." We thank Mindy and her bloke and leave them to continue looking at the toys in Woolworth's.

On the way back to the hotel, we stumble across the Flavel House Museum, where Mikey's dad worked – an impressive gothic-looking building with turrets and intricate designs hanging off it like Pat Butcher earrings. This place is *small* – it's not hard to just *run into Goonies* locations. Just around the corner there's the bowling alley where, at the beginning of the movie, Chunk flattens his face, milkshake and hamburger against the glass as the Fratelli jailbreak car chase ensues down the street. We have to, of course, press our faces against the glass, although the owner doesn't let us spill our milkshakes because he's just had new carpet put in. I'm loving these locations so much that I almost lick the glass, but then imagine a thousand other pilgrims pressing their greasy hooters onto it and realise I'd only be licking their nose-oil. Don't want that.

But *what* a day.

———————

Luke and I decide to hit Astoria for a few beers in the evening, to celebrate our discoveries and try to get to the heart of the place; to find out what it is, other than the photogenic curly old bridge that brings film-makers to Astoria. Even recently, *The Ring 2* was filmed here, so it's clear that its charms are enduring.

But we're not expecting the sort of carnage in store for us.

We go to a bar called *Merry Times*, hoping to indeed have some Merry Times. The barman turns out to be called Taylor. He's a middle-aged gent with grey hair and a grey tash with slight orangey tobacco hues. He's just finished his shift and is already making a really good show of being half-cut.

"Welcome to Nowhere," he slurs. One of the first things I speak to him about – bearing in mind that I'm a Bud or four down the khazi myself – is that he fought in Vietnam. I unabashedly, with four-beer unabashedness, ask him if he killed anyone. Yup, subtle. He says grimly that he *did,* and a few minutes of awkward silence follow before he begins with tales of cradling his dying friends and all that war stuff. I remain moderately scared of him for the rest of the evening.

So, thinks Luke, is it *called* 'No Name Road', or does the road actually have no name?

Dante's Viewpoint, Death Valley. Luke poses on the edge of the cliff, just before petrol-gate.

Leo Carillo State Beach, CA. Me and Tom doing the famous *Karate Kid* 'crane kick'.

Marty McFly's house, LA. Me asking Tom if there's 'anyone at home McFly?'

The tunnel from *Back to the Future*, LA. Tom and I share the tiny skateboard.

Tom stuck up the tree George McFly spied at Lorraine from in *Back to the Future*.

Tom pays homage to *Teen Wolf*...surfin' USA.

Me and *Teen Wolf* – with Mark Arnold, who played Mick in the movie.

Me and Tom waving from Kevin Arnold's house in *The Wonder Years*.

Lunch and cunnilingus with Hightower, Hooks and Callahan.

A dreadful attempt at the *Thriller* dance, outside the house used in the video, LA.

Proof that No.5 *is* alive. With Eric Allard, the guy who designed and built the robot Johnny 5 from *Short Circuit*.

No more Truffle Shuffles for Jeff Cohen. Beers with me, Tom and Chunk from *The Goonies*.

Breakfast with Howling Mad Murdoch (Dwight Schultz) and his radio sidekick, Don Ecker.

With Jason Lively, who played little Rusty Griswald in *National Lampoon's European Vacation.*

Me and Tom sitting at the very table used in *Top Gun*, at the Kansas City Barbecue in San Diego.

The bar is full of overweight men and women, most of them just sitting there in couples staring at each other, expressionless, having a "merry" time, while others play darts without a trace of a smile. Drinking, it seems, is more of a requirement than a pleasure here. Taylor insists on making us feel at home by playing Spandau Ballet's "True" back-to-back on the jukebox three times, thinking it's some sort of stately British anthem one's Queen might smooch to. People in Astoria seem to be friendly, but a little rough around the edges: scruffy and brash. I suppose they're only used to seeing *each other* and aren't used to dressing up for outsiders. Nonetheless, what we've found is a vaguely charming thoroughfare for people heading elsewhere: only populated permanently by people either born here or stuck here.

After a while, Taylor becomes three-quarters cut and convinces us, with the steely eyes of a drunk veteran who could kill us with his mere eyebrow, to get a cab up to Annie's – the local strip joint at the top off the road. Not usually my cup of tea, but what the sod – it's been a while, if you know what I mean.

We walk into Annie's and see a woman on-stage, down the other end, whom I initially and genuinely double take in mistake for Rick Parfitt from Status Quo. In fact, all of the women are growlingly dreadful, and *completely naked* – a very confusing scenario for a female-starved gentleman. Old tinsel covered in dust (amassed skin cells of dirty old men looking at dirty old women) drapes over anything that looks like it needed decorating ten years ago. We sit through a few excruciating "dances" (or staggers) that occasionally involve having legs placed on our shoulders and a huge female mullet – not being sure sometimes whether it's her *upper wig* or *lower wig* – moving towards our crotches. Thankfully, without actual contact. The place is drum-empty and super-seedy; the girls are grim and cost a-dollar-a-dance. Around a dollar more than I'm prepared to pay. We get out of there with Taylor's permission and he takes us back to his bar, opens it all back up and gives us our own free lock-in as Spandau Ballet return for an encore.

I get talking to a local single mother who – in true American *let's talk about my life and my feelings in ridiculous detail* style, let's me know very early doors that she has a terminal illness. I pull my sympathy face, of course (an elaborate combination of constipation and losing at cards); it's a horrible thing for a single mother, but I try to change the subject to something less terminal as soon as possible. In the toilets, I dutifully warn Luke about her situation, knowing she might spill it all over him too, and leave him to go off and have a chat with her.

He does more than *chat*, though. Uh-oh. He persuades her to come back to our motel and share his turn on the double bed. Which, by the way, is the bed directly next to the double bed Tom and I – due to the revolving system – are having to share. I force myself to sleep, desperately trying not to hear the kissy wissy slurps or the secret whispers and *Carry On* giggles. But in the morning, after *whatever-her-name-is* has crept out for the Astoria walk of shame, back to her child (I heard her leave but pretended to be asleep), Luke gloats and brags and postures like an arrogant gorilla over his bagging of a local lady. Perhaps spitefully, because he's had the flaming gall to have sex within a couple of feet of me, I remind him that she has a terminal disease. It's like telling him for the first time. He was too drunk in the toilets to absorb it properly. His face drains and withers, as though he's just had his willy freeze-dried off. His brow immediately sweats that *guilty-scared sweat*, the *sitting in the HIV clinic* sweat, and all I can do is assure him that it's not a transmittable disease. I can't quite remember what the disease *is*, because I was too busy being incredibly lurchingly drunk, but I do remember that it wasn't something you can catch up the willy hole. "It was muscles or bones or something," I say. This doesn't necessarily reassure Luke and he sits quietly as the glory turns slowly into sex-horror. Eventually, he speaks. Quietly and remorsefully.

"She said she didn't normally do one-night stands, but I persuaded her by saying, 'You only live once.' Oh my God." A sort of sordid, naughty spray of giggles from me and Tom fill the car in that *I mustn't laugh but I can't help myself way* that you'd be thrown out of a classroom for.

Luke doesn't mention this episode again. We do, often, but Luke doesn't.

After a fair amount of stilted silence, we stop off at Ecola State Park, where in 1985 The Goonies were filmed on their bikes from a helicopter – racing towards the restaurant that the Fratellis hid out in before going underground looking for One Eyed Willy's treasure. It's here where the bad kids in the car trapped Mikey's hand, while he was on his bike, and dragged him down the twisty, slopey hill at speeds his little feet couldn't peddle at.

The curvy road cuts through dense forest and is perfect for us to get the bike out once more. I'm surprised Tom's up for this. He sits on the little bike in the road and puts his hand on the door. From the driver's seat of the Oldsmobile, I grab his hand, tightly, and trap it. A park ranger, done up in all the ranger gear, looking all inquisitive, draws up next to us and asks if everything's alright. We say, "Yes, and thank you very much please Park Ranger," and feign interest in the woodland and wildlife and "isn't this tree amazing with its bark and leaves and that". He buys it and drives off a bit smiley.

So. I start driving down the hill, one hand on wheel, the other gripping Tom and dragging him alongside me on the bike. Slowly. But. A perfect chance for me to avenge the Fort Warden day of torture, don't you think? This is my perfect moment, as Martine McCutcheon would warble. Nostalgia-based retribution. First gear. I play it cool. I don't want Tom to have second thoughts and get off before I screech away and scare the piddling kidneys out of him with eighty-eight miles per hour on a bend. Maybe. Second gear. I want to see him sick at least one kidney up. Wind dries his mouth out, he closes it and the screams become confined. Third gear. Thirty miles per hour. Tom's face starts going grey-green. Either he's crying or there's slight G-force strain starting to pin his cheeks into a grimace. Thirty-five miles per hour. Expressionless now, somehow serenely terrified. A sudden belt of compassion – seeping through a face full of evil chuckles and piggish snorts – forces me to stop. Tom flies off the bike and manages to satisfy momentum by running down the road on just legs. "You bastard" is all he can say for half an hour or so, varying it with "You cock" a couple of times.

But at least we stayed true to the film. That was my *only* aim, right?

We find ourselves in Roseburg, Oregon, hunting for the residence of a Mr Chuck Eisenhamm of Bellwood Lane. After asking a few locals where the hell Bellwood Lane is, we run into a woman who used to be his neighbour. She warns us that he's an "interesting" man and directs us to his place.

When we arrive in the suburbs, we find Chuck's detached, bog-standard, perfectly nice house empty, but it's just a few minutes before a car with a dog in the back and an old man at the wheel pulls up uber-slowly beside us. There are pictures painted on the side of the car of some Alsatians, with the words "The Littlest Hobo" underneath.

THE LITTLEST HOBO (1979–1985) (TV)

Cast: London the Dog (London the Dog)

Notes:
Perhaps this show is best remembered for its theme tune, the words to which any self-respecting eighties-phile will know … *at least* the chorus. Every episode, the ultra-intelligent hobo dog would find a new owner, help them out "until tomorrow" and then "just keep moving on".

Chuck was the loving owner of London, the dog that starred in the Canadian kids' TV show, and I arranged to visit him to talk about the show – via an elaborate set of emails through a third party and finally a couple of phone calls.

Chuck shuffles – oddly contorted by age – out of the car and seems a little confused as to who we are, despite the fact that I spoke to him on the phone just yesterday. He has that generic old man face, which after a certain age becomes devoid of any distinctive features. I can't wait for that. I can't afford for my hooter to get longer, I'll be able to sit and chew on it.

"Where's the girl I spoke to on the phone?" he asks. Here we go, I think. I wondered why he kept calling me "dear" on the phone. He thought I was a woman. That's why he appears confused now.

Americans *always* think I'm a woman on the phone. Better than mistaking me for one in person, I guess, but my phone voice must just be at the right octave to allow for such humiliating a misunderstanding. I mean really, it's crushing. Apparently, American women can be called Spencer, which is all I have to cling to in my desperation to retain some respect from the situation. Maybe I should have just turned up in hot pants and a bra-top and gone with it to minimise the old boy's confusion. I follow Chuck into his home, which stinks of dog, piss and old man – one of the worst combinations, especially when you're never sure whom the piss leaked from or which one of them smells more of dog. The whole thing really is quite awkward, he doesn't seem to know quite what's going on and isn't that bothered that we're here as he carries on with what he usually does at home. It's like he's let us in and decided to ignore us. Where do I put myself? Do I sit down or what?

We break the five-minute silence and ask him where he'd like to be interviewed. He swiftly slumps into his favourite seat (I assume it's his favourite by the fact that it's much more stained than the rest, with some sort of black dribbling syrup all down the bottom bit between his legs). Looking around the place, there are mementos and reminders of *The Littlest Hobo* everywhere: big faded oil paintings of Alsatians on the walls and plaques with twee poems about man's best friend scattered everywhere.

His only remaining dog, Rora, a big fat black dog, snarls around us all suspicious and arch, as Chuck speaks to it in German. I ask him why he speaks to the dog in German.

"During the war I spoke two languages when I was doing a show with the dogs. It was in Canada and they have two provinces there that are German, so I spoke it and did shows for them."

"So Chuck, Rora here is the grand-dog of London, the original Littlest Hobo, right?"

"No, no. There are no living descendants." Oh balls. I really want Rora to be a relation. He then starts barking German instructions at Rora in a very stiff, Hitlery sort of way.

"So where are you from?" he asks.

"We're from London in England."

"Oh yeah, that's right. Where's the woman that called?" For Christ's sake Chuck, why don't you just ask me to tuck my willy between my legs? Having to explain to someone that you're the woman on the phone is *really* humiliating. I do so, laughing, but inside I'm dying.

"Do you wanna take a picture?" he says to Luke, who's holding the camera.

"This is a video camera Chuck, it's already recording." This is getting a bit silly. He nods like he understands but clearly doesn't. Poor old sod.

"So what can you tell us about *The Littlest Hobo*?"

"Well, I did the first one, which was a full-length feature, down in Hollywood. We only had one dog then. Then I kept working with them. I was playing professional baseball. At that time I was with San Diego."

"We had the show all through our childhood, Chuck, and it's very popular in England."

"Oh really? Yeah, we had dogs that lived to be sixteen, that was London. And then I kept five dogs for the next twenty years, doing shows all over. I would usually use just one dog for the TV show, usually the dog which hadn't been on a long run or doing a show."

"Were they all related?"

"Yup, all of those were related. I had twenty over thirty-five years."

I don't think he really knows what a cult-status the show holds, even now, in England. He seems to have an *inkling*, so I push that bit further and ask him to sing the theme tune to us and almost immediately he starts warbling triumphantly; though without the correct throat equipment, as many old people do, with their tattered vocal chords. He seems to be singing similar words to the "Maybe Tomorrow" song we all know and murder after a few pints, but it's doubtlessly a different tune. I can only think that he's singing the tune to the original series back in 1958.

"Did you ever appear in the show?"

"I played in about fifteen episodes. We did a hundred and eighty-four pictures in total."

I ask him about his techniques in handling dogs.

"I would say London had around a five thousand word vocabulary. About two thousand more than the average for dogs. In three different languages." That's pretty impressive. I'm not sure I could think of five thousand things I'd want a dog to do.

"So London was the dog that we saw on the screen most of the time?"

"That's correct. London was a star. London was the top dog. But each one of them was given an opportunity to be great. And they *were* great. They were great dogs because they would never *not* do something and embarrass you. I also was very careful not to get them to do something that would embarrass them. If they couldn't do something, they would come up to me and apologise."

"How can you tell that they're apologising?"

"You can tell by the way that they hold up their paws. You know?" Not really, but I believe him, this man knows his dogs alright.

As he gets more used to us being there, Chuck seems to warm up (unlike Rora, who remains frosty) and out comes another rendition of the original *Littlest Hobo* theme. In fact, Chuck gets so comfortable that he decides to give us a quick display of his power over Rora. He asks the dog to take a tissue and put it in the bin, which Rora refuses to do until enough time has passed that Chuck could have got up and put it in there himself. Chuck shouts at the poor little stinker to bring this and take that and the dog lumbers around seemingly not really getting what's going on or why Chuck can't put his own snot-rag in the bin.

We get a quick tour of his house, which is basically a series of rooms with more oil paintings of dogs, although among the canine depictions, there's one huge painting in the bedroom of a naked lady in a *very* erotic position. Absurdly erotic. This comes as a bit of a surprise. Put it this way, I take a picture of it. Then he sits on the bed in front of the erotic lady and out comes another rendition of the alien, not-my-pub-version *Littlest Hobo* theme tune. Chuck has an infectious, devilish grin and I can tell that he was probably a bit of a lad back in the day. On our way out, he puts his veiny old hand on my shoulder and says he's been looking forward to our visit for a couple of months. I wonder whether he hoped he was going to get his leg over with the woman he *thought* I was, or whether he *still* thinks I'm a woman. But he clearly loves talking about the old days and maybe doesn't get much of a chance to do so any more and that triggers a boom of compassion. Bless him, he's been looking forward to us coming and I feel proud that we've made him feel good by showing an interest in the work he loved.

Just as I did with Ben and Franny Rose, I can see that Chuck has involuntarily scaled down his activity, knowing that the best days of his life are behind him. He's just *surviving* – waiting for his time to go. For a man who's had such an interesting, varied and successful life I find it hard to feel sad that Chuck has got old; we've caught him near the end of a *great* life, and even great lives have to come to an end.

What's strange is that the eighties were only twenty years ago, and those twenty years seem cheap to us because we're still relatively young. But for Chuck, the last twenty years have been expensive, and it's weird seeing a man who's contributed to our childhoods now barely able to dodder out to the kitchen without having to have a sit down. I realise that this must rush up on you pretty quick.

Chuck showers us with old black and white promotional pictures of *The Littlest Hobo* team of dogs – London sitting proudly in the middle. He admits with a little extra moisture in his eyes how much he misses having the Alsatians around.

"Would you say Rora is your best friend, Chuck?"

"Yeah, he's a good boy." He turns to Rora and starts stroking him. "Are you a good boy? Are you a good boy, London?" Chuck doesn't notice that he accidentally called Rora "London". And I don't correct him.

We wave goodbye to Chuck, knowing that more than just a chapter of our childhood is probably going to close before long.

But we carry on. Because Goonies never say die.

CHAPTER ELEVEN SOUNDTRACK:

Stand
By Me

Ben E. King (1961/1986)

Cry
Little Sister

Gerard McMann (1987)

Chapter Eleven

When the night is long...

Roseburg, Oregon to Santa Cruz, California

In choosing the scenic but bladder-burstingly long route eastbound through the Lassen Volcanic State Park, we didn't expect this mother to lead us up a mountain and squiz us around roads narrower than my head. Tom drives with his eyes fixed forward, without sparing even a flash of eyeball for the sheer drops on the passenger side – which I lean away from in a token attempt to keep all our weight *on* the mountain. Old ski tracks scar the remaining ice and snow on the slopes and the alpine trees stretch their branches towards the sun like begging lepers. We pull over at the top and tread through the snow to get a view across the entire stonking valley, where neighbouring peaks form various shades of dark silhouettes, layered into the distance and suggesting days on end of travel between each of them. It's really big, this America.

Our journey leads us finally to a bridge that spans Lake Britton. From here we can see another bridge, further away, that sends the shivers down my spine. We immediately dump the car on the hard shoulder, barely remembering to lock it, and sprint up to the railway line that runs alongside the road.

We start wandering down the tracks, quite quickly surrounded by dense woodland, until a smaller bridge challenges our path to *the* bridge. Suddenly, my initial burst of location-hunter's adrenalin ebbs away and trains, snakes and bears all become a *most* present danger – causing my lips to purse like a cat's bum and forehead to wrinkle like custard skin. This first bridge puts us in the sort of spot the characters our pilgrimage is based on were in: to go for it, together, or to wimp out and go back...?

We skip across the ailing, rotting wood bridge, clearly with something less noble than that childlike sense of fearless adventure the boys had in *Stand By Me*.

STAND BY ME (1986) (Movie)

Director: Rob Reiner
Writers: Stephen King (novel), Raynold Gideon , Bruce A. Evans (screenplay)
Producers: Bruce A. Evans, Raynold Gideon, Andrew Scheinman
Awards: Nominated for an Oscar
Cast: River Phoenix (Chris Chambers), Corey Feldman (Teddy Duchamp), Wil Wheaton (Gordie Lachance), Jerry O'Connell (Vern Tessio), Kiefer Sutherland (Ace Merrill), Richard Dreyfuss (Writer), John Cusack (Danny Lachance)

Notes:
I really remember the morbid fascination kids have about dead bodies. I remember spending an afternoon adventure in Leyton, trying to get the courage up to open a cardboard box in the street that my mate Paul claimed had a dead cat in with worms coming out of it. That fascination has slipped away now, especially as I've been unfortunate enough to actually find a dead human body in a forest. But the adventure the kids have in this film is typical of the sort of rite of passage adventures we all wanted to have during our summer holidays.

It's one of those situations where once you *start* on the bridge, you've *got* to get across quick, because there's no side bit to hide on: if the train comes, the train gets you. There are all sorts of swears flying around as we skip across the planks, the gaps between which offer flashes of speeding cars on Highway 299 way below. I don't like it. I don't like it. *I don't like it.* Breathlessness masks a slight sob as I meet the other side, and immediately, concerns about bears and the like keep fear levels rocket high. What a wuss. I really am a wuss.

As the railway line curls round a corner we walk right down the centre of it, further away from the road and off into the wilderness. It feels just like the cricket-infested atmosphere the kids experienced in the film – a tranquil, baking hot nowhere; one of those places removed enough that you can reflect objectively on life's mess. The bend continues and eventually shows us what we've journeyed for – the Lake Britton bridge. The *Stand by Me* bridge.

Although work on the McCloud River Railroad began in the mid 1890s, a thirty-two-mile extension that brought it out here to Burney wasn't complete until 1952. Originally it was used for the lumber business, but the industry has shrivelled and now it's mainly a treat for train lovers, who can go on a vintage train ride and have their steak dinner on it too.

Suddenly, everything seems to ring true. I really feel as though I'm in utter wilderness that's only occasionally invaded by the odd train, a few curious kids ... and us. But more importantly right now, this bridge clearly can't accommodate pedestrians *and* a train at once – which is exactly the gristle of the most exhilarating part of the movie. We've had a warm-up with the flimsy *little* bridge earlier, but this is *it*, this is the daddy. In the distance on the other side is a bend in the track, with the curve showing us a white bit of cliff wall that's now much more covered up by vegetation than it was in the film. But we're at the other end of the bridge, where the kids – sprinting away from the train – finally managed to leap off into the undergrowth. Although we quite fancy trying the same jump, it's simply too far. The kids must have used a crash mat, at least, to get down there. Or they were just much braver than us. I notice that the rocks are in the same position next to where the kids landed and I can't help but have a lie down in the dusty dirt by the big boulder you can see clearly in the scene, and look up to see what the actors saw when they were here.

I stay down there quite a while, actually. The others start to wonder whether I might be having a David Icke moment or maybe even a stroke, but actually I'm thinking about how the plot of this film – more than any other film we're covering – actually correlates with our own journey. The tagline for the movie says:

> "For some, it's the last real taste of innocence, and the first real taste of life. But for everyone, it's the time that memories are made of."

Those boys were on their last childhood adventure, that last episode of absolute freedom. And seeing as this nostalgia craze has sent my head back to those days, longing for them, I too seem to have created my last childhood adventure. Again. I've designed this journey as a last irresponsible gasp ... and that's where the plot, the location and the sentiment all snap together to make this place special. We came with every intention of re-creating exactly what the kids did in the film: a daring run across the bridge followed by a heroic leap. But now we're here, my brain says no. My knees agree *no* and my soul begs with my heart to go along with the rest of me and say *no*. No way. The bridge is high. It has big wide gaps in between the wooden slats, showing us the distant sloshing water of Lake Britton. No way. Tom ventures a little way further onto it, but every noise seems to convert itself mentally into an imaginary approaching train. I feel like he's going to be the dead body the kids in the film travelled miles to look at. It seems almost impossible that anyone could actually *run* across those wooden planks, they're so irregularly placed that it would be easy to lose your footing and get stuck or topple sideways over into the river below. Well, maybe not *that* easy, but for a big tart with rampant vertigo.

I wonder about how Rob Reiner got those kids to get *on* the bloody bridge, let alone *sprinting* across it. Maybe they put boards down. Apparently, aside from genuine support and encouragement, Reiner used scare tactics to get the best performances out of the kids. Even though the train wasn't *actually* behind them as they sprinted screaming along the track (it was added in post-production), he was there shouting them shitless so they'd be *really* scared and not just *acting* scared. Also, apparently, in another scene where the kids scrambled out of a pond with leeches stuck all over them, he surprised them by using *real* leeches, so their reactions weren't only those of good actors but also those of really scared children with leeches stuck to them: tactics that he'd *never* get away with in today's climate.

I wander away from the bridge absent-mindedly singing "Stand By Me", noticing my voice bouncing back off the surrounding valleys and that it's a little flat, which is disappointing. We feel as though we've just visited the actual set from a movie, like we've gone to a soundstage where all of the props and set have been left just the way they were the day filming finished. And I can now *never* watch *Stand By Me* and feel all sad and nostalgic about days gone by. That film is now as much a part of my present as the wee I need so badly it might start squirting out of my belly button.

On the way back down the track I think a bit about River Phoenix. I always feel a bit twitchy when I know I'm standing in the same spot that someone who's died once stood. I don't know why it makes me feel weird, maybe it's that a fleeting moment of a tragic life had taken place on that spot, or that this is one of a limited number of places he *ever* could have been which makes it in some way significant. Or maybe it just gives me the creeps.

The 180-mile drive to San Francisco, on the day that marks one month of our trip into the eighties, is a stretch we thought we'd canter in two or three hours and then enjoy the tourist delights of the Golden Gate Bridge and all that.

The warning signs are there though, when we slip off Highway 5 and onto a road that hasn't been graced with a number or name on the map. Then about five minutes down the road we drive past a home-made, badly painted sign saying "Road With No Name". Which doesn't really work, because now its name is Road With No Name. Is it a name or a statement? Confused now. Desolate scrub is occasionally broken up by towns that declare on their welcome signs a population of less than fifty. One of those towns, Marshall, looks as though it's experienced something of an economic turndown or maybe a plague epidemic: its population of fifty-eight has had the eight rubbed off and half its buildings boarded up and cordoned off.

We have no choice but to speed out of this big mistake and strive for the ocean on the way to San Fran, because our next movie location sits on the coastal road in between. But In our way are miles of bastard, sun-browned, flammable mountains. We've already wound ourselves halfway up the first mountain when we spot a small sign saying that this would be the end of paved roads. I put my foot on the brake in astonishment and immediately skid on the dust and sharp stone track we've already bumped onto.

Fifty yards down the road, another polite sign warns us that the road is also to become a little narrower. Are they slowly squeezing us into a muddy bit of guttering? Within minutes we're driving the car on a tightrope road made of shingle, with a sheer drop leftwards down into a woody valley. Every turn forces me to scream a sweaty "Oh Christ" and my toes are so clenched they'll probably heal themselves webbed. The pinnacles of these mountains are spectacular, with views right across the singed California landscape and off to a smudged blue distance stretching across the Pacific. However, by now we don't care about spectacular, these roads feel like driving up the inside of a slinky, and I've never fancied doing that. The constant curves are turning my face gargoyle and my guts threaten to show the other two boys that I sneakily finished our last chocolate bar at breakfast, and that it *wasn't* the maid at the Motel 6 who took it after all.

This to-ing and fro-ing goes on for hours. Hours and hours. And even when we hit the coast our heads are spinning too violently to even *want* a look out at the rough old sea.

We get to Goat Rock Beach in Sonoma County and step out towards the sea. A sign warns us that this is one of the most dangerous beaches in California. It's deserted and bloody right too. The sea shouts angrily at the seagulls, who all look niggly, irritable, hungry and a bit pissed off that the wind keeps blowing them somewhere they don't want to go. The gusts fiercely pelt us with sand that stings on the legs like little needles and we can't hear a word each other is saying, which actually, after so many hours in the car, is a sweet, sweet relief.

Then we get there – the place where the final scene of *The Goonies* was shot. All the jubilations and the families being reunited and the TV crews interviewing them: this is where it happened. You can recognise it by the formation of rocks poking out of the sea just off the coast. The sun adds hazy twinkles all around them and there's definitely something mystical about the beach that must have turned the film-makers on. The weather conditions become more hostile and there are only so many times we can stare out at the rocks and shout "Hey yooooouu guys" in Sloth-style at each other and the fat wads of seals strewn on the rocks like oozing salt-covered slugs. I'm minutes away from needing hospital treatment for a case of entire-body chapping from the wicked wind, and despite the sun shining its heart out, bless it, the wind and ocean spray take the climate down to Margate. And who wants to be in Margate?

–––––––––

San Francisco seems to be all about the hills, which various parts of my body object to while attempting to scale them. However, the views from the top of one peak across to the tops of other peaks down the bay are remarkable: it's like looking down one of those big wavy water slides. From the Nob Hill area – which is very well-to-do thank you – you can pan your head across the bay to see the Golden Gate Bridge loping off through its mist towards Sausalito; Alcatraz plonked on top of a random rock; and behind it the Oakland Bay Bridge totally out-spans the Golden Gate, looking in my opinion much more impressive. Further along, the Coit Tower – a stubby cylinder on top of the opposing Telegraph Hill – offers a tasty alternative view of the bay.

But I knew the Coit Tower would be a problem.

Elle and I began our journey here in San Francisco. All young and out in the world on our own and intrepid and holding hands. Everywhere I look there are reminders that just make me want to close my eyes and be somewhere else, away from the regret and loss and chest pain. *Especially* the Coit Tower. So proud we were, to have found our way *all* the way to America, to the top of a hill to look down at our travelling achievements. We were so scared of the world then. Now? I'm more scared of myself. As I look out across the bay at places we went to, it's like she's with me, her Chanel No.5 lingering, gloating. *I shouldn't have come here*, I think, but you know how it is, some things hurt so good (if Marc Almond really must interject); like picking a scab, sometimes we can't help re-opening wounds just to see if there's a wound still there. And there is. But there shouldn't be. It was *years* ago. Could I *really* want her back now? Do I even *know* her any more? Probably not. It occurs to me that this might not be about her, it's about *someone*. *Anyone*. It's about missed chances and lost love and altogether, my faults and failures and me being this number of years old, and alone.

On leaving San Francisco, we whizz towards the beach resort of Santa Cruz. The journey is short and before we know it we're trotting around town trying to work out whether the vampires who roamed the place in *The Lost Boys* are actually a menace to the area in real life.

THE LOST BOYS (1987) (Movie)

Director: Joel Schumacher
Writers: Janice Fischer, James Jeremias, Jeffrey Boam
Producers: Richard Donner, Mark Damon, John Hyde
Cast: Jason Patric (Michael Emerson), Corey Haim (Sam Emerson), Dianne Wiest (Lucy Emerson), Bernard Hughes (Grandpa), Kiefer Sutherland (David), Jami Gertz (Star), Corey Feldman (Edgar Frog), Jamison Newlander (Alan Frog), Brooke McCarter (Paul), Billy Wirth (Dwayne), Alex Winter (Marko)

Notes:
I'd like to nominate this film as the campest horror movie ever made. There was so much black leather, men with earrings and gaudy music knocking around it's unbelievable. A topless saxophone player and long man-perms. But the eighties was a time when men started to really embrace their feminine side: a time when it became OK for men to wear pink. I remember when it suddenly became alright for men to wear white socks!

Because the Santa Cruz council were concerned about the city's portrayal in the movie as "The Murder Capital of the World" (daubed in graffiti on the back of the city boundary sign as the Emerson family drive in) and of course the image that comes with it being full of damn vampire-types, the film-makers had to change the name of the place in the film to "Santa Clara". However, there's no disguising that Santa Cruz was the setting for the film and I think in being so vain the council may have denied themselves a few extra visitors.

With cloud lurking obstinately and temperatures not really beachy, we wander around thinking we've somehow tripped out to Southend for the day. Santa Cruz has that same moribund feeling of a British beach town in decline, stripped of its client base by cheap flights and the promise of sunshine elsewhere, with a tired, old-fashioned and worn out promenade in the last throws of popularity – stripped of its client-base by cheap flights and the promise of sunshine elsewhere. Those Southend smells of popcorn, hot dogs, candy floss and anything you can imagine fried float through the air along with the screams of people flashing by on a rickety old roller coaster that seems so outdated I'm sure I've had hairier rides on the London Underground.

The opening bits of the film has Echo and the Bunnymen's version of "People Are Strange" plastered appropriately over shots of punks and freaks and weirdoes lazing around town. There's still an essence of that in downtown Santa Cruz, where the pierced and tattooed hang out, but it feels a half-hearted comparison to the film.

As twilight starts stealing the sun, we go across to the wooden pier, where in *The Lost Boys*, the mother (Dianne Wiest) goes looking for work. The pier is desolate bar the odd family walking by: father in a vest with mustard down it, mother still trying to wedge herself into the boob-tube she bought in 1988 and kids with too much hair gel, gold chains and voices you'd like to cut out of their throats. Just like Southend. From here there's a view across to the thrill-laden boardwalk. From this angle, that signature roller coaster lofts above it all with its dips and curves that have been promoting nausea for the over-popcorned since the 1920s. The boardwalk begins to illuminate through the ash-grey dusk, and gradually, this overcast Southend-twin turns into the eerie vampire-haunt you see in the film: loud noises of electronic games mingling with traditional fairground organ music pumping out of the rides; bloodcurdling roller coaster screams hanging in the air.

A 1920s pavilion sits on the edge of the beach; with concrete pillars holding up an arched walkway that Michael and his new vampire friends burn through on their bikes and down the stairs onto the sand. The comic shop where Corey Haim first bumps into the Frogg brothers isn't there but the feel of the place is the same. It feels edgy, like something horrible could happen any moment: whether it's a murder or an over-excited kid honking up a donut.

In the film, a wild-crazy party rages on the beach, which is where Michael first meets Star (Jami Gertz). It's one of those supposedly spontaneous 1980s parties with fires burning in big oil drums and women spontaneously going topless. We somehow manage to get Luke to re-create the musical performance at the party in the film by an oiled-up bare-chested muscleman singing "I Still Believe" with a saxophone. Although Luke's own bare-breasted version is funny, it doesn't help with the nausea I've been experiencing since going on the cable car across the boardwalk. Incidentally, in the movie the cable car is shown with a model of a caveman sitting in one of the cars: he's still there, looking tired and flaky.

On the far side of the boardwalk is a bridge that seems to cause much debate among location hunters. There are some, including locals we speak to, who claim it's the bridge used in the scene where Michael and the vampires hang underneath as a train goes over. A punk rocker lady with more tattoos than a Saturday night out in Camden assures us with all her heart that it is. It certainly looks a likely candidate – sitting there looking all bridgey, but doesn't quite match up with the one in the film and I think maybe she's been sucked into the romance of it all. Walking on the bridge though, it feels like it. I can feel the scene playing out around me ... maybe I should go with my location-hunting instincts on this one.

We umm and ahhh until Tom can't stand the not-knowing and back at the hostel manages to track down the location manager of the film, who confirms on the phone that the bridge bits were shot at Six Flags Park in Los Angeles. But at least it *looks* like it was modelled on the real one in Santa Cruz. Probably. Still, a sign hangs on the bridge saying "Warning – no jumping or diving from the trestle". We decide to adhere to the sign's instructions.

I'm desperate to get bitten by a vampire and then meet a girl like Star (Jami Gertz, who is still really tasty and now in a US sitcom with the fat English bloke from *The Full Monty*). But, it's getting late and I have some chips instead. Chips or blood? Chips please.

On our second day in Santa Cruz, exploring further into the world of *The Lost Boys*, we venture further afield than the obvious boardwalk area and its constant threats to make me eat donut.

As with the bridge, there's a fair amount of local debate as to where certain parts of the movie were filmed. One of those disputed locations is the cave that Kiefer Sutherland and his gaggle of blood-swiggers hung upside down all day long in before emerging at night to play in the sand on their bikes. It's quite obvious that the inside of the cave – where all the noodle and worm eating took place – was a set in a studio somewhere. But there are some caves in the University of California Santa Cruz area that are rumoured to be where they shot the vampire hunters' escape after they disturbed the fanged ones. It seems to be one of those student word-of-mouth urban myths, but we decide to check it out because it seems very much a spot everyone locally knows and goes to to scare themselves as youngsters – and therefore by proxy it's a necessary part of the Santa Cruz pilgrimage.

The scene in question takes place on some metal stairs that the Froggs clamber up frantically – occasionally slipping in that annoying way that horror film characters do just to raise your blood pressure a little. By asking various grotty students along our way, we're eventually directed to a lay-by on a main road near the campus. In a thick wood and just ten metres from the lay-by is a concrete box covering an entrance to a cave. The concrete has been smashed open and the metal stairs they all say were used in the film lead you down into a type of darkness I've never enjoyed visiting. So I don't – on grounds of vertigo and cowardice. It's grim down there. Graffiti around the entrance suggests that others have dared, but I tell myself they will have all been glue sniffers and drunk twonks off their bonces and wouldn't have known what they were doing anyway. Tom and Luke bravely (or stupidly) plunge themselves down the hole, suspecting they might find bats and vampires and homelesses. But of course because it's dark, the silly sods can't see a thing, which adds to the terror. Using the genius of a camera with flash we find out later that it's just one small chamber, a lot like the one they made for the film. Tragically, there are no vampires or ghostly apparitions or drunk piss-tramps in the back of shot. Just cave.

We think for a second about going back later at night with a Chinese takeaway – like they did in the film – to truly experience the *The Lost Boys* thing, but that second is very fleeting, and anyway, the hostel has an 11pm curfew. Thank Christ. But more importantly, it's clear that this is purely a piece of local mythology, a student folly designed for mates to challenge each other to visit the shit-scary place late at night.

––––––––––

Before we left England, Tom tracked down Jamison Newlander through his cousin (who is listed on *www.imdb.com*) and managed to get a message to Jamison to contact us if he wanted to have a chat about the old days. And he did. So, we arranged to meet him in a park to rather randomly play football with him. I'm not sure how it landed at a game of football, but there it is.

When he turns up at the park, this short chubby little man bears little resemblance to Alan Frog – the character he played in *The Lost Boys*. The Frogg brothers (the other, Edgar, was played by Corey Feldman) were the feisty teenagers who worked in a comic shop that Corey Haim wandered into early in the movie, and who helped with the vampire hunting sporadically throughout the film. I didn't, for some reason, expect Alan Frog to be this plump little amenable man, but he is ... and his his little wife looks almost exactly the same as him. It's a peculiar situation; we all shake hands enthusiastically but still with a curious look in our eyes as if to say, "I've no idea what I'm doing in this park with you".

Jamison seems an ordinary sort of bloke. He's no longer acting and is considering a plunge into the writing world, having had some small success with some plays he's written. But essentially, he's just some bloke that appeared in a film twenty years that we quite like. So, Jamison has brought the football and off we go – striding up and down the park breathlessly and pale for half an hour before the California sun gets to us, the effects of too many beers over the last five years drags our stomachs to the ground, and we collapse behind them in heaps.

To be honest, Jamison is a crap footballer but professes to be nothing more and we appreciate his efforts in coming all the way to the park to meet some nostalgic Englishmen who emailed him out of the blue. As we lay flaked – Jamison being mopped by his sweet wife – we take the opportunity to chat to him about *The Lost Boys*, before *The Lost Boys,* and after *The Lost Boys.*

'Have you still got a lot of memories of the film?"

"I do, yeah. It was sort of like being a rock star. I felt like a rock star when I was shooting it and when it came out of course I felt like a rock star. I think about it a lot because those experiences and those years and what I did in those years affect how I deal with things in regular life. I think a lot about those years actually."

"So was it your first movie role?"

"Sort of. I had been doing a couple of commercials, but it was definitely the first big movie that I did. When I got it, I didn't even know that it was as big as it was. I just remember looking around and thinking *that's the guy from...* And there was Dianne Wiest and the Coreys and everything. And I'd just seen Corey Haim in *Lucas*, which I actually auditioned for myself. I auditioned for a lot of roles the Coreys ended up getting."

"So you weren't bitter then?"

"I wasn't. These guys were industry people, you know? They were marketed; they knew what they were doing. At that time I was more honoured to be working with them."

"How did you get the part of Alan Frog?"

"I just auditioned actually. I don't think my agent was a great agent, but he was shifty. He chain smoked and everything, the classic agent. It was a call back and I hadn't been to the original audition and he said, 'Just don't say anything about that, just go in there and pretend you're on the call back.' So I had a bit of luck and I knew Joel Schumacher from an acting class that I'd been on. At the time I got recognised quite a bit, it was pretty cool actually. But I never got to the level of people giving me free stuff."

"How did you get on with the Coreys?"

"Actually the three of us were really very close, while we were shooting it and probably for six months after. We were really tight actually."

"So Corey wasn't mashed up on crack pipes at that point?"

"*The Lost Boys* was kind of before that. I did see a little bit of it later in our relationship. Not crack, but I think I did see the beginning of the slide. I was kind of going back to being a high school kid and they were going off to do their sort of Corey-Corey thing."

"And you opted out of "the slide" I take it?"

"I guess I did. It's not like I never experimented. But with them I didn't feel comfortable."

"So when you were on set or hanging around off set, what did you get up to?"

"We just kind of listened to music; we all had our first girlfriends at the time, so we'd hang out with them. We didn't even really drink at that time. We would just hang out around the pool."

"How about the older guys in the film, Kiefer Sutherland and Alex Winter, did you get on well with them?"

"Erm, we clearly hung out in different groups. Jason Patric was just the nicest guy, he hung out with us. Brooke McCarter, the blond vampire, and Billy Wirth, the dark haired vampire, they were really nice guys. They partied much more than us and we couldn't hang with them. I think they just partied. I didn't realise that at the time, but being on a film set is just about partying I think. There was this one time when Corey Feldman stayed up all night before a day of shooting and I can only assume he was partying with all the older kids. Kiefer Sutherland I didn't really see that much."

"How about Jami Gertz? She was really fit."

"Yeah, and I'm sure she is now. She's done a lot of work recently. From the beginning, when I met Jami Gertz, I don't think I'd ever met someone who was more beautiful." The wife, Hanny, shoots a devastating look across to Jamison. "My wife is more beautiful, of course." He repairs, grinning cheekily, as if to say that, actually, Gertz is probably better. "But she was really cool. I guess I knew I didn't really have a shot with her. I think if anybody had a chance, it would be Jason Patric. They had a definite flirty thing. But I don't think it happened; she might have been seeing someone else. She was really quite beautiful."

"Are you still in touch with Corey Feldman?"

"Yeah, I got in touch with Feldman again recently. I called him because my film was coming out but he wasn't around. But he called me back about a month later and he said there was a Swedish camera crew that's coming over to film us playing poker and I should come. Just at Corey's place. So I said yeah, why not. So I bought some cheap cigars. I lost every hand. *Every hand.* And I was thinking about leaving but I went back for one round and won eighty bucks."

"Has he changed much since the filming?"

"You know, on seeing him I realised why we got along so well. Because his persona that you see in the movies ... I think they try to make him seem like he's full of himself. But he's actually really just a nice guy. I think that he's got issues with celebrity-ness, if that's a word, but he's a really nice guy."

"So what would you say you've been doing mainly in the time since *The Lost Boys*?"

"Well, I did another couple of things and went off to college after that. But I studied theatre and I did theatre for a while afterwards in New York. I think that writing is the new direction for me. The problem with acting is that I don't really audition well. But with writing I have a little more control over the creativity. Acting is so much like you have to do it how they want you to do it. I just got a job corporate writing, but I think it's going to take a little more time to find my dramatic voice. I had great success with a play recently; it's actually a virtual reality film noir..." Ah yes, that famous genre. "...I looked at it in the theatre and thought that maybe I've a little way to go." I can't help thinking that Jamison's having a little bit of a struggle explaining what happened to him since the film, and I detect a trace of sadness. Maybe he's not totally thrilled about how things turned out, even though he's still only in his early thirties.

"Do you ever get any recognition now?"

"Not at all. It's very rare. But maybe if I had longer hair and a beret, maybe."

Over two days, Santa Cruz has grown on us. What's left of its weird punky stoned people now mingle with families on holiday; making it a strange but forgiving place – just the place depicted at the start of the movie. The writers must have written the script with Santa Cruz in mind, because in the same way Nelson fits *Roxanne* and Hope fits *First Blood*, Santa Cruz definitely fits *The Lost Boys*.

The only thing I couldn't stand about Santa Cruz was all the goddamn vampires...

CHAPTER TWELVE SOUNDTRACK:

Theme from Dynasty

Bill Conti (1981)

Do You Really Want to Hurt Me

Culture Club (1982)

Chapter Twelve

Deserted

Santa Cruz to Las Vegas

About to set off on the hottest, most desolate sections of our journey, we decide to get the car oil changed to avoid a silly breakdown among the deserty rubble. Especially as the little light on the dashboard has been flashing at us since Chicago and we've all been in denial about it.

The journey east allows us to leave civilisation and mobile phone reception for a few days. We travel to Yosemite National Park, of which I really don't know what to expect. Trees I know, but the shape of them or their surroundings I don't.

On arrival, I'm shocked to happen upon a type of landscape we haven't seen the likes of so far: full of immense sliced cliffs with brittle peaks iceberg sculpted to jut menacingly ... it's the sort of place where you can imagine Skeletor investing in property. This is serious, grown-up, life-or-death landscape. Huge granite slabs spray waterfalls fiercely over the edges; trees smother the friendlier surfaces of rock in such numbers that from a distance they look like moss; and the occasional evidence of past forest fires flash by – charred skeletons of trees in eccentric poses like frozen snapshots of their dying moments.

At the National Parks Service office we meet a slippery kind of man called Scott Gediman – the media relations guy. He's the one who has to mournfully give press conferences telling journos how a man dressed in a duck costume managed to tragically bump into the floor while base jumping, or how half the park has burnt down. They never seem to deliver *good* news, these guys. Scott's nice enough to stick his hard-starched park ranger hat on and drive us out to some 'points of interest'. I do like a "points of interest."

We brief him though that our mission is one of eighties nostalgia, and it's a *particular* spot we're after. But he had *such* a great time hanging out with Mel Gibson when they were making *Maverick* at his old park, Glen Canyon, that he figures we'll lap that up all the same. Oh, the hilarious stories of Gibson. Gibson this, Gibson that. How about when Gibson had a sandwich, or when Gibson had a drink of water. What a lovely Gibson. Scott's an incredibly pleasant man, but he becomes much *less* easy going when talking about the time he worked with John Travolta on something or other. He properly dislikes Travolta.

Then he gets us to the place we came here for: El Capitan. El Cap to its friends. This is the cliff edge used in *Star Trek V*, when Captain Kirk climbs the mountain and then falls off.

STAR TREK V: THE FINAL FRONTIER (1989) (Movie)

Director: William Shatner
Writers: William Shatner, Harve Bennett, David Loughery
Producers: Ralph Winter, Gene Roddenberry
Cast: William Shatner (Captain James T. Kirk), Leonard Nimoy (Captain Spock), DeForest Kelley (Dr Leonard "Bones" McCoy), James Doohan (Captain Montgomery "Scotty" Scott), Walter Loenig (Commander Pavel Checkov), Nichelle Nichols (Commander Uhura), George Takei (Commander Hikaru Sulu), David Warner (Sgt John Talbot), Laurence Luckinbill (Sybok), Charles Cooper (General Korrd), Cynthia Gouw (Caithlin Dar), Todd Bryant (Captain Klaa), Spice Williams (Vixis), Rex Holman (J'onn), George Murdock (God)

There's not really much we could ask Scott about the filming – he wasn't here and it is after all just a cliff (well, 910 metres of granite formed by glacial action and one of the world's favourite rock climbing sites ... or something, but essentially still just a big cliff). It's impressive, no doubt, a great big looming sheer face with brave bits of tree and shrub growing at the top like a close-shaved afro.

I *have* to ask it. It's rubbish, but I have to.

"Scott, I've seen how chubby William Shatner has got since back in the early days. How did they dangle him off a cliff? Did they *really* have a *dangling Shat*?" I'm such a child; I really enjoyed saying that. Without batting an eyelid, he replies.

"Well, they had stunt doubles. He never actually went from the top."

"They never had a Shat up there at all?" I give him another chance to *Shat* back at me.

"No, no." That shuts me up. At that very point, bolts of lightning start stabbing at the peaks and thunder collapses around us as if the great Shat himself has been stirred and angered. This prompts Scott to go off and deal with the important things, like local news stories about bears stealing picnic baskets: leaving us to wander about the park staring at granite and trees and dodging lightning.

Later, we check into the Midpines Hostel, a few miles outside the park. It's a cute little place with a load of wooden huts on stilts perched around the mountainside among trees and rocks. It has its own dog, which is called Ying Yang – because one ear pricks up and the other stays flat. He stinks. Youth hostels can be a bit of a lottery – some can be moody cockroach dens full of the semi-homeless, others can be friendly chilled out vegetarian-magnets. This one is a henna tattoo sort of affair, with signs everywhere asking you to put your rotten veg in one bin, tin cans in another, and not to wash too often so they can save water and eventually the planet.

After a long day on the winding Yosemite roads, beer is in order. Before we know it, we're playing guitar and singing eighties TV theme tunes, mainly *The Littlest Hobo*, conspicuously smashing the cosy log cabin hostel bar atmosphere, and being eaten alive by mosquitoes as German teenage grotbags eye us contemptuously and a Japanese couple grin along vacuously. Dissolve to two hours later and a few jugs of beer down to idiotsville, and we're sitting on sofas with Bonnie and her big sister.

Bonnie is fifty-eight and admits that she has a son in his thirties ... older than me ... but that doesn't stop Luke. Nope, that libido is bullet-proof; nothing can put it off, not even her white roots or the sheer size of her booty. Somehow we end up in their room. She's already been giving us back massages (which actually made me *more* tense), and when Luke massages *her* back, she starts making grotesque sex noises. I get scared, really scared. This is all wrong. So wrong. With my half-drunk rationale kicked in, I decide that running away will be the best option. It's always the best option: run,

run as fast as you can. So I flee, away to bed, leaving Luke to grab-a-hippy-granny.

I don't think it went as far as the last escapade, because a few minutes after getting to bed they both arrive at our room and I pretend I'm asleep while Bonnie says, "Spencer, I'm sorry, I didn't mean to scare you." Which makes me feel bad about running off. But at least it gave Luke a chance to get a snog.

Luke's record on the trip thus far includes a granny and a terminally-ill single mother. Shameful. Brilliantly shameful.

Luke hides in the car with a blanket over his head like an ashamed criminal fleeing a courthouse. He's desperate not to catch a glimpse of his geriatric partner from last night. Tom and I purposely dawdle and faff to increase the chances of him having to face up to his horror, hoping she'll come down on her walking frame to say goodbye without teeth in. But he luckily avoids a gummy farewell slobber and we speed up the dirt track back towards Yosemite.

Today we just need to get across the park in order to hit our second national park in two days: Death Valley, an altogether different proposition to Yosemite. Just as the day starts warming up and the curvy roads begin turning the fried eggs in my stomach into scrambled sour balls of methane, a massive tailback halfway up a mountain seizes our progress. Some plonker has driven their motor off the side of the ravine. Apparently, they're OK, but their car looks like a Salvador Dali sculpture. This puts us way behind schedule and jeopardizes our homage to *Star Wars* at Death Valley.

STAR WARS (1977) (Movie)

Director: George Lucas
Writer: George Lucas
Producer: George Lucas
Cast: Mark Hamill (Luke Skywalker), Harrison Ford (Han Solo), Carrie Fisher (Princess Lea Organa), Peter Cushing (Grand Toff Markin), Alec Guinness (Ben Obi-Wan Kenobi), Anthony Daniels (C-3PO), Kenny Baker (R2-D2), Peter Mayhew (Chewbacca), David Prowse (Darth Vader), James Earl Jones (Darth Vader voice)

> **Notes:**
> OK, OK, it was 1977. But if you grew up in the eighties, *Star Wars* and its sequels were very much a constant presence. The toy figures were a playground epidemic. They were compulsory. Everyone simply *had* to have as many figures as possible in order to be taken in any way seriously. And if you had an AT-AT, *and* knew that it stood for "All Terrain Armoured Transport", then *you da man*.

We storm(trooper) down the highway, trying to make up lost time, with the Sierra Nevada Mountain range standing like a wall to our right: snowy triangular points in a distance with flat desert in between, broken only by balls of dry green-brown shrubs. Irritable cacti wait like lonely little men posing. The temperature gauge on the car starts edging its way towards red and only when we slink out of our air-conditioned biosphere do we realise quite how *hot* that desert is. It's ludicrous, unbearable and almost unbreathable. Even strong gusts of wind are like being held at gunpoint by a hairdryer. I jump back in the car before my arm hairs singe – I hate that smell – and we continue cutting our way through the soupy heat haze, heading towards what looks like a constant imaginary puddle of water at the end of the road.

Death Valley must be so called because it's an absolutely impossible bastard to live in. Worse than South London. Nothing but shabby drabby browning old plants and lizards that couldn't spit on a stone. The valley scoops down to some two hundred feet below sea-level: like a great scar gouged out of the earth. Salt lakes give some parts of the basin a white crusty appearance that from a distance could be mistaken for ice ... which would be odd given the incredible heat. We spot a coyote lolloping half-heartedly across the road in front of us and then skanking around by the cacti; staring us out from a middle distance, limping and scruffy. It looks fucked like the scabby old crows and everything else that has actually managed to carve out a life for itself in this formidable rock heap.

It's easy to see why Death Valley was used to depict the planet Tatooine in *Star Wars*. Its landscapes range from lunar to *much* further afield. There's only a couple of spots we're heading for, because actually, just being here gives you enough of a feeling to be able to imagine R2-D2 trundling along haphazardly on the gravelly surface and Luke Skywalker zooming about, all flash, in his Landspeeder. But also, in fact, Death Valley was only used to fill in for some shots they hadn't picked up in Tunisia; apparently they couldn't afford to go back over to North Africa and had to settle on knocking them out in the US.

Lots of people make the journey through the park to identify the places shots were taken from, and they're not hard to find because the film crew stayed close to the road. They actually had an elephant with them, you see. The elephant was playing one of those Bantha creatures, and really, if you've ever tried travelling around with an elephant in the back, you'll know that they moan and whine and jab you with their trunk the *whole* time.

We get to our first stop, Artist's Drive, a winding track that eventually leads to a multi-coloured section of rock called Artist's Palette, which overlooks the valley. It's here where you see R2-D2 all on his own, happily wheeling along a road. Among fans, this area is called "Artoos Arroyo" (with an arroyo being an empty watercourse or creek). Tom and I sit on a rock and play stupidly with the *Star Wars* model figures we brought with us. In this baron, otherworldly expanse, at last, Tom's Boba Fett play figure seems at home. Inevitably it all ends in something of a wrestle in the dirt when Tom won't let me be Luke Skywalker and then declares war on my Ewok. Liberties. Covered in dust and small grazes, we pack our toys away and rush thirteen miles off the CA 190 before the sun sulks its way down behind the rocks; up towards Dante's Viewpoint on the edge of the Black Mountains.

In all our Tatooine fervour, we kind of forget that we're running just a little bit low on petrol. Just a little bit, but more than we'll allow ourselves to acknowledge. Like that moment in a film when you shout, "Don't go into the desert without petrol you cocks," we continue as classic movie victims would, keeping thoughts of the drama of running out of fuel at the very back of our minds. Up at the top, the view from Dante's Peak searches right down the valley, across to Furnace Creek. In a shot from this precarious ledge, Lucas had the Mos Eisley Spaceport painted in, in post-production. We've reached the top just as the sun is tiring and casting a weepy light from the peak of an opposing mountain. It's stunning – one of those visions that will always stay with me, despite the fact that any memory of actually being here will likely be entirely replaced by the photographs and videos I'm taking.

Having stood staring over the edge all misty and wistful for a good twenty minutes, imagining having a beer in the Mos Eisley Cantina, we head off on the fifty-odd-mile journey towards our awaiting beds in Tecopa. But after not more than ten miles, the petrol gauge plummets down to red and the fuel sign lights up on the dash. The glory of a blood-orange sky has bruised into the first gasps of black night and we're in the dark, in Death Valley, in the shit. I start having visions of that manky old coyote wolf thing coming back for me. I knew he had my cards marked. Or Jabba the Hut sending his men out to put me in ice like he did to Han Solo (I'd quite like that though). This really isn't a good situation – there are *no* other cars on the road, and that sense of nothingness we drove out to experience has suddenly changed from being a touristy past-time to a life-threatening saga. Every time the engine grumbles in any way other than a perfect purr, I promise to become religious, in some way, if we ever get out of this nightmare. I start making plans for staking claim to sleeping on the backseat, and why it definitely can't be me who goes walking off into the pitch black distance looking for petrol ... because of ... erm ... I'm allergic to the dark ... or something. I start scheming about how I can stitch the others up to save myself. I even think about how I could skin Tom and use his pelt for warmth. I'd rather that than wear his stupid red leather jacket.

After half an hour of squealing outbursts followed by rounds of collective moody silences and definitely *no music* on the stereo to confuse the tension, the car just about drags its lifeless chassis into a small town called Shoshone. We whoop, we sweat some cold sweat and we nearly wet ourselves. Stuck in Death Valley at night? Sod that. No such nonsense. We have to pay a local geezer to put some petrol on his Visa, using the automated paypoint because the petrol station is closed. We even give him a bit more than it costs. It was a real close call.

Idiots.

––––––––––

The road out of Tecopa the next day is deserted, straight and arduously long. It's the sort of road that makes you feel like you're not moving at all because the scenery remains the same.

Las Vegas is visible from more than twenty miles away – the Stratosphere tower starts poking its pointy top out across the desert from the north end of

Las Vegas Boulevard: otherwise known as The Strip. The whole place is fake. Not only the re-created worlds that each of the hotels drag you into wallet-first, but the very existence of the city itself. That dry, inhospitable Nevada desert isn't supposed to play host to millions of greedy tourists visiting hotels that claim to be glamorous microcosms of France or New York or Ancient Egypt or Rome ... its supposed to be hot and empty with lizards. It's not natural and I don't like it. I don't like the unabashed money-making techniques that the hotel owners employ – even the little things like at one point on The Strip there's only one way to cross the road, and you have to go through a hotel to get to the walkway to cross. Blurgh. It makes me feel like they think I'm an idiot, wafting smells and shoving gambling opportunities at me every five footsteps. It's fake fun, that's what it is, designed not actually with fun in mind – just *money* – and how they can get at mine. None of the casinos have clocks or an ounce of daylight so you have no idea how many hours you've spent throwing your hard-earned money into their pots. All of the cheap food and special deals are sneaky incentives to get you emptying all the money you think you've saved into their coffers anyway. What's even worse is that people willingly go there to be raped of their cash. I know a lot of people like it and I'm sorry, but you'll see there are other reasons at play for me when it comes to Vegas...

Walking down The Strip is an uncomfortable thing in more than one way for me. The blokes walking around in their holiday singlets, the women and girls in flesh-flashing bra-tops: all of them here determined that they're going to have *fun*. It just feels so desperate. Some people walk around grinning, others fuming that they've lost money. Emotion runs high.

But it's not just all of that, or the fact that I'm sucked into watching water jets dance to Celine Dion outside the Bellagio, though that in itself is enough to send a man off the edge of El Capitan. It's not even so much that Elle and I came here seven years ago and stayed at the Circus Circus hotel at the other end of The Strip to the meagre Motel 6 we're now crammed into.

It's that she's sent me a text.

I haven't heard from Elle since *that* day in London, where she said goodbye at a zebra crossing and I wandered, aimlessly snivelling myself into the Trocadero toilets. It was months ago. And now, I've been away, reflecting on it all, thinking about her, and she sends me a text. It just says: '*Hello*'.

That's all. I fumble off a reply immediately, heart clumping away like an old Fiat. I know that she's already said *no*, I know that it *went* years ago, but the fact is that somewhere inside I haven't accepted that. Turns out she's drunk with an old college friend, which gets me all suspicious, like she'll wake up tomorrow and wonder why the fuck she's done that. Because of the time difference, I'm only just thinking about lunch and she's off her nut on Chardonnay. But I don't care, whatever I can get, I'll take it.

Another couple of messages ping around, like the opening stages of a flyweight boxing contest. And then she sends: "Can I call U?"

And before I know it the phone's ringing and it's her number and *shit shit shit* and I'm in Las Vegas where we were, together, and it all seems so poetic and maybe this is where my life takes a 360 degree turn and becomes like some Hollywood love story that was meant to be.

Hello? She's slaughtered, no two ways about it. She must have been drinking for hours to get *that* conquered. We talk about nothing in particular for quite a while. It all flashes by so quickly, I can't even remember, it's like I'm talking to someone famous ... I suppose she *has* become some sort of celebrity from the pages of my *OK! magazine*-style glossy nostalgic view of the past. I get off the phone and buzz around the hotel room, appearing to tidy up but actually not moving anything anywhere apart from my trembling frame from wall to wall and three wees. *Could this mean something? Could this mean something? Could this mean something?* I think, over and over.

"Im going to call again." Another text. Off goes the phone again. *Shit shit shit,* again, and what should I talk about to my drunk ex who I want back? Not about the wanting back bit, that's for sure, it's not the moment, it's not welcome, is it. Is it? *Is it?* Oh Christ.

"Hello?" This time we talk about Vegas; she loved it, I hated it, but we talk about the hotel and a couple called Dee and Ed who stalked us to join them for dinner as we hid under the covers giggling every time they knocked on our door. We talk about the coach ride out to the Grand Canyon, where the driver hated me for some unknown reason, just my face, and how we went and watched a hotel's free pirate show every night because we were so skint. All those memories are so much more real with her chipping in from another pair of eyes.

"I miss u." Twenty minutes later, that turns up. *She's drunk, she's drunk* I think, but after all the turmoil and nostalgic tsunamis I've put myself through, this would be the ultimate cure, wouldn't it? The past coming back from the dead, the *real* past returning to my now, back to where it belongs.

Luke and Tom get hold of some tickets to see Simon and Garfunkle. Not sure why they want to put themselves through that, but they go off for a bit of "Bridge Over Troubled Water" while I go out and find alcohol to help me process what's going on and build a bridge over my own troubled waters. This is *big*. I head up The Strip to Casino Royale. Elle and I walked through here a few times and I know where the bar is. Beers and beers and cocktails and chatting to a girl who looks like Janet Street Porter and more beers and a cheeky rum and yup, there I am, crumpled, bleary, disgraceful and walloped, gloriously. I don't get a great deal of thinking done, maybe a bit of hoping, but I mainly end up talking to whoever lets me. It all goes a bit hazy around midnight when I'm taken to another bar with yards of cocktails and a band and a little bit of rainbow-coloured sick. Luke and Tom came along after their three hours of adult-oriented folk rock, but even they call it a day and head back.

I start heading back to down The Strip, *so* sure of where I'm going, stumbling, careering, until one of those bridge diversions sends me all over the place and leads to me just standing, holding onto the anti-suicide bars on a bridge above The Strip, with the dull ache of a hangover emerging as fast as the sun at the end of the road between the hulking hotels and casinos stacked up on either side. Just standing here, hanging on, looking. *How did I get here?*

Phone rings. It's Elle.

Shit shit shit, I'm bladdered and it's the morning over there and she'll be hungover but a bit more rational while I'm a bumbling beer bag full of rubbish on stilts, oh balls I can't answer, I can't, I can't, I ... "Hello?"

She's cold and stern and terse and ever so definite. Drunk she was, drunk, didn't mean it, she's sorry, ever so sorry, she shouldn't have done it, shouldn't have called me, her friend said not to do it, had to take the phone off her in the end, just a mistake, back to normal, no more of that thanks. It's like she's saying it in slow motion, and even though the booze is raining through my brain, I get it. It finally clicks in, I understand. She *really* doesn't want me. In the throws of drunken terribleness, she had taken a swig of nostalgia and allowed herself to finish the bottle. But in the cold light of day, this *isn't* what she wants.

"Do you mean never *ever*?" Like a child.

"Never." With that, a blub bursts out of my mouth, some sort of volcanic emotional pop explodes my chops and following behind it streams a diarrhoea of sobs and wails that I've absolutely no control over.

"You mean never ever ever ever *ever*?" Now this doesn't even sound like me, it's just not me. I'm really not one of these blokes who likes getting *stuff off his chest* using whichever emotions are at hand; I'm not that sort of bloke. I'm terrified of emotions; they bite. I feel like a right tit even writing this, I'm sitting at my computer, alone, as red as a redcurrant, humiliated by myself.

"No. NEVER," she says, annoyed now, setting me off even worse. As I continue to rain all over this fucking end-of-the-world bridge in this cunting fake bastard-baked city, the line just quietly clicks.

"Hello? Hello? HELLO?"

Bumbling around, breaking my heart all over Las Vegas at dawn on the wrong way back to the hotel, I *know* that my reaction was ridiculous. But I also know that this moment has been a long time coming, a final final nail in that past's coffin. The pain is immeasurable, what with my heart shattering into splinters and falling down into the pit of my stomach. But I also know that this might be a chance for me to at last let go, and make my way, off in another direction.

Oh, and by the way, some of *Rain Man* was shot here, at Caesar's Palace.

But I don't go and look.

Just get me out of here.

CHAPTER THIRTEEN SOUNDTRACK:

Happy
Birthday

Stevie Wonder (1980)

The Power of
Love

Huey Lewis and the News (1985)

Chapter Thirteen

Great Scott!

Las Vegas to Los Angeles

I'm not sad to see the oversized hotels of Las Vegas as a distant shimmering shitty clump in my wing mirrors; it's a place that will only remind me of substantial sadness. I'm not especially sad either to see my twenties fade away: today is my thirtieth birthday. Whoopee doo, I could rip a tissue. Ironic I suppose that this landmark should come right now, while on a tour aimed at trying to wipe the past clean so I can prepare for the second third (hopefully) of my life, especially after the spectacular finality of last night's drunken disaster. All of these coinciding fates.

So with Vegas once again a remote desert figment, we stop at a middle-of-nowhere petrol station, in the searing midday sun, huffing and puffing the gloopy steam passing as oxygen, and I call my parents so we can all say *Happy Birthday to me*. At the end of the conversation, my mum asks, "Are you OK though?" I say yes, I'm fine. But I know that really, I'm not. I'm all over the place. As the desert speeds by, I think about how we can never sit content for a moment. We can't be happy with what we've got *right now*, it always has to be a look back at when things were different or a look forward at when things might be OK. I promise myself to try and live more for *now*, because now is really the only time that actually exists.

Ploughing south on Highway 5, I know we've bumped into the outskirts of Los Angeles as we pass through the forcefield of smog that drapes over the city. It's like entering a whole different atmosphere: mountains in the distance become vague grey outlines as the sun struggles to soak through the particles of crap and cancer hanging in the air. Being the epicentre of entertainment, Los Angeles was always going to be the busiest part of this trip. We've already spoken to agents and location owners and have a pretty thick timetable planned, so it's handy that we're met by an old friend of mine, Sally, who's putting us up and kindly steering us around the city she knows like the back of her own show reel. Sally is your archetypal Los Angeles wannabe actress – drawn by Hollywood's glittering sidewalks to have a crack at the big time. I've no idea if it'll happen for Sally, of course I hope it does, but I know it must be tough waiting, being blown out, waiting, being blown out, waiting … it's the same pattern I have with girlfriends. Sally and I have a slight past, romantically, but we've lived in different countries and it's never really come to anything. But there's always *something* there whenever I see her.

She's arranged for one of her friends, Bob, to come and meet us at an English-sort-of-style pub in Studio City (home to out-of-work actors). Bob is, of course, an out of work actor. He's a large man in the John Goodman mould. Unfortunately for Bob, John Goodman already exists, that's how they got a mould. But it's the ambition that rides sparkling in his eyes that astounds me – this guy must have had a hundred rejections daubed all over him and still, he goes back for more. He laments at length about a sitcom he appeared in recently that's been axed. His big chance may have just fluttered by noticed by only a handful, some of whom were network bosses that didn't like what they saw. We drink his artistic woes away, along with the unmentioned last gasps, the clinging mouldy dregs of my youth. But among the melancholy splattered up the walls all around me, I decide one thing for sure: LA is going to be a romp, a binge, an immense nostalgia bender to help me get over all the heart-smash. Balls to it all, let's have it, let's live this poxy thing, I'm going to tear this city apart and start revelling in it, grabbing it, a fresh start like a fresh start's supposed to be.

It's time for us to jump in the motor and see LA buzz eccentrically around, trying to drive through the baking hot skirmish that is Hollywood. Our first location hunt starts at a place which back in England helped whet our appetites for the trip in the first place. How better to kick-start our LA odyssey than to go for *Back to the Future*'s jugular. Marty McFly, I'm coming for you baby.

Bushnell Avenue in the South Pasadena area of Los Angeles seems attractive fodder to film-makers: an idyllic, tree-lined, probably middle-class street with homes of different shapes and sizes that I guess represent the *anything's possible* aspect of the American. There's a bit of dough in the area. The street looks familiar, and I start to get those shivers I get when it feels like we're in the area of a location, like Derek Acorah in a castle. It all seems to fit. And suddenly, we're right inside the crazy bonkers Flux Capacitated world of Marty McFly.

BACK TO THE FUTURE (1985) (Movie)

Director: Robert Zemeckis
Writers: Robert Zemeckis, Bob Gale
Producers: Steven Spielberg, Frank Marshall, Kathleen Kennedy
Awards: Won an Oscar for Best Effects and Sound Effects Editing
Cast: Michael J. Fox (Marty McFly), Christopher Lloyd (Doc Emmett Brown, Lea Thompson (Lorraine Baines McFly), Crispin Glover (George McFly), Thomas F. Wilson (Biff Tannen), Claudia Wells (Jennifer Parker), Marc McClure (Dave McFly), Wendie Jo Sperber (Linda McFly)

Notes:
It's long been known that *BTTF* first starred Eric Stoltz as Marty, but when it didn't work out he was replaced by Michael J. Fox and the footage they shot with Stoltz has never surfaced. I can't imagine Hill Valley without Michael J. Fox.

I first watched this movie with my cousins in Southend; at least three times a day on a pirate video. My jaw didn't get off the floor. I'd never really considered time travel until this film said to me "imagine if time was bendy" and thereafter I made all sorts of day-dreamy plans for tweaking things I'd done and said. But mainly I was going to go and watch Spurs win the double. It was enthralling, exciting, intoxicating but unfortunately, impossible ... which I still find a disappointment.

This specific aspect of Marty McFly's world we're barging our fat noses into is his 1955 existence. At number 1727 we find the house where Lorraine (Marty's mum) lived with her parents, the Baines's. My eyes hawk up to this all-American family home's top right window – you know the one where in the film we see a shot of Lorraine getting undressed. Glory be. God Almighty, did I fancy her. Her real life name is Lea Thompson and I when I was young

I once wrote her a letter. No reply. Her loss. Well, she did get to keep the knickers I was asking for, so I guess she didn't entirely lose. Right across the road there's a tree, a significant tree, because one of the branches was where George McFly climbed up to grab a glimpse of Lorraine undressing.

Just as I stand here in silence, contemplating the moment, I hear a scrabbly kafuffle and a small piece of bark lands on my shoulder. I look up for something to blame and yes, of course, Tom's crawled his way with shaky Clive Dunn aplomb, up to the very branch George did: proving that it really is a *kafuffle* getting up there. He's got a look on his face that says he doesn't *want* to be up there, but that he knows he *must* be up there. That face a dog has when it's humping your leg, it doesn't know why it's doing it, it just knows it really *needs* to. Not that Tom's shagging the tree, he's more sanitary than that. I watch in awe of his devotion. He looks unsteady, unstable, incapable and has grazed his arms in the process – striping them with slight blood-to-surface strips of raw red. In the meantime, the man who lives in the house by the tree has wandered out with a knowing smile. He's seen goons like us before.

He seems very proud of his home's brief appearance in the film: a tad out of focus behind Michael J. Fox as he approached the tree that George was clinging to. The guy wasn't here at the time, but has the DVD and says he likes to occasionally pause it at the bit where his house appears. Somehow that feels sinister. But then I realise that I sometimes have to share a double bed with a man who's right now having his own private Hajj up a tree, and if anything's sinister, it's us. He stands with us for a while, chatting about *Back to the Future* and clearly realises what this film means not only to people of my age, but generations above and below.

"A lot of people climb the tree and get up there. A guy came by in a DeLorean one time." Bastards beat us to it. I suppose twenty years have passed. The man then starts talking about selling his roof tiles on eBay as *Back to the Future* relics, which I politely don't tell him is a ridiculously ambitious money-making idea.

Meanwhile, Tom has begun his descent, which given the nature of the tree's bark must be like trying to slide down the leg of a fat man with chronic eczema. The guy becomes silent and concerned while Tom dangles over the spot where George McFly landed before being pushed out of the way by history-meddling Marty, who then got mowed down by Lorraine's dad – his own Grandfather – and subsequently woken up in his Calvins by his own mum drooling over him. Anyone's nightmare. If you think about it, *Back to the Future* could be described as a a time-travel incest story". It's pure filth.

With Tom down from the tree, shaken and scratched, another neighbour walks by. This lady is in her thirties and has some sort of supportive back brace on that makes me stare rudely. The guy we've been speaking to knows her and starts asking about *Back to the Future*. He sort of interviews her for us.

"So what do you remember?" he asks quite professionally.

"It was exciting; I was young, probably twelve or thirteen."

"Did you have a thing for Michael J. Fox?" I ask. That's enough from you Mr Neighbour

"Oh, of course. I met him; he was smoking on my front lawn. I saw when his dad fell down from the tree here. That scene was exciting to watch. At that point it felt like movies were being shot on this street all the time. You always find *some* neighbours that don't like it though. I'm sure the realtors take full advantage by saying this house was in this movie."

The glory of being in the place where possibly my favourite, most imagination-provoking movies took place gets even better when we find that just three doors along from Lorraine's house stands a neat looking gaff which had been messed up substantially to be used as Biff's 1955 residence. I really wanted to meet Biff, and unlike your Michael J. Foxes, who are unreachable even to the industry-connected, thought we might stand a chance. Back in England I found an email address for him and threw a slightly adapted but standard sycophantic mail to him. He replied:

TO: Spencer Austin
FROM: Thomas F. Wilson
SUBJECT: Re: Eighties!

I do wish you great luck with your project, Spencer, but the fact is, I don't talk about the eighties any more, as I am quite busy in the new millennium. I've frustrated many that have come before you, my friend, but alas, I have yet to do anything like what you're up to.

I do wish you good luck with it.

Tom.

Pah. I sort of wanted to hate him for it, but fair enough. And then he became an *internet smash* with a YouTube clip where he sings a stupidly funny song about people asking him about *Back to the Future*. Just search "Thomas F. Wilson" on *www.youtube.com*.

Anyway, the guy we've been speaking to in the street tells us that the people living in Biff's place weren't entirely happy at what the film company did to their house. "The people are still in that house and they say, 'When we agreed to have them film, we didn't realise they were going to make our house look so bad,' and I said that 'Yeah, but they made it look again,' and they said, 'Yeah, but we're embarrassed that our house appeared in a movie looking so bad,' and I said, Yeah, but you probably got paid so much money, you probably sent your kids to college on the money you got!'" Some people, tsk.

The Gamble House in Pasadena is a hugely historic spot that in England would be considered relatively modern, having been built in 1908. It was built for David and Mary Gamble, of Proctor and Gamble soap-making fame and now belongs to the City of Pasadena, which allows visitors to tour it and such. "An outstanding example of American Arts and Crafts style architecture", says the website, which is snootily careful to make *no* mention of *Back to the Future* anywhere on the site.

The relevance of this big wooden shack is that it was used as the exterior for Doc Emmett Brown's 1955 home in *Back to the Future*, and the garage he and Marty run down to in the film is now the souvenir and gift shop. As far as I can see it's an enormous wooden house and apparently was only given to the city because prospective buyers thought it was too dark inside and would have painted the wooden walls to brighten them. So really, it's a big shack that's quite dingy.

Without bothering to gratify them with an entrance fee to the house – our money's too cheap for them – we continue on our way to Burbank, to the McCambridge Recreation Centre. The people in the office at the centre don't know and don't care that a scene was shot here and bemusedly allow us entry to sod around in the hall for five minutes. We didn't intend to watch an hour of girls basketball, but that's what we have to do, happily, before gaining exclusive access to the gym at which Marty McFly auditionedin front of Huey Lewis (of Huey Lewis and The News in a cameo appearance) in *Back to the Future*.

We elect – with the democratic process of "Bagsy it's not me, it should probably be Tom" – that Tom should be the one to play writhing air guitar on stage in front of the twenty sweaty, sniggering female basketball players now standing iat the back of the hall. I, meanwhile, stand in the very spot Huey Lewis sat when he shouted that classic line at Marty, "You're too darn loud!"

"You're too darn loud!", I shout at Tom, even though he's perfectly silent, as air guitar should be.

From the recreation centre, we wade our way through hordes of school kids in long shorts and baggy T-shirts and walk not far up the road to a quieter street away from the noise of summer holidays. At 516 University Avenue, we find a standard family home that's unspectacular to the point of being perfect. It's gloriously suburban: absolutely nothing happening but happy families. Which is why this house was perfect as the Arnold household in *The Wonder Years*.

THE WONDER YEARS (1988–1993) (TV)

Awards: Won a Golden Globe

Cast: Fred Savage (Kevin Arnold), Daniel Stern (Kevin Arnold – the narrator), Jason Hervey (Wayne Arnold), Dan Lauria (Jack Arnold), Alley Mills (Norma Arnold), Josh Saviano (Paul Pfeiffer), Danica McKellar (Winnie Cooper), Olivia d'Abo (Karen Arnold).

Notes:

No no no, it's not true. Marilyn Mansun did not play Paul Pfeiffer. It's a rumour that's been knocking around wildly on the Internet for years, but it's not true. Josh Saviano, the actual actor who played Paul, grew up to do a major in Political Science at Yale and now he has been admitted tothe Bar in New York and works for a law firm. Apparently though, the character Paul Pfeiffer was an inspiration for Millhouse in *The Simpsons*.

Every boy was, in some way, Kevin Arnold. To whatever extent, we all experienced the problems Kevin had in growing up: everyone had their own Winnie Cooper or their own geeky friend just like Paul. *The Wonder Years* was a tremendously observant commentary on *growing up* that roamed seamlessly between comedy and drama.

When I hear just the first line of Joe Cocker's marauding, bestial version of "A Little Help From My Friends", it triggers thoughts of that Super 8 film in the opening titles of *The Wonder Years* and being in the street where that was shot provokes a whole different type of location-hunting nostalgia. *Back to the Future* locations provoke bladder-worrying excitement, *The Wonder Years* house is like visiting a personal childhood home – growing up with Kevin Arnold was for me like watching my own home movies. We stand in front of the house waving at the camera in that frantic childish way people did in Super 8 films. For some reason this feels personal, which can only be a tribute to the programme and the effect it had on people. My reaction to finding the *The Wonder Years* house has surprised me. I never realised that the reason I liked the programme so much was because, all along, Kevin Arnold had been, approximately, me.

––––––––––

The First Hollywood Methodist Church is slap bang in the middle of Hollywood: a huge old building with spires and stained glass windows in all the correct places, making it look incongruous among all the new development in the area. For all its reputation and word-of-mouth international fame, Hollywood is a shit heap. Before the celebs started getting out of this part of town to allow the drug dealers and pimps more space, apparently this old church had quite the star-studded congregation. But you can tell the area isn't the best now, by the fact that the church has an elaborate telephone entry system that's backed up by huge metal doors that would need a ram raid to get through.

This is the place where *Back to the Future's* "Enchantment Under the Sea" scenes were shot. A church wouldn't be the first place you'd suspect of being the location, but there's a gym within the grounds and, sure as hell, that's the place. The exterior scenes, incidentally, were shot at a school nearby.

We're buzzed in by a lady name Grace, and wander into the offices of the church, almost choking on the smell of must, to find her huddled in a corner surrounded by a desk full of chaos and cobweb. She must be in her mid-eighties and shows no signs of allowing space on her desk for a computer. She greets us enthusiastically and begins talking about the time when Michael J. Fox and the gang visited the church. She's been here for some thirty-five years and remembers visits by various film crews.

"So do you remember much about *Back to the Future*, or does it all blend in with the rest of the filming done here?"

"Oh yes, uh huh, yes." Well which one? Never mind.

"Did you meet many of the stars?"

"Oh yes. A lot of them stayed here during the daytime and they had a cart where they could rest." The phone rings and Grace shakily deals with an enquiry by asking them to call back later. She rejoins us and looks suddenly aghast at the camera (that's already been pointing at her, *on*, for twenty minutes).

"Oh no! Not on film!" she giggles with that coyness we all used to have in the eighties when the novelty of a video camera arose.

"I was a singing star. I was supposed to be in a film with Grandma Moses up in Grand Hall." Bless her, she's a real sweetheart, but that flies right over my head and Tom tries to politely steer the conversation back to living memory.

"Did you meet Michael J. Fox at all?"

"Oh yes. He was here a lot. He used to sit on the steps here with my husband." The phones rings again and before she's actually picked the phone up, starts to say, "Hollywood Methodist Church, hello..." I think the camera and us and everything is confusing her a little. "My husband didn't smoke, but just by the gym is where Michael would smoke."

"What did they chat about?"

"Oh, I don't know."

"Men's stuff?" Not sure whether I mean whippets, pigeons or pornography.

"I imagine so. My husband was a meteorologist so I don't think he was interested in movies." All the while, a little poodle-shaped dog sits on the chair, stinking and stained, whining with extreme back leg quiver.

"It's great to have you guys. Now you're right in the heart of Hollywood, right?"

Grace directs us through the haze of church dust to the gym, which as we enter takes my breath away. It shouldn't do, it's a manky old hall, like the ones you'd imagine a Scouts' gang show to take place in, but it really has barely been touched since *Back to the Future* was shot. The stage looks just the same and it really isn't much work to imagine all the "Enchantment Under the Sea" décor draped over the walls. Tom and I sprint for the stage, vying for the lead singer's spot where Michael J. Fox hammed a mime of "Johnny B. Goode". It has just the aura we expected: like a trip back to the 1950s. I leap around doing all the guitar moves Marty exacted, while Grace giggles like a moped.

It seems a lot smaller, but boy am I filling this stage. I've got presence; I'm like Joe Longthorne. I lie on my back playing my imaginary guitar, hold it behind my head and back round to twang the strings with my teeth. I'm all over it.

After my first set, I sit on the edge of the stage for a few minutes while the boys check around the back of the hall. I remember little moments, like to the left of me where Marty checked the photograph of his family and found that his hand was disappearing; right under my bum where Marty stood after an inappropriate wailing session on his guitar and said, "I guess you guys aren't ready for that," and the spot in the middle of the hall where George first kissed Lorraine.

The boys start shouting round the back of the stage, so I slip off the stage and wander dreamily round to the door. Here are the stairs leading to the fire escape that Marty McFly ran through after he finally got his parents together. In the film, they stood by the door telling Marty his music was "interesting" and that they wanted to call their kid Marty, which meant that of course even before the story started he'd already been back and affected his own past, otherwise he wouldn't be called Marty. Christ, time travel is confusing. Keep time linear, that's what I say. Let's start a campaign. It seems strange that I can get a thrill out of a fire escape. It's a bit seedy, getting all sweaty over a grubby Hollywood fire escape.

The only way we can get to visit the back lot at Universal Studios in LA is to go as paying customers – to ride the tourist train along with all the other screaming kids. The press department at Universal were having none of our amateur documentary-maker nonsense, they want our forty-nine dollars and whatever else we have to spare for candyfloss and hot dogs.

I forgot that theme parks are like being caught up in the apocalypse. It's as close to utter civil unrest as I've ever seen. Everyone is in competition with everyone – even *within* families – to get first in line for something: rides, food loos, face painting and even to get out at the end of the day is a *must win* sport. The whole day is about standing in a queue for two or three hours at a time and paying fifty dollars for the privilege.

So we queue up for two hours to get on what I hope is the Universal back lot tour. If I get to the front and find some prick in an E.T. costume offering just a photo, I'll twist that long neck around until his head goes black and falls off. But luckily for E.T. (or an out-of-work actor stooping to new lows), a big long cart is at the front of the line and I get on it to be patronised for an hour about how the experts make films, by an over-energetic wannabe who thinks he's one of those experts.

Despite the whole turgid theme park thing, the back lot tour takes me somewhere I've *always* wanted to go. I can see the *Back to the Future* clock tower from ages away, and before I know it, we're slap in the middle of Hill Valley. As was. It's bizarre. In front of the clock tower there's the big green square, which our irritating yet admittedly informative guide tells us was dug out and replaced by a lake for the movie because in those days they couldn't simply slap a CGI one over the top. As we face the tower, to our left is a row of shops where in the film we see Biff chasing Lorraine a bit before he gets shit poured all over him. Behind is the café where in 1955 Marty discovers his dad for the first time, and in the future, he discovers his own son in the 1980s café. This makes me feel ten again. The train goes too fast for me to take it all in, all the scenes that were shot here – Old Biff getting in the DeLorean, Marty buying the Almanac, the Hoverboard chase, save the clock tower and ... *slow down train,* I need to do the Hill Valley thing, *slow down.* It doesn't though, and before I know it, that crappy mechanised Jaws is rearing its polystyrene head at me.

With little time to spare, we head out to Puente Hills Mall, northwest of Los Angeles. Once arrived, we wait patiently for the sun to come down, because we really couldn't try to conduct our experiment during daylight. Oh no, and also, the Libyans would recognise us. We *have* to wait for night-time before trying to hit eighty-eight miles per hour at Twin Pines Mall.

But even when the sun sets sourly over the trees, the car park remains full. We hoped to get the rental car up to eighty-eight in the very spot that Marty powered the DeLorean back to 1955, but all we can manage is twenty miles per hour and only then after the cruising cop car popped round the corner for a couple of minutes. What a fizzle. What a dud. I've had all these visions of skidding around the place at top speeds, when actually, the place is full up with cinema and restaurant goers ruining it for us. We do, however, find the spot at which Doc's van was parked, and where Marty arrived at the mall on his skateboard. From the higher view, where the Twin Pines' sign was in the movie, the structure of the mall looks the same and, really, just like any shopping mall. We run around frothy-mouthed for a few minutes, standing in the spots where Doc was shot and where the DeLorean burned off into the past before going inside to check out the sort of local shopping available to Marty.

Inside the mall, it's all corn dogs and baseball jerseys and mess and shouting and hordes and quite, quite unbearable. It's really grubby. I didn't want Twin Pines to be grubby, but it is. I'm sorry. We leave discontentedly at fifteen miles per hour, some seventy-three miles per hour slower than I'd hoped.

This is the first time I have ever, and I suspect will ever be towed along by a car, on a skateboard. In fact, I think this might well be the first time I've ever been on a skateboard, so to jump to being pulled along by a car on one is probably a bit precocious. What's more, the skateboard is the cheapest, kiddiest one we could find (for no reason other than budget), and the smell of its melting wheels becomes more apparent the further through the tunnel we get.

So, we're at Griffith Park in Hollywood, named after the Welshman Colonel Griffith Griffith, believe it or not, who once had an ostrich farm on the land and then shot his wife (how deliciously LA). The park is a hilly affair, with winding roads through foresty areas that Sally knows so well that my bearings flake away after turn two. It's home to Los Angeles Cultural Monument No. 111 (better known as The Hollywood Sign); the Griffith Park Observatory (famously used as a location in James Dean's *Rebel Without a Cause);* the Batcave seen in the opening titles of the original *Batman* TV series; forest fires, lots and lots of forest fires; and of course, the tunnel that Biff drove through with Marty trailing on his Hoverboard trying desperately to secretly grab the Sports Almanac and save humanity.

Except I haven't got a Hoverboard. Like I said, I've got a flimsy children's effort that's more like a flip-flop mounted on a Matchbox car. Sally takes liberties with the speed, and because it's an open-topped Jeep, I can hear her cackles responding to my wails. I'm in that situation where I've got to stay on or get hurt; there's no *jump off* option, it's too fast for that, plus the camera's on and I'm trying to show off. "Just go slow," I told her, "I'm scared" I told her, and now look, she's ripping through this dank hole in the hill and the very last thing I'm thinking about is how Marty McFly did the same thing all those years ago. *You bitch, you cow.* And now there's a car behind us, which makes the peril of falling off even worse. I take a quick glance back and the sheer terror on my face seems to amuse the passengers of the car crawling behind. *It's not funny* I think. Luckily, the film-makers made the tunnel seem about three times longer than it actually is. The scene goes on for *ages*, when actually, it's quite short and my misery is over quite quickly; Sally slows down and the adrenalin rush forgives her. I celebrate like I've just come back from war, managing even to flip the skateboard up into my hands like Marty McFly did. I looked ridiculous, but I did it. In the car, I sit exhilarated, recounting to myself the legend of my high-speed skirmish, which actually turns out to have only been fifteen miles per hour. It felt a lot faster.

We've saved the best to last, in my opinion. It's so iconic of the movie. I wanted to live here when I was a kid.

"I've lived here since 1972. I remember *Back to the Future* being filmed. I've got all the pictures," says the lady who actually lives next door to 9303 Roslyndale Avenue. She's been called by her neighbour, who spotted me knocking/thumping Tom on the head while screaming, "Anyone at home McFly." I really did twat him about, it sounded like a coconut. It knocked him off the skateboard. The lady was a bit surprised, but she's seen it all before, and although she doesn't mind people coming to look at Marty McFly's house, she doesn't really like to spend all day standing outside the house talking about it. That's why, when she detected the English accents, she called her neighbour, who's from Manchester. So out the neighbour came, all mousey and clinging to the haircut she arrived with in the seventies, chucking out an accent that combines Manc and Californian to create a sort of mutated icky tongue slap somewhere between Clint Eastwood and Su Pollard.

"It was fun meeting Michael, I danced with him."

"Sexy dance?"

"Oh no, just messing around. Are you on a school trip? How flattering. I'm thirty.

"Do you get many people coming around here for the McFly house?"

"Oh, every day. That's why I thought you were college kids, 'cos usually it's college kids and last week there were some dressed up like Christopher Lloyd, with the wig on and all that."

"Have you seen someone with a DeLorean come around here?"

"Only once, a guy came round with a DeLorean," That pesky guy, he must be the one they told us about at Bushnell Avenue. I feel weirdly competitive with him. No, let's say it, I hate him, and I hate his stupid DeLorean.

"What was Christopher Lloyd like?"

"He was very nice. They were all great. They did the first one, it took about three days, and then they came back and did a couple more days on number two. It was all really quick, but it was really good to see. And we got the money for it. And we got to eat anything that they ate, in the field at the back there. And they gave everyone passes to see the movie, because of the inconvenience. Oh yeah. The guy across the road, he wouldn't be quiet, he kept working in his garage until they paid him. He said, 'Pay me, it's my job.' The second time they came, we'd changed the front of the house..." Bear in mind that this is *just* the next door house, not even the McFlyhouse, "and they had to put it back to how it was the first time using oatmeal and rice or something. They had to put branches back in the trees because they wanted it the same." Oatmeal and rice on the side of your house? I start wondering whether they got done by a prank pretending to be filming another *BTTF* movie.

"And how did the DeLorean take off," I say, keeping so deadpan that she thinks I'm a genuine idiot rather than just a stupid one.

"Oh honey no. It just run down the street, you guys are into movies, you should know that." Yes, we should. But you know, when you're in it, living it, sometimes reality begins to blur just a tad.

Today's been a therapeutic crash bang wallop day the way nostalgia should be. A proper celebration.

Los Angeles is going to be a mad two weeks...

CHAPTER FOURTEEN SOUNDTRACK:

The
A-Team

Mike Post (1983)

Chapter Fourteen

I love it when a plan comes together

Los Angeles

The Disney-owned Golden Oaks Ranch in Newhall isn't open to the public, but I suppose they were impressed with the extraordinary lengths of our trip and our exceptional begging skills and gave us a rare invitation to go along and look at the ranch. We've seen lots of movie-location websites saying you must not enter onto this property because old man Disney will throw you into jail, and that'll be no theme park ride I can tell you. So we feel quite honoured to get the chance to stick our big noses into Walt's business.

There's not much signage outside the Disney Ranch other than the aforementioned threats to throw trespassers in jail for six months. *Six months,* just for having a look at their ranch. Feeling all privileged, we drive past the sign and into the heart of the ranch. It's basically a wild, dry, greeny-brown piece of land with big plains of long weed, clumps of trees, and orangey sun-baked dirt roads. A proper ranch; nothing too spectacular other than the fact that film-makers can come here without the threat of being disturbed by the public or stopped by the law from performing dangerous stunts.

In the office, among maps and still photos of movies all over the walls, is a foghorn loud cowboyish type called Steve, who takes great pleasure in showing us a pair of spurs that were signed and given to him at the ranch by Tiffany Thiessen, because he lent her his scruffy dog to use in her first film as a director (*Just Pray*, released in 2005). He gloats proudly and, admittedly, I'm jealous. I would *die* for Tiffany Thiessen. At worst I would even *be* her scruffy dog.

Steve warns us that a visitor to the ranch a while ago hurt himself on the property and sued them for thousands. He's not going to tolerate any more of that litigious lunacy and tells us that if we injure ourselves he'll probably shoot us like bitches, so that we can't take them to court. Fair enough, I think. I like the cut of this man's jib. It does all seem quite un-Disney though. Steve gets on his walkie-talkie and makes a call for his colleague Juan to come over and drive us around the ranch as a sort of mini-unofficial tour. Juan turns up quick-smart, with his ranger's outfit on and a Mexican accent that's so strong I can barely make out *hello* through all the spitty palatal friction. He clearly doesn't understand too much of what we say either, he must think we're trying to do machine gun noises at him, what with all the glottal stops and cockney clicks.

"What will we see on the ranch today, Juan?"

"Yes." He nods and smiles politely. This tour might be tricky.

We jump in Juan's four-wheel drive and start a squiz around the ranch. He takes us past tens of barns and houses that were built for movies and TV shows that we've never seen. I'm happy to sit through Juan's stories of an Oprah Winfrey movie being shot here in order that I can eventually see the barn from *Back to the Future*. That barn, after all, is the reason we've travelled to the ranch. Marty is transported there in the DeLorean from the Twin Pines Mall, and the terrified Peabody family fire a blunderbuss at him – the only way to deal with anyone you believe is an extraterrestrial. So that means that the Peabodys went from owning a small ranch to developing a mall in the same spot thirty years later. A small piece of trivia is that when Marty arrives *back* at Twin Pines Mall after all the fuss of the film, the sign says "One Pine Mall", which is a reference to the fact that he knocked a tree down in his first journey back to 1955. So when the Peabodys came to name the mall, history had been changed and there was only one pine left to inspire them. I love the confusing non-linear time layers of this film.

Juan stops on the edge of a plain and a wooded area and starts talking about *Back to the Future*. Confused, we quiz him further to find that the barn and ranch house has been knocked down about six years ago. *The outrage, the cocking outrage. I feel personally insulted. They can't just go tearing people's eighties down, this is a breach of human rights.* I accuse Juan of destroying movie history and he admits that he was a bit choked himself that the barn had to be pulled down. That barn had been there for years and years, and way before it was the Peabody Farm in *Back to the Future*, it had been in TV shows back in the fifties. And we're just too late to see it. Gutted. I've had visions of me bursting through those barn doors and everything.

Juan drives us around some other bits and pieces: the lake from Disney's *George and the Dragon*; roads that the first series of *Dukes of Hazzard* were shot on; a bit from *Cat from Outer Space*...

My first ever visit to the pictures, a grimy old cinema in Leyton, now a B&Q, stinks of wee, Dad can't afford popcorn, kids screaming and fighting. I'm bored within twenty minutes, I'm too young for this, I don't really get it, but my God that alien cat with the collar with the bright colours is sooo cool for those twenty minutes...

But even the entire cowboy town of impressive facades from *Roots* can't get our peckers up. *The barn is gone.* On our way back to the office, we're silent, like a squadron that's lost too many good men. We drive past a barn that looks enough like the *Back to the Future* barn that we tempt ourselves to shoot it and pretend it was the one, but our journalistic integrity forces us not to. However, as we're peering through the busted up old wooden doors, Juan mentions casually that this barn was used in *The A-Team*. He doesn't know which episode or when, but we trust him, he's all we've got. Plus, the A-Team were *always* getting themselves locked in barns, so it's a good bet. Remarkably, Juan leaves us to it because we're close to the office, and just tells us to stick to the roads and to make sure we leave. But we're not going to leave until, of course, we've *been* the A-Team in that crazy fool barn.

It's a rickety old affair, probably not safe, but we imagine ourselves being locked in here. Stinks of hay and dung and wood that's been wet then dry then wet then dry. It's a bit hard to carry off the being trapped bit believably though, because I can just slide out through a hole in the side and our storyline completely disintegrates. The barn's not exactly the most astounding of discoveries, but one that conveniently sets us up for our big breakfast tomorrow morning. This plan has unexpectedly come together (crazy fool).

In order that we could get to meet Dwight Schultz, we had to contact his partner on a radio show he hosts called *Dark Matters*. Tom emailed Don Ecker – world-renowned Ufologist – through the website, hoping desperately that the message would get to Dwight.

THE A-TEAM (1983–1987) (TV)

Awards: Nominated for 3 Primetime Emmys

Cast: George Peppard (Col. John "Hannibal" Smith), Dwight Schultz (Captain H.M. "Howling Mad" Murdock), Dirk Benedict Lt Templeton "Faceman" Peck), John Ashley (Narrator), Melinda Culea (Amy Amanda Allen)

Notes:

Apparently, the "crime they didn't commit" that we're told about at the beginning of every episode was stealing gold bullion from the Bank of Hanoi during the Vietnam War.

Don replied to the email – despite Tom discovering that he'd accidentally referred to Dwight as Dirk (confusing him with Dirk Benedict who played Face and couldn't meet us because he's away) – saying that a meeting might be possible. Tom was careful to make out that we were just as interested in *Dark Matters* and Don as we were in Dwight and his portrayal of The *A-Team* legend, Howling Mad Murdock.

And today is the day. We've managed to arrange a meeting with the pair at a small diner some way out of central Los Angeles.

Dwight and Don turn up and it takes a second or so to mentally peel back the years and remove the grey beard on Dwight's face before Mad Murdock appears in front of me. This straight-laced, serious but friendly man wears studious metal-framed glasses, a carefully backcombed neat hairstyle and seems to want to be taken seriously. I didn't expect him to come steaming in howling off his head on Prozac, but I had forgotten that he would of course have piled on the years since I last saw him on telly. The years haven't been unkind, and perhaps there are suspiciously too few wrinkles on his perfectly sheeny, uncrumpled forehead to be true, but he looks well, and happy, and that pleases me.

Annoyingly, Don and Dwight want to sit and have breakfast before we do the interview – which normally means that all the good stuff gets talked out to an audience of boiled eggs and toast and the interview looks like the continuation of a conversation no one heard half an hour ago. But actually, it's a good way of getting all the UFO and conspiracy theory stuff out of the way so we don't use too much tape up on it.

I am actually naturally quite interested in all that stuff, and we talk for quite a while about aliens and how Iran are on the verge of sending nuclear bombs into all the major cities of America. That's the point at which Don uses the term "towel heads" and a round of uncomfortable looks shoot across the table, carried by a marked pause, as if Don and Dwight are testing whether we're going to be onside with that sort of anti-Muslim sentiment. We don't show any signs of approval, and the towel heads aren't mentioned again.

"So the radio show you guys do together now, *Dark Matters*, seems to cover all sorts of things from UFOs to politics ... what's it basically about?"

Dwight steams in with his explanation, "Well, the idea is Dark Matter is something that is speculated about. We can only see around five to ten per cent of the visible universe and we can tell from the speed at which galaxies rotate that there's something else out there, causing them to rotate so quickly." Jesus, this is heavy stuff; and it's just a basic *synopsis* of the programme! "So, we only see ten per cent and ninety per cent is unknown. And we use that analogy with the news and information in the same way. Ten per cent of what you see and hear is not *it*. You have to take that and infer what is *really* going on. Most people take that news and believe it. But that's not it; the real news is what you *haven't* been told.

"You see, *Dark Matters* was originally going to be a TV show," continues Don. These two have got this patter down. "We were in negotiation with the Sci-Fi Channel, back in September 2001. We had interest and what we were going to take a look at is a lot of what we do now. A lot of conspiracies and that sort of thing, what *really* happened. But when 9/11 happened and we were attacked, Dwight and I had a conversation and felt that it was not right then to go forward."

"I think the radio is a better format," chips in Dwight, "it's three hours. The television experience is a lot of quick sound bites, a lot of inference. The radio has become very important in that sense. We have been told that we can say what we want to say and the show is what we want it to be."

"How did your career take this course: from the A-Team in the eighties to conspiracy theories now?"

"Well, once you hit my age... I'm fifty-seven, so it's a pretty tough time for an actor. I was lucky to have a career as long as I did. I still do a lot of work in voiceovers, a lot of DVD games. The entertainment business has changed so drastically. There's no need for actors in the US. If they want a truck driver, they'll just go get someone who drives a truck. They don't need someone who can act. So, my career went in the typical way that I was thirty-five and then fifty-five and unless of course you're Paul Newman, most of the actors I know have fallen out of television, or if they're lucky, doing what I'm doing – a lot of voiceovers."

"That says a lot about the superficiality of American media and entertainment." Don tries to steer, slightly into the realm of a conspiracy.

"But I have always been a radio fan," continues Dwight. "I've slept with a radio in my ear since I was twelve. I would listen to *New York*, drifting in and out, all night. Don will tell you, that's how I found him. I listen to the radio constantly. I don't watch TV, don't go to movies. I listen to radio."

"No, that's not exactly true, we went to see *Saving Private Ryan*" interjects Don with a big grin on his face, teeth slightly overlapping the bottom lip in an endearingly daffy way.

"But you see, this was it, not only was I a Conservative in Hollywood, which is totally devastating, I mean you can't work."

"You have to keep it quiet?"

"Well, I made a lot of unfortunate mistakes by *not* keeping it quiet. But anyway, that hurts your career, immensely. Nobody wants to work with you. Then I also am interested in the subject of UFOs. So, not only am I a Conservative, but I'm a nut. Yeah, you're just a joke."

"So what's the most pressing Dark Matter at the moment?"

"Personally," starts Don, "my own feelings about that are the possibility of another imminent attack within the United States by Islamic fascist thugs who want to destroy this country and murder innocent Americans." Uh oh, he's off again.

"By the millions," adds Dwight.

"And do you think this might happen soon?" quivers Tom to Dwight.

"Well I hope not. It's hard to say. I think that our government has in many ways aggravated its responsibilities by failing to tighten up its national borders."

"And what's the biggest news in terms of UFOs, Dwight?"

"Well it would have to be what happened in the skies of Mexico, when a Mexican military aircraft suddenly encountered eleven UFOs surrounding it for fifteen minutes. What makes this unusual is that the aircraft picked up these objects on its infrared and radar equipment, but they were invisible to the naked eye."

Don continues the story, they're very slick, it's like they're broadcasting right now. "The Mexican Chief of Staff released it and caused a great furore. Why would he release it to a UFO investigator as opposed to the scientific community? His response was 'well I didn't really know of anyone in the scientific community who's actually interested in this'. Which is absolutely true. The scientific community has no interest in it whatsoever. Officially. But *were they* upset that they gave it to a UFO Investigator!"

Tom manages to pull the whole thing back into some sort of order by getting back to *The A-Team*. "No-one *ever* dying on the show is quite an admirable attempt at family viewing," Tom says. Which is quite a surprising fact, considering the sort of press the show got at the time, about how it was the Anti-Christ and was making good kids turn bad.

"It was a cartoon," replies Dwight. And I guess he's right, it was a larger than life caricature that had nothing more or less disturbing than *Dogtanian and the Muskahounds*.

"I have actually been asked, 'Did you use real bullets?' That was a real question." He bows his head and giggles with a flash of the mental Murdock emerging. "Some of the silly things that you're asked, you know? 'Are you *really* crazy? Are you? *Really crazy?*' You're asked that question five thousand times. At one point, *Captain Kangaroo*, a kid's show in the sixties ... what'shis name? Bob Keeshan. He's now gone. He held a press conference and blamed drug addiction on The A-Team. We were responsible for violence and drug addiction..."

"Was it a fun set to work on?"

"No. Well, it was to an extent but because they [the network] hated the show ... we had a number one show for two years..."

"They didn't take to it even after it became successful?"

"No, they did not want it to be number one. They wanted *St. Elsewhere*, *Hill Street Blues* ... what they called quality programming, to be the number one. They even wrote an article in a paper saying they weren't proud of the show, it's not the kind of thing they want to make. So here we were, the number one show, being treated like failures. And that was not good. We had none of the wrap parties or crew jackets, *nothing*. When the show ended, nobody came to the set to say goodbye, they just came and took the trailers away one by one. They loved the money we were bringing in, but nobody admitted watching it, that's the problem."

"Everyone in England of our generation would find that a disgrace. We *loved* that show." Tom's incensed.

"Well *we* found it a disgrace. You rarely get a chance to be the number one show and you think of it as your opportunity, your chance, and then it ends up like this. A show that they hated, they wanted to get rid of. I was going to get fired. They told me I wasn't good and was gonna be fired. And they *hated* the programme. NBC hated the show, it was not their idea of quality entertainment and they wanted it to fail ... and it was the only show they had in the top ten." He finishes smugly, with a little bitter edge, "When I went to *Star Trek* on the other hand, they treated you like you had a successful show, and that was a pleasure. I often think back and wonder what it would have been like to have been treated like that on a regular basis."

"There was quite a lot of controversy around Melinda Culea, who played Amy..."

"Well, yeah, she wanted to carry a gun. She didn't want to do what her character did, which be a reporter. And so when she was fired there was this great misogynist accusation that 'I was fired 'cos I was a girl', but then of course when we told the reporters that actually the first person to be fired was a guy [Tim Dunigan, who originally played Face before Dirk Benedict took over] they all shut up. She was fired because she didn't want to play the role that had been created. It would have been like me saying I don't wanna play crazy any more. You know, it's nuts."

"We heard that you and Dirk had to do loads of long hours because Mr T insisted on working nine-to-five."

Dwight nods knowingly."Well, Mr T was the biggest draw. And George [Peppard, who played Hannibal] was the movie star. The way TV works demographically, George brought in a certain demographic. And T at the time had just been in *Rocky*, so there was a huge demographic. I was an unknown. Dirk had been in *Battlestar Galactica* so ... the way the network would look at it was that these people would pull in a section of the audience. George certainly considered himself the star, and that didn't sit well with T, because George made a big show of being *the star*. T was not very talkative, but he would demonstrate his displeasure in certain ways; by ignoring certain people on set, that sort of thing." All sounds a bit handbags to me.

"Do you still see T?"

"No. I see Dirk, frequently. I talk to him a lot. He's actually doing a film in Germany. It's the first time he's worked in a long time."

"Have you ever been on one of his cruises?" We read before we came that Dirk Benedict was running cruises on his boat, where fans of his could literally go and spend a few days sailing with him. I'm not sure how much he was charging, but it seems an odd way for a celebrity to interface with fans: by literally being paid to go on holiday with them. In fact, he's not the only one, we found out that *The Hulk* actor, Lou Ferrigno does them too.

"No. I don't want to be on one of his cruises," laughs Dwight knowingly. Hmmm. "It would be one of *my* cruises by the way. Let's just say I've been offered but I don't want to go. You know, being locked up on a boat with a load of fans, not my idea of a happy time." Well, I have read on a website that Dwight was actually scheduled to be on a fan-cruise called "Dirk Benedict and Dwight Schultz's European Adventure", but the website says it's been postponed...

"Is it true that Mr T recently had cancer?"

"I don't know. We tried to find out. There was a controversy about that. Dirk and I both tried to find out and we were both rebuffed by his agent. I had a manager at the time; I had my manager try to find out too. We then set up a time to meet with one another. T was gonna come to my house, Dirk flew in. T was supposed to be there and he didn't show up. And that was the last time Dirk or I heard from him. And then we heard that he was ill, and that he had gone on *The Howard Stern Show* and said he was angry with us that we didn't care about him being sick. I don't know what the thing was."

"There were also rumours that he turned to God and is now known as Pastor T or something like that..." adds Tom.

"He has been known to garner publicity."

"Were you in touch with George before he died?"

"Oh yeah. I kept in touch with George. He lost his lung to cancer and then married the nurse. But he succumbed to cancer. He had a very small funeral, one of those where very few people were invited. But he was a huge movie star. He was like the hottest actor in all of Hollywood for quite some time."

Tom gets out his collection of pristine A-Team figures that he's brought all the way over from England. "They made toys of you that actually didn't look like you."

Dwight inspects one with his head tilted down and eyeballs hanging over the top of his glasses. It's the figure of Murdock in an orange Jumpsuit. "He's quite gay observes Dwight. Tom gets out two alternative versions of Murdock and asks if these are any better. "That's close. I look gay here too though."

I grab hold of the figures of Mr T and Hannibal and pretend they're arguing, "I'm the star of the show, no I'm the star of the show, no I'm the star of the show," which thankfully gets laughs.

Dwight then holds up the three Murdock figures, slings his glasses off and puts them next to his own face. "You wanna talk about the universe? One dimension, two dimension, three dimension!"

"I take it you got residuals for those toys?"

"No, I wish we did. They find a way of cheating you out of *everything*."

And so there's Dwight Schultz; a little bit bitter about the industry and his experience on *The A-Team* and by the sounds of it, who can blame him?

It's a bit sad that our fond memories aren't necessarily shared by those who've provided us with them.

CHAPTER FIFTEEN SOUNDTRACK:

Sho' You Right

Barry White (1987)

Chapter Fifteen

Don't move, dirt bag!

Los Angeles, still

Last night, Sally invited us to a friend's birthday celebration at a tacky Mexican Texican place just outside Universal Studios. I was a bit *oh alright* about it, this Los Angeles malarky is exhausting and I was zonked and didn't fancy a plastic salad with an E number vinagarette giving me instantaneous mouth ulcers. I had to be just a little bit *dragged* out.

Turns out her friend is called Megan. Turns out there's something about Megan that intrigues me. She's quite tall, with curly brown hair and a squeaky voice. Great big, pretty eyes, she's got. Part of the intrigue is that I'm *allowing* myself intrigue for the first time since Elle-gate. And for the first time since long, long before that, the intrigue isn't making me compare that person to her, or to have that stomach-churning twang of pointless guilt. Turns out I just quite fancy someone, good and proper and without the weight of an impossible ex hanging on my shoulders like the end of the world. Just maybe the whole Las Vegas debacle has *dealt* with the Elle demon. Problem is that, as I mentioned, Sally and I have an ongoing history that's bubbled under for a while, and although she's lovely, we've been friends for too long for it to concrete into much more. Ten years of friendship is too much to risk. Plus, I'm staying at her house and it's just not appropriate to feel this way. So I decide to try to lock it all up a bit and not feel anything, if that's possible.

As I sit here with my rancid melted Plasticine and battery acid cocktail and salad that's literally half an entire lettuce sliced down the middle, I watch Megan have a go on the bucking horse rodeo thing, you know, where it tries to make you fall off.

Giggling, tossing her hair back and emitting squeals only dogs can hear, there's something free and uninhibited and natural and innocent about this girl; she's impressive, she's cute. Shit, I like someone. That means I can't talk to her, I can't, my mouth will rust, my mental dictionary will break down, she'll think I'm boring and a bit thick and probably that my nose is too long.

With my confidence bulldozed into rubbly bits of broken me, that's as far as it goes. Just an eyeful of intrigue, leave it there.

As an antidote to the toxic waste cocktails from last night, I pour a gurgling gutful of breakfast omelette and over a furlong of coffee through my gate to bog it all down. We drive bloated and caffeine-scatty down to Sunset Boulevard to hunt out a café at which we've been instructed to meet Bubba Smith, who played Hightower in *Police Academy,* for a lunch we're not in the least bit hungry for. But it's not about the food, is it now.

Moses Hightower was a largely silent character that the writers could rely upon for gags that needed *a very large black man.* It was a pretty simplistic device that in true *Police Academy* style was repeated over and over again. You know the one – where someone gets all feisty and then Hightower stands up and shows what a huge black man he is and the person gulps and retracts everything nervously.

Anyway, with a talent for *Englishing* his way through the brick walls of snarling agents, Tom managed to get to talk to Bubba on the phone back in England, and since we've been in LA, has managed to piss him off a bit by not retrieving a voicemail message in time or getting back to him accordingly. It's not really Tom's fault, just a miscommunication faux pas, but Bubba was smarting about it on the phone earlier. He might be nearly sixty, but you really don't want to piss off Bubba Smith.

We arrive about half an hour early at the café, hoping to get a chance to set up our cameras so they can accommodate a man of his size in the same shot as men of our size. Bubba is six feet, seven inchesof massive. Plus we want to make sure we're not late, because that might push Bubba over the edge. I don't want to go over Bubba's edge.

As soon as we walk inside the place, we see a huge grinning face with a gap in between the front two teeth that could only belong to Bubba Smith, and even though his face looks like a ballooned-out *Bo' Selecta!* mask of himself, you can still tell it's Hightower. The man I remember from *Police Academy* was a little more muscular than this manatee sat in front of us now, but he *is* nearly sixty and keeping a frame that size down in weight must be a nightmare. He has a hairdo that I just can't stop staring at. It's been straightened, cut short and plastered down flat onto his head to give a sheen that looks like varnish. You know like when a restaurant puts varnished plates of food in the window to show what their dishes look like? Well Bubba's hair is like a hair version of that. It's really shiny and I'm *desperate* to touch it.

Bubba says that he's been to the gym, as usual, and came straight to the café to wait for us. Bless him, it's really kind of him to make the effort, after all, who the hell are we? He almost immediately launches into a speech about how he doesn't hang out with actors or footballers (from his days in American football, for which he is a national legend, but more on that later), and all he likes to do is go to the gym and then go home. A simple life. He then slings some gaudy yellow T-shirts and caps at us that have "Bubba's Online Casino" printed all over them in the largest font imaginable, without saying a word about the business venture for the rest of the time we're with him. That's his bit of plugging done for the day and I've duly included it. The cynical side of me wants to think that's why he's come to meet us, for a plug, whereas the human tucked away inside me somewhere wants to think he's simply brought us a memento. Who knows, he's a quiet man with a tough exterior and it's hard to tell.

Bubba mentioned on the phone earlier that he would "call some of the guys" from the *Police Academy* crew, but we took that as seriously as when an old friend you bump into in the street says "I'll give you a buzz". So when Marion Ramsey comes charging in, also a bit early, it's an enormous surprise. Marion played Hooks, the lady with the squeaky voice, and she looks hardly different at all. I suddenly feel all a bit emotional that they've come just to see us.

Immediately, Marion goes ranting off about her last boyfriend, who was English. After an angry bombardment about how he used to complain that everything "had to be about her", and how she'd replied by Saying, "Honey, I am the diva," I find myself apologising for the Englishman and then for the English in general, which she seems to accept in a mock regal snooty-nosed sort of fashion. Marion *is* a diva, and her giant swanning, prancing entrance shows she clearly loves to play up to the role. It's not Hooks-like *at all*.

By the time Hooks has piped down, an attractive blonde lady has sidled up to us and I'm just about to order coffee from her when I realise that she's Callahan. Callahan, the Academy instructor with the jokey boobies and the unquenchable sexual appetite. Beside me. Leslie Easterbrook, that's her name, and for people my age she was pretty much our first experience of S&M. It was a real education and I'm absolutely terrified, petrified to find her standing next to me. Leslie actually looks *more* attractive than she did in the film – I'm not sure if she's had some work done, but if so they've made a pretty good job of it. She glides in, all showbiz and *mwah mwah* and glitz, and before I know it we're all posing for a photograph and there's Callahan, you know, *Callahan*, holding my hand in that way where the fingers are all interlocked and sweat-swappy.

While the *Police Academy* lot hug and kiss and continue brief conversations they had on the phone, we set up our cameras ready for this mammoth interview. Eventually, all settled, with LA style salads, wraps and room-temperature mineral water all ordered, we get going.

"What was the camaraderie like on set?"

"It was awesome," begins Marion. "We would look out for each other, help each other out with scenes. One particular movie, they wrote a speech for me and I thought it was more *her* character [points to Leslie], even though there were more lines, so..."

"I started out with a teeny teeny part, a medium small part, but after Marion got through with giving me all her lines..." confirms Leslie, half joking.

"Yeah, I think Hooks is more ... she doesn't say a lot... Whatever little bit she says means a lot more. If she says less, her actions speak louder than her words. It's like Bubba, his character doesn't say much but when he says something, it's off the hook." Bubba sits quietly, decidedly *on the hook,* while Marion does most of the talking. I think that's why he wanted them to come along, so they can take care of all the rabbiting while he fills his face.

"Is that Hooks voice still inside you somewhere?" asks Tom.

"Honey, believe me, when they come to me with a contract, she comes *rolllllling* out."

"Can we hear a little bit of the voice?"

"You mean *that* voice?" she says, as Hooks, all squeaky and meek and a million miles away from what Marion is really like. We applaud; we have to, her face says so.

"But then by the end, you're shouting, 'Don't move, dirt bag!'" Tom attempts that angry Hooks line with unnerving accuracy.

"You know that was *my* line, but I gave it to Marion," Leslie says, and then laughs and shakes her head. It was a lie. I think there's a smidgen of diva competition going on between these two that's cloaked away somewhere in all that *mwah mwah love you so much* – this is Hollywood after all.

"At least you *remembered* that line," says Marion to Tom, "I get a lot of people coming up to me and they say, 'I've seen the movie a million times,' and I'm like, 'Well then, what's the line?' and they remember everything else *but* that." Only Marion could quiz fans on their knowledge of the lines just to check whether they truly are her disciples.

"How could people not remember that?" Tom slurps out of his smoothie and into outrage.

"Thank you," says Marion with firm vitriol. Tom feels the need to make sure it's known that *he is* the world's most devoted *Police Academy* fan. And probably he is.

"I have a football team back home and we're called The Academy, and all of the shirts have the name of a *Police Academy* character on the back. The shirts are exchanged each season, so that if you were the toughest player, you'd get the Hightower shirt, or most improved would get the Hooks shirt." The actors sit literally open-gobbed that this sort of thing goes on. So am I, it's the first I've heard of it. "And the player who's been a big girl gets Callahan."

"That's wonderful," the ladies mouth, as Bubba breaks his silence by clapping and giggling really loudly. They're fascinated by it all.

"You guys *really do* like the movies!" says Leslie incredulously.

"Yes, they're legendary."

"You remember when we went to Nasaka?" Bubba erupts, in that drawly booming, slow but captivating way he has. He's kicking into life, now he's knocked the guts out of his chicken dish.

"We did go to Nasaka, yes," confirms Leslie.

"You remember we went to that bar? They started drinking and singing so I said, you know, we gotta work tomorrow, so I went back to the hotel. It's the first time I've ever seen a Japanese pimp. And he came up to my room and he said, 'You want girl?' and he had this girl. I said 'ugly girl', and he said, 'Got more downstairs!' I said, 'No, that's alright.'"

"He never finishes that story, by the way." Leslie whispers mischievously over to us.

"No, no, if I'd have hooked up with one of those girls, you'd have *known* it".

"Those Japanese journalists kept asking me about my..." says Leslie, pointing at her chest.

"Yeah I know," Bubba confirms, as though it still annoys him.

"I just said there are better ones in the company," Leslie concedes humbly and points at Marion's chest. But Bubba wants to clear this one up.

"I said, 'What's wrong wit' you freaks?' You know, I said, 'Haven't you seen some titties before?'" This man is a legend.

"He didn't embarrass me *at all,*" Leslie says sarcastically.

"One of his assistants pulled me aside and said, 'Bubba um, it's just that Japanese women don't have big breasts.' Oh, I said, 'So they ain't used to seeing no titties, right?' And then they told me about you know when you put a wig on?" He motions towards his head, "Well, they put a wig on their..." moves his hand to the crotch area.

"What?" exclaims Leslie. This is all turning a bit weird, merkins are suddenly the topic of conversation.

"Did any of you date on set?"

"Are you kidding?" Lesley reacts defensively, as though it's a ridiculous idea.

"Wait a minute, Marion recalls. "Sharon dated Brian."

"Little Brian Tochi? [who played Nogata in *Police Academy 3* and 4]" asks Leslie. "Oh, that's about as serious as it got, they just went to dinner." I assume she's talking about Sharon Stone, and if so, it's quite an odd match. "He played *my* boyfriend, I was furious." she adds, tongue in cheek.

"So who else do you still hang out with?"

"Michael Winslow. I told him to come back here today. He called from Detroit and I told him to switch his reservations and come back here to meet the boys," says Marion. How flattering. But why us? Are we the only fans that have made this sort of effort? *Surely* not. "He's so creative and *so* funny. He's written a film that he stars in and we're all supposed to be in it."

"What's it about?" asks Bubba, with a slightly cynical tone.

"It's about a dog that solves crimes." Bubba opens his eyes wide and nods his head as if to say he thinks Michael's a lunatic.

"And there's G.W. Bailey, we just did a Celebrity Golf thing. She golfed, I didn't." Marion points to Leslie.

"Who was the biggest prankster on set?"

"Bubba," Marion says immediately. Bubba shakes his head with disgust at the allegation. "He would always call me and say..." She puts on a monotone, deep voice. 'Marion ... Marion ... come over here.' And I would walk over to him and say 'What?'" He would just start to chuckle, because I only come up to a certain part of him. And everyone else would get it and start to laugh and then I would get it and be like ohhh, he did it again."

"You know, you get bored around there. I remember the first one we did, I had to *tell* Michael," says Bubba.

"Yeah, you did," agrees Marion, like a congregation member agreeing with the preacher. That's how much Bubba holds court when he eventually speaks. You can't help but wait for his next words, because they could be *anything.*

"He kept making those voices. And it was hot out there. And we were sitting in those chairs." Bubba's face is stone cold deadpan, dry as a bone. He talks slowly and it's clear that he's talking about an incident that really riled him. "And he made a Pacman noise, he did a Pacman. And, you know, maybe it was the sun, I don't know what it was, but I thought it was a real Pacman. And I thought, well maybe I could play some Pacman. And I turned around and it was him and I just grabbed him by the neck. And I said, 'They *pay* you to do this. You don't have to *do* this all day.' Boy, I hated it." I love that Bubba lost it because he fancied a game of Pacman. I sit giggling privately about it for quite a while.

Marion adds her penny's worth about him too. "In Florida for number five, he was doing Rodney Dangerfield and horse noises all the time. He had the extras in hysterics. It was so hot, I just wanted to cry. I remember just looking at him and thinking, *my God, how can he do this?* I just wanted to pass out."

"And he was always the first one *to* pass out," adds Leslie. "We had to *make* him eat. His mind moves so fast and he's so creative that he forgets to eat. He's *so* buff though."

"He's still buff now?" sniffs Bubba competitively. There's definitely an edge of something between those two.

"What was it like when Steve Guttenberg said he didn't want to make any more, was it a surprise?"

"Not to me," says Marion knowingly. "To me it was just disappointing. You know, above just another movie on my résumé, it was a family. It's the best thing that ever happened to me, *Police Academy*. And it was the people. The people that stayed all the way through."

"How long were you shooting before you knew you were onto something?" I ask.

Leslie fires up first. "Well we knew within the first week or two that it was really special. First of all, it was an ensemble, we just seemed to really click and connect. And putting together a black and white cast, there was this whole period of time when it was black films or white films and here we were as this gang who really started to bond. We didn't know we had a hit, but we knew we had a good experience. We flew back together [touches Bubba on the arm] and had a wonderful time on the plane. And then when they started painting the picture up on the sidewalk, we were calling each other ... and I've got a Polaroid of a few of us who got together: David Graf [Tackleberry], bless his soul, who's sadly no longer with us; Scott Thompson [Copeland], who's up at my house right now; and we went up there and climbed the scaffolding and held onto the pictures of our own feet. And just this excitement that we had, because of the bond. We knew we had something funny, but we had no budget, my stuff was all shot in one take. They just said, 'This is what the script says, what do you wanna do?' And all the stand-up comics and all those of us who came from the theatre were able to put our piece in."

"We added a bit that is my all time memory," says Bubba.

"Was it you turning the car over?" asks Leslie.

"Yeah, but not the actual turning over the car. The significance of it. I watch *a lot* of movies and that was the first time I'd ever seen a black man standing up for a black woman at the risk of losing his job. And I told Hugh [Wilson, the director] that was *so* cool, because most of the time it's so hard to get a job. And now this calls her 'jigaboo' And if you notice, I was up there with Steve thanking him for teaching me to drive. I was up there laughing at you [points at Marion] running over Harris' feet and then he shouts You jigaboo'', and the camera turns straight to me. I turned and everybody went 'Oh, shit'. I turned the car and that's when G.W. fired me and I'm walking away with her following me going, 'Hey, hey'." His impression of Hooks is a weird thing to see. Quite unnatural.

"Was it a real car you flipped over, with an engine inside?"

"Yeah. There was no budget to take an engine out."

We start to ask what happened towards the end, when the films started looking tired and repetitive and when there just got to be too many of them.

"I wasn't in seven," says Marion, snarling a bit.

"They called me and told me they couldn't write her in," explains Bubba. "She called me up crying, saying she didn't understand why. And I said I'm out too," he booms defiantly. Bubba says that he called *Police Academy* producer Paul Maslansky to have it out with him.

"I made you," apparently claimed an angry Maslansky in the heat of the argument.

"Now look, mother fucker..." Bubba coolly replied. "You didn't make me; I was already made when I got to you. All you did was enhance the brand."

"It was very low budget, number seven," starts Leslie, almost apologetically. "It was the strangest concession that they made. And I was in need of money. I always seem to have a lot of things going on around me that fall apart with people close to me. And when I met the writers and I found out; they told me that I was the only female character they could write for. So that explains a little bit about why Marion ... it was low budget, made for video. When it opened I know it was a major release in Great Britain and Germany and all over the world, but not here, it went straight to video. There was some conflict in even getting that done, there was no press when it opened, but it was really bleak without the two of them in Moscow. It was really bleak in Moscow at that time anyway." She seems a little guilty that she went ahead and did the movie, despite all her friends getting ditched.

"Leslie, you appeared in *Baywatch*, didn't you?"

"Yeah."

"How was the Hoff? He's a legend in England."

"Oh, wonderful. Oh my gosh, I had to kiss him. He teased me about it and I teased him. I played the older woman and had to lay this kiss on him, so we did this scene and everybody's quiet, it was just a kiss. But he kissed me back. It was great ... it was fun. Afterwards I said it was so sweet of you and he said, 'I actually enjoyed it.' He turned it on and I responded."

"Did he slip the tongue?" I know, I know, I'm sorry. I just *have* to know.

"I don't know, I don't remember the tongue. I just remember how romantic it was and how focused he was." I bet he was.

The bill comes and these guys have got more to life than free lunch all day, so they start to wind it up.

"Thank you guys so much, your interest in the films seems to be really genuine and thanks for lunch, I mean, free food!" closes Leslie, slightly formally. "And if we do number eight, I'll do as much as I can to get you guys in the movie." Wow.

"We love you, thank you so much for being our fans and we hope to make many many many many many many many many more *Police Academy* films," says Marion while Leslie walks around the room kissing everyone and saying thank you so much and thank yous are flying around everywhere and kisses and it's all such a love in that I nearly pucker up for Bubba.

After Leslie's gone, we expect the other two to drift off pretty soon. But Bubba has bedded in. His backside has worked its weight and fused to the chair; he has the ballast to keep him sitting here for a while yet. Marion shows no sign of leaving either. It very quickly becomes the Bubba Smith show: he seems a lot more relaxed after the camera's gone off and he can talk about things unsuitable for even most adult audiences. Somehow, Marion gets talking about Bubba being "The Love Doctor". I thought she was just saying that because he'd had a fair few girlfriends, but it turns out he's a little more experienced than just a *few girlfriends*. The man is an insatiable libido on legs. He's everything Barry White could only sing about.

Love Doctor Bubba goes straight in with the cunnilingus. No messing around. He doesn't even give us the foreplay of discussion about how to cajole a woman into bed; he dives straight down between the legs, so to speak.

"You have to just flop your tongue right out..." he says slowly and expressionless in his Texan twang, flopping his tongue at the end to demonstrate. I find myself slightly tongue out too, the way you do unwittingly when you're watching someone do something on the telly. "And just let it drop onto the clitooorrrrrris." This giant from movies of my childhood is giving me a lesson in oral sex. I look nervously across to Marion to make sure her face hasn't turned sour through the rudeness, but she doesn't look in the least nervously back. She just nods in agreement. What the? I suspect she's heard all this from Bubba before.

"Some guys try it with a pointed tongue tip. *No.* You gotta cover the whole thing with your tongue." We giggle nervously, I'm sorry but I just wasn't expecting this. Bubba remains deadly serious and I reckon could go on for hours, mainly because he talks so slowly that each sentence seems to take five minutes to complete.

The conversation eventually sections itself off, with Marion chatting to Tom and Luke and me sitting watching Bubba demonstrate lady-licking to thin air. Bubba takes the opportunity to move closer to me and asks quietly, "So, what problems you got with women?" I'm being love-doctored. *But you're Hightower.* I'm not sure why he assumes I have problems with women. I must have that *can't-pull* face only a mother can just about decipher. But he's guessed right, I am a nightmare.

"Erm, meeting them."

"You know..." he sets himself up for a long one, "...the best thing to do is *shut up.* Just let your eyes catch theirs and then go over and talk to them quietly. You might get rejected six times out of ten but I can take that."

"But what if you can't take that sort of rejection?" I sneak in a George McFly line, undetected, because really, I don't feel like spilling my real emotional guts all over Hightower. If I start on the Elle episode, me and Bubba could be here for *days.*

"Then you don't get any woman." Point taken. I suppose it really is as simple as that.

Marion catches a break in the conversation and takes a chance to pull us all back together. From here onwards she seems to take on the role of presenting links into Bubba's stories, which keep us sitting here for another three hours. We begin back at college, where Bubba was *the man.* He tells us about the first time he planned to sleep with a girl. He'd heard so many stories of his older brothers coming home having been with girls that this moment was one he'd really been building up for. He went to the girl's house and they ended up in the bedroom, where she started undressing. To cut a short story short, he ended up messing in his pants instead of in her. Unfortunately, when he got home, his mother noticed the stains on his pants and said "Bubba, have you been premature?"

"Yes, Momma," he replied.

But it would seem that once he got going, he worked his way through half of the college. He tells us a story about a girl having sex with his knee while he watched the television, which frankly gives me the hump. I can't get women to have sex with the right bits, let alone the extravagance, the nonchalance of offering up a knee. Thankfully, he moves on to his football career and how he was a massive deal in the sports world back in the 1970s. Again, he was *the man*. During his bout of national superstardom, Bubba was paid by Jackie Kennedy to look after her kids (while security guards hovered constantly) and had his phone tapped by order of Hoover, who saw such huge fame of a black man as a threat to public order. During a trip to the White House for some posh dinner or other, he spoke to Hoover and asked, "Get any good stuff?" Hoover knew straight away that he meant the phone tapping, but Bubba didn't care, he wasn't doing anything wrong. I didn't realise quite how famous Bubba had been in America, and here he is now, sitting eating my lunch, being my *love doctor*.

At a party during the big time, Bubba says that someone once trod on his toes, by accident. Even if it was an accident, treading on the toes of a six foot seven inch man with *in-growing toenails* is guaranteed to land you in trouble, even if you *are* Richard Pryor. Bubba felt the anger bubble up as pain hit his brain and he grabbed Pryor by the throat (even though, he re-iterates, he's *not* a violent man).

"What did I do big guy?" Pryor blurted in a terrified high pitched voice. As Bubba tells the story, I can just imagine that shocked look on Pryor's face as he was elevated by his throat at the hands of a man Bubba's size. Bubba seems to think that Pryor eventually got his own back though: in the next comedy album he released, he told a story about a really stupid friend called Bubba. Bubba seems convinced that it was a dig at him and quizzed Pryor about it the next time they bumped into each other. Pryor denied it, but to this day Bubba feels maligned by it.

His stories of womanising are incredible and vast and outrageous. They make me feel like some sort of library-dwelling, carrot-juicing Mr Bean. There's one where he was sat in a plush penthouse with his girlfriend, and just out of her sight, three girls climbed onto the balcony and started signalling Bubba to make his excuses and go and meet them. He pretended to be tired, called the girlfriend a taxi and had his wicked way with all three girls. How could I have possibly guessed that this monster was having his cake and eating it all over the place when I watched *Police Academy* all those years ago? I sit open-jawed at the casual way Bubba feeds us stories that twenty years ago the tabloids would have plastered all over the nation's breakfast tables.

By the time his stories have been three hours in the telling, we're brewing up reasons to tell Bubba and Marion why we have to make a move. Eventually our standing over the table with jackets on and bags on our backs spurs Bubba to his feet. It takes him a few seconds, but once up straight, that man is *big*. The punishment his body took as a footballer has left its receipts, however, and when he walks he looks just a little precarious. Marion gushes about how she's loved meeting us and that she'll put a word in with Paul Maslansky to get us cameos in *Police Academy 8*. I love that it's mentioned as a "cameo". It'd be more like lucky *fans who got to walk past in the background*. We rave over the prospect anyway, of course, and thank our heroes wholeheartedly for so much of their time.

CHAPTER SIXTEEN SOUNDTRACK:

Who's Johnny

El DeBarge (1986)

Chapter Sixteen

Number Five IS Alive

Los Angeles

Now that we're completely Police Academied out, Bubba Smithed up to the eyeballs, it's time to move on to another of our eighties favourites.

SHORT CIRCUIT (1986) (Movie)
Director: John Badham
Writers: Brent Maddock, S.S. Wilson
Producers: Mark Damon, John W. Hyde
Cast: *Ally Sheedy (Stephanie Speck), Steve Guttenberg (Newton Crosby), Fisher Stevens (Ben Jabituya), Austin Pendleton (Howard Marner), G.W. Bailey (Skroeder), Tim Blaney (Voice of Number Five)*

Notes:
It took a lot of persuading Nanny Green to take me up to the (sadly now demolished) Odeon in Gants Hill to see this."I don't want to see a silly robot film," she said, "I'll be bored to tears," she said. But it was the school holidays: I forced her to take me and I demanded popcorn too. Despite those hard old Odeon chairs and the smell of bleach emanating from the dank cinema corners, she loved *every minute of it.*

We managed to get in touch with Eric Allard through some of the *Short Circuit* fan-sites, of which there are surprisingly many, and found out that he still has one of the Johnny Five robots made for the film. You see, Eric designed and built Johnny, he's Johnny's daddy, and the *actual* Number Five is still alive, in his Venice Beach lock-up.

Eric agreed to meet us at his lock-up for a meeting with his little Johnny, and when he turns up, late, I almost mistake him for The Dude, as per Jeff Bridges in *The Big Lebowski*. If not a dead physical ringer, he certainly has that more than easy-going air about him that makes you think he probably enjoys the good things in life a bit *too* much. Eric *lives* the beach; Hawaiian shirt with a pattern you wouldn't want to look at through a hangover, scruffy overgrown but somehow cool surfing old-timers hair, and tattoos in what looks like Arabic; that sort of affair. He's got the laid-back vibe of someone who doesn't take too much seriously; he doesn't flap at anything these days, he might not have made his money, but he's learned how *not* to earn money the hard way. He sort of eyes us suspiciously to begin with, checking out whether we're going to be weird and geeky or "suits" here to take his robot from him. But after *hellos and nice to meet yous*, he pulls open the doors to his lock-up, revealing machinery. A lot of machinery. Robots and engines and lots of heavy duty stuff with wires and clumps of bits I'll never understand. It smells of dust and grease and oil and electronics that have been obsolete for fifteen years; certainly not the shiny hub of cutting-edge creation. His stuff is *storage*, not ongoing projects. Loads of stuff is under covers that have half an inch of dust and dirt piled on them; it seems like a museum to a life Eric doesn't lead any more.

"So, this is where it all happens?" I ask.

"Actually, it didn't happen here. It used to happen at a much larger facility but I've given it up. I've moved on, I'm doing other things..." he replies with a mild edge of dignified resignation.

"There he is, it's Johnny Five! He's just been sitting around for years," Eric announces as he rips the dust cover off one of the mounds. Off comes a big sheet and underneath sits Johnny, perfectly kept and still shiny with his binocular-style eyes and wearing the same neckerchief he wore in the movie. Here come the flashbacks: *sitting with Nanny Green, in Gants Hill cinema, rooting for Johnny Five, go on my son, and I can see that Nan's enjoying it, which makes me love it even more because an adult has*

validated my kids' film, making it seem like it must be reeeeallly brilliant.
I've run out of popcorn though, which is devastating. But sod back then,
now here he is, right in front of me, Johnny Five, the same heap of wires
that kept me and Nan entertained all those years ago with his madcap
action adventure and his touching desire to prove he has emotions. But he
looks empty now, a mere shell of his former self with vacant eyes and a
paused expression.

"How many robots were there?" Luke asks.

"There were fifteen. Eight remote controlled versions and seven with no
motor in, they were the stunt robots. This was one of two of the remotes that
were most advanced. The only difference was that it had articulated fingers."
With that, I take a firm grip of his metallic hand and move his arm up and
down.

"Hi Johnny Five, I'm Spencer Derek Austin, very pleased to me you. We
met in Gants Hill once, a few years ago. Nanny Green sends her best wishes
and says that she's very glad that you got out of your pickle." OK, well, I
don't say *all* of that out loud. Johnny's arm makes all those robotic
mechanical noises you always think *must* be sound effects. I think Eric likes
to see this, people's faces when they meet the robot, he looks all proud, with
that *look what I done* face.

"How long did it take you to put the whole thing together?"

"It was actually from the time I got the job to the time we went into
production, which was about fourteen weeks. We made fifteen of them in
that time. This is *actually* number five of fifteen." The genuine *Number Five!*
"I remember we did a test and you've never seen so much smoke pour out of
something. Every wire just fried and we had thirty-six hours, so we went
ahead and got a new electronics supervisor and we got it built. They were *all*
used a lot, but this one was used mostly. He did the lion-share of the work,
he's genuinely number five and he started his life with a *real* short circuit!"
Oh, the utterly edible irony!

"His eyes are looking a bit lifeless at the moment," I say carefully, as
though standing over a patient who's his relative.

"Yeah, he needs a rebuild. One of these days, when I retire, I'll give him
a complete rebuild." Like the bathroom walls you're supposed to paint or the
banister you're supposed to repair; Eric *must* get around to rebuilding that
damn robot.

"I was just wondering how much you might expect to get for this on ebay?" Not that I'd have space in my rucksack, but he'd be a brilliant flatmate.

"I don't know but I might have to find out before too long. I've been an artistic type all my life, who puts *everything* into a project without paying much attention to business. I've been considering it, but this is one thing I've been holding on to." I hate that, seeing talented people who just haven't got the savvy for numbers.

"Were there no residuals on this fella?"

"Nope, nothing." Seems a familiar tale.

I ask him if he has fond memories of working on the films.

"Yeah, I gotta tell ya. You know, it's amazing because it was my first big break. They sent me the script and I knew, this is my break, *this* is my break. So I spent the weekend doing a thirty page proposal, breaking down every scene, working out how many robots we'd need, how many stunt robots we'd need, how many puppets we'd need. All of the pieces, like two days I spent. I went in the next Monday for what was supposed to just be a meeting to *see what you think,* and I laid *that* on them. They couldn't believe it, you know, that was it. And I understand that when I left the meeting, John Badham said, "that's the guy who's going to build my robots". I wish I'd known it at the time. But I went ahead at twenty-five bucks an hour as a parts man and built the robots."

"Did you interact much with the actors?"

"Oh yeah, in fact, my brother, who's a world class computer nerd, met with Steve Guttenberg a few times so Steve could work out how computer nerds act. A lot of his mannerisms came from him. The whole cast, Ally Sheedy, Fisher Stevens, they were all great. That was the best film experience of my whole career. Nothing else has ever equalled it. Even the second one, you know, the artistry of portraying Johnny Five on the screen was not as good as the first one. It was the best experience, and it was really because of John Badham. He respected what I was doing for him. He knew I was a hopelessly attention-deficit disorder kind of guy, you know, he knew how to work with people. He was in the shop two or three times a week through the whole twelve-week period we were filming it. There were six guys working in the shop and he knew *all* of their names."

"Would you do a third one if you were asked?"

"Yeah, yeah, I've got a great script for one actually. But it's a little hard to get into the club. Even if you have a great story and a good script ... I'm not in the club. It's basically about these megarobots..." Eric goes off on an incredibly long description of this story about nuclear bombs and silicon chips, and to be honest with you, he lost me early doors on the word "servo". He froths with passion, but it just goes a little over my very simple head. Eventually it sounds like Johnny Five gets involved and probably saves the world.

We ask Eric about some of the other stuff he's worked on, and it turns out that he was one of hundreds of techy people to have worked with Michael Jackson on that eccentric triumph *Moonwalker* in 1988.

"Did you have much to do with Michael Jackson?"

"Yeah, three of us went to a movie place and watched the movie to see where the robotic bits were going to go. And it was kinda weird because Michael had these sunglasses on, and when he went to talk, he took these sunglasses off and balanced them on his bottom lip." Eric demonstrates, with the lenses literally moved down from his eyes to cover his mouth and precariously balanced as he speaks. "And he started talking and I'm standing there all the time thinking ... and these other guys with him aren't reacting at all ... and I'm just thinking are these fucking things gonna fall off or what? It was *really* bizarre. And another time I met him at one of the other shops, there again he had his mask on and the whole thing, it was kind of eccentric. And then the third time at a recording studio, where he was doing an album at the time, he was so relaxed and personable and just a normal guy even with all the make-up on, you could see *that* was *his world*, he was in his element there. But he was a very charming, very nice guy."

All in all, I get the sense that Eric feels a bit bitter about the industry and how the money men always seem to get their way. He's a bit cloudy about what he does now, but I do hope he gets another crack with that nuclear bomb version of *Short Circuit 3*.

CHAPTER SEVENTEEN SOUNDTRACK:

(Just like)
Starting
Over

John Lennon (1980)

Holiday
Road

Lindsey Buckingham (1985)

Chapter Seventeen

Previous Lives

Los Angeles

Around lunchtime we spend about an hour trying to find the offices of a lawyer, even though we haven't done anything wrong. It's the first of two meetings that we've managed to cluster into the same day, with guys who found the big time very young and then went on to live normal, successful lives in other areas. Two guys with a positive outlook – that's refreshing in Hollywood. I can draw inspiration from them. You know, what with turning thirty and trying to let go of various elements of *my* past, maybe I'll draw something from the way they handle *theirs*. But apart from that, I'm *dying* to meet them.

"Jeff, is this right? The north bit of the road isn't connected to the rest of the road?" Jeff confirms on the phone that this is the case, and directs us succinctly. It's hot and the roads are bitches. But we have to get there, because we've only got a twenty-minute slotand he has another meeting this afternoon. I get all thirsty and snappy and headachy and might have a shout. But we've *got* to get there, I'd never forgive myself for missing out on this one.

Jeff has moved on since his fame in the eighties and is keen *not* to appear on camera, so we leave that contraption behind. But seeing as we've come *so* far, he's graciously agreed to meet us for an informal chat. It's amazing how many of these people feel *obliged* to do so, as though we've journeyed light-years to be here. I feel like more of a scroungey chancer than they perceive us to be, but that's fine by me. So, we get to the office and ask for Jeff. It's not an exceptionally plush office, just your standard *ring-binders and hole-punches everywhere* sort of basic office fodder; my basic nightmare. His secretary sits us down, calms us down, offers tissues for the sweat streaming down our faces, and I look around the walls at the movie posters. One is an original *E.T.* poster signed by Steven Spielberg: "To Jeff, you are my favourite Goonie." Only a few seconds later, a tiny man with a tight and curly but definitely diminishing bonce of locks with a carefully sculpted goatee beard skips through door. It only takes a second or so for my recognition module to kick in and spot that this guy still has traces of the eye glints and facial moments of the character he played in *The Goonies*: it's Chunk.

"Hi, I'm Jeff Cohen." I know, I think. I can totally see that now. *You're clearly Chunk; you've got the mole and the nose and the face, just like Chunk. Not the fat, not any more, but you still really are Chunk. Look at you. Chunk.*

"Why don't we go sit outside? It's nice out. Do you want a drink? I tell you what, you're English, do you want a beer? Come on, you've got to have a beer with Chunk." Well, if you insist. Of course, he's got a well-stocked fridge brimming with beer so cold it'll stab you between the eyes. He must have been doing the *yes, I'm Chunk from the Goonies* routine for nearly twenty years, but he doesn't seem tired of it.

So we sit on his sweltering Beverley Hills rooftop garden above the office, around his dark wood patio furniture, just hanging out, just knocking back some suds with Chunk. Oh yeah. Look at me, I'm da man. That's right, that's where *I'm* at, just chewing the fat with Chunk. He speaks to us like insiders, like co-conspirators and not the freaky geeky weirdies that he could easily handle us as. And for this twenty minutes of beer-fuelled Chunk, he makes us feel like we all lived the eighties *together*.

There's not even a flicker of visible regret in Jeff's demeanour that makes you think he rues not becoming the massive superstar actor that reaction to his role as Chunk suggested he might have been; in fact he seems glad his career moved onto something with a tad more reliable longevity.

"That's a surreal life, I'm glad at some of the choices I've made," he says. The roller coaster lives of the Coreys Feldman and Haim are good examples he cites as to why he's glad he didn't stay in front of the camera. It allows him to look back on *The Goonies* with fondness and affection; he loves the attention he gets in the street, or when he walks past someone who's wearing a Chunk T-shirt (although he jokingly enquires as to why he hasn't received any residuals from the Chunk T-shirt *Tom's* wearing. He is a lawyer after all). Meanwhile, I drink my beer far too quickly, due to the excitement of it all, and get more of a headache. I can also see my reflection in Jeff's mirrored sunglasses, which is unnerving.

"You didn't grow up to be a fat man then," I plonk with the verbal clumsiness of an oblivious grandad (with a headache).

"Thank you," he says graciously. "Everyone wants a chunk of Chunk." He's a slick talker, and everyone's favourite fat kid who's not so fat any more: he must do OK in the wooing department.

During filming *The Goonies,* Jeff tells us that Michael Jackson was on set quite regularly.

"He didn't touch me! Maybe he wasn't into the fat kid thing, I wasn't quite what he was looking for. He preferred the Culkin-esque types." He says that Corey Feldman at the time was a *massive* Michael Jackson fan and that, one day, Jackson gave him a pair of his sunglasses. Corey kept those precious glasses wrapped in tissue paper and cradled them like the tiny baby Jesus, only removing them for a look or a quick wear once or twice a day. One day, Jeff got hold of the glasses, hid them and wrapped something else up in the same type of tissue paper. He put the thing on the floor, shouted over to Corey, and stamped on what Corey thought were his precious precious Michael Jackson glasses. Corey went ballistic until he realised that it was a gag, and then went ballistic again.

With his lawyer's clock a-tick-tocking and sun-prone forehead cooking like a Spam fritter, we start ploughing quickly through the cast members with that irresistible question for each one: "What were they like?" We ask Jeff about Robert Davi, whom Paul Gleason told us the other day was a right royal pain. Jeff confirms that, though as diplomatically and lawyer-like as he can. He says that the Fratellis (Davi and Joe Pantoliano) throughout filming were in competition to hog the camera: *especially* Robert. He speaks with sadness about Jonathan Matuszak, the guy behind the Sloth mask that scared the crap out of me as a kid, who died in 1989 of heart failure.

We get to talking about Jeff's good friend Ke Quan, who played Data in the movie. He tells us about being sent abroad to promote *The Goonies* with Ke, and how because Ke had already been in *Indiana Jones and the Temple of Doom,* he was used to all the pampering and star treatment. While Jeff had his jaw swinging open at being sat in limousines and put up at the Savoy, Ke remained unimpressed because he'd had a longer limo and a more expensive suite when he was promoting *Temple of Doom.* Jeff and Ke have remained good friends and Jeff has taken to representing Ke in his current incarnation as a martial arts movie choreographer, which is all quite nice.

Jeff is a level-headed man who appreciates that he had an exceptional childhood; but now, with more than equable success in a different career as an adult, he can look back at all that *Goonies* stuff as a happy chapter that's now closed. I think for others, who didn't or couldn't cope with the early fame thing so well, closure never came; they never accepted that it was over. I draw relative comparisons to my life, and think about how now that I've finally accepted that Elle has gone, maybe I'm headed down the right road, the Cohen road. That's not to say Jeff doesn't still lead a showbizzy life. He tells us about a party he went to recently with Ke, where at one point he was standing chatting with Spielberg when Tom Cruise came up and said how much he enjoyed *The Goonies*. Even Spielberg was amazed that Tom Cruise had watched *The Goonies*. As he chatted with Cruise and Spielberg – as you do (though I like to call them Spielbers and The Tommulator) – the actress Jenna Elfman tried to nudge her way into the conversation, and where Jeff would normally grab an opportunity to slather over someone as eye-wateringly attractive as Elfman, he found himself moving round to block her off. All was well, until Ke started talking about *Temple of Doom* and Jeff got frozen out, at which point the Elfman option was more attractive. Even the parties in Hollywood are smothered in politics and snidey game play; I'd be far too cockney for all that subtle professional espionage. I'd probably end up trying to fight Gary Busey.

Before we leave, Jeff drags us into his office to show us pictures of his family. This peculiar but relaxed meeting is getting a bit personal. I just hope he doesn't start telling us all about cunnilingus – my experience of celebrity oral sex education is that it can take *hours*.

We swap business cards and exchange all those showy promises to keep in touch that I know won't happen. But that's fine, because *The Goonies* chapter of my life is over now. I love it like my toes, but it's time to move on.

"Shit, are you OK?" I say to Jason, half panicked, half trying not to show that I really want to allow a torrential laughing fit to screech out like an evil Skeletor cackle. Jason just took a spectacular tumble, an outrageous point seven on the Richter scale; almost a triple pike in Sally's front garden. He doesn't say a word though, simply gets up, brushes his knees off and carries on walking up the path; not even looking partially annoyed by it, not even mildly disgruntled, almost as if it was always going to happen and he accepts that. Maybe he falls over a lot. With Tom and me especially partial to losing it with giggling fits over the simple comedy standard of a fall – to the extent that I most definitely rate *You've Been Framed* as easily the best show on television – we have to spend the next hour trying to contain ourselves and not play it over and over in our minds. I'm doolally over a faller, I love it.

"You guys let it fly, whaddya wanna know?" In Sally's living room his voice catapults around the kitchen and bounces off the telly with everything else slightly rattled by the volume. He's a booming, confident friendly giant. Instantly likeable. It's hard to relate him to the gawky teenager he portrayed all those years ago: Jason played Rusty Griswald in *National Lampoon's European Vacation*. Back then he was sort of skinny, with these big bulbous blue eyes and fiercely ginger hair. Now he's a great hulking beast, certainly with a few extra pounds around the waist and a pork scarf under his chin. His hair has calmed down to more sand than rust but his eyes are still bulbous and warm.

"*European Vacation*. An absolutely classic film. What do you remember?" asks Luke.

NATIONAL LAMPOON'S EUROPEAN VACATION (1985) (Movie)

Director: Amy Heckerling
Writers: John Hughes, Robert Klane
Producers: Matty Simmons, Stuart Cornfield
Cast: Chevy Chase (Clark Griswold), Beverley D'Angelo (Ellen Griswold), Dana Hill (Audrey Griswold), Jason Lively (Rusty Griswold), John Astin (Kent Winkdale)

Notes:
What happened to Chevy Chase? In these movies he was unbeatable, the ultimate comic movie dad. What does he do now? These movies were *naughty:* delivering dead grandparents to other relatives, dragging a dog behind the car along the motorway, boobs and porking. But somehow there was no way a parent could look at them and tell you "you can't watch this". They were a harmless exaggeration of a family life that we could all identify with. Everyone had at least one of those family holidays that's just doomed from the start.

"It was my first big role. I mean, I'd grown up doing this stuff my whole life since I was eight years old. Did a bunch of commercials as a kid in Georgia, still just a regular kid, you know. Family moved out to LA when my dad was on the *Dukes of Hazzard*."

"I read *you* had a couple of roles in the *Dukes of Hazzard* too."

"Yeah, I did the pilot episode. I filmed that in Georgia when I was a kid. Funny thing is, and I didn't know this myself until I read it recently, my character's name was Rusty. So I was Rusty then as a kid, I played Rusty in *European Vacation* and then I did a two-hour *Movie of the Week: Gun Smoke* with James Arness, and I was Rusty in that." I wonder if his acting has got a bit rusty. Ha. Sorry.

"What did your dad do on *Dukes of Hazzard*?"

'There were one or two seasons where the mechanic, Cooter, left and then his cousin, L.B. Davenport came in. That was my dad and that's why we moved, because he was filming at Warner Brothers.

"Do people still recognise you as the *European Vacation* Rusty?"

"It's one of those movies that *has fans*, you know, which is great. I meet people like you guys who are younger than I am. It's great to do one of those movies that's sort of like one of those cult classics that they play every year so people can see. I get guys that come up to me and say, 'Dude, sign my hand, write *I think he's going to pork her!*'" This is of course in reference to the scene where a romantic couple are getting it on at the dinner table and Rusty says, "Dad. I think he's going to pork her." Dad replies with "He's not going to pork her, Russ," but then concedes, "He may pork her, but you finish your breakfast."

"It was great, overall an unbelievably great experience. He was Chevy Chase. *Chevy Chase*, who as great as he is now, at that time was phenomenal. I was doing a movie with *Chevy Chase*," he reiterates in mock boastful fashion, and rightly so. "And he was cool to me. He wasn't like, you know what I mean?" Erm, I think so.

"You mean he wasn't patronising?" clarifies Tom.

"I think only because I was working *with* him. Everyone else got it though, oh yeah, he's got a bit of an attitude."

"Was it quite weird having seen the first film [*National Lampoon's Vacation*] and then suddenly you're playing Rusty yourself?"

"Well, you know, it was. 'Cos I figured they only did that in soap operas ... here's the *new* Rusty, or here's the new whoever. But obviously I didn't care.

Anthony Michael Hall was great in the first one, and too bad he didn't get to go to Europe, *I* did, but at the time he was working *a lot*. He'd gotten onto *The Breakfast Club* and *Sixteen Candles* and *Weird Science*, and I'm not a hundred per cent sure, but I think he was under contract to Universal and this was a Warner Brothers film, and so they had to re-cast. It was fortunate for me because we looked similar enough and I liked to ad-lib. Quite a bit of that movie was ad-lib. And that's my specialty, I can B.S. with the best, and that's all it is. And the reason they wanted that is because Chevy will throw you stuff, you know, it's not even what you're doing but it's so funny and they wanted people to play along with it. And that's how a couple of the scenes were started. The scenes on the train ... and was from improv and Amy Heckerling [the director] was bright enough to go oh, this is a good scene, let's make something of it. We were doing the scene, I was doing my thing with the headphones ... and he was doing his and he tells me "shhhh". And I turn to him and he grabs my arm and does the Indian burn ... and aagh ... it's the real deal. None of that was ... I didn't know he was..." Jason has a very lively mind, excuse the pun, but he has, and he seems to flit around; managing to get a story out without really finishing many sentences. "And another scene I remember real clear ... the traffic circle ... with the "Look kids, Big Ben, Houses of Parliament." My favourite scene. Most people's favourite scene. It was just pure genius: the Griswalds in their silly little car, going around and around the roundabout at Parliament Square in London. Even now, when I'm in a car, at almost every roundabout I end up saying, "Look kids, Big Ben, Houses of Parliament," and almost anyone who's in the car with me knows exactly what I'm talking about. In fact, quite a lot of them admit to doing it themselves. Hysterical, do you remember? Because he was sort of laughing and crying at the same time. *'I can't get left!'* It probably took twenty plus takes."

"So you were literally going round and round and round?"

"Well, no. We were in a sound stage, but we were laughing and we were supposed to be asleep ... and then I would feel Dana [Hill, who played his sister Audrey] start to shake and we were quivering. At least one of us couldn't keep it 'cos he was just too funny."

"You got one of the lucky scenes too, in Germany with the topless girl..."

"Oh yeah, are you kidding? A sixteen year old kid getting paid for that? She helped me get a fine appreciation for good looking women. I did what I had to. Somebody had to do it and I said alright, I'll do it. I think that's why people like the character. Most people, guys and girls, can appreciate the horny teenage kid. I was lucky enough to play that likeable character."

"When you were in England, you worked with loads of famous British comedians; did you know who they were at the time?"

"You know, Eric Idle of course, from Monty Python. The idea I think was to hire local celebrities because they have their own local draw, which I think was a smart move. Willy Millowitsch was also a big German actor."

"You didn't know who Mel Smith and Maureen Lipman were at the time?"

"No. But they let us know, it was like so and so is working on...and they work a lot here ... and so on. When you work on a film, and especially when you're travelling with your core group, it really is like a family."

"Did you see many of the Griswolds much after shooting?"

"Yeah, I kept in touch with Dana. But you know what happened with Dana? She died a few years back. She had a long battle with diabetes. But we did keep in touch. Chevy, you know, I got the Christmas card every year from *his people*. You know what I mean? I don't know how much time *he* spent stuffing envelopes. I actually ran into Chevy not that long ago at a golf tournament. So I mean, we do run into each other occasionally, but we don't go for a family dinner."

"How come you didn't do any of the other Vacations afterwards?"

"Well, if you look at it, the time line doesn't ring true. Because of the kids' ages, they bounce around. When it came time for the *Christmas Vacation* the kids were even younger than we were. So that was kind of a prequel, supposedly. And then it came time for *Vegas*, they thought heck it doesn't matter, the kids are all different ages anyway. I think another reason they didn't use Dana and I was because it had been another three or four and instead of being sixteen we were twenty, you know what I mean?"

"I don't really remember the Rusty characters from the other films," slurps Luke, looking at Jason like *he's the one*.

"'Cos you got the real Rusty right here. I think Chevy even said on one of the DVDs, "Oh, it doesn't matter about the kids, no one cares about the kids anyway." I was like oh, really. It was different writing as well, my script was written by John Hughes, who's a master of teen film, and so he played up those aspects and in other ones they didn't."" Yup, John Hughes haunts us every step of this trip.

"So what's next for you?"

"I'm a family guy now." He proudly gets out the Lively family picture, the kids and all that stuff. "I do projects, I produce and direct, my dad's got a sound-stage. A lot of independent stuff.

"You worked with Corey Feldman, right?"

"Yeah, I should have called him for you, have him come with me." Errr yeah, you bloody should have. "Yeah, Corey Feldman, Corey Haim, any of those eighties type kids, we all grew up in the same business, same town, and we used to hang out. I didn't hang out all the time, sometimes. I'm glad that things are going well for him [Feldman] now and that he's got his life on track. This town's rough. For so many people that are successful there are so many others that don't make it and they really have a hard time dealing with it. Especially if they achieved some level of success younger, you know. Kids that I knew here, I've got two friends ... P. Pruett, this guy was great looking, super talented ... you should have seen the beautiful girls at this guy's funeral ... died of a heroin overdose ... Christina Applegate there, boo-hooing. This was one of our good friends. Rodney Harvey ... Rodney and P. Pruett were both on *The Outsiders*, the TV series ... both of those died of a heroin overdose. And you have to think that the town had a good bit to do with it. Just because of what all the people go through. Not that it doesn't happen to other people in other lifestyles, people get hooked on drugs and die everywhere, but I think it's an easy escape for people who don't know what to do later on. And that's why it's nice to see Corey has got things back together. We used to all get together, like Corey Feldman, Rodney Harvey and Matthew Perry, a whole bunch of actors; none of them were huge, just actors trying to earn a living. The business, I'm sure not gonna knock it, 'cos I don't think that. I think you ultimately choose the path that you take. And I was fortunate enough to have some great doors opened and got to do some things that most people don't get to do. Especially at that age. It's a good thing as long as you keep a sense of reality."

Again, just like Jeff, Jason closed his bygone chapters and moved on. I'm learning my lesson really quite sharply now. I *could* be all bitter and Miss Haversham about the past, sitting for years in a darkened room wearing my Frankie Goes to Hollywood "RELAX" T-shirt and leg warmers, playing *Jet Set Willy* on the Spectrum, *or* I could see it all fondly from a distance and be quite happy about where I'm headed. It's my choice and, really, it *is* a choice. I'll be alright, I'll move on. I'm no Haim, not these days.

CHAPTER EIGHTEEN SOUNDTRACK:

Surfin U.S.A.

The Beach Boys (1965)

You're the Best

Joe Esposito (1984)

Chapter Eighteen

Teen Spirit

Los Angeles

Just like Jason Lively said; for every one of those young stars who go on to be a grown-up success, there's one who didn't. And fresh from the inspiration he and Jeff gave me on how to move on; we dip over to the other side, the world of *not doing so good*, when we visit Mark Arnold, who played Mick: Michael J. Fox's heavy-eye-browed, chisel-jawed, basketballing, womanising bloody annoyingly good-looking antagonist in *Teen Wolf*.

TEEN WOLF (1985) (Movie)

Director: Rod Daniel
Writers: Jeph Loeb, Matthew Weisman
Producers: Thomas Coleman, Michael Rosenblatt
Cast: Michael J. Fox (Scott Howard), James Hampton (Harold Howard), Susan Ursitti (Lisa "Boof" Marconi), Jerry Levine (Rupert "Stiles" Stilinski), Matt Adler (Lewis), Lorie Griffin (Pamela Wells), Jim McKrell (Vice Principal Rusty Thorne), Mark Arnold (Mick McAllister), Jay Tarses (Coach Bobby Finstock), Mark Holton (Chubby)

Notes:
Teen Wolf was actually shot *before Back to the Future*, but ended up being released *after* it. In it, Michael J. Fox as Scott didn't know that his whole family were werewolves. He just hadn't noticed. So, it was quite a surprise when puberty started throwing in little added bonuses like wildly excessive body hair (think Richard Keys on Sky Sports) and fangs. Then the writers added Stiles, an eighties-style entrepreneur type, who saw his school mate turning into a werewolf and decided to earn a packet out of making him a local superstar.

I first saw *Teen Wolf* at the old cinema in Southend: all red curtains and organ music and seats that'll break your arse bone after five minutes. My aunt took me with my five cousins, all of whom are brothers and all are younger than me. It was chaotic, to say the least. I've never known such a din at the pictures; this movie got a packed theatre of E number addled Essex kids so excited that it was like being at a local derby football match. The adrenalin was phenomenal, we were totally out of control for that *Teen Wolf* fella, he was *wicked*; and I'm sure at various stages of the film, we all totally forgot it wasn't actually real.

Before wandering into an area of LA that we really don't fancy too much (to meet Mark), we decide we should refresh our memories of *Teen Wolf* by scooting around a few of the locations used in the movie. Just to get that wolfy flavour back.

We've already been to Bushnell Avenue, where Tom climbed the tree in honour of George McFly, but the street's movie archaeology isn't confined just to *Back to the Future*. While we were there the other day, we discovered that the very same house used as Lorraine's in *BTTF* was also Scott's house in *Teen Wolf*. I didn't mention this before. Sorry. Nor did I didn't mention that when we left Bushnell Avenue, we hoisted a tree-scratched Tom up onto the roof of the Oldsmobile (Luke or I may have buckled the roof into a metal hammock with our weight; Tom's a slip of a thing, so up he went) and drove along with him standing up, surfing the car just like Teen Wolf did on the van in the movie. As far as I know, Tom didn't perform the acrobatics wolfy did, but he was up there for, ooh, around ten yards before I heard words being screeched like "stop" and "bastard" and "decapitated" Amused by the fuss, because really, I wasn't going that fast (was I?), I kept on going a few yards, happily humming "Surfin' USA", the song Teen Wolf dances to atop the van, before practising my emergency stop (I haven't done one since my driving test). Something flopped forward onto the bonnet. It was Tom. *Hello there, Tom.*

So, that was our first taste of Teen Wolfiness, and today, with Mark expecting us in a couple of hours, we go via Tony's Liquor Store.

"Give. Me. A. Keg. Of. Beer." Tom says slowly, gruffly (well, Rula Lenska gruff more than werewolf gruff), and unfortunately without even a hint of the menace that Teen Wolf conveyed. To be fair, Tom's not *actually* a werewolf. This is the very liquor store where Scott managed to extract a keg from the eanie-meanie owner who *never* let the kids have beer. It was all part of Scott using *the wolf* to become Mr Popular. The store looks the same, a sort of shabbyish box building sitting there all on its own on a busy street with the same old "Tony's Liquor Store" sign on the frontage. Inside, the till has moved a bit closer to the door, but all in all, it's an offy, that's all. It sells loads of booze, simple as that. Leave it there.

The Asian guy in the store finds the video camera suddenly dropping in on his Monday afternoon and Tom saying these unusual things quite amusing. He barely speaks English and has no idea that we're referring to *Teen Wolf,* or that the scene was even shot in this store.

"Teen Wolf?" I ask. Not that it's a question, but it comes out like one.

"No." He giggles away with it all, quite happily. It seems a delicious folly for all of us.

"The movie?" Still not a question, but I'm asking it anyway.

"No." This is even funnier, apparently. "Give. Me. The ID Please," the guy says, replicating Tom's tone and intonation. He does it very well actually, and finds the whole thing really quite playful and pleasant. He's giggling like a night out with Cannon and Ball. So that was that. A peculiar incident, really. We leave keg-less (because we didn't actually want one anyway), and maybe he'll speak of the strange men with their camera and funny accents for weeks to come. Or maybe he's forgotten us already. I can't really decipher quite what sort of social interaction just happened.

Over at Lennox Middle School, we find someone to let us into the school gym. The bleachers are the same, but actually folded up flat against the wall and the dressing rooms are the same sweat-misted set of coat hooks and loud-slamming metal lockers we see in the film. It's all just the same. We head straight for the coach's office, which we can see through a window in the corner, and that hasn't changed either. I remember the scenes where Scott goes in there to talk to the coach about dropping out of the team.

We find a basketball and it somehow feels really weird to be sprinting about on the same court as Chubby and Scott and Mick, and of course, the Wolf. It's a little bit like getting a run out at Wembley. I've gone all conspicuous and naughty, all unnecessary. Feels a bit silly that I'm doing this. My head feels enormous because the school coach guy is watching; it's a real whopping pumpkin this time, massive. It takes about three minutes to get just a little bit exhausted, wheezing like an Alsatian in a Fiat Panda in a car park in the summer, so Tom gets out his really bad wolf mask. I'd never get that on my prize-winning pumpkin, especially with Coach standing there all judgemental. So I stand under the hoop, being a dejected (markedly less dashing) Mick in our version of that furiously slow-motion climax that had the Southend cinema I watched it in screaming like a *Grange Hill* civil war, in which he Scott shots a last-minute winner to prove that he *could* be a winner without his special powers. Probably another of those eighties movie moral messages that say *hey kids, anyone can achieve anything if you put your mind to it* and *you don't have to be a superhero to be a hero.* Didn't work on me. It just made me want to be a werewolf, even more than before.

And so on we drive, like I said before, to a part of LA we don't fancy that much. It's run down and has those tell-tale front garden chicken wire fences you see on *Cops*. It feels like a difficult, tense area and we wonder whether we've got the address wrong. Surely Mick from *Teen Wolf* doesn't live amongst this? This is when I start to wonder whether life's not been especially kind to him since *Teen Wolf.*

We find what *must* be the right address and see a very thin, worn-looking man sitting out on the porch. It's Mark Arnold. He greets us with a face that seems like it needs approval. He's in his late forties now, but Mark still has that classic, angular good-looking face, the dark, strong features; but now there are heavy scored lines; deep wrinkle tracks in all the places that aren't worn in by smiling. He invites us round the back of his tired-looking house. He seems neither proud nor ashamed of it, nor gives the impression that it's especially *his own*, it just feels like a place to stay, for now. We get round to the back garden, which has nothing in it, it's just a grass and concrete space. Just a few plastic patio chairs. We set up our cameras. I can't quite put my finger on it, but the minute I met him I sensed something weighing heavy on this man's mind.

"Of course, you played Mick, Michael J. Fox's arch nemesis; do you still have fond memories of the film?"

"I do. It was a quick shoot, about a month. Michael did it while on hiatus from *Family Ties*. I think it's a film that nobody... You know when I read the script, I was an actor looking for work, when I heard the title, I thought hmmmm, it's not a great title and then I read the script and it was better than the title, and then I saw the movie and it was a better movie than the script, I think. In that sense I think we kind of lucked out. In any project like that, whether it's a play or anything where a lot of people come together to collaborate, a lot's gotta go right. It was a pleasant time. It was a quick shoot and it was a lot of fun."

"Although it came out afterwards, it was actually shot before *Back to the Future*, wasn't it?"

"Yeah, we started it, Michael was shooting it on his hiatus and then Eric Stoltz was let go on *Back to the Future*. And Michael was cast in that about a week and a half before the end of shooting *Teen Wolf*. So by the end of it, he was doing *both* films. He was being shuttled back and forth."

"I've read Michael J. Fox's autobiography; he mentions *Teen Wolf* a couple of times and isn't particularly complimentary about it, why do you think?"

"You'd have to ask Michael, but I remember him saying one thing when we were filming that he could just see it now in the trades, the headlines would be '*Fox's dog as Wolf*'. So, you know, I mean it was in a *hair suit*, I mean it's a risky thing for him to have done. And he's gone on to do some great work. He did some great work in this, it's just that it's kind of silly and it's a werewolf movie. I'm certainly not ashamed of it, but *I* wasn't in a wolf costume."

"At what point in your career did you get Teen Wolf?"

"It was fairly early on, out of college I got a TV Movie of the Week and then some soaps in New York. Then I didn't feel comfortable in the soaps, although I had some good success, I did *The Edge of Night* first and then moved over to LA. I was looking for work, wanted to keep challenging myself. *Teen Wolf* was a low budget film and I guess I was very fortunate to get into it. Michael auditioned me and ... it's just really hard to get a job, it *is*, there's too many actors, and you're just grateful for anything you get." Mark's talking in a low tone and has quite a depressive outlook on the industry and how tough it is to get work. As he speaks, his tone gets a bit lower and it's like he's talking himself into a bit of a funk.

"Was it weird being auditioned by another actor?"

"No, it was actually nice. Because it was on camera and it was you know, it wasn't a studio picture and there wasn't a lot of approval going on. It was a large role for a virtual unknown in that sense."

"In England, people still have really fond memories of the film, is it the same here?"

"Yeah, in the sense that it's on TV the whole time, it's on cable, it's on Turner all the time."

"Do you watch it?"

"No, I mean I may watch it for a minute if I pass by it. Other people have favourite bits, but I don't really. It's just part of the mosaic of what you do."

"He was a nasty piece of work, wasn't he?"

"Mick? Yeah, he was this guy who's a convict; there was a line in there that he was a convict, that he had been held back by a few years. That was to explain my age I guess." I don't know what's going on, but Mark just seems like he's turning more morose as he speaks to us, perhaps it's all this reflecting on the past, maybe it makes him maudlin, I don't know, but it's tangible to us sitting here in his perfectly sunny back yard.

"Mick went out with Pamela Wells, played by Lorie Griffin. Was there any off-camera wotsit going on?" Suddenly Mark starts to grin.

"Not for me..."

"Oh really ... anyone else?" Tom gets the sniffter of a bit of something or other.

"Maybe ... maybe ... I can't tell that ... it's not for me to say ... I can't tell that ... all I can say was that it wasn't me." We goad him and plug away, almost just as happy that this is a subject that gets him smiling a bit, but there's no cracking him. "You know, there's often that sort of stuff when you're filming. Especially when you're that age. But no, not for me." Doh.

"Do you still get recognised for *Teen Wolf?*"

"I get recognised for *Teen Wolf* more than anything else. My experience in soaps tells me that your recognisability factor is as high as the frequency you're on TV. So the deal I went through was that when I was doing soap operas I'd get recognised a lot. And then when I stopped doing them there was a period when people would say, 'Didn't I go to high school with you?'because that was the period they watched the show so they associated me with that period of their lives. But I *didn't* go to their high school. But now I get recognised for *Teen Wolf* more than anything else because of the frequency it's on TV. It's never left the air in all these years and I don't know why. Guys like you come up and say, 'Oh God man, I loved that movie' and and it has to do with that age bracket getting older. I knew it was popular then, because it made a lot of money, something like $50 million dollars, so you knew it was popular then. It's like a rock and roll song; if there's a song you really liked in high school, you'll always have a fond memory."

"There's a scene at a party where everyone's writhing around and dancing ... is that how you remember eighties parties?"

"I might have been locked in a closet at sixteen playing spin the bottle. But with all shaving foam everywhere? No. I mean, those party scenes are always ... well, I've never been to a party like that."

"It seemed to be essential that women flashed their boobs spontaneously in eighties party scenes."

"Well, yeah, they did, and we were glad they did. I think they flash more now, I think women are more comfortable with their bodies now." Amen. It's just mine they're not comfortable with.

"Did you see *Teen Wolf Too* at all?"

"I did not. I don't know why. I heard it wasn't very good."

"If someone came to you today and said we're doing *Teen Wolf Three...*"

"The geriatric version?"

"There's a million dollars on the table ... are you in?"

"Of course I would. I'm not stupid. I wanna work. But no one's gonna ask me to do it. But work's work."

"So what *have* you done since *Teen Wolf?*" I'm nervous of asking this question, I can tell there's a story to tell here, and it's just a case of whether he wants to off-load it all on a couple of strangers.

"Well it's been very up and down. Partly at my own hand. After *Teen Wolf* I did another soap. And then I kind of ran out of money and went back to New York and I did regional theatre for a while and had a nice little career in that, but it doesn't pay a lot of money. Then I moved back out here and I kind of drifted out of the business for a while. I started working at a post-production company for a while, making TV commercials and movie trailers and I sort of climbed that corporate ladder and I was being groomed to be a writer-producer for that. But it's not what I wanted to do. As good as those guys are, it's good money, it's part of the studio system, it's high pressure, I left that and right now I'm currently kind of rebuilding my career. I got to a point in my life where I really thought of what's important to *me*. I want to do things that make me happy, that give me pleasure in terms of my soul and in terms of my creativity. I also started to write, I had a short play that was produced off-Broadway, which was fun. I wanna do more of that, but I've been reconfiguring my life and I'm getting to the point now where things are getting interesting. It's been a long road back. I kind of kept my hand in the business in that I would occasionally do a play and some commercials to make some money. But I kept drifting out of it and I just couldn't understand it, it felt weird and it was frustrating and it was very unforgiving; this business can be *very unforgiving*. And then several events happened and I just thought *what am I going to do from this point on?* So I decided to kind of head back in. I'm currently doing two plays and I've been working consistently all year, in theatre. Once again, you're grateful for any job that you have and we'll see how it goes."

The camera goes off, and as we've found with a lot of these interviews, the subject often opens up even more when the camera goes off than they would have done if we'd never brought the camera along in the first place. There's something about the moment the camera goes off; a sense of relief. And the same goes for Mark.

He starts by apologising for his performance on camera, he feels like he may have paved over cracks with generic *I'm OK* stuff that doesn't really represent his situation. What follows is an awkward privilege that we're allowed in on, a moment when a man who's had some tough tough luck decides to talk about his ordeals to two complete strangers (one of whom has only just respectfully taken off his rubbish werewolf mask). In fact, it's such a privilege that I don't feel any of it should be discussed here, I'd feel cheap and sensationalist and it would be wrong. But as he talks us through it all, unhindered by the cameras, he's close to tears: bitter, sad, regretful tears that make me truly feel for the guy. Was that five minutes of movie fame as Mick worth it? I wonder. But at least now, he's getting up off his knees and attacking the world from a new angle, and I really hope that works for him.

As much as Lively and Cohen showed me how the past can be assigned to pleasant memories and a good life *can* exist in the present, Mark Arnold has shown me what can happen if you don't move on. And it scares me.

The second part of our day exploring eighties teen stories leads us to the Californian coast. While we're there, it would be rude and foolish not to want to run topless and slow motion on the Will Rogers State Beach, in honour of The Hoff and the team on *Baywatch*.

BAYWATCH (1989-2001) (TV)

Cast: David Hasselhoff (Lt Mitch Buchannon), Jeremy Jackson (Hobie Buchannon), Pamela Anderson (Casey Jean Parker), Michael Newman (Mike "Newmie" Newman), Chris Fiore (Brad), David Chokachi (Cody Madison), Brooke Burns (Jessie Owens), Alexandra Paul (Lt Stephanie Holden), Yasmine Bleeth (Caroline Holden), David Charvet (Matt Brody), Gregory J. Barnett (Jim Barnett), Erika Eleniak (Shauni McClain), Billy Warlock (Eddie Kramer), Monte Markham (Captain Don Thorpe), Gregory Alan Williams (Sgt Garner Ellerbee), Michael Bergin (Jack "J.D." Darius), Gena Lee Nolin (Neely Capshaw), Nicole Eggert (Summer Quinn), Kelly Packard (April Giminski)

Notes:

Pornography. Simple as that. *Baywatch* sold in 148 countries, and in the same way that in some places Fashion TV is seen as a legitimate, artistic channel, but is still a way for men to get cheeky looks at the female form, *Baywatch* was cloaked in its stories and melodrama as a method of delivery for the drug of semi-naked flesh. Bravo to it too.

Well, the topless and slow-motion bit was a mistake. It's not a great pleasure looking at your muscle-less flaps of boob and belly from the confines of the bathroom; let alone when you're running along the *Baywatch* beach, in slow motion. On the tape, it actually looks like with any one of those bounces either a tit – flapping up and down like half-filled water balloons attached to a sprinting dog's collar – or the entire belly button area – like a huge vibrating uncooked donut – might actually just bounce so hard it'll tear off. I need to get in shape. What if The Hass had been here, looking for extras for a comeback series?

The beach is pretty packed: tinny radios playing in various groups; the smell of coconutty sun creams that put your brain directly into beach mode; the sound of distant kids' screams being fuzzed over by the gentle but authoritative rhythm of the foamy lapping waves. A place to lazily worship the hazy LA sun where occasionally a heroic breeze coolly defers the burning heat and the sand gets in your boiled egg sandwich. It's what you would expect of a beach in California: those with bronzed, sculpted bodies swan around so self-conscious that they probably find it impossible to relax their stomach muscles. But actually, the beautiful bodies are outnumbered by those plagued by the American disease, the obese, straining to keep enlarged bits of themselves tucked into bikinis or Speedo trunks pulled up high enough to kid the wearer into thinking the belly is invisible. Some of them are so habitually tanned that they've gone a boot-polish brown that when oiled looks like a pan of fried sausages and when dry like an old leather coat. There are Frisbees and windshields and us, wobbling for *Baywatch*, anaemic skin flushing rash-red with burn within minutes; really showing everyone that we're first-timers here ... and wasn't *Baywatch* just *brilliant* early Saturday evening porn.

We find the main control centre at Station Fifteen, which featured heavily in the show, and it looks pretty much the same – apart from some stairs that led down to the beach have been ripped out since the show finished. The occasional lifeguard hut on stilts up and down the bay seems emblematic of the show. Having humiliated ourselves quite enough with the obligatory (but awkward) sprint down the beach, we get talking to one of the lifeguards who was around at the time of filming. He's your basic bleach-blonde muscle-monster with gingernut biscuit brown skin and that air of chilled indifference. The guy seems to stare off into his *good place* – somewhere between the beach fatties and the horizon – as he talks fondly of those days when the TV producers shipped in the silicone to bomb up and down the beach posing as lifeguards.

He says that, generally, everyone was very nice: Pammy and Erika and especially in this guy's eyes, Yasmine Bleeth, "Man, she was just perfect." I tend to agree. We ask if any of the lifeguards there had ever had a crack at the actresses, who, given the show's worldwide popularity, must have been some of the most admired, desired women in the world *in history*.

"Nahhh, there was none of that. The nearest it got was one of the guys dated an extra a couple of times and that was it." For some evil, selfish reason, I'm pleased that those uniformed beach bums never got their salty lifesaving mitts on my Yasmine.

The guy chuckles when we merely mention David Hasselhoff. Silly question, but what was *specifically* so funny about The Hoff? Well, on the *first* day of shooting *Baywatch*, The Hoff got caught in a riptide and had to be rescued. I would love to have seen a struggling, flailing Hass all dressed up in his lifeguard uniform, air-conditioned-gym muscles flexing uselessly against the giggling waves; having to be dragged out by a *real* lifeguard, snot streaming down his chin. Somehow they managed to keep that episode of the *Baywatch* story *out* of the papers.

Further north and up in the Malibu area, we find Paradise Cove, where we'd read that a pier was used to film the scene in *Indecent Proposal* where Woody Harrelson and Demi Moore reunite. In the film, they sit back to back on some sort of bench, and stage a gooey reunion by holding hands without seeing each other. Blurggh. But we just thought we'd swing by on our way to the next beach, a throwaway stop-off. The pier is closed. Barbed wire and everything. It has no bench and there is nothing to suggest that the film was shot here. Fair enough, let's go.

I begin walking away but Tom *really* wants to film it. I see no point; the film wasn't even shot in the eighties and there's nothing to actually film other than an old broken pier through chicken wire with bits of shredded up old carrier bag flapping away in the breeze. Tom's not happy. He goes bright red and if he goes any redder his head may explode, like in *Scanners*. The problem is, the more livid he gets, the more Luke and I laugh. You see, I mentioned early doors that I was worried about Tom's over-obsession, his fastidious rather than romantic view of the tour and how this might clash with my admittedly sopping wet emotional journey. And now it's coming to a head. With the battering romp of a schedule that LA's provided us with, Tom's fed up with being denied his obscure locations, the tenuous and unspectacular ones that Luke and I are fed up with constantly having to go to just to indulge him.

We have a nostalgia gulf. It's the positioning of the compromise line that's the problem: Tom feels like we're not passionate enough to want see the *everythings,* while we think he's bonkers mad to *want* to see the absolute *everythings.* We feel like we're indulging him enough; he doesn't. And now, at this poxy *Indecent Proposal* non-eighties *probably wasn't the pier they used* location, Tom's about to blow up and we find it so silly that we can't help but giggle. However, the tense stand-off in no-man's land eases, Tom's not one for anger after all, and he tucks it back with all the other repressed emotions. The thought of getting onto the *Karate Kid* beach shoves his fervour into the more positive pursuit of finding the Leo Carillo State Beach. Phewww.

KARATE KID (1984) (Movie)

Director: John G. Avildsen
Writer: Robert Mark Kamen
Producer: R.J. Lewis
Cast: Ralph Macchio (Daniel Larusso), Pat Morita (Mr Kesuke Miyagi), Elisabeth Shue (Ali Mills), Martin Kove (John Kreese), Randee Heller (Lucille Larusso), William Zabka (Johnny Lawrence)

Notes:
There are no official stats – it would be impossible – but I suspect that even above *Rocky, Karate Kid* was probably responsible for more playground injuries than any other film. That crane kick. The amount of times either the kicker would mess it up and fall arse over wotsit on the hard concrete ... ending in tears ... *or*, the kickee would take a foot to somewhere higher than the kicker intended ... ending in tears. Personally, I still have a chipped tooth from a random crane kick attack at lunchtime.

The sky is just starting to bruise as we arrive at the Leo Carillo State Beach; an idyllic spot in a curvy sun-blessed cove, with gulls flapping serenely and the waves fizzing their way gently over the sand like a spilled glass of lemonade on carpet. This is altogether a different beach to good old Will Rogers', this one has a touch of the wild about it: it's rocky and pebbly with long wild grass poking out of the sand wherever it can. There are little cliff edges hanging over the coast that are easy to climb from where you can look out across the more choppy sea and whippy breezes.

The silhouetted image of Daniel in that crane pose is one of the signature motifs of the eighties. Even the girls at school didn't mind having a go at the crane kick; it was awesome. So we stand on any old log – we haven't found *the* log yet – trying to keep our balance in something approximate to the crane position. Arms stretched out with limp, bent wrists and one leg kicking out, doing the crane kick, oblivious to people and their dogs laughing at us. Even the dogs are laughing. Lucky, then, that we've arranged to meet someone who can teach us to do the crane kick in a little more dignified, technically accurate manner. On time, along comes a squat, muscular little forty year old man named Darryl Videl. An incredibly personable fellow who has just popped away from his job somewhere in the region of computers to meet us. He's clearly of Asian decent, I clumsily assume somewhere in the China region and has a thinning pate of jet black hair that I suspect was once very thick.

He pops his trousers off and quickly hauls on a freshly washed and ironed karate outfit. As he does so, we politely avert eyes and ask him to tell us the story of how he developed the famous crane kick for Ralph Macchio and Pat Morita to perform in *Karate Kid*. This man *created* the crane kick. Not only that, but he played Vidal – Daniel's semi-final opponent in the movie.

"Did you actually train Ralph Macchio?"

"Well, what they did was, I used to compete in the Los Angeles area a lot and I won this one division in LA and the director's assistant came to me and asked if I wanted to get involved in this movie, and of course I did. So after they got the group together, they had Pat Johnson, who was the stunt co-ordinator, he run classes for like six weeks with all the Cobra Kai boys and Daniel. So we got to train together for quite a few weeks."

"Were they any good?"

"Actually, they were fairly athletic guys. The guy who played Johnny, William Zabka, was pretty athletic, so he did a fairly good job of fitting right in and doing it."

"And what did you think of Ralph Macchio's karate abilities?"

"Well to be ... er ... I don't wanna..." Ha ha, Macchio was shit! Turns out Karate Kid was shit at karate!

"He was an actor..." I say to help him phrase it politely.

"He *is* an actor, and you know when we were watching the filming it was very unbelievable. But when it came out on film, it looked pretty believable. I mean, most martial artists will look at it and say it looks set up but it came out better on film than I imagined. At the time he was *a lot* smaller than me."

"Were you good friends with him?"

"No, by no means..."

"You hated him?" I bait.

"No, I would never say that. Actually, I only talked with him a few times during the production. He was always coming to training and then leaving so we never got too personable."

"And what about Mr Miyagi, because you doubled for him didn't you?" Actually, we tried to get in touch with Pat Morita before we left. I had his home number and he had a sweet little recorded voicemail machine message. I left him a few messages but decided to leave him alone when there was no reply. He's since died, sadly.

"Oh, he was great. Just like you would imagine him, with his humour when you see him on television. He was really a great guy. In fact, because we worked at the beach, we spent a week or two together, he was fantastic, very nice, I liked him a lot."

"Did you keep in touch?"

"Well, it's funny, when it was my thirtieth birthday, which was thirteen years ago, my wife got hold of him and asked him to call during my surprise birthday party. And he called me, during his busy schedule, and he talked to me and remembered me – it was pretty surprising, a real neat surprise. I doubled for him when he was on the wooden post during the crane technique scene, that is me."

"So you devised, or created the crane kick?"

"Well let me clarify that because it seems to be a little confused. There is a Kung Fu style called Tai Crane, where they have different crane techniques..." Darryl's hands draw back and he goes all karate-fied, in a way only experts can do without looking like you're trying to take the piss out of Bruce Lee "...where they're standing on one foot, that's really the basis of the crane. And then when we came to do this movie, I was talking to Pat Johnson and he told me they wanted to have a technique where someone was doing a crane style stance and jumping and kicking and then landing on that same foot. And I said, "Well, we would want to do it this way and probably land on the other foot ... so we made up this sequence of moves that you see ... and that's what we did. I don't wanna say I made it up, 'cos a lot of people stand on one leg and do a kick, but the sequence of this ... going to here..." He's showing us the moves now, all agile and jumping up and down and I know when I do this myself it's going to get that uncooked donut attached to my midriff vibrating again, "...and then doing the kick ... is something we put together."

"Have you ever taken anyone out with the crane kick?"

"No. I would say that the crane kick is not a very practical technique. Because if you were standing on one leg while you were fighting me, I would just come in on you. If I move in, you're in trouble." During exhibiting how he would "come in" on Tom, he sticks his heel in Tom's belly button. I suspect it doesn't hurt *that* much, but Tom goes down anyway, like the proverbial Portuguese footballer.

So come on Darryl, we say, show us how to do the bloody thing properly, and show us like we've only just learnt how to walk. He does just that and, in fact, it's incredibly easy. Well, he makes it *look* easy, I *feel* like it's easy but actually make it *look* like the most difficult manoeuvre man has ever attempted. I make it go on longer than a David Copperfield special. The whole move begins with some sort of karate hands squatting stance that attracts a fair amount of derisory stares from the snooty dogs and their owners. But I look through them like I've entered into a meditational trance; I'm in *the zone* (probably Zone 4, somewhere near Blackhorse Road) and from my uneasy *shit in the desert* squat, I rise with the delicacy of a hamburger and angle my arms and hands into that crane arrangement that the movie made so distinctive. Then the scissor-kick movement lashes a leg out, and before I know it, I've landed on the other leg and have successfully completed the Darryl Vidal crane kick. Wallop.

"Do you think you could beat up Bruce Lee?" I ask, all het up after my triumphant crane.

"Well I'm bigger than him..."

"How about Jackie Chan?"

"You know, it's not really about who can beat up who." *Yes it is* I think. "But if I came up behind them, I could probably take them both at the same time."

Darryl becomes a civilian again, in civilian clothing, and my tweaked hamstring sings like a tuneless harpsichord.

"Go find the stump and *don't fall off*," he says as we wander away to try and find the right bit of the beach to bring our newly acquired crane kick skills to.

Unfortunately, the stump's not there any more; I *would* have fallen off though. So we just crane kick ourselves towards sunset over the sea.

CHAPTER NINTEEN SOUNDTRACK:

Take My Breath Away

Berlin (1986)

Thriller

Michael Jackson (1983)

Chapter Nineteen

Editing Killed the Radio Star

Los Angeles to San Diego

"Look, it's the wankers," greets Dirk Sutro in a ballpark cockney accent as we shuffle nervously into the studio. Dirk is the smooth-talking presenter of arts programme *The Lounge,* here at WPBS radio station in San Diego. Word has got around about our quest and we've been invited to come on the radio and tell all of San Diego how mental we are. Look at us and our lofty heights. I've never been on the radio before.

"You do know what that means, Dirk, don't you?" I reply, pretending to be a little bit put out, but actually smiling at the mouth corners too much to pull it off.

"Of course," he says, conceitedly but chummily. Well, fair enough.

Dirk's a middle-aged guy with a grey twiddling beard and stands at what seems to be over seventeen feet tall. Enormous. His monotone voice is so garglingly deep that it's like it's being excavated from his stomach as it trickles along the script with all the hallmarks of a Jack-drinking Hamlet-cigar-smoker on a couch in a jazz club since last weekend type of guy. It's no surprise that he wrote the guidebook *Jazz for Dummies* ... he oozes *jazz.* Stinks of it. Yeah, dig it, baby, doobydabop, jazzzzzz. (As you can tell, I'm *not* so jazz.)

As we sit in Dirk's dark, techno-functional studio, waiting for his opening music to funk and sax its way through to a laid-back introduction, I wonder what the be-Jesus I'm doing here, with all these headphones on and microphones shoved up my face. I feel like it's got a bit out of hand and now I'm having to explain myself to America, on the radio. My *personal* journey of both celebrating and letting go of my own childhood is suddenly San Diego's business and I feel just a little bit exposed; the subject of a freak show news report. *And would you loooook at the size of my head. I'm sure Dirk can't stop staring at it.*

We start talking about all the ridiculous predicaments we've been in ... Toronto and the Blue Oyster Bar debacle, the nuns at the *Rain Man* institution, the stories about Stallone in Hope, staying at the Roxanne house, having our heads shaved in Port Townsend, and meeting the stars in Los Angeles ... and it's surprisingly easy to talk about, so much has happened. *He said this and I said that and Tom climbed Hightower* and blah bloody blah – Dirk can barely control our ceaseless jabbering and neither can we, with talk-spit firing into the microphones like water cannons, I had no idea we'd have so much to say. We're like school kids, rushedly and with very few complete or correct sentences, telling Headmaster about how the water balloon that hit Mrs Thompson and made her top go see-through wasn't our fault.

Up to this point we've veered around the place so hurriedly that we haven't had a chance to actually stop and look back at what we've done. A tingle of static pride tickles my ribs and sends a little flush of alrightness through me: we've gone out there and done something people only talk about dreamily in pubs after a few pints. Sod it, I'm going to have a little self-indulgent burst of pride, and if they all want to point and stare (at their own radios), then *they're* the weird ones. Nobody has any business pointing at a radio anyway.

My mind drifts off during the break, as it's prone to doing without me asking, and I think about how much Los Angeles has exhausted me. It's totally fiddled with me, stitched me right up the corners, I'm a collapsee. It's been a near-brain-bursting whirlwind of a movie nostalgia bender. And I needed it to be. It's been medicinal; Las Vegas seems a long time ago now. Elle seems a long way away, in every sense. But for the last few days we've been running on empty, knackered and hot, and having covered much of the stuff we'd been really looking forward to, we've started to draw a few blanks. Especially yesterday, up in Glendale...

We drove to 1345 Carroll Avenue, which one shady night in 1984 ran alive with hundreds of zombies and a Michael Jackson, who chased "girlfriend" Ola Ray into a house at the end of the song, told her it's all alright, then gave the camera a demonic glowing eye glint. Yup, this was the house used in Michael Jackson's *Thriller,* where she tried to get away from scary old Michael and his only partially (at this point) surgery-devoured burn-victim face. These days of course, he wouldn't need the hours and hours of make-up, they'd probably actually take make-up *off* and just press record.

Thriller (1983) (Pop Promo)
Director: John Landis
Writers: Michael Jackson, John Landis
Producers: George Folsey Jnr, Michael Jackson, John Landis
Cast: Michael Jackson (Michael), Ola Ray (Michael's Girl)

Notes:
Of course, we weren't legally allowed to watch *Thriller* – it was a Certificate 15 and we were all 10. But doubly of course, we all saw it *as soon* as it came out. It was virtually a race at Henry Maynard Junior School to see who could persuade their parents to let them see it first, and whoever got to see it, we'd huddle around as they revelled in telling us how scared they were and how we're not going to be able to watch it because it's far too horrendous. But just like the knackered old ghost train, with a camp Dracula and a couple of unravelled mummies showing you the machinery inside, once you got there it was fine. Just a load of old zombies, dancing. But still, what a song, and a great bonus Vincent Price ending to boot. For some reason, I'll never forget queuing up for dinner tickets with Munaf from my class, and him singing us his sports brand-influenced adaptation of the *Thriller* chorus. "Cos it's a Fila, Fila Nike. No-one's going to stop me from going to the football match tonight." It was rubbish and I've no idea why I remembered it. I bet Munaf hasn't.

We stood outside the house, looking up at it, feeling all little and apprehensive, like we were ten again. It looks *very* sorry for itself, but then again, in the video it was supposed to look a bit derelict and haunty and it still does. Its front porch is all hanging off, bits of guttering dangling, decomposing –

all the wood flaky and weather beaten like an old boat, with bits of paint like clinging on scabs. It's perfect for *Thriller:* tall, foreboding, wrecked, creepy and zombified. It has that classic look a house has when you can't tell whether it's derelict or occupied by squatters. The big giveaways, though, are huge pieces of filthy patterned cloth acting as curtains, covering the windows, even during daytime: a classic squatter décor touch. But there was no confirmation to be gained, nobody was home.

So, what else could we do, once we were there, other than re-create the video? It would be a shameful waste, a scandalous abuse of traveller's privilege for us to stand outside the *Thriller* house and *not* perform the *Thriller* video for the neighbours. We'd prepared for this moment. After rehearsing our routine back at the house in the morning, we felt slick and ready to throw some gruesome shapes that attempted to resemble the quality of choreography in *Thriller.* Albeit a bit camp and tame now, it was ahead of its time back then. And it went a little something like this...

It went badly.

Firstly, there was a lurking snidey pointy-nosed photographer, with the big tripod and professional tool belts with special clobber and what not, taking shots of the house next door. This made me feel massively uncomfortable, like an enormous pillock, pricking around with Tom, who's finally using *that* red leather jacket in the situation he'd purposely bought it for. The weedy, droop-shouldered photographer clearly didn't even begin to understand why we were there and what for, and his face was one of ultimate suspicion with a little bit of scorn to make our whole exercise feel even more trivial and pathetic.

Then, a couple of people walked by without batting an eyelid. Being a sensitive pup, I had to take that badly. Their failure to even shove glance at us meant that: a) we didn't look good; b) they'd seen this silly shit done before in their street by geeks like us; or c) they were so genuinely scared at our undeadness that they couldn't bring themselves to make eye contact. Or d) once again, we didn't look good.

Whichever of those was true, it knocked my performance off-skew and self-consciously, I flounced around like a less talented Weird Al Yankovich doing a Michael Jackson pastiche. I couldn't even look uncoordinated and half dead enough to pull off a zombie. What a shower. *Step right, step right, scary werewolf hands up to the right, step left, step left, scary werewolf hands to the left, and shimmy, and shimmy, and shimmy* ... was what we were *supposed* to be doing. Right from the off, Tom and I pranced off in separate directions at the wrong time, missed the beats and couldn't stop looking over at the beardy photographer, scowling between his clicks. Oh, the shame. Michael, I'm so sorry.

What made it even worse was that I tweaked my hip trying an elaborate move where most of the action happens mid-air (like a horror double-pike) and nearly had to go down. I've no idea what bit of the hip tweaked, but it *tweaked*. A disgraced zombie, I trudged back to the car, gutted that I even managed to be bad at being dead.

We did the goodbye bits with Sally, a rueful *that's a shame* goodbye to Megan, and drove out of Hollywood feeling as though we'd got to know the place a little bit. Despite it's plastic facade and all the sweet and sour that comes with the desperation of too many people trying to get too few jobs, we liked the feeling of Los Angeles. But it was time to move on, and we started South towards San Diego...

Dreamy transition wipe back into the radio studio (use some imaginary harp music or something to ease it through)

Back in the studio, Dirk opens part two by announcing our intentions in San Diego...

"You're in town for a visit to The Kansas City Barbeque..."

The Kansas City Barbeque is the self-proclaimed "sleazy bar location from *Top Gun*". With Dirk having told the world we'd be here, we are sure people in San Francisco, down Mexico way godammit, will be jumping in their cars to get to San Diego for a glimpse at the strange men who've got their lives snagged on something in the eighties.

As soon as we arrive, we can see that the owners have decided to go *heavy* on the *Top Gun* link. Neon signs, murals of aircraft, posters, pictures and anything that could possibly reinforce the idea in patrons' heads that *Top Gun* scenes were filmed here, and that's why it's cool to be here. Plus they sell meat dishes bigger than any animal could actually *be,* and Americans seems to like that sort of thing.

TOP GUN (1986) (Movie)

Director: Tony Scott
Writers: Jim Cash, Jack Epps Jnr
Producers: Bill Badalato, Jerry Bruckheimer, Don Simpson
Cast: Tom Cruise (Maverick), Kelly McGillis (Charlie), Val Kilmer (Ice), Anthony Edwards (Goose), Tom Skerritt (Viper), Michael Ironside (Jester), John Stockwell (Cougar), Barry Tubb (Wolfman), Rick Rossovich (Slider), Tim Robbins (Merlin)

Notes:
Is it homoerotic or is it just that campness that was inherent in the eighties? In a cameo in the film *Sleep With Me*, Quentin Tarantino famously made a case for the theory that *Top Gun* had a homosexual sub-story. And when you look back over that topless volleyball scene, you do start to wonder whether it was shot for an audience slightly wider than the worshipping teenage girls and their mums.

It looks like a summer place, all awnings and outside seating made for those long sunny days when the smell of a smoking barbecue and the taste of cold hopsy beer is what it's all about. Honest-looking, hand-painted signs and pot plants, all enclosed by a little fence that keeps the drinking confined.

Outside the bar, we meet the owner, Martin Blair. Martin's a tall, grey man somewhere in his fifties who speaks slowly and with such concentration that there's little outward evidence of brain activity actually showing in his eyes. But there must be; he's played the whole *Top Gun* thing just right since the eighties.

"I guess when they came – it was in July of 1985 – the whole landscape of this area was quite different. They actually shot two scenes here. They had actually located a place for the bar scene but the restaurant wouldn't close down for the day, so the location director was out looking for another place. They came in, got beers and said, 'Hey, do you mind closing down for the day.' So we agreed to do it."

"I take it they must have given you a decent amount for that?"

"Well, you know, it's a funny thing; they said we'll give you whatever you would make in a day. So we said sure, that's fine; it was more out of interest to see something filmed. We'd only been open for two years and it was really different downtown. Everything was warehouses, there were no high rises, no convention centre, this was really a dead-end area of town, not nearly like what it is today. They didn't need the interference and publicity and this was far enough off the beaten track that it was a plus for them. I chatted to Meg Ryan lots between takes. She was very nice. She had just come off the soap operas. This was her first movie break. She'd been very happy because they'd filmed the scene before where her husband, Goose, had died. And the producer kept retaking it and saying alright, *cry* ... and she was very happy because having been in the soaps she could just cry on cue for about six takes, so she thought that was a plus for her. She was a very nice person. Tom was pretty quiet..." Here it is, yet another report saying that Cruise was really quiet on set. "But I suppose any time you're twenty years old and earning a million bucks, you've a right to be a little bit... Paramount said he just gets into his character, so there's not a lot of periphery type stuff. He was short, so I couldn't be an extra, they wouldn't let me in."

"Was there a massive buzz after the film, did everyone just pour down here?"

"Eventually that summer they did, word kind of spread. It was *all* filmed in San Diego, so there were half a dozen places in the next year that people were interested in seeing. It certainly did a good job for the *Top Gun* Naval school, they saw a huge increase. But they moved away around five years ago, down to Nevada."

Walking around inside the restaurant, Martin takes us to look at his nooks and crannies. The place is so smothered in memorabilia, even on the ceilings, that very little light can get through the windows to the far corners. It's dark and smoky, with the neon signs providing that sleazy edge. The bar is sort of in the middle, which means there are lots of stools around the edge of it. This is the sort of place where you *should* sit up at the bar, preferably on your own, after a break up or being fired, and *drink a lot of whisky.*

"This is the corner where they were sitting in the first scene and in the last scene this is the jukebox," says Martin, pointing out a hazy table in the front corner, near enough to the window that light shafts through to show the dust floating and the odd puff of fag smoke in the air. It's all just as it was in the movie, just where Meg Ryan and Tom Cruise et al. sat getting drunk, with the jukebox still sitting there patiently waiting for someone to put new records in it.

"So you haven't moved the jukebox ... and does it play 'You've Lost That Loving Feeling'?"

"It used to, but the bartender heard it so many goddamn times that he broke the record and the jukebox hasn't worked since. For twelve years."

Over in the other window corner, I spot a piano. The "Great Balls of Fire" piano "And this is the piano that was used in the film," Martin confirms. "Great Balls of Fire. At that time, they had a problem because they didn't know how to play the song, he didn't know the words, so if you look at it carefully he's banging away at the piano because he couldn't actually play, and they're looking at sheet music with the words on. The little kid they sat up here on the piano was of course a twin, because young kids in Hollywood can only work four hours, so they had to have twins."

"How come the piano has moved from over there, where it was in the film, to this bit, just behind where Cruise sits and has a drink?" I ask. The piano is a lot closer to the jukebox.

"It was in the way over there." Well, that tells me. Silly question.

"Can you play the song?"

"Oh hell no, I don't think it plays any more. I don't think it played then."

"Luke's a pianist, do you mind if he has a go?" Luke's moment, his *put your money where your mouth is, sunshine* moment of truth. He was giving it *Charlie Big Spuds* about being able to play the piano earlier and now it's his chance. I wait, hoping he's terrible so I can slaughter him for the next few hours.

Oh dear. Les Dawson played more in tune than this. *Great Balls of Bollocks,* more like. Admittedly, the strings inside are probably as droopy as a bulldog's lips, *and* he didn't know the song before he came here.

Before we lose Martin's favour, we close the lid on that beaten up old tinkler and turn our attention to the bras that visitors from other countries get stapled to a particular part of the ceiling. I'm not sure how something like that gets started. Who was the first who thought it was a good idea to staple their lady's underwear to the ceiling? I definitely wouldn't go into the Rose and Crown at home and stick my Y-fronts to the wall. But ladies do it, and there's an almighty collection of braziers to sit and gaze at.

Given that the bar is an inviting den of knick-knacks and tapped beer, Luke and I decide to perch ourselves on some stools and knock back some friendly frothy suds while Tom wanders off to take pictures of things he doesn't recognise. Especially as Martin's already got us sitting here in identical Kansas City Barbeque T-shirts – on the house – it only seems appropriate to get to know what it's like to spend a night in the *Top Gun* bar.

The sun disappears and this "seedy bar location from *Top Gun*" becomes a dark, dingy drinking hole populated by the odd silhouette and an occasional German sailor smoking shadily in a corner and stinking of haddock. It's great, the staff are lovely and the beers just keep coming. I get to the point at which if I had my bra on today, it would be on the ceiling by now. We write our names on the wall and get right into the boozy spirit of the place. And what's even more great is that Martin has ordered the staff to pick up the tab for us. Result. Super. Smashing. Great. Embarrassed that we've had quite so much to drink that it might look like we're taking the piss, we walk away with our free T-shirts and a complimentary haze of inebriation.

In the car the next day, our radio interview is being aired on KPBS. I thought we'd gone out live. I certainly had that tingle of *I could really fuck this up* while were doing it, so it's all a bit of a surprise to be hearing it now. So *that's* why the screaming hordes never turned out to worship us. Hearing your own voice is bad enough, but hearing yourself say things that make no sense is even worse. During the interview, Dirk asked us about Ali G, and as a big fan of the show he attempted to do the voice. He was rubbish at it, and I did a Dick Van Dyke in Mary Poppins impression to compare his attempts at an English accent. All quite innocuous banter. However, the interview has been edited so that Dirk's Ali G is cut out entirely, but my Dick Van Dyke is left in: on its own and utterly out of context with anything we spoke about or were going to. In short, it made me sound like a rambling lunatic.

"Cor blimey, Mary Poppins," I shout bizarrely, in the middle of a conversation about *Police Academy*. How humiliating.

It seems that the second half of the show went downhill further when Dirk got Luke to do the dance from *Thriller* in the studio. It being a radio show, the performance doesn't really translate to anything other than the grunts of an out-of-shape Englishman Michael Jacksoning poorly in a confined space. It actually sounds a bit porny.

When the show finishes, there's a deathly silence in the car.

CHAPTER TWENTY SOUNDTRACK:

The *Boys and Girls* are *Doing It*

Vital Signs (1989)

Regulate

Nate Dogg and Warren G. (1995)

Chapter Twenty

Mostly Excellent

San Diego to Santa Fe

Just when we thought we'd seen about all the possible variations of landscape America has to offer, the Interstate Highway 8 slides us east through huge mounds of clumsy boulders: mountains formed entirely of seemingly loose rocks piled precariously on top of each other. It all looks rather slapdash and ready to tumble into itself at any moment. As California slips out of our lives for the last time (on this trip at least), Arizona takes the baton and decides it wants to show us desert. Arid, empty desert with little else than cacti and the odd shack in the middle of nothing. When we stop for chips and drinks, we realize the extent of the heat outside. As soon as the car door opens, it's like when you open the oven door, and roasted air melts the expression off my face. This Arizona desert air is chokingly hot – not humid, just piercingly scorchy. I've never felt my internal organs sweat before, but I'm sure my kidneys are.

Occasionally the journey takes us higher, where actual sandy dunes – like a proper desert – and rocks outbid vegetation easily. Then we dip into lower areas that water has managed to slide into and a bit of grass with the odd tree are allowed to survive. After one of those touch-and-go situations with petrol, this time less scary because we're so petrol-toughened, we get to Phoenix, dump our stuff, make a serious complaint to the lady at motel reception that the city is too hot, and dash back into the air-conditioned car. Given this spiteful, bastard sun, it may be a little ambitious to think we're capable of tackling an open-air water park. Stupid, actually. But Tom *loves* these places, he's a tiny little over-excited boy about it; twitchy and anxious;

can't wait. As we go along in the car, Tom clutching his little towel rolled up with trunks, I see something in him that I haven't actually felt in myself for years. It's that overwhelming excitement which so many things back then could provoke in me: Spurs on the telly, Pizza Hut garlic bread, the cinema when the film board certificate came up, *Game for A Laugh*; the simple pleasures were new and gut-pummellingly thrilling. I was an excitable little boy, I'd squeal in expectation at stuff, I'd even on occasion wet myself with the giggles. Now? Nothing really gets that stomach-tightening rush of undiluted adrenalin surging through my veins at the prospect of pleasure any more. I seem to have lost that over the years without even noticing, until now. My enthusiasm for life has ebbed away, been sucked out of me by the tube and the council tax (what's that for again?) and forty hour shifts on a stupid Breakfast TV show and the harsh realities of the hard knock life. But in another way, I feel a bit sorry for Tom. Not in a pitiful sense, but just that he's still got the burden of trying to satisfy that raw expectation; he feels the need to do things like this trip to keep him fuelled. We're all chasing *something* on this trip, and more than ever, I realise that Tom's chasing an *extension* to his childhood rather than a *conclusion* to it. And that's maybe why sometimes I want to punch him on the nose, while *he* thinks I'm a traitor to the mojo of childhood.

It's a good job he can jump into the pool to hide that he may have wet himself a little bit with excitement. I'm not so excited about walking around with my milky tits out, but am happy to do so in the name of location-hunting?? Sunsplash Golfland, on the edges of Phoenix, is the water park where Bill and Ted took Napoleon for a day of historic water fun in their *Excellent Adventure*.

BILL AND TED'S EXCELLENT ADVENTURE (1989) (Movie)

Director: Stephen Herek
Writers: Chris Matheson, Ed Solomon
Producers: Ted Field, Robert W. Court, Stephen Deutsch
Cast: Keanu Reeves (Ted Logan), Alex Winter (Bill Preston), George Carlin (Rufus), Terry Camilleri (Napoleon), Dan Shor (Billy The Kid), Tony Steedman (Socrates), Rod Loomis (Sigmund Freud), Al Leong (Genghis Khan), Jane Wiedlin (Joan of Arc), Robert Barron (Abraham Lincoln), Clifford David (Ludvig Van Beethoven).

> **Notes:**
> Few films lodge themselves so much into public consciousness that their dialogue melds itself into every day language. But this was one of them. If you were around when this film came out and didn't occasionally slip "Most excellent" or "Be excellent to each other" into conversations, there was something wrong with you.

The park is teeming with drenched over-excited kids, sun burning against a vivid blue desert sky backdrop. Shrill shrieks of delighted terror peak over every big spindly slide structure and the fake castle facade with sun-faded paint that's been there since Bill and Ted; noise shooting down the flumes and bobbing around in gurgles in the half-hourly wave pool eruption ... it's a place of serious, vigorous *pleasure*. All the sounds and smells take me way back, for a wistful moment, to the days when Walthamstow had an open-air swimming pool called Whipps Cross Lido.

> *Summer 1979, sitting on the smoky old Routemaster bus, the Number 257, with my little towel, tight Speedo-style trunks already on, too tight, itchy willy under my trousers, trembling with anticipation. Oh the fun, the fun, the fun is coming. A bit nervy, breathy, jittery in the belly when I get through the old iron gates and the first delicious whiff of swimming pool chlorine and coconutty sun lotion hits me. It's chaos, a true day of London summer madness we've been waiting months for; all the big kids dive bombing and punching and swearing and smoking round the back, being whistled at by the lifeguard and throwing each other into the old 1930s fountain. "No horseplay," he says. "One more chance," he says. There's a sense of all-or-nothing fun, grab the sun, our one hot day in the year when Mum can get time to come, an enormous occasion. It's my day, deserve the special treatment: a packet of Refreshers, some KP Skips and a warm can of Coke with complimentary wasps – in between tempting myself over to the so so scary deep end meant for grown-ups. Mum sits up on the grassy hill, sunning herself, keeping the odd eye open to make sure the older ones aren't drowning me...*

The grassy hill of the Whipps Cross Lido is still there, but now it's all just one *big* hill, where they filled in the pool with soil. The whole lido has been consumed once again by Epping Forest, eaten up and turned into undergrowth, as though we were never there screaming out little gullets out. But this place right now, in Phoenix, is like bringing that old lido back out of the ground.

We wiggle self-consciously down a few chutes and slides with me dressed as Napoleon: an all-in-one white suit (which is actually just a long T-shirt) and shower cap (which is actually a bald wig we had knocking around in our dressing-up bin liner). Bill and Ted brought him out of the past and took him to a water park. Most excellent. The attention this outfit attracts isn't necessarily playful and curious – some of the faces staring at my shower cap (bald wig) are of utter disgust and disbelief. I feel a right prat, but at least I get to wear a top that hides my breasts. As I stand up at the top of one of the rickety old slides, on my own in the Napoleon get-up (as the boys stay at the bottom ready to film me flump down it), rap music blares out of the speakers at sound levels I thought reserved for harrier jets, and the *entire queue* stares at me. They're not even laughing at me or taking the piss, they're just staring. I get to the top, where the lifeguard on duty sits and signals you to throw yourself down their *premier* white-knuckle flume – the very one that Napoleon screeched down in the film.

"What are you doing?" he asks, high volume, to reach over the rap music. I ask if he knows about Bill and Ted bringing Napoleon here in the movie. Napoleon loved the water slides. *Loved* them.

"Bill and who?" Come on pal, I think, you can't be *that* young.

"*Bill and Ted's Excellent Adventure?*" I say, like a question, almost pleadingly.

"What?"

"The movie?" *Please, please remember it and validate me wearing a nightgown and shower cap.*

"What movie?" Oh fuck off now.

"*Bill and Ted's Excellent Adventure*, it was shot here," I say, with resigned indignity and a smidgen of annoyance. Which must look very silly, at the top here, in my outfit.

"Was it? Are you a movie star in England?"

"Yes." What the fuck, there might be some scraps of pride left here after

all. I'm Hugh Grant; I'm Mr fucking Bean; I'm, I'm Grace pissing Jones.
Whatever.

"Awesome."

"Yeah, awesome."

"Yeah, *awesome*. Go dude!" he confirms, again.

"Yeah, go dude!" Must be something they're saying these days.

"Go!" he says again, we're really riffing with this dude-talk.

"Yeah, awesome!" What the hell, let's chuck another awesome into the
mix. Maybe a high-five next time. Do they still high-five ?

"*Go. Go down the frickin' tube, dude.*"

"Oh, go as in *go* down the flume?" I turn around and now the staring
queue is a *scowling* staring queue. I'm eating into their flume time and dude,
you just don't do that, it's *not* excellent.

"Oh, shit, right. Aggggghhhhhhh." I hate water up the nose. It shouldn't
be up there. But up it goes, down the back of the throat, all chloriney. I
convince myself I'm going to lap up the sides of the flume and spill over
onto a family of picnickers twenty feet below, a tragic peanut butter
smothered death. It goes on forever, fast, faster, the joins between the sections
of tube catching the same bit of back each time. Then *Kerrsplash*. I enter the
water like a space hopper full of sand, face screwed up like a greengrocer's
twisted brown paper bag. Tom and Luke nurse me out as you would grandad
after a fall in the bathroom. Pathetic. But I have to admit, a little bit awesome.
I got tingles. I finally got the tingles back. I got a flood of tense expectation
and that burst of being alive that's been absent for so long.

Heading north towards Flagstaff – the gateway to the Grand Canyon – we
streak through scorched, rusty orange deserts into something more like
Montana: pine trees clinging to humpy lumpy hills smothered by huge skies
that stretch like cling film over a bowl of broccoli. You'd think that on these
large, empty, straight roads in America, drivers would indulge themselves in
a little more speed. But no. Maybe it says a little something about the way
we live our lives: we weave, sprint and dodge while the Americans cruise,
wait and chill. They've got the sun and the space and the time whereas we're
cramped up in the rain and in a rush. Passing through Flagstaff, fat pies of
rain start splatting the windscreen while veiny fork fork-lightning jabs

spitefully out of the leaky black cloud. We realise that this is the first time we've seen rain since Calgary, *ages* ago. In England, this duration of rainlessness would have the the water board banning stuff. But as fast as the rain comes, it goes, and leaves no trace of wet on the roads we're heading into, like we've driven through a massive open-air carwash.

Some of the locals we spoke to in Phoenix reacted to us going to the Grand Canyon next by saying "but it's just a big hole". Peering tentatively over the edge when we get there, with vertigo waving itself gloatingly in my face, I can't deny it; it really is a bloody big fat hole. In fact it's so wide that my eyes can't really comprehend the distances involved or which bits of rock are in front of or behind the others. I totally lose any ability to perceive depth of field and it just seems like a mass of visually unfathomable rock. But it is the royal highness of canyons, the daddy mac, an absolute majesty of a hole.

I've been here before; Elle and I did a cheapo coach tour out here from Las Vegas. I got closer to the edge back then, because Elle held my hand like a toddler approaching a drunk scary Santa so I could shuffle tremblingly near to the rails in a semi-crouching position I like to call my *vertigo tripod stance.* I skulk around the path, well away from the edges, hoping the vertigo bitch won't grab my knees and turn them into pieces of old rope that will just collapse in a knotted heap and send me rolling impossibly over the ridge. Vertigo makes you believe that the most unrealistic, impossible falls over the edge are probable. I really don't do Grand Canyons. But thinking back to that day with Elle, I don't get any of the chilly goosebumpy aches of loss that I've had in some of the other places. I'm just *OK* about it. It *happened*, and, well, *this* is happening now. I'm just happy to be in the present at this moment and that feels like another little breakthrough.

Heading west to Page, we run into huge misty sandstorms, clouds of thick swarming grains hover over the desert, cloaking multi-coloured striped hills. Then out of nowhere, those hills turn crocodile green; big sleeping dinosaurs slumped by the side of the road, all puffed out. A real-life tumbleweed bobbles across the road in front of us just like Bobby Davro at the Walthamstow Assembly Hall; swirls of sand sweep in front and behind us. The occasional hand-painted sign advertises Native Indian stores that they promise will appear in a few miles. "Friendly Indians, 2 miles." Then another saying "Oops, you missed us", four miles later, trying to *nice* their way into my wallet. We miss them on purpose, thinking that anyone who has to make the point that they're *friendly* probably isn't actually that friendly.

We rampage through Zion National Park, where scenes from *Romancing The Stone* and *Jewel of the Nile* were shot. We'd never find the actual spots, and really, this is just part of the cross-state transit for us. But Zion is a visually *smack in the gob* striking place: massive cliffs of yet more stripy red rock formed in awkward poses and curious angles. One looks like it's a man doubled over after being punched in the stomach, probably after a pub fight, another looks like it's hailing a taxi and has been doing so for thousands of years. One looks a bit like Ross Kemp, but that might just be the shimmery heat haze playing tricks.

Heading further north into Utah, livid dark cloud hovers in patches as we sit in the car entirely numb, adjusting to the openness of the country. At Canyonlands National Park, the rangers value their experience at ten dollars per car. We pay and chug up to the visitors' centre to find out exactly which edge *Thelma and Louise* drove off at the end of the movie. Inside the wooden centre, there are two young kids standing at the counter, left hands aloft, taking an oath to become junior park rangers. At the end of all the worthy chanting and promises to save the world, the park ranger announces to all the strangers inside that they've just sworn in some new young recruits. No going back now kids, you're involved, you're a part of it, sucked in, you're a *friend of theirs*. I howl and whoop with the rest; it's always a shame to miss out on a chance to whoop with a little *too* much vigour. Americans can *never* tell you're doing it with sarcasm.

The park ranger, still buzzing high from the ceremony, comes over and we ask where the *Thelma and Louise* bit happened. I always feel a bit of a plum going to these places and asking about film locations while everyone else makes enquiries about types of rock and shrub. The ranger smiles and perhaps quite enjoys telling us that we're in the wrong park for *Thelma and Louise*. Shit, that's ten dollars worth of wrong park.

In the end, we're glad we made the mistake, because Canyonlands is an amazing place. The Grand Viewpoint gives you a lofty red-brown vista across what must be Mars. A massive flat valley below: cracked open in parts, with sub-valleys within each that look like they've been cut out or rotted out by acid – in weird shapes, like jigsaw pieces of land are missing. This is pure

Luke plays the 'Great Balls of Fire' piano from *Top Gun*.

Tom in 'downtown' Cerillos, NM. The old town used in *Young Guns*.

South Fork Ranch, Texas. The Ewing house in *Dallas*.

Luke filming me, Tom and PR lady Sally inside Southfork Ranch.

Georgia. Climbing out of the window, *again,* at what's left of the original Duke's barn from *The Dukes of Hazzard.*

A sneaky peak inside the old Duke's barn. Tom was devastated.

Tom and I try to get into the parenthood thing at the Cabbage Patch Dolls' Babyland General 'Hospital', Cleveland, GA.

Our feeble attempt at the *Dirty Dancing* 'lake lift' at Lake Lure, NC.

Tom at the top of the stairs of the Philadelphia Museum of Art, where *Rocky* completed his legendary montage.

Me and Tom try to recreate the *Trading Places* scene where Eddie Murphy feigns being disabled, in Rittenhouse Square, Philadelphia.

It's not that easy being on the road. Especially with a cowboy hat on.

Katz's Deli, New York...the very seats where Harry met Sally.
Tom's Sally. I'm Harry. Come on then Tom...

'That's not a knife...', the exact spot where the machete-thwarted mugging took place in *Crocodile Dundee*.

The *Ghostbusters*' HQ – an old fire station in New York.

Me and *Jaws* finally meet in Martha's Vineyard. Actually, it's Tom holding up a fin fashioned from a pizza box.

With Carroll Spinney, the man behind Big Big and Oscar the Grouch from *Sesame Street*.

Roadrunner territory, and I can't help pinging a loud "meep, meep" across the valley. It's so dramatic and extreme that I wonder what the hell happened to form such an end-of-the-world piece of landscape. I read about it on the information board on the viewing platform and still don't understand it. As soon as anything older than 1700 is mentioned I lose all perspective of time and turn into a spaz.

These few days feel like endless rapid transit, transient come-and-go days where we speed through hours and hours of nothing but still manage to rack up three states. Utah makes way for Colorado, which shows us some ugly black mountains they call San Juan and more greenery than we've seen for a while. Colorado slips craftily past and, as we creep through New Mexico, I'm surprised that it remains reasonably green. I imagined orange desert and amusing phallic cacti the whole way.

Santa Fe, the highest state capital in the USA, emerges early evening and the rest of the day *has* to make way for sitting in the motel room watching re-runs of Seinfeld re-run re-runs. The trip is coming up two two months old now, and sometimes you've *got* to lock the world out and pretend you're at home. At last, our massive journey across what felt like two or three other worlds is over. At least for a bit.

––––––––––

Despite the New Mexico sky bundling clouds across what should be a perfect blue desert sky, we wander down the Cerillos Road, out of Santa Fe, to a Spanish colonial living history museum: El Rancho De Las Golondrinas. During the 18th and 19th centuries, this ranch was a major stopping place for people heading in or out of Santa Fe towards Mexico. What was a major through road is now a small out-of-the-way dirt road that we've only just managed to find tucked off the highway. We walk towards the open gate, past an American flag clanking noisily on its pole: the only noise breaking the silence in this wild spot that can't work out whether it wants to be desert or forest.

We walk through to the courtyard of the ranch, which is surrounded by adobe buildings – those constructions smothered in mud that seem a little unnecessary these days. But the heritage types seem to like making old buildings and then pleading for money when it turns out they're a monster wallet-sucker to keep up. It makes for an interesting visit though, so I decide to like Mike – the guy that runs the ranch, who is trying really hard to keep a bit of his country's history intact.

Mike, like all the volunteers that help run the ranch, wears period costume that he seems just a little too comfortable in. It's a sort of billowy white blouse-thing with one of those string neck ties that serve no purpose these days other than to suggest there's a line-dancing club nearby. The hat really takes the biscuit – a wide wicker thing that really doesn't deserve a head. Mike has an old face and speaks slowly, he's like a drawling cowboy dressed in a frock. A very odd combo, but they *were* the Spanish and who's Mike to argue with history?

"In 1710, we were part of Spain of course. And Mexico City was the capital of Spain. We were one day's trip out of Santa Fe and known as an official stopping point..." My attention dips in and out of his monologue. I walk along wondering when we're going to see the locations used for the movie *Young Guns*. The place *feels* right: lots of wooden cabins, in all different styles, some original, some imported from other parts of the state and rebuilt to their original specifications. With all the mud and shack and the feeling of a real living Wild-West town, the place reeks of *Young Guns*.

YOUNG GUNS (1988) (Movie)

Director: Christopher Cain
Writer: John Fusco
Producers: John Fusco, James G. Robinson
Cast: Emilio Estevez (Billy the Kid), Kiefer Sutherland (Josiah Gordon "Doc" Scurlock), Lou Diamond Phillips ("Jose" Chavez y Chavez), Charlie Sheen (Richard "Dick" Brewer), Dermot Mulrooney ("Dirty" Steven Stephens), Casey Siemaszco (Charles "Charlie" Bowdre), Terrence Stamp (John Tunstall), Jack Palance (Lawrence G. Murphy)

Notes:
Admission: I only saw this movie recently. Back in the real eighties, I was all about time travel and robots and the impossible, and cowboy films were old and boring and reminded me of impossibly dull Sunday afternoons when Dad wouldn't play Scalextrics because there was some crusty old Western on BBC Two. I hated them. So maybe it's a good thing that I only saw it recently; now that my extra years have given history more of a context in my brain.

Mike keeps skirting around our questions about *Young Guns*. We keep asking about the whereabouts of the ranch house where Terence Stamp's character John Tunstall lived, but Mike consistently refers only to a pig pen from the film. Sure, we remember a pig pen, at the beginning of the movie, but that wasn't really the meat of our visit, we wanted ranch house ... big fat ranch house. We get to the pig pen and Tom crawls inside with his cowboy hat on and prats around pretending to be Emilio Estevez, who hid in the pen when Jack Polance, as Murphy, turned up to threaten them. "Do you feel special, Tom?"

"Yeah, I do a bit."

"Because you look *very* special."

Tom has trouble getting out of the pig pen, due to a restrictive bit of fencing on the other side. He scrambles around, tries to squeeze through a bit and then sits looking at the sides of the hut, clearly thinking that he might be in there for a while. Meanwhile, I laugh proper whooping cough laughter.

"Actually..." says Mike, slowly and with a deadpan face as he looks at Tom pitifully squirming around in the pig shit, "...we put that fencing there to stop the movie fans from climbing in."

There are buildings all around the pen, but we can't get a positive identification on any of them as the Tunstall house. Mike seems intent on trying to make us more interested in Ron Howard's *Missing*, one of many films that has recently been shot at the ranch, but I think that's because he pretty much knows the pig pen is the only remnant from the movie. So, to sum up: we've travelled all the way to Santa Fe, and our main attraction turns out to be a pig pen. I look around me, at this mocked up 18th century New Mexico town, and wonder what in the name of *Cheggars Plays Pop* am I doing here.

Thirty years old, and while people my age at home have their own offices and hefty pay-packets, girlfriends, regular sex and friends ... I've just journeyed eight hours to visit a pig pen that was used for thirty seconds in a movie made twenty years ago. I must be fucking insane.

On the way out, Mike tells us that he met some of thestars who have filmed at the ranch since *Young Guns* were here. Apparently, a young actor introduced himself to one of his colleagues.

"Hi, I'm Val Kilmer."

"Hi, I'm Pete Smith."

"Yes, but I'm Val Kilmer.". That would probably have been the point at which I would claim to be Mick Hucknall. Kilmer would have had no return on that.

Staying dedicated to the *Young Guns* theme, we drive further out of Santa Fe to a tiny village named Cerillos. The town was portrayed as Lincoln in the film and Mike tells us that it's still pretty much as you see it in the film, which is weird, because it looks like an elaborate old cowboy town set in the movie.

We just about find Cerillos, a pin prick of a village that's almost into hamlet territory, and drive down Main Street, although there's nothing too *main* about it. A group of perpetually masticating old people sit on wooden benches in composed silence by the main cluster of wooden buildings that are more Wild West than John Wayne's spurs. The place is so butch, it makes me feel like a scrawny-titted tart, mincing around in my plastic strappy traveller's sandals.

Using the old church as a marker, which had the sheriff's office opposite in the film, we match up our camera shot with the moment in the film where the Young Guns go riding up the street. Everything looks just the same, give or take the odd period trimming added by the film crew or an old faded Coke sign that's emerged since. Electrical wires hang overhead now, because the crew went as far as to bury them invisibly underground for the duration of their stay. This place *is* real and it didn't take much to make it look as though it was a hundred years ago.

One of the two hundred citizens, an old boy sitting with the masticators at the wooden shops, says hello and asks how we are. We're fine thanks. Tom jumps at the chance to ask if they remember *Young Guns* being filmed in the town.

"Oh yes," butts in a little Mexican-accented lady wearing floral everything, and sitting on a bench high enough that her ant-thin legs dangle to a rhythm she must be playing out in her head. I imagine it's "La Bamba". Bloody "La Bamba". She croaks with that Mexican accent that you think is only reserved for borderline racist depiction in *Speedy Gonzales* cartoons and doesn't really exist real life.

"My house was the sheriff's office in the movie. And right here they killed Jack Polance." Not literally of course; even in the eighties, murder was illegal.

"They even said thank you," says the original *how are you* old boy standing opposite wearing trousers up to his Adam's apple, a massive baseball cap and ultra-magnified glasses so big his face is basically invisible. "Oh, the kids were very nice," says old invisible face, of the actors.

"Oh, they were the nicest people ever," adds dangly La Bamba legs. "Kiefer Sutherland ... all of them were at my house. And they had a big New Years party outside my house by the church. And they were all drunk. They were going all over my roof."

"Was it whisky or beer?"

"Oh, it was Sprite. I saw them drink it." What? Sprite laced with something? "They were just pretending."

"Oh, so it was for the movie, they weren't *actually* drunk?"

"Oh no, no. It was for the movie. No, they were very respectful. *Very* respectful." Damn, that would have been a good story. "Some of the movie stars wanted for us to go to Hollywood, me and her." She points to an old bag of bones barely conscious next to her; a lady who plucks her eyebrows and paints them back in again, like Aunt Sally. I've never understood why some women do that. "They had to hide in my house because they were really tired and the kids were just after them all the time. I told them to go to the back room so they could rest and eat. So I fed them in the back room. Emilio Estevez got sick, he got pneumonia, and he was in the hospital for a while. It stuffed the whole thing up for a while. It was cold, it was February."

"Did they give *you* any food?"

"Oh, if we wanted it. But I was cooking for my friends because they came to see the movies. And the actors sent my friends over there to the food trailers and they ate my food. They ate my beans and my chilli."

Suddenly, old painted eyebrows comes to life in a *Bagpuss*-awakening moment, clanks inside the shop and storms out with a director's chair they left for her. We're ceremoniously asked to take turns in having an approximately five-second sit on it.

We leave the crazy gang to sit in their shaded boardwalk, masticating, and selling their hand-painted Christmas baubles to no one. I find the charm of the place is its emptiness, its utter disregard for development. They've left all the modernisation to Santa Fe and kept their place the way they liked it, and I admire that. We burn off safe in the knowledge that I can still enjoy the odd water park and that a pig pen isn't the only attraction in New Mexico.

CHAPTER TWENTY-ONE SOUNDTRACK:

Theme tune to

Dallas

Jerrold Immel (1978)

Loadsamoney
(Doin' up the house)

Harry Enfield (1988)

Chapter Twenty-one

Oil, Money and No Tomorrow

Santa Fe to New Orleans

The journey east from Santa Fe sees us strangle right across the neck of northern Texas from New Mexico to Dallas; it's like driving through Essex from Billericay to Onga thirty times over. Hundreds of miles of flat green fields with skies that start off blue and end misty-grey dreary; flobbing grimy gritty rain whenever they fancy. The thrill of a road trip isn't *always* the road. I bought four new CDs to make the journey a bit less suicidal, but we're not even halfway through Texas when Aimee Mann whines out the last shreds of misery on her second album. Thereafter we search through local radio stations: trying to weave past the country music, which becomes torturous after around ten seconds of twangy wailing about undying love for a horse called Mary Jane.

Somewhere in nowhere, we stop at a lonely looking petrol station and I waddle tight-leggedly – to protect a taut bladder – through the sound of nothing towards the shop. A haggard old cowboy stands behind the counter of the cluttered little shop, instantly restoring my faith in stereotypes as he grimaces over his glasses and even further over his bushy tash to make me feel as unwelcome as possible. I fantasise about holding the place up, maybe with a banana in a paper bag that looks like a gun, and going on an end-of-the-world countrywide bender like Thelma and Louise (with less bosom). So much in the eighties was about *live now, fuck later*. But if I tried it, I really wouldn't have a later. So without a word being said by anyone I edge apologetically through the café section with a table and a fat sheriff sitting with his gleaming badge. I part a veil of dangling beef jerky to make my way to the toilets. Every step is being watched, scrutinised by them all. We're all just looking at each other, no smiles, no nods, just watching. After weeing through a willy that wants nothing other than to shrivel, I walk back past the wall of eyes, back through the curtain of jerky and out to the glorious freedom of baking hot nothing outside. I now understand what "redneck" means. America really does have an awful lot of middle-of-nowhere.

A relatively short drive through Oklahoma City to Dallas brings us into the home of gallon hats and meat in every meal. Skimming past the city, we arrive at Southfork Ranch, half an hour's drive or so north at a place called Parker. The shiny clump of the city's high-rise downtown buildings shimmer promisingly in the distance – just like in the opening titles of *Dallas*.

The metal archway at the entrance to the ranch tells you you've arrived at Southfork, and it looks just the same as it did from the helicopter shot in the opening titles of the programme; quite unpretentious, just an opening to drive through. The place is wide open, fields and livestock and buildings are in the distance down the driveway. How odd. I'm at the entrance of J.R.'s place. It's hard to separate the TV world from the real world. J.R. lives here. But he doesn't really. I'm confused.

DALLAS (1978-1991) (TV)

Creator: David Jacobs

Cast: Larry Hagman (J.R. Ewing Jnr), Patrick Duffy (Bobby Ewing), Victoria Principle (Pamela Barnes Ewing), Linda Gray (Sue Ellen Ewing), Steve Kanaly (Ray Krebbs), Ken Kercheval (Cliff Barnes), Carlene Tilton (Lucy Ewing Cooper), Barbara Bel Geddes (Miss Ellie Ewing), Susan Howard (Donna Culver Krebbs), Howard Keel (Clayton Farlow), Priscilla Presley (Jenna Wade)

Notes:

Who shot him? That was an insane time for television. The tapes were being handed over under armed guard on the TV news; it was in the papers; canteens, staff rooms and even in the playgrounds everywhere. Who bloody shot J.R.? For us kids, it was exciting because it was one of the rare times when grown-ups became obsessed with telly, with make believe. And even though we didn't really follow the soap or know what was going on, we were sucked in by proxy; we all wanted to know who shot J.R.?

Down the end of the long drive, we find a visitors' centre and conference hall: developments which must make opening the ranch up to the nostalgic public financially viable, but which disappoint me. I want it to be where J.R. lives, that's all.

Public relations lady Sally Peavey's voice hurt my ears, all the way from Texas to London on the phone. Shrill and excitable; it punched through my eardrums each time it hit the note that made the telephone distort. She was overfriendly to the point of comedy; a cartoony caricature full of *y'all a*nd *darrrlin* and *oh mahhh* – an effect I don't think is an accident. Southfork *represents* Texas internationally, and they crank it up so far it pokes out the other side. Sally greets us at the visitors' centre, a new building that smells clean and wants you to buy its merchandise, *now*; all the *Dallas* videos, books, Texan curios and more jerky. Sally must be mid-fifties, big blond perm and bright white teeth rebounding off the sun when she smiles. Dolly Parton, basically. She's lovely and a good laugh and just about gets that *Dallas* is now a piece of eighties culty kitsch.

First things first: I make it clear to Sally that I simply can't, *won't* go on a tour of the *Dallas* ranch without wearing a J.R. stetson. It would be improper; a liberty. So she takes us straight to the racks of cowboy hats sitting on hooks waiting for heads to live on. I'm shocked that there isn't a single hat resembling the one J.R. wore. I'm outraged. Sally manages to find one that almost gets there and I sulkily settle for that. It's the wrong colour, but I am at least now a cowboy and insist that Tom and Luke call me S.A. for the duration of the tour. They refuse.

Tom has turned up in a wig, hoping he can pull off the Patrick Duffy curly-topped look. But when he starts putting hats on top of the wig, he looks far too much like Harpo Marx to be taken in anyway seriously as a genuine soap-opera actor. We have to lose the wig ... in any case, it's already been used as David Hasselhoff's barnet when we were in Calgary with KITT, and I feel uncomfortable at the thought of The Hoff merging into The Duff.

Sally leads us through the *Dallas* museum and I follow behind at my own pace, swaggering, drawling and screaming "Sue Ellen" whenever it Tourettes its way up (which inevitably results in the odd spray-mist of spittle. But I'm a cowboy, it's OK, we spit; that's what we do).

The museum is a cute little thing, a world of soap, with pictures and little videos and *the gun* that was used to shoot J.R. One of the biggest storylines in the history of international television; something that got the whole world talking, and the gun that caused all the kafuffle is right in front of me in a glass case, looking all plastic and not at all capable of firing even bits of potato, let alone a bullet. Lucy Ewing's tiny wedding dress is draped over a midget mannequin and Cliff Barnes' voice fills the room from speakers with melodramatic J.R. hate. Everywhere you walk, you can hear the theme tune setting the mood, taking you back to your own living room back in the eighties...

> *...a plate of boil-in-the-bag cod in dill sauce with peas and crinkle-cut oven chips smothered in vinegar and Daddy's Sauce. Eat quick, it's tinned fruit salad with evaporated milk for desert night. Oh no, not stupid Dallas. Boooorring grown-up telly. Mum will want to watch it and I've got an episode of The Adventure Game on video I want to watch. I hate J.R., hate him, I wish someone would shoot him...*

Out the back of the museum, we get on one of those trams that theme parks seem to love packing people on to travel ten yards. Sally throws some figures at us as the tram chugs along: the ranch has 300,000 visitors a year and Larry Hagman drank four bottles of Champagne a day while he was on set shooting the show. Way to go – beat that Cilla Black. Of course, apparently that's all changed since the brand new liver, but Sally seems quite sure that he still occasions the odd glass of something.

Sally's well up for playing Sue Ellen whenever the J.R. voice in me takes over and starts shouting at her. My accent ranges from Swedish to Namibian, but the words are all there. Probably because I've got some favourite quotes that I plundered from the Internet written on a bit of paper under my new hat.

"He bit me, Sue Ellen, with his teeth. Cliff Barnes, that rodent." I'm just a little bit more like Dirty Den than J.R. "Well I'll be damned if you can come in here any time you want and use me like some stud-service!" I continue. Sally apologises. "Like my daddy always said: if you can't get in the front door, just go around to the back." Not a euphemism. I hope. "You take another shot at my daddy, and I'm gonna knock that nose of yours five inches of the centre!" I aim that one at Tom. "Never interfere with a man who's correcting his wife!" Luke gets that one. "A marriage is like a salad. The man has to know how to keep his tomatoes on the top." Not sure I get that one, but Sally damn well agrees with me.

We arrive at the Southfork mansion and enter around the back, where the swimming pool and balcony immediately spark recognition. It looks so familiar, just as I remember it on the telly. At the back door entrance, there's a huge glass breakfast table with chairs around it. As we walk up to it, movement sensors trigger the *Dallas* theme music and it starts blaring out from the speakers. Sally tells us that this was the original breakfast table that appeared in many scenes in the programme. I can just see J.R. standing here with Bobby, Miss Ellie and Daddy, having an argument about losing Southfork for the seven hundredth time that series.

As we walk inside, Sally says very quickly, and under a slight masking cough out the side of her mouth, that the interior of the house was never used for filming. Eh? I stop with a Texan "whoaaaa" and ask her to repeat what she just said. She confirms it. It's clearly a fact that visitors would prefer not to know, it sort of marginalises your visit, and it nearly got buried under that cough.

"Originally it was someone's home..." says Sally. "It was built in 1970. They started filming the exteriors in 1978. So this looks nothing like it did on the set. Every summer they would fly in, stay in hotels in Dallas and every day come in and film the driveway scenes, barbeque scenes, pool scenes, breakfast table scenes ... everything they needed for the entire season and then it would all be spliced together."

They have tried to bolster the experience by using the inside of the house as a twee shrine; each room is devoted to a character from the show and is decorated as they think they would have liked it. It's hilarious. The actors might never have been in the room, but attention has been paid to every minute detail to help the visitor imagine the characters living here. *Sue Ellen has her own bidet.* There are no props from the show or waxworks of the characters, just duvets they thought the characters might have had on their beds and ornaments they'd probably quite like. Bobby's bed has deer antlers attached to them, which I think is a bit kinky for him. It's a cute tribute to the programme, but clearly one that's been created to keep visitors from rioting when they realise they've driven all the way out to Parker to see the outside of a house.

Tom gets his top off – he still likes doing that – puts on his Bobby wig, drops his trousers and goes into the shower. It wasn't the shower from the actual show, but we're in Southfork mansion, and it's a shower, so that's enough for us.

"Bobby? Bobby? Where are you?" I slur, my attempted J.R. coming out a bit like a drunk stroke sufferer. Tom emerges from the shower with his surprised face on.

"Bobby, you're alive, you're alive. It was all a dream," Sally squawks, stealing my line with crystal-shattering shrillness. Oh, the fun.

We go out onto the balcony, overlooking the pool and the entire estate.

"They came here to film *War of the Ewings*," continues Sally after her brief dip into tragedy. "And they're all real nice. Except I met Larry Hagman and I said 'do you have anything you'd like to donate to the museum?' He said 'Darlin', are you gonna pay me?' Just like J.R. would. Anyway, this is the famous balcony that Kristin fell from. Kristin's the one that shot J.R. in the show and she was played by Mary Crosby, Bing Crosby's daughter." The balcony isn't high at all, and I would jump into the pool from it if I didn't have my new hat on.

"The stunt double actually broke her leg. They tossed her over, caught her in a net and just flipped her over like a fish."

Sally tells us that the scenes in the swimming pool would often be shot with someone holding onto the swimmer's legs so that they didn't move very far, thus making the pool look huge. Which it isn't at all. Another cheeky move by the director was when they shot Jock driving in and out of the ranch; they would smother the ground and tyres in flour, so that it looked like dust was puffing up from the back of the car. It was deemed that it was much more *"Dallas"* to have dusty dry ground.

Humming the *Dallas* theme tune, we jump back into the car, I leave my hat on, and we speed three hours south to Austin: altogether a different piece of Texas.

On the way, I start thinking about J.R., which leads me to think about Gordon Gekko and all those other money-mad characters that eighties film and TV portrayed in droves. No wonder we grew up as a material-obsessed bunch of *want want wants*. Maybe my addiction to the eighties is because back then life was all about now, all about having what you want right this moment and doing *anything* to get it. But was that healthy? Here I am now: I achieved everything I set out to achieve, I'm a (relatively) successful TV producer, I've had good money, property, things, *loads of things*; just like we were told we should strive to get. But somehow, that's doesn't feel enough. Happiness can't be bought, and where do I find that Mrs Thatcher? How many more of us Thatcher's children who were brought up during the capitalist revolution are now wondering: how much wealth or how many possessions do you need before you get happy? Because we're a little bit lost. Some of us go to hide on beaches in Thailand, some buy a farm in the country, others get so stuck thinking about the times before we had the responsibility of maintaining wealth that they go traipsing around North America trying to get it back. We're in a spiritual void, and people like J.R. led us there. I'm hardly about to go and hurt myself, but I do feel the newer generations are going to have to start looking to something other than money for happiness.

Back then, of course, I had no idea I was being brainwashed by the telly and film. I was a consumer, just being drenched by it all. But now I'm starting to unravel how I got to the point I'm at now, and although I can't blame the media I loved so much, I can certainly cite it as an influence. So, I'm glad that we've arranged to meet someone who can help me understand how film helped make me an unwitting part of the capitalist explosion; a movie expert who's spent time identifying how politics seeped into our recreation and directed us towards the way we've lived our lives since the eighties.

"It started off 'cos I got paralysed and it would drive me crazy if I wasn't communicating with the world somehow, so I started a site about film," says Harry Knowles. He runs the website "Ain't it Cool News" – one of the most popular film sites that glorifies the geekification of film. He's a *proper* buff. The king of buffs. He's so important in the buff world that his opinions on casting are heard by the studios; he's made friends with the directors and actors and seems to have made himself a powerful force representing the consumer. If he writes about something, the studios care what he writes because he's got so many readers. It's a triumph.

Harry's house is a shack of eccentric glory. On a quiet Austin road, the front is overgrown by bushes and shrubs, hiding the fact that inside is something quite bizarre. Harry sits in his wheelchair, which he was confined to in 1994 at the age of twenty-three after being hit by a cart full of science-fiction memorabilia. He's a bit greasy looking with long ginger hair and glasses and a bright Hawaiian shirt that along with the chair and the hair, has become his trademark. He's enormous, probably tall but definitely quite overweight and is thoroughly surrounded by movie stuff; piles and piles of memorabilia. Videos, DVDs, every piece of wall is covered in posters and pictures; there's no light coming in, it's got that stale, timeless darkness of a movie theatre. Harry must need it to feel at home. Dust is everywhere, piled on top of the piles of DVDs and books; it feels like a place created to enable escape, away from the world, untouchable, another dimension ... just like the place your brain goes to when you watch a movie.

He starts telling us about what happened when he first started the site. He was at a movie theatre that, for some reason, Quentin Tarantino was visiting.

"This usher at the theatre comes up to me and says, 'Mr Tarantino would like to see you up in the office'. I was like whoa, I hoped I hadn't done anything wrong. At the time I was walking with two canes and I limped my way to the manager's office and Quentin's in there and he says, 'So you're Harry Knowles, I was wondering which person out there in the audience was you'. I said 'Oh, hey, nice to formally meet you,' and he says, 'You know I'm just such a fucking fan of your writing maaan'. I said, 'Oh, how did you know I was writing?' He said, 'Everybody is sending me updates about it.' He said. 'I said 'Everybody? Who?' He said like 'Oh, Sam Jackson, Steve Spielberg...' and I was, like, whoaaa!"

Harry talks fast and energetically, sometimes leaving sentences halfway through to get onto the next. It's an impressive display of consciousness, but it's hard to steer him onto subjects and keep him there. But we get onto the eighties when he sees Tom's t-shirt.

"I see you're wearing a Goonies T-shirt. We did a screening of *The Goonies* down in a cave down here in Austin. And to gain admission to the cave you had to pull up your shirt and do the Truffle Shuffle, and once you got down into the cave, there was Corey Feldman, who was down there to actually talk about the movie. We're gonna do another one where we bring in Sean Astin. I met Sean Astin when they were doing *Lord of the Rings* in New Zealand. We were having drinks, we were talking about how I'd supported his casting as Sam very early on, based entirely on his performance in *The Goonies*. Because I think Mikey is probably the greatest go get 'em kid in the history of cinema. Because he believes in the empowerment of children, you know? You take someone like Elliott in ET, he was just like 'Oh, my best friend, I don't want my best friend taken away.'" He puts on a flaky, girly voice to show what a weed Elliott was compared to Mikey. "I mean, Mikey was the prototype of the liberal go get 'em activist kid who wanted to defeat the evil Republican overlords who were trying to turn the world into yuppy hell." He laughs, often, in that dudey sort of way that's like a motorbike starting up. But really? *The Goonies* was about Mikey beating the Republican overlords? "It's a geeky geek film. I swear if I ever met Data from the film ... I just think he's the bomb."

"So what, to you, *defines* eighties movies?"

"I think eighties films ... one ... they loved widescreen, which made things feel big. Probably my favourite director from that period is John Carpenter. Because he was just *the man.* I mean from *Escape from New York, Big Trouble in Little China, Star Ma*n ... all those films were just *so* good. And at the same time you had like Spielberg doing his, like, monumental, like, *wow.* But it was sort of like the death of Lucas, 'cos that's when he sort of petered out, in the eighties. John Hughes was, you know, a God. Definitely creating what I thought high school was supposed to be. I was watching those movies as a kid, going ohhhhh, I have to find a girl to give me her panties in high school ... or, if I get into detention I can have friends. The eighties was also before evil people like me came about, who give reports on movies in advance. And so movies just came out of nowhere. I mean, like *Ferris Bueller.* I just wandered in ... I had no idea what I was walking in to. And it was boom. Movies like *War Games* were the things that made me want to get a computer. *Tron*, which freaked me out about computers. The seventies were probably artistically the best decade of film for the United States. The eighties were blockbuster mentality. You know, when *Beverly Hills Cop* became a marketing machine. When all those *Saturday Night Live* comedians came into their own and just started ruling. You know, I mean Belushi just owning every movie he was in in the eighties; they were so consistently good."

"Have you got any particular favourite films from that time?"

"*Teen Wolf* was awesome. Over here it was thought of as the lesser of the two Michael J. Fox films that came out right at the same time. *Teen Wolf Too* sucks balls, but *Teen Wolf,* you know, was just fun. The thing about the movie that's insane is that nobody minds that he's a werewolf, you know? It's just like not a big deal. But that's what's insane about a movie like *Howard the Duck* ... which I actually love... It was a total failure because they should probably have motion-stop animated Howie instead of having a guy in a suit, which was just terrible. But to me, the scene with Lea Thompson in bed with the duck ... I thought it was just *hot*. Maybe it was because I was a fat geek thinking if she'll fuck a duck, she'd fuck me, you know? That sort of rules."

"What about *Police Academy*?"

"*Police Academy*? That brings in the whole Steve Guttenberg thing. Guttenberg ... people think of him as being a bad actor. Guttenberg gets all sorts of crap. I disagree. I love him in *Short Circuit*, in the *Police Academy* movies; in *Cocoon* ... I was distracted from his performance by the idea of fucking a glowing woman. I thought he was sort of an every-guy. So many actors today *look* like performers. Steve Guttenberg looks like some loser you might have found somewhere. There's a genuine authenticity to him being just an eighties guy."

"The other thing was that there was an overall transformation that took place in the eighties – you were phasing out the psychedelics and the disco of the seventies and sort of pop came in. And in this country Reaganism was so empowering to the public in the sense of don't worry about tomorrow, buy now. It was that rampant consumerism. But what it did do was it created an air of let's not worry about the ramifications of tomorrow, so most of the films of the eighties were affected by that policy in a lot of ways. There were films about living for today and not worrying about tomorrow. I actually feel that Sylvester Stallone had more to do with the fall of Communism than Reagan. I think the commies saw *Rambo* and *Rocky 4* and thought fuck, we'd better give up. I saw *Rocky 4* in a mall theatre in Texas. It was military leave weekend and the place was packed with soldiers. And that end fight with Ivan Drago ... the audience was like 'Kill the fucking Russian bastaaaaard' at the top of their voices. I was sitting there thinking *man*, if there was one Russian in the room right now, they would be dead. This was really legitimately terrifying. When *Rocky 3* came out, I used to walk to the theatre in town, watch the movie three times and then come home. I was a movie geek, you know."

Harry seems a bit like he's rambling, but it's just that he's got so much to say, so much knowledge that he wants to spit out that it ends up as streams of bits and pieces. But I get what he's saying, and I can't believe I didn't start thinking about how the eighties film and TV influenced me to go and live the life I've lived so far; to get all this way only to want less and be happy.

With the Austin heat feeling like it's grabbing at my skin and giving me Chinese burns wherever it can, we crank up the air-conditioning in the car to full-pelt and get on all the appropriate roads to sink us further south towards New Orleans. The dry baron Texan land becomes a distant memory, and a damper climate takes over, which is clearly a big hit with the tree and bush population. Lush green trails us all the way down to Houston and, everywhere we stop to change driver or eat plastic fast food, we can smell damp in the air: like breathing concentrated rain.

Houston appears and disappears as no more than an overpass amid dozens of wiggling Scalextric style ramps and roads piled on top of each other while monster clouds throw javelins of lightning down to the ground like an angry Fatima Whitbread.

The French Quarter. The quarter of the city where drinkers slug poisonous mixtures of oversweet alcohol like it's the end of the world. In the French Quarter, nothing really matters and tomorrow will never come. Hyped-up travellers clutch at plastic cups of booze, swaying and laughing, bumping into each bar along Bourbon Street; screaming for more, dancing and begging each other for a flash of boob in exchange for cheap shiny plastic strings of beads you can buy on every corner. The road is narrow and revellers revel on the balconies of the Spanish buildings (they're not French, oddly), penned in by intricate patterned black iron railings, watching the streams of over-excited hangover-tempters flash by as muffled sounds of bands and karaoke and cheesy MCs vibrate through the foundations of the street – each bar with its own little set-up of eyes flashing across the room, everyone sussing everyone – underscored by symphonies of shrieks and giggles and a live band playing rock and roll. Nudey-bar neon spreads gaudy illumination across the road and, in the haze of three-for-the-price-of-one bottles of beer, the light trails and smears across my eyes to make the whole place seem somewhere in a smudgy dream tucked well out of the way of reality.

This is the adult theme park. The world where gin makes anything seem possible, where childish fantasy seems fact and everyone in their own mind is the king of Hollywood. At last, somewhere to go that isn't real, there's no responsibility for anything: you don't have to be yourself in Bourbon Street, you can be whatever you want to be, we're all drunk, and who cares. To the sober it must look desperate, sad, and foolish – to the drunk it's the moments of a lifetime. It's tense and exciting and edgy and by Jove, tomorrow that's going to hurt.

But I'm a child of the eighties, there *is* no tomorrow...

CHAPTER TWENTY-TWO SOUNDTRACK:

Good **Ol *Boys***

Waylon Jennings (1980)

The Time of **My Life**

Bill Medley and Jennifer Warnes (1987)

Chapter Twenty-two

The Time of my Life

New Orleans to Lake Lure

Hangover. The moment of wake up; realisation that *it's on*, it's go; the suspension of reality has been suspended and the world is back out there again as harsh and bastard fast as it was before... and it slaps you right in the chops. It's not as simple as a pick-up-as-you-were, this time it's with a headache and the fuzzirific thoughts and *the fear*.

By day, the French Quarter is like a grubby TV set once the studio lights have been turned off. It's rancid and old and the only people on Bourbon Street are the street cleaners removing traces of another night of carnage with bleach guns, while stragglers wobble home with beads still around their necks and a yard of half-full cocktail that'll be dumped somewhere the moment the sick starts pumping up. I walk to the car slowly so as not to upset the contents of my guts, or to remix the alcohol and send it round my blood again for another journey around the brain. An eleven-hour journey down to the sunshine state offers no refuge. Brutal. Inhospitable. The journey thrusts us into an even balmier clime. The thick air is torrential even when it's not raining. We drive through tree-lined highways that offer none of the rugged landscape we'd been so used to in California and the North: this is flat and green and all the same, which is some relief for my stomach.

We emerge from the motor somewhere near Tampa, probably, for a stretch and a packet of cheesy hangover-feeding Cheetos; post-booze-flinchy and a bit paranoid. I *am* Hunter S. Thompson (without the Samoan). Early evening we get to Macon, Georgia, where a motel and a cool pool are waiting for us; having disregarded the entire day as something we were just going to sit and watch go by in mild pain and confusion. I have no idea what's in Macon or where exactly it is. But I sleep there very well.

Our couple of days starting to rise up the east side of the States are a story of masculine and feminine; butch and high camp. But to start with, it doesn't get much more butch than in Covington, Georgia, our next destination.

Covington prides itself on being the "Hollywood of the South". I'm not quite sure who decided that was the case, seeing as a handful of vaguely memorable films and (importantly) *The Dukes of Hazzard* seem to make up the sparse list of credits for the town. Nonetheless, we clamber out of the window of the car – out of respect for the Dukes. *The Dukes of Hazzard* was true boys stuff: fast cars, stunts, spitting and Daisy Duke. Ah, Daisy Daisy Duke.

THE DUKES OF HAZZARD (1979–1985) (TV)

Creator: Gy Waldron

Cast: Tom Wopat (Luke Duke), John Schneider (Bo Duke), Denver Pyle (Uncle Jesse Duke), Sorrell Brooke (Jefferson Davis "Boss" Hogg), Catherine Bach (Daisy Duke), Ben Jones (Cooter Davenport), James Best (Sheriff Rosco P. Coltrane), Waylon Jennings (The Balladeer), Sonny Shroyer (Deputy Enos Strate)

Notes:

The Dukes of Hazzard Barnstormer. I wanted it for months. A General Lee toy you had to wind backwards on the floor and then let go to see it whizz off. Thereafter, hopefully it slammed itself through the plastic doors of a little barn with tiny haystacks you could arrange according to your preference. It was a little one-dimensional as far as toys go, it pretty much just crashed into a barn, but back then it was even more desirable than the Stretch Hulk that I couldn't help sticking a pin in to see what the goo inside looked like. Those adverts made all those toys just *so* irresistible.

On the edge of Covington we find a little visitors' centre and figure we may as well drop in before we hit the main square. For a Saturday afternoon, there doesn't appear to be many people in Covington, let alone a whole lot going on. As we walk into the visitor's centre, we hear the voice of a lady talking to her son as she bends down to get some stuff out of a cupboard. The large blonde lady stands up on hearing our entrance and turns round to reveal herself to be a himself. I'm jarred by this, especially considering I was just having a little look at her/his behind. I begin asking all sorts of questions of myself.

The man has bright blond dyed hair and the most finely shaped eyebrows since Sherilyn Fenn in *Twin Peaks*. I wonder if the child is someone else's or maybe something he produced before his epiphany. In a small town like Covington, it's probably quite hard to keep sexual orientation a secret. We ask him for a map of Covington, believing this to be a pretty common request that wouldn't create much fuss at all. For the next five minutes he flusters around his collection of leaflets and concludes that he doesn't have maps. The visitors' centre hasn't thought to produce a map of the town. We ask about *The Dukes of Hazzard* and he shows us a toy car signed by Bo and tells us that our best bet would be to wander down to the square and visit a shop called A Touch of Country, which sounds ever so quaint.

We leave Danny LaRue to flap around his jumbled leaflets and head off to the main square. Covington is oh so quiet, with a little park in the square that has trees hanging lazily to mask a view across to the other side. In the middle of it all stands a statue of some old cowboy with a gun who's doubtless done something to make the town what it is today. In the first episode, the General Lee drives through this town square, so it's a very special place.

A huge courthouse occupies one corner of the square, looking over everyone with a warning demeanour and Tom vaguely recognises it as *the* Hazzard County Courthouse. He can't be sure, and so spends half an hour photographing the bloody thing anyway. This is one of Tom's days where he wants to drink every bit of Dukes location legend *or* myth *or* pure conjecture, despite not remembering or recognising *any* of it. He calls it *making the most of it*, while Luke and I think it's more *making a meal of it*. We battle our way through a group of bored kids on skateboards, whizzing around with accents that the local authorities really ought to try to stamp out for their own good, and make it to A Touch of Country – a store that sells furniture, knick-knacks, ice cream and houses a *Dukes of Hazzard* museum up the far end.

We walk into the ice cream bit and approach an elderly man behind the counter wearing one of those fifties style diner uniforms like something out of *Happy Days*. The men in these parts are *real* men though, and refuse to offer any facial expression to go with their tough-talking manner. This man slurs his way to telling us to go the hell up the far end for *Dukes of Hazzard* stuff and he doesn't care a damn if we video it. Ok then. Up the end, we find a little glass counter with *Dukes of Hazzard* memorabilia, like the Barnstormer toy that I so coveted as a kid. Seeing it gives me a pang, a little flashback to the moment I unwrapped it on Christmas Day.

> *Tear it, rip it, get the stupid paper off... Barnstormer! Yes yes yes yes yes yes ... dance, must do a celebration jig, run round the tree, dive on the sofa and squeal into the pillows. The Barnstormer! Yes yes yes... Next present?*

There are photos of the stars are all over the walls – some of them standing with the local people who are still a little obsessed with the show and looking decidedly starry-eyed. Especially the ones next to Daisy. A lady with bizarre eyebrows stands behind the counter; it's like she's plucked them all out and drawn them back in. I'm not sure what the deal with eyebrows is in Covington but I begin to suspect that the one and only local beautician hasn't got as far as the eyebrow unit on her course yet. The lady introduces us to a car door that appears to be from the General Lee itself. I hoot with nostalgic glee and begin touching every part of it so I can be sure I've touched something that Bo and Luke have touched.

After letting me do what is almost a Christmas present unwrapping jig, she tells me it's just a random car door that a local bloke has done up to *look* like the General Lee. I feel cheated, a bit silly, and hiss something about *what's the point of that*. Behind me an old boy has walked over and introduces himself as the father of the guy that made the car door.

"Ain't nuthin' like the Dukes a Hazzard," he declares. I agree enthusiastically to make up for my previous disapproval of the car door.

The man speaks with such a three-foot thick accent that he might as well speak Hindi with a Geordie accent, because it's pretty unintelligible. I'm not sure even *he* can make out what he's saying. I manage to make *some* stuff out; that he went to the "Dukesfest" a week or so ago and met Dukes fans from all over the world. Dukesfest is one of those conventions where everyone wears T-shirts with pictures of their favourite things on them. I'm amazed to hear that neither Tom Wopat nor John Schneider (the original Bo and Luke) turned up to the convention. Not even Elizabeth Bach (Daisy Duke) turned up. Ah, Daisy Duke. Daisy Daisy Duke. Those legs, those unbelievable legs. This show had everything: cars and legs.

I actually spoke on the phone to Elizabeth Bach once, when I was working on *It'll Be Alright on the Night* with Sir Denis of Norden. I was a mumbling stumbling jibbering pillock-tongued nonsense-vendor. How on earth was I expected to call Elizabeth Bach and maintain control of my toilet functions? I said *hello* just fine, *hello* went well. But it's just that when she started talking with that Daisy twang, it changed something in my tongue muscle. The same thing happened when I called up Chrissy Robinson from *Neighbours*; although that time I just didn't trust myself *not* to do a Stefan Dennis impression.

Anyway. The old boy keeps trying to make me buy a Daisy Duke key ring that I really don't want. He thinks I should *definitely* have one; really *wants* me to have one. I refuse politely six times. He tells me that, just like most households in the area, he has a framed picture of Daisy up on his wall. That's brilliant. They *all* have a framed picture of Daisy Duke on their walls. She's their Princess Diana. Priceless. It's like me keeping a photo of Kathy Beale from *Eastenders* on the mantelpiece.

Before we leave, the museum lady with the eyebrows tries to sell us retro *Dukes of Hazzard* digital watches, which she says she can't guarantee will work because of the damp, but will charge us fifteen dollars for. Then she gives us some maps with the locations they used for the show marked on them. With those and a belly full of milkshake, we leave and promise to come back if we ever return to Covington.

Luke and I look over the map and see some places that really would be interesting *only* to the Dukes connoisseurs who've tragically memorised *every* scene of every show made. If you search on the Internet, you'll see them. One guy has meticulously matched up the most inane of shots (like a bend in a road or a junk yard the General drove through) with the same places as they are today. A sort of sinking feeling lowers into my stomach; because I know that Tom's obsessive compulsive location box-ticking tendencies are going to mean us being dragged to every little shred of Dukesness on the list.

We plod behind him as he strives to reach destination "A": a car lot that featured on the show. After trudging for fifteen minutes in the mid-afternoon sun, we reach the car park of a bank where the car lot had once been. Tom, at this point, admits that not only did he not remember there *being* a car lot in the show, but that he wouldn't have recognised it even if it had been still here – which it isn't. *Good grief, Charlie Brown.*

"Can you tell me where I can find a Daisy around here?" I ask a stranger.

"Well, the policy around here is that a girl has to wear a skirt below the knee. But you might find some Daisys on a Saturday afternoon around the shopping centre."

Seeing as this man appears willing to put up with my flagrant but playful stereotyping, I really put the boot in and go for it. "Do you make moonshine?"

"No, but a lot of it *was* being made. It looks and smells horrible. At one time the South River, on the other side of the county, was known as producing more moonshine per square foot than any other river in Georgia. And there were several killings in the county because they said you were taking too much of their water. And the good part of it was that the water they were fighting over was sewage water from the city of Atlanta." Jesus, these people had rucks over the right to drink poo? "You'd look at it and you'd see big clumps of sewage floating down. And they'd make moonshine out of it." I somehow get the feeling that I'd try it anyway.

We head towards a place called Snellville – the directions for which are hazy and muddled. At one point we stop at a local store for directions and a lady outside asks us where we are from.

"You can *tell* it's England." Her husband snaps at her.

"Hell, ahhm a Southern gal, ahhh don't know nuthin' but Georgia!"

After an hour or so of driving up and down the same roads we manage to find a wiggly little road that winds down to a gravel dirt track, which itself kinks its bone-dry way like a secret path deep into the heart of Georgian farmland. This is the real deal. Tourists don't go to places like this, you just wouldn't; it's so hidden away and off the sensible track. But we're not ordinary tourists, we're *idiot* tourists. Gunshots fire away in the distance and kids zoom past us on quad-bikes, which seem to be the preferred method of transport in these small lanes.

Finally we find the address that, according to the map, is where the building used as the Dukes' farmhouse stands. This is supposed to be the pièce de résistance of our Dukes tour, the great bazooka bonanza finale: the actual house where Jesse and Bo and Luke and Daisy lived. However, we're confronted with a broken up old barn/shack type thing that's struggling to keep its walls and roof aligned and vertical. There's no recognition sparking in my brain whatsoever. It's just a log cabin on the verge of condemnation with signs painted in red on it saying "Keep Out". Hot and irritable, I'm on the verge of storming off. Then, one of the kids on a quad-bike trundles past and Tom stops him to ask with a hint of wobbly desperation in his voice if this was the place used for the show. The kid immediately points very positively at the old shack and screeches off without a word.

Still, we can't believe it. Tom decides to take the bull by the horns and venture up to a farmhouse sitting some distance off a driveway nearby. It's a bold move; there's a long walk of shameful trespassing before he gets to the house where he may or may not be welcome. I expect him to stagger back with a body full of blunderbuss shrapnel, but in fact he comes jogging springily back with the flared nostrils of a location hunter with a lead. It would seem the owners of the farmhouse also own the shack and confirm that it was the Dukes' home in the show. We all trek up the driveway and speak to the man who owns the place, while his wife peels carrots over the sink. The house is a very large new build that's not too out of touch with the original style of farmhouse for the area, and on being invited in, we find an interior of *much* mahogany; it's like being inside a tree.

"Oh yeah, when they had a reunion last year they had forty cars on my lawn," says the owner. "The only thing is the hut's in such bad condition. OK? It had asbestos and we had to remove it. OK? They used it for the first five shows. OK? If you go down this road down here, you'll find a little wooden bridge and that's where they used to jump." We are in *proper* Hazzard County, and Jesse's old place exists. OK? Not sure what the OK bit's all about.

"Nuthin's changed, it's all still dirt roads. After the first five they re-created the barn at the Disney Ranch. I bought the place afterwards. Most of the people that live on this road are the same people."

"Are the locals big fans of the show?"

"Not really, it was just something that was going on here. When they had the reunion, *a lot* of people came over."

"Did they shoot the interiors in the barn?"

"Yeah, yeah."

314

"Is there anything left in there?"

"No. Somebody stole the mantelpiece and a couple of the windows." Not things you can just slip under your jumper.

"Did you get starry-eyed when the stars came down for the reunion?"

"No, no, I don't get starry-eyed." This man looks like he hasn't pulled a facial expression since 1973. There's no wiggling his tickle. He's very generous though, to allow us in and entertain us wanting to look at his rancid old barn.

"It's probably gonna have to come down."

"Really? When?"

"I don't know, probably fairly soon. All the beams are rotten. I was actually gonna restore it but we took a look at the condition of it and it's termite infested and everything."

"So we could be the very last people to video the old Dukes' barn?"

"Could be. A world exclusive..." Finally a little smile cracks open his face.

"This land was deeded to a soldier after the civil war and it stayed in the same family until I bought it. Some of that family were *born* in the old cabin. The film company didn't make *anything*, it was all already here." So they really did just tap into the local Georgian culture to present us a caricature of it. The man instructs us that it's fine to drive the car across his lawn to the shack. We're not to go in the place though, as at any moment it could fall on us, which might hurt a bit and smear asbestos residue all over our faces. "Watch out for snakes too," he says, which almost puts pay to my approach up to the place. I brave it though, and we climb out of the car windows yet again, which is getting harder each time because a knobble of bone on my spine is beginning to scrape on the same bit of the window each time and chafing is becoming apparent.

We dare approach the building, scared that it's a bit like the latter stages of a game of Jenga, and peer through a gap in the wooden beams; the walls just seem to be logs arranged on top of each other. Inside, the place is trashed all over the shop. It's like a heroin addict's flat, all stained and shit all over the floors. All that's in the room is a mouldy old armchair that may or may not have been used in the show. We take a look at a still from the show and can see that the building is smaller than it was then, but I can match up the chimney and see that the General Lee was parked where a tree is overgrown now.

I'm chuffed that we've found the Dukes' farmhouse. *And* might well be the last people to shoot at the place. If you'd have told a five-year-old me that I'd be the last person to point a camera at that house before it became wood pulp, I would probably have asked what wood pulp is.

We manage to tear Tom away ... nearly in tears ... muttering something about buying the place and restoring it and moving Jesse and Daisy and the boys back in and it would be just like the old days and ... and ... and...

Another multi-state day begins with a drive down to Cleveland, where I've arranged to meet Margaret Strong, the Press and Publicity lady at Babyland General Hospital – the birthplace of the Cabbage Patch Kids. This brief tangent away from film and TV is intended to add a different popular culture texture to our trip ... and also the idea of a hospital for Cabbage Patch Kids sounds hilarious.

In 1976, art student Xavier Roberts began using an old German fabric sculpture technique to create quilt dolls, and by 1978 he was making money "adopting" the unique dolls to people in the southeast of the USA. Suddenly in 1981, the Little People Originals were featured in Newsweek and *kabooom*, off the world goes on a ravenous frenzy for the quilty little monsters. By 1983 three million had been sold and supply hadn't even met demand. In 1985, the first Cabbage Patch Kid went to space – true – and by 1990 sixty-five million had been "adopted" worldwide. That's one for *everyone* in the UK.

My first memory of the Cabbage Patch Kids (the word "dolls" is banned from the hospital – they say "kids" or "babies" is of watching the news sometime in the eighties and seeing grown adults – mostly parents – rampaging through a department store, fighting over these ugly dolls ... sorry, I mean kids ... which their children had *demanded* for Christmas. The parents *had* to get one or face a bitter parent–child divorce in the law courts. I'm not sure which I find more terrifying – the fighting parents or the dolls ... er ... babies ... themselves. These pug-faced deformed toys absolutely swept the world off its feet and I'm not really sure *why*. Ugly little bleeders. Their success was so absurd that someone was moved to create The Garbage Pail Kids – a collectable series of cards, which also came with a stick of bubble gum that tasted of Germolene – that offered a pastiche of evil alternatives to the sugary Cabbage Kids.

We start seeing signs for Babyland General Hospital a few miles before we hit the small town of Cleveland. The billboards have the faces of Cabbage Patch Kids plastered all over them and already I have the fear and the faint indigestion. These things really creep me out.

At the hospital, we park the car next to all the family vehicles: the people wagons and the older, longer cars owned by grandparents that have borrowed the children for the day. Tom keeps us waiting by the car as he changes into his suit – he feels it's appropriate that he looks the part if he's going to apply for the adoption of a child, even if it is born in a cabbage and looks like Les Dawson. Margaret has told us to meet her in the "Father's Waiting Room", which is their cute name for *the reception*. And there she is, a sweet little ear-to-ear grinning American-Asian lady who's made the effort to come in on her day off to show us around dressed in her nurse's outfit. After introductions, I make it clear that although Tom and I might look like "My Two Dads" applying for adoption, we're not gay.

"That's fine, doesn't matter. You just have to promise to love the baby. *Anyone* can be a father." I'm sorry, I know I'm a cynical old wotsit, but this place is ludicrous. It's like a *real* hospital, all white and clinical; I mean there are waiting rooms and Tannoy messages and machinery – lots of *proper* hospital machinery.

Just as we get there, a message comes over the Tannoy that the delivery of a new baby is just about to happen in the Cabbage Patch. Margaret springs to life, all excited and naïve-looking, and drags us through the hospital – past the room with newly born Cabbage Patch Kids in incubators and the room where the older Cabbagers are having their school dinners – to the Cabbage Patch, a large hall with a centrepiece that's essentially a stage made to look like a cabbage patch with a huge tree in the middle. Dr Justin (dressed in full doctor's garb) is there, ready to extract a new baby. Dr Justin is as camp as a bauble.

"These are the mother cabbages," explains Margaret, pointing at the cabbages around the tree. "We're waiting for the nine leaves apart, once they're a full nine leaves apart then they start to go into labour." Are the nine leaves a euphemism for the *you know what*? I'm standing in front of the "Magic Crystal Tree", waiting for a cabbage to go into labour. I can barely control myself from laughing; it's all so over the top, I just can't believe we're all standing here waiting for one of those dolls ... kids ... to be *born*.

"We have two drugs that we use during labour, that's *Imagicillin* and *TLC*, which, of course, is tender loving care." Blurrrrrrgh. Sorry Dr Justin, but this is the funniest thing I've ever seen. I try not to make any noise as my shoulders heave up and down with the giggles. Everyone's taking it all really seriously; a whole hall full of kids and parents standing there riveted and concerned.

"Mother Cabbage in labour, *code green*," announces the Tannoy voice.

"This is a very special delivery," says Dr Justin. "This is what we call a planned parenthood. The new mother is right here in front of me and she's hoping for a little baby boy." He points to a fourteen-year-old girl standing at the front, looking quite tense. Oh my Christ.

"The procedure we're performing today is an "Easyotomy". Since we've been doing Easyotomies here at Babyland, we've never had to do any c-sections..." Fuck me. This is unbelievable... "which we're pleased about here because we all know that a c-section is really just a cabbage section, right folks?" The crowd ripple with a nervous giggle and then murmurs with all the enthusiasm of a Butlins kids' club. Dr Justin then gets us to join in with breathing exercises and starts to pull the Cabbage Patch Kid, naked and upside down, out of the mother cabbage. He announces proudly that the little girl has already decided to name the baby Devon Alexander. All I can do is stare at Dr Justin, utterly agog, tears of laughter hopelessly welling.

It's just a money-making tourist attraction and I know Margaret's PR role is to act as though it's a genuine facility, but the whole set-up is *so* realistic; there are people walking around with their adopted newborns wrapped in blankets, looking as though they really have acquired a precious being. Everything at Babyland is geared towards cutesy; the ickle cots and the darling little cribs and the soft sound of happy children playing over the loud speakers. Every time I look over to Margaret, her face beams with gooey pride; she really believes this is the cutest thing *ever*. It probably is, but I'm not the geezer for all this malarky. Dr Justin invites the girl down to get the baby thing dressed, and from behind a glass window at another part of the hospital (the whole group of voyeurs follow to the other wing for the next stage), we see him x-ray, weigh and professionally put a nappy on it, with powder, as he strokes its chest with a hand clad in a very dainty ruby ring.

We then follow the proud new mother through to the "Adoption Room", where she has to take an oath saying that she'll give the little kid enough TLC.

Then it's off to the "Discharge Desk" (what a rigmarole, couldn't she just have bought a *real* baby from Africa? There'd be less paperwork), which involves a parent or guardian producing a Visa card to the strength of $199.

"Is this your first baby?" Margaret asks the girl, whose wearing a T-shirt that says "Strange is not a crime".

"Third. I've done this a couple of times." So, she's probably spent nearly $600 just to have Dr Justin pull her doll thing out of a cabbage. Remarkable.

"OK," says Dr Justin, "So, your baby was born with a butterfly on his stomach, so I'll give you a prescription for a lot of TLC, give him a lot of love in the first week and that should clear up. Any problems, give me a call here at the hospital." He holds up an *actual* prescription and a birth certificate is handed over along with the official adoption paper. The girl is told to hold her hand up and repeat the oath.

"I promise ... with all my heart ... to give this special Cabbage Patch Baby ... all my love and care ... and in every way possible ... be the best adoptive mom ... in the whole world." At that the whole room breaks out into applause. America. Only America.

Margaret pulls us back through to reception, where a cute girl in a nurse's outfit mans the reception desk. I feel so embarrassed about being here, with two other blokes, that I nearly go over and explain to her that I wouldn't normally be here. We try to exit from the reception, but a sign discourages people from that route and urges them through the other exit that happens to be situated at the other end of the gift shop.

Needless to say, we don't end up adopting one of them.

Along the highway, the only adjustment to the thickly treed surroundings we've been passing through since Florida is that hills are beginning to emerge which at least give us a bit of distance to gaze into as we sit in the car for hours. In between those hills and winding roads that turn my intestines into knots and ruffle my gizzards, we pass through small tourist towns populated by families, occasionally interrupted by gangs of bikers exploding along the street on their great growling Harleys.

We're heading towards the North Carolina holiday town of Lake Lure, but along the way in Chimney Rock, we find The Wicklow Inn, which proudly has a wooden wall from one of the *Dirty Dancing* holiday camp huts attached to it. The owner, with Jimmy Saville-white hair, seems to think it quite normal that she's attached one side of a log cabin to the side of her hotel. The film-makers sold off parts of the set to a lot of the places around here, and they saw fit to display them for a bit of extra attention from tourists.

Although the towns of Chimney Rock, Bat Cave and Lake Lure have been tourist destinations for years, they clearly owe something to *Dirty Dancing* for their perpetual roaring trade.

DIRTY DANCING (1987) (MOVIE)

Director: Emile Ardolino
Writer: Eleanor Bergstein
Producers: Mitchell Cannold, Steven Reuther
Cast: Patrick Swayze (Johnny Castle), Jennifer Grey (Frances "Baby" Houseman), Jerry Orbach (Dr Jake Houseman), Cynthia Rhodes (Penny Johnson), Jack Weston (Max Kellerman), Jane Brucker (Lisa Houseman), Kelly Bishop (Marjorie Houseman), Lonny Price (Neil Kellerman), Max Cantor (Robbie Gould)
Awards: Won an Oscar for Best Music and Best Original Song ("The Time of My Life")

Notes:
I didn't really get into this movie until the early nineties, when my first girlfriend's obsession with the soundtrack gave me the excuse to listen to it. *Dirty Dancing* is a real guilty pleasure for blokes, we're just not *supposed* to like this sort of stuff. But really, gloves off, male pride aside, it's got to be one of the best movie soundtracks ever. There you go, I won't be saying that again, but I've said it.

Dirty Dancing is a coming of age tale about a girl moving into womanhood during a family holiday in the Catskills. Johnny (Swayze) isn't what Daddy intended for Baby, and the relationship between father and daughter changes forever.

Laid-back Lake Lure sits pretty on the edge of a lake that was actually man-made – a vision of Dr Lucius B. Morse, who in 1926 built a dam on the Rocky Broad River to create the lake. It's an enormous effort; deep lush green trees cram around the royal blue basin on which float tourist boats as the mansions clinging onto the bank hide themselves and their famous owners.

Tom has spoken on the phone to the people at Lake Lure Tours about a visit to a location used in *Dirty Dancing*. They seemed to want to help, so we head straight for their hut on the side of the water. Amazingly, they want us to take a big motor-powered boat out on our own so we can visit the spot in our own time. They basically give us the keys. I hate boats, and look at the young girl offering us this beast as if she's asking me to fly my own plane back to England. She gauges my expression correctly and decides to throw in a boy, who can drive the boat for us.

Brandon is an outgoing young fellow with the traditional rolls of American flab and one of those teenage wispy moustaches that looks as though it's about ready for its first trim. He can't wait to call us "blokes" every time he refers to us, finding it the funniest thing since "mate" and "blimey". He loves the idea of our trip – another of those younger people who are fans of the eighties despite being born sometime during them – and bundles us on the boat like an excited puppy.

The sun begins to creep towards the lake as water-skiers plough through the glistening ripples and shove waves our way that lap up over the side and quietly drench me. It's serene here; lots of people, but they're all relaxed and slow paced. That's what they came here to be.

We get to the *Dirty Dancing* cove: the very place where Johnny got Baby in the lake and held her up above his head. Just on the bank is the remains of Johnny's cottage – but all that survived an arson attack are the stone foundations at the bottom. We watch the scene on our video camera and match up the landscape to approximate more or less exactly the spot where the lake-lift happened. I throw Tom into the lake and bust a gut laughing while Brandon sneaks behind me and does the same to me, which is fair enough apart from the murky lake water that gets up my nose. I've said it before; water of any description has no business up the nose.

My shrieks are not for cold water – it's nice and warm – they're for whatever it is at the bottom of that lake. Some sort of gloopy, sandy, silty stuff allows my feet to sink in and send signals to my brain that all sorts of vile water creatures are probably snacking on my toenails, making nests in my leg hairs and laying eggs between my toes. It's not ideal, to be fair. It must have been a hell of a day for Swayze and Grey when they stood here to shoot that scene. They actually filmed it in October, which meant that some poor bastard on the film crew had to go around painting the browning leaves in the back of shot green again. Tom's spared that duty due to the fact it is actually summer now. Apparently though, there are no close-ups of this scene in the movie because they were so cold that they're lips had gone blue. But I wonder if that's just a piece of web-mythery.

Anyway, the mysteries of the underfoot texture *have* to be ignored; we have work to do. I've suspected all along that I haven't really got the biceps to lift Tom over my head. I sort of understand that most likely, it's beyond me. But Tom's never going to get *me* over *his* head, I'm too bloatsome, and Luke has to hold his precious camera. So here I am. I've got to try my best to show any remaining masculinity I might have, after sacrificing much of it to come to a *Dirty Dancing* location in the first place. I work through my natural aversion to holding another topless man around the waist and hoist the skinny fella into the air.

Well, I say *hoist*. It's not really a hoist. It's more of a vertical shove that couldn't possibly maintain weight. It's more like a bit of a push. I can't muster the power to hold him above my head and although we manage to get him kind of horizontal – the way Swayze and Grey did – the weight is too much and I end up keeping him aloft by balancing his stomach on the side of my face. This is the least erotic homo-erotic situation, and not one I'd like to get anywhere near repeating. We try over and over again, and each time it's less likely I'll get him up their because my unfathomable biceps are filling with more lactic acid every time I get to the stage where I straighten my arms. Every time, we get to the point of collapse, where either I fall over and go under the water with him on top of me, or I roll him off and plunge *him* under. It's obvious which route I take and each time Tom complains that I'm not supposed to throw him, which I get the giggles over because sometimes he's going quite a way under, maybe scraping his chin on the silty nonsense down the bottom. In between "takes" (if they can be called that), things skulk around down below and slither around our legs causing shrieks and blood-curdling whines that are probably hugely over the top.

After around seventeen tries, I decide that I've had enough of Tom's tits being rested on my cheek and we call it a day.

Technically, unsuccessful.

But sod technically, I'm proud that I came out here to this oversized ditch, where one of the most loved and famous scenes in eighties movies was shot, and goddamit I gave it a go.

Nobody puts Spencer in the corner.

(Sorry).

CHAPTER TWENTY-THREE SOUNDTRACK:

Eye *of the* Tiger

Survivor (1982)

Raining in Baltimore

Counting Crows (1993)

Chapter Twenty-three

Suspects, Witnesses and lots of Stairs

Lake Lure to New York

North north north; we pummel the roads and just get the hell up north. Up we get into Washington, where we have no business other than to briefly throw me down an enormous staircase. Of course.

At the end of M Street in Georgetown, we find a steep staircase – seventy-five stairs to be precise (it took a while to count) – which can't fail to trigger cramp in anyone's movie memory muscle. The staircase is in northwest Washington and looks like something out of Victorian London.

THE EXORCIST (1973) (Movie)
Director: William Friedkin
Writer: William Peter Blatty
Producers: Noel Marshall, David Salven
Awards: Won two Oscars

Cast: Ellen Burstyn (Chris MacNeil), Max Von Sydow (Father Merrin), Lee J. Cobb (Lt Kinderman), Kitty Winn (Sharon), Jack McGowran (Burke Dennings), Jason Miller (Father Karras), Linda Blair (Regan), Reverend William O'Malley (Father Dyer).

Notes:

The Exorcist may not have been born in the eighties, but it was doubtlessly one of those movies that hung over to such an extent that for many people my age, it was like watching a brand new film and thus part of our eighties experience. It was a *thing* in junior school: "Have you seen it?" Rightly, most parents wouldn't allow it, but those who did get to see it told of horrors that made you want to sick up your Spam salad.

The stairs are wedged between rows of houses and take you down to the next level of roads in the slanted area of gradient-ridden Georgetown. They're narrow and daunting and not necessarily consistent in stair width. Graffiti covers the top and bottom, the word "exorcist" featuring many times, lest we're mistaken that *these* were the stairs used in, yes, *The Exorcist*.

There's really only one thing I can do at *The Exorcist* stairs, and probably the one thing that after twenty-odd chapters of my voice you're *dying* for me to do. Fall down the buggers. It wouldn't be possible for me to visit the stairs and *not* fall down the bloody things: just like the vicar did in the film. So, I stand at the top; just in front of me is a sinister little brick-built archway that frames the stairs in amongst the rest of Georgetown below, and a lake off in the distance. I look down at the first paving slab right in front of me. Someone has written "Get Exorcised Here."

I'm not sure about exorcised, but I suspect I'm about to get bruised and chafed and lacerated and maybe, if it goes *really* terribly wrong, circumcised, again.

I trip myself up and begin my descent. Roll after roll after roll ... it's not fast; in fact it takes forever to get all the way down. You don't think I'd go down there full pelt, do you? What am I, some sort of mug? In the movie, the stunt man had thick rubber lining the stairs, so there's no way I'm going down normal speed on pure concrete. I do it very, very slowly, striking all sorts of theatrical falling poses for the camera so that when we speed it up later, it'll either look really real, or comically satisfying. Nonetheless, the slow motion tumble still grazes and claws at my flesh and I'm sure the smell of my burning skin wafts across all of DC.

I get to the bottom, exhausted, having strained every muscle in my body trying to prevent the fall from picking up pace and turning into what the newspapers would report as being a "death tumble". Oh no no, if I'm going to fall victim to a death tumble, it certainly wouldn't be during a homage to a film made in 1973.

"I can see why the vicar died, coming down those things," I say to Luke, forgetting what actually happened in the film.

"He didn't die," replies Luke coldly, like I'm a spaz.

"Oh, well, he *should* have done."

From Georgetown we drive into Washington so that we can get lost and inadvertently enter unsafe areas with our laptops and camera on show. We're good at that. Northeast Washington really isn't a place I want to spend time: every single window has bars on it. I drive fast and with white knuckles that look like rows of miniature skulls, until we're well away – stopping randomly at a Motel 6 in Capital Heights – wherever that is.

In the morning we smuggle our stuff into the car, get out of Capital Heights as fast as we can and leave the DC area without seeing so much as a tint off the dome of the Capitol building or a glint of smarm from the White House. Heading north, we crash into the side of Baltimore. It feels like a mini-New York, with the same edgy, manic feel – like anything could happen to you at any minute – but just on a much smaller scale.

Before we get to our next movie location, just on the edge downtown in that bit of a city where all the bypass bridges hang over and nobody knows quite what to do with the land underneath; we have a wander around the big buildings in the city centre.

Further up the road, we spot an old-looking red-coloured Gothic building standing in such an eccentric pose that we have no choice but to head towards it. What a delightful little mill around the city this is. We may even have got there had a policeman not grabbed us like a couple of naughty hoodies, and forced us to sit in the gutter on the pavement with hands on head, while demanding our ID (*but my hands are on my head, officer*) with what I perceive to be unnecessary aggression and a little bit of hand hovering over the holster. What the fuck is going on? My heart's gone to techno-beat level, my face must look like a knotted old rope dyed red, I don't understand, I'm in the gutter, scared.

After I get my bearings back, I find myself still sitting in the gutter. I feel humiliated, perched on the kerb like someone who's done something awful, while everyone walks past staring and pointing and *assuming*. Have they found out we're TV producers? I knew working on *RI:SE* would catch up on me one day. It seems we're being aggressively guarded by the policeman while he waits for back-up. We look at the copper with, naturally, bewildered faces. This is an outrage. In seconds, another two police cars screech up and my passport is being handed round like a cheap rumour. The cop comes over and fires questions at us at a speed clearly intended to force an error and confirm guilt. We can't get anything wrong though – fact is that Tom pictured one building because it had cute smoke in front of it, with no knowledge as to what it was at all. Turns out it was a bank. Some fucking do-gooding wanker saw Tom and called the police, claiming that they'd been watching us walk around taking pictures of financial institutions. What a prick. Do I really look like fucking Al Qaeda, walking around in my brightly-coloured football shirt? If you're reading this, you, who called the police, I'm going to find you and lock you in a pissing safe.

It's not long before my arse starts to whine about the kerb and I spot that the policeman's colleagues, over by the now numerous squad cars, are looking at him like he's some sort of imbecile.

"What do you think you're going to do with them?" one asks incredulously, with a little smile curling round the edges of the sentence.

"I don't know, they were photographing financial institutions." The other one looks at us, looks at him and huffs, comes over to us and asks us to enjoy our stay, hands back my passport and goes no way in apologising to my arse for the trauma it's sat through, let alone my poor clonking ticker. As we walk away, a female colleague shouts after us, "He's an arsehole!" and they all stand there laughing like the end of a *Scooby Doo* cartoon at the embarrassing predicament their idiot colleague put the three Englishmen through.

IMPORTANT MESSAGE

George W. Bush: I demand a full pardon and public apology on the front of every newspaper in the USA, saying that you accidentally put three innocent men – The

Baltimore Three – through a pavement Guantanemo hell. And I would also like a free dinner at Denny's as a gesture of goodwill.

With our appetite for Baltimore, let alone its poxy financial institutions, dampened to the point of drenched, we sop our way back to the car and just *drive* past the Hollywood Diner, a metallic building wedged underneath the bridges. It hasn't changed a fig since the filming crew of *Diner* visited, along with, I think, the best performance we ever saw from The Guttenberg. But I'm not in the mood.

We have a whole day to dawdle around Philadelphia; to get to the bottom of how it contributed to our experience of eighties movies. Our research came out with the headline of *Rocky*. Curious that the production be split right the way across the coasts, but anyway, Philadelphia is the true home of *Rocky*. And before you start, I know, *Rocky* was made in 1976, but I think we all know that the sequels and in truth Rocky himself resides very deeply in the eighties. The story is set here and there's even a statue of the great slurring buffoon outside the Spectrum Sports Stadium. I know of no other eighties movie star who has a statue standing in his or her honour. Can you imagine a bronze Howard the Duck in Los Angeles? Maybe a Marty McFly *should* be petitioned for, I'd support that.

The Art Museum is probably the most popular but least visited attraction in Philadelphia. Because of Rocky, bus-loads of tourists seem to pull up outside, empty out for five minutes, fill back up and bugger off without so much as a once-over of a Monet. All because these are the stairs that Rocky ran up while he was training in that world famous, much-spoofed montage where he ends up jumping around at the top like a nutter.

The museum's website makes no reference to *Rocky* and the only official confirmation that this was the place used for that incredibly famous movie moment is two small Stallone-sized bronze footprints and the word "Rocky" carved in capitals into the paving slab at the top of the stairs. It's certainly a photogenic spot: looking out from the top towards downtown Philly, there's a statue of someone important standing serenely in the way of towering shiny buildings grouped up in the distance. I stand watching the *Rocky* fans huddle around Rocky's footprints waiting for their turn to stand on them and raise their arms like champions, and don't know whether to be proud and validated

– that my experience of eighties films has a hangover for other people too – or whether to feel sorry for the art museum, playing second fiddle to an idiot boxer.

So we wait for a lull in the *very* constant flow of tourists/pilgrims embarrassedly running up the stairs, red-facedly doing the two-armed leap into the air at the top.

Then I go for it.

I sprint like a Jack Russell: tongue hanging out, feet clapping up those stairs in nothing short of a scamper, *come on Balboa, get a piece of me.* I get to the top and tear around the place like a demented Premiership footballer. Celebrations I've never *thought* of before are pouring out of me: sexy dances, vitriolic air-punches and wide-mouthed grins-near-to-tears. I let it all out. I thoroughly show up everyone else's efforts, which I think are just too close to the original *Rocky* – I thought we may as well play with the format a bit. I think most people feel a bit sorry for me.

After that little public out-pouring of bizarre dance and jubilation – almost performance art – I think it best that we make for the downtown area to give me a bit of a cooling down period. We move along to an area in the city where Rocky wouldn't have been seen dead. Rittenhouse Square is larger but identical in essence to Soho Square in London; a piece of tranquillity in the middle of madness, all surrounded by grand old building, with a wrought iron fence carving out the green serene plenty-benched square park in the middle from the flanking houses. It's populated by three different types of people: 1) city workers grabbing a hasty low-carb lunch trying to kid themselves that they can relax in this leafy tree-lined square when actually all they do is sit checking their watches every couple of minutes to make sure they're not late back; 2) tourists who are too proud to admit they're lost and are acting as though this is just a little break from all the walking around but actually they're stuck here; and 3) homeless people with bottles of something in brown bags and voices like they've swallowed Michael Winner.

We add a fourth "type" to the park's inhabitants: 4) eighties movie-location hunters trying to work out which corner of the park it was where Eddie Murphy pretended to be crippled in *Trading Places*.

TRADING PLACES (1983) (Movie)

Director: John Landis
Writers: Timothy Harris, Herschel Weingrod
Producer: George Folsey Jnr
Cast: Eddie Murphy (Billy Ray Valentine), Dan Ackroyd (Louis Winthorpe III), Denholm Elliott (Coleman), Ralph Bellamy (Randolph Duke), Don Ameche (Mortimer Duke), Paul Gleason (Clarence Beeks), Jamie Lee Curtis (Ophelia), James Belushi (Harvey)

Notes:

Trading Places was not my favourite movie, which is something that Tom and Luke and probably *you* will gang up on me over. They loved it. They thought it was funny and I thought it was stupid. OK, so for the first half of the film there's something of a serious message in their about race and privilege and maybe something even more philosophical relating to the nature/nurture conundrum ... but the fact is that Eddie Murphy's best gag was that he had to fart in the bath to have a Jacuzzi at home. Come on.

And then? And then they get on a train. Everything was vaguely believable and I thought the premise might go somewhere until it turns into a *Russ Abbot's Mad House* sketch with a fake gorilla and an even faker gorilla and Dan Ackroyd badly painted like a black man. I thought it was a load of eyewash. The best line in the movie was delivered by the best man in the movie, Denholm Elliot. That line? It was "Eggnog."

Despite my reservations about the film, I'm keen to re-create the scene from the Rittenhouse Square where Eddie Murphy is on a skateboard type-thing and pretending to be crippled. Tom does the same thing as Murphy – using the skateboard we came through the *Back to the Future* tunnel on – and just like happened in the movie, I opt to lift him up from the board and throw him, almost crushing all of his vertebrae in the process, sending him rolling along the grass like a 1990 Jurgen Klinsmann. People walking past smudge a slight grin across their faces.

In the movie, Eddie Murphy is lifted up by the cops and proclaims it's a miracle that he can walk. He escapes out of the square and down what we discover to be Locust Street, only to be caught up by other cops in a car. It's here that he bumps into Dan Ackroyd outside the gentleman's club and the gristle of the movie is born; where the rich meets the poor and the whole *Trading Places* escapade kicks off. Well, the entrance to the gentleman's club is still here, looking as prim and poncey as it did in the film; except it's not a club for old farts but actually a music school. We try to contrive a scene where I bump into Tom just like Murphy and Ackroyd. The result is a sickening clash of appalling acting styles: one being over the top and the other being even further over the top. On impact, which we badly act as not expecting, I collapse to the ground like a fainting Victorian lady and Tom stammers out a hammy apology that would have got even an *Eastenders'* extra the boot. So we give up on that.

On the edge of town and in the middle of a nest of over and underpasses threading urgently between each other is the 30th Street Train Station. I've no idea about historic architecture, but I would describe this immense building as a little bit art deco but not half as flamboyant, which really makes it just a bit grand but largely functional. Its height is something to get the neck flapping for a start, and the windows spanning from top to bottom in strips with light flooding through seem to be the most striking aspect of the place. This station certainly has that eerie, echoey feeling of many people not even half filling a massive building full of marble: 'but creating the illusion' of a huge noisy crowd. In *Witness*, Peter Weir portrayed this feeling of mass detachment at the station perfectly.

WITNESS (1985) (Movie)

Director: Peter Weir
Writers: William Kelley, Pamela Wallace, Earl W. Wallace
Producers: Edward S. Feldman
Awards: Won two Oscars and one BAFTA
Cast: Harrison Ford (Detective Captain John Book), Kelly McGillis (Rachel Lapp), Josef Sommer (Chief Paul Schaeffer), Lukas Haas (Samuel Lapp), Jan Rubes (Eli Lapp), Alexander Godunov (Daniel Hochleitner), Danny Glover (Det. Lt James McFee), Viggo Mortensen (Moses Hochleitner)

Notes:

Oh dear, cop kills a cop, kid in the toilets sees the cop kill the cop, which provokes another cop – Harrison Ford as John Book – to look after the kid (who's now the *witness*) and his mother by blending into Amish life while slowly falling for the mother (Kelly McGillis) – who can blame him – as the killing cops try to find and destroy all of them. Actually, I make it all sound quite bog standard, but it's not. It's a beautifully shot and timed piece that gets you right into the Amish way of life.

We really want to shoot some of the station, but are scared to ask, because firstly, we don't want to draw attention to our interest in such things as train stations (especially after the incident in Baltimore), and secondly because we think we might be told that we can't. Tom figures that he'll try to film it surreptitiously anyway, which I think is a disastrous decision and a recipe for arrest.

Tom goes to the toilets and finds that everything has changed since Lukas Haas, as Samuel Lapp, sat in the end cubicle and witnessed a brutal murder. So, in true dogged Tom-style, he finds any old cubicle and films himself sitting on the throne, waiting patiently for a murder to happen. He strangely lasts around thirty-seven minutes before he's heard quite enough men pissing, shitting and farting. To me, that's around thirty-six minutes and thirty seconds too long.

While Tom's filming himself on the toilet, Luke and I find the scary statue that Samuel Lapp was intrigued by – the one with an angel or something basically holding someone up by the tit. The statue is actually a memorial for people who died in the making of the railway, but it appeared to have an altogether different meaning for Samuel.

After Tom's spent all that time sat in the public toilet cubicle, muttering to a camera on his lap, it would seem a shame not to expand on the *Witness* story. So, we decide to head out further west into the countryside of Pennsylvania, to Lancaster County. If the film is anything to go by, Lancaster County is to comprise baron farmland occupied by the disconnected Amish people in small quiet villages. The Amish are a unique phenomenon: people who choose not to partake in the simple American pleasures of electricity or motor cars or prostitutes, in the name of religion.

The Amish people believe in taking what God said *literally*. God was a long time ago, therefore electricity, cars, television and radio and all the things that he would consider a poison to the people are all no-no's – he wanted them to "be not conformed to this world". The Amish and Mennonite people (or "Plain People" as they're known) keep themselves to themselves and rank among the most productive in the USA, producing such stuffs as soya beans and tobacco. They arrived in Lancaster County from Switzerland and Germany back in the 1720s or 1730s, and I guess not a lot has changed for them since. Many however have moved away from the area due to both high land prices and the dreaded tourists.

We fully expect to get lost in the winding country roads that aren't enormously dissimilar to the English Home Counties; stared at because of our motor car and talked at in a Germanic tongue. But what we find is a bizarre tourist trap. One of the first things we see as we enter Lancaster County is a huge cartoony model/statue of an Amish man all dressed up in his gear: dark coloured suit, dark shirt, straight jacket without lapels, short trousers with suspenders, a broad rimmed black hat and a hearty beard (which means he's married. They refrain from a moustache alone because a tash often signifies military and they don't like all that). They've managed to make these people an attraction and it's not clear whether the Amish are the victims or the architects.

The Amish appear to be reasonably undeterred by the attention their every day activities attract; just a journey down to the local shops in their horse drawn carts brings out the points and stares from tourists who can't tell the difference between people trying to live their lives the way they choose and those living in a history theme park. Clearly, the area is all about the Amish, but all they do is go about their business while people gawp. I find the whole set-up tacky; but then by coming here in the first place myself, I'm no better than everyone else who's hoping to catch a glimpse of some people who have genuinely rejected the ways of modern society. And by golly am I keen to see them go about their ways. It's fascinating, the costumes, the horses ... I admire them at the same time as being a bit scared of them. It's like they're ghosts of a bygone time, spirits floating around town as though they've never died.

A sign on the road says "Welcome to Intercourse", and you can't help but snigger at something like that. Intercourse is genuinely the name of the place, and Tom is moved to buy three caps and a T-shirt stating "I Love Intercourse."

Among the hordes of holidaymakers buying Amish quilts and still pointing at the horse drawn carts, is a small supermarket called Zimmerman's In *Witness*, Harrison Ford's only link to his life back in the city is a payphone, but the local Amish people raise eyebrows when they see John Book talking on it dressed in his Amish costume, talking on. The exact same telephone sits in the same booth in the same position as it did in the movie. Given that the telephone companies seem to enjoy updating their phones so often, the fact that the same phone is there must mean that the owners wanted to keep that bit of movie history in tact.

We go into Zimmerman's and chat to the two spotty Amish boys working behind the counter. They seem to have done their homework and confirm that the phone is the same one, while also pointing out that the scene in which locals abuse the Amish with ice creams happened just up the road. That's when the locals smear ice cream all over their faces, but the Amish do nothing; they're peaceful people.

We get Tom to buy an ice cream, with loose promises that if we re-create the scene, I'll go easy with the daubing. So foolish. *I let rip with that damn Cornetto.*

"You want to be Amish do you? DO YOU? You can't do a thing Tom, I could walk on your nuts and you'd have to take it, because you're a PEACEFUL MAN!!!" I shriek like an absolute madman, as the cone jabs at his face until it's just a wafery stub. Tom's just smiles.

Further out we go, away from the epicentre of the Disneyish Amish viewing villages, to just outside Strasburg, where we veer off the trodden path and into the realm of small roads, farming equipment and the smell of shit every hundred yards. We're looking for 658 Bunker Hill, but it's not signed. We take a calculated guess and drive down a lane that runs down the middle of a field flanked by really tall plants of some kind. Maybe corn. Eventually, a farmhouse appears in the distance, as do three little dogs who start visibly wagging themselves from quite a distance. It appears to be a working farm.

As usual, with his fearless nervousness, if that's a possible combination, Tom volunteers to go up to the house and knock on the door, while Luke and I sit in the car at a distance.

Even from where Luke and I sit, we can see the porch where John Book sat as he recovered from his bullet wound. It's definitely the right place. A load of the film was staged here. The flour mill, like many others that are smothered over the landscape, sits where it was, provoking memories of the pulsating grain-based scenes that took place in there when Book was having a right old punch up with the snidey cops; the white wooden house looks just as shabby and plainly functional as it did in the film. Right in front of us is the home of *real people*: no bright paints or fancy decoration to satisfy their own egos or to impress others, just an honest, practical nest made for a family's simple existence. I admire them. If my life were free of ego, desire and competition, if I was just more accepting of my future and past as being things that are already laid out for me, then maybe I wouldn't worry so much either.

Eventually, Tom comes back and pronounces the family not in. But he does want to go up to the barn where John Book kept his car and take some pictures. I oppose this, because I'm doubtful the family would allow us pictures – due to their beliefs – and am sure they would like it less if it happens while they're away. And anyway, the barn is well onto the property, to the right behind the house, and if going up to the door was dodge, traipsing through the manure to the barn would definitely be too much. There's location hunting and then there's respecting people's property and privacy. Does he listen? Off he bounces, with the video camera in hand and me seething because I can do little else but sit and wait.

So after a few minutes of Tom out of vision and round the back, I gasp air-conditioned car air as I see the family returning in a car. *Oh Christ, here they come, here they come, the scary Amish, and Tom's in the barn.* Luke's face goes all twitchy and scared and as they go past our car, eyeballing us suspiciously, I could strangle Tom for getting us into this situation. Maybe I could do it in front of them as an apology, like an offering ... then I realise they're peaceful people, not Satanists. I find myself getting out of the car and waving with a very unconvincing smile at the Amish people in their full costume who've got down to the house and are piling out of the car in more numbers than the car looks capable of containing. Tom's still in the barn and I don't know if he's heard them return or not.

Suddenly, I wonder why they're in a car. They don't like cars, it's their *thing*. Then I realise that the car is being driven by a non-Amish. Oh, I think.

Just like the Arabs who sneak the odd beer, or the Jews who love an occasional bacon sandwich, this lot treat themselves to a trip in a car once in a while, with a cheeky little cheat that they're not driving it themselves. Hmmm.

I mutter awful words in association with Tom's name as I try to work out what I'll say to them about my friend in a Mr T T-shirt hiding out in their barn. They could call the police, and I don't want to have to deal with them lot again. Just as I'm about to go up to them with my apologetic face, Tom appears from around the corner without the camera. He smiles at them nervously and approaches their car like a naughty dog waiting to be smacked. I back off, retreat, edge back to the car ready to ditch him when it all kicks off. I turn round to Luke, who's sitting in the car, and give him eyes that say *start the fucking engine*, but seeing as there aren't really any eye gestures that say that, he just looks back at me vacantly.

Tom's lucky to find the women and children are friendly, while the men nod formally and walk straight into the house. Phew. It turns out that the family have lived here for two years and are happy for us to photograph the barn. Jeez, I'm such a drama queen, there's me dreading the county jail where thought I was going to be beaten up by a biker in my cell, when the next minute we're being welcomed to come and photograph a manky old barn for fun. This is a weird trip.

One of the playful little boys walks us up there and, while Tom sneaks off to retrieve the camera from the corner of the barn – he hid it in there in case they turned out to be horrified that we'd try to capture their images on film and steal their souls – I have to create a minor diversion, which involves questions about which languages he speaks (Pennsylvanian Dutch), whether he's ever seen *Witness* (No), and does he think I'd look good in an Amish costume (yes, I called it a costume, I didn't mean it, it just came out). He says *no*, I wouldn't.

We thank the Amish family profusely and speed off their property, past the spot where John Book drove into a bird table, until the little white house and memories of Kelly McGillis' flash of boobs fade into the countryside.

CHAPTER TWENTY-FOUR SOUNDTRACK:

Ghostbusters

Ray Parker Jnr (1984)

It Had to Be You

Harry Connick Jnr (1989)

Chapter Twenty-four

Who you gonna call?

New York

On the day we finally bite The Big Apple, we approach the city through grimy, straight-down rain; the miserable, spiteful tail of a hurricane that's caused all sorts of problems in Florida since we escaped. The New York skyline starts poking stoically, nuzzling through the cloudy dinge in metallic peaks, the whole thing looking compact and iconic, but still tragically conspicuous in my mind by the absence of the twin towers. Approaching New York gives me a little fuzzy static of excitement, mixed with nerves. Driving into New York is *scary*.

I'll never forget the summer of 1987, driving from Toronto to New York with my parents. New York was different then, it was pre-*zero tolerance* and had a moody knife-at-your-throat electricity that made you feel intimidated and suspicious; especially my dad, who drove a hire car through the city while hyperventilating and clinging onto the steering wheel like the edge of a cliff. Then in 1997, ten years after that, Elle and I arrived at Port Authority on a Greyhound bus at dawn on Christmas Eve. Within minutes we had a bag stolen that contained forty rolls of exposed films from our entire trip. So New York provokes mixed feelings for me; it's only ever provided fear and loss. But that's all in the past. I'm ready to paint all over those memories, in red, and post new ones up in my brain. Incidentally, a few months after Elle and I returned, we received a reverse-charge phone call from New York, with a guy saying very slowly in a thick Bronx accent, "Hello. This. Is. Black. McKnight. In. New. York. Do you speak London or English?"

"Erm, both."

"OK, I found a bag. It has camera film in it and your telephone number. I'm a Christian, I want to return it to you." He spoke it like a telegram. I couldn't believe it, but in return for a not-so-Christian "reward", he delivered the forty camera films to someone we knew at the World Trade Centre and two days later we got *all* our photos back.

Getting rid of the car in some moody long-stay lot means wholesome footwork between locations in New York's crammed metropolis. It's not quite LA, in terms of the quantity of production these days, but a lot of movie and TV has been *set* in New York and many of the old places are still here. We begin with a mish-mashed romp around the city...

First up is a lengthy walk across Central Park, the ultimate urban park that manages to totally remove you from the insanity surrounding it. On the other side and out of the park, we get to the corner of 79th Street and Park Avenue, where a very ordinary block of flats pokes unimpressively to a reasonable height. It's not exactly a *dodgy* area, it's just indistinct, perched in the northwest side of Manhattan, where apartments are at a premium and everyone's crammed in at extortionate rates. In the show, the Drummond family apartment looked a lot plusher than the exterior suggests, but it's older now and that blocky, concretey type monster was one of those eighties things that we all regret. It's an ugly building, but very definitely one that makes you sing:

> *Now, the world don't move to the beat of just one drum,*
> *What might be right for you, may not be right for some...*

Which we do, really quite loudly, nearly scraping our voices up to and above the level of the traffic police sirens.

The sight of that building sparks off all sorts of memories from my after-school bouts of television watching with a little box of Sun Maid raisins and the gas fire burning my feet; excited because I might be allowed to watch *Diff'rent Strokes* and *The Adventure Game* before bed.

DIFF'RENT STROKES (1978–1986) (TV)

Cast: Gary Coleman (Arnold Jackson), Dana Plato (Kimberley Drummond), Conrad Bain (Phillip Drummond), Todd Bridges (Willis Jackson), Charlotte Rae (Edna Garrett), Shavar Ross (Dudley Ramsey)

Notes:
I didn't know, until I read up about it, like a good boy, that the show's story goes that millionaire Phillip Drummond adopted Arnold and Willis as a promise to their mother, his housekeeper, as she laid on her deathbed. I'd never even thought about *why* the boys lived with Mr Drummond.

Since the show finished, it has become as famous for the plight of the actors as for the show itself. Well, Gary we surely *all* know about. *Watchu talkin' 'bout Spencer*, of course we all know he famously attacked someone while working as a security guard. *But*, did you know that he got married to a twenty-two-year-old lady in 2007 and claims that sex isn't part of the marriage because he's a virgin?

Todd Bridges has a well-known history with drugs but now travels the USA speaking to school kids about the dangers of such. But, did you know that when he was a kid, he was the first Afro-American child to appear in a recurring role on *The Waltons*? These days, he mostly takes part in reality TV shows, which a couple of years ago saw him beat up Vanilla Ice in a boxing match. Brilliant.

Dana Plato's story is much more tragic. Drinking and drugging at fourteen – even during filming the show – she ended up appearing in soft porn, working in a dry-cleaners and getting arrested for holding up a Las Vegas video store with a pellet gun. She also got done for trying to forge a valium prescription. The day after being interviewed/savaged on *The Howard Stern Radio Show* in 1999, she was found dead from an overdose in the caravan she was living in with her fiancé. It was ruled suicide, but many – including Gary and Todd – maintain she wouldn't have done that. Poor cow. Raise a glass to Dana Plato; someone who contributed to our eighties and sorely paid for it.

Talking of cosy winter evenings, in Greenwich Village, at 10 St Luke's Place, my brain sparks off immediate images of homely, avuncular Bill Cosby dancing rather oddly in contorted and eccentric poses to jazz music.

The doorway looks just *so* welcoming and familiar, almost like I could go up and knock for Denise. The Huxtables were such a warm, compassionate

WHO YOU GONNA CALL?

THE COSBY SHOW (1984–1992) (TV)

Awards: Won 3 Golden Globes

Cast: Bill Cosby (Dr Heathcliff Huxtable), Phylicia Rashad (Clare Hanks Huxtable), Malcolm Jamal-Warner (Theo Huxtable), Keisha Knight Pulliam (Rudy Huxtable), Tempestt Bledsoe (Vanessa Huxtable), Lisa Bonet (Denise Huxtable Kendall)

Notes:

It's said that Bill Cosby's son, Ennis, provided a lot of the inspiration for some of the storylines featuring Cliff's son Theo in *The Cosby Show*. The Huxtables and the Cosbys had the same balance of family members and both Theo and Ennis (in real life) were diagnosed as dyslexic.

In 1997, long after *The Cosby Show* finished, Ennis Cosby was murdered when his car ran a flat and a robber shot him in the head on the side of the motorway. Mikhail Markhasev is still serving a sentence in jail for the murder.

Malcolm Jamal Warner – Cosby's on-screen son Theo – meanwhile is now a musician and, going by his website, a very funky fellow too.

Anyway, why was it called *The Cosby Show*, when Cosby played someone called Huxtable?

---

family and *so* many of those scenes happened just outside this door that I feel I'm *entitled* to be a part of it. It's a quiet, leafy street, a bit like Sesame Street, and on the other side of the road is a little park where small kids run about quite happily and safely. I want to live here, with Lisa Bonet.

We stand outside and think it might be a good idea to try and pull some of the moves that Mr Cosby did in the opening titles of the show. As I put the face on that Bill had – that tight-lipped jazz grimace – and prance around at the bottom of the stairs leading to the door, imagining the music (which was actually composed by Bill Cosby, with Stu Gardner), people walk by. I assume they know I'm doing the Cosby pilgrimage dance. At least I hope that's what they think.

Moving along on this whirlwind titbit trot, at 1 Centre Street, by the subway stairs and with the aid of our tiny DVD player, we manage to find the *exact* spot where Crocodile Dundee was approached by a young punk with a knife – provoking that immortal line: "That's not a knife, this is a knife."

CROCODILE DUNDEE (1986) (MOVIE)

Director: Peter Fairman
Writers: Paul Hogan, John Cornell, Ken Shadie
Producers: John Cornell
Awards: Nominated for an Oscar and a BAFTA
Cast: Paul Hogan (Michael J. "Crocodile" Dundee), Linda Koslowski (Sue Charlton), John Meillon (Wally Reilly), Mark Blum (Richard Mason), Michael Lombard (Sam Charlton), David Gulpilil (Neville Bell)

Notes:
Before Paul Hogan went on to become the star of this immense film – which in the USA, almost made up its $8 million budget in the opening weekend – he worked as a painter on Sydney Harbour Bridge. Hmmm. I worked in the warehouse at Sainsbury's and I'm *still* waiting for my break...

I have no intention of attempting to recreate that line. No way. It would look silly and hackneyed. *And* I haven't got a huge machete-type instrument to accompany the punch line. So, with the confidence and experience of what's now *hundreds* of movie locations under our collective belt, we decide to go off-road and perform our very own, very English interpretation of that moment.

Here's the scene: it's mid-afternoon on a week day and slightly bustling. The big building's impressive columns are thick grey concrete, casting a grimy, shadow to the subway entrance. I suppose the film-makers thought this was appropriately intimidating, in a grim urban sense, for a man used to the green outback of Australia to look and feel out of place in. Along I walk, towards the subway stairs. Tom walks across my path, wearing the red leather jacket (that's uncannily similar to the one worn by the real punk in the film). I stop at the very spot that we've marked out with chalk, where Mick Dundee stopped in the film.

"I say, you wouldn't have a light would you old boy?" Tom squawks with plummy proficiency.

"Why, of course, old boy," I reply, with a slab of cockney poking out like a Chad's nose. I can't do posh really, it's all too many sounds to pronounce for me. I sound more like the Artful Dodger.

"Oh, and I'll have your wallet also please, I've got a knife you know," Tom smarms, while holding up a plastic McDonald's fork.

"Dear boy, *that's* not a knife, *this* is a knife," I retort, with calm assurance and a plastic McDonald's knife. See what we did there?

New York begins to get sunnier, and just like in the movies, the weather reflects the mood. Morale is high, and for the first time I find myself thinking ahead and actually *looking forward* to getting back to London and starting over.

After that little mill around the city, we decide to hone in on one particular movie that most people are very fond of. A fair walk away, (via the apartment block used for *Friends*), at 14 North Moore Street, we find a stubby-looking out-of-place fire station that seems like it could be the last building left on a street that no longer exists. The red-brick building with its white frame around big red castle-like doors sits narrow and lonely, completely detached but certainly dignified and distinctly Victorian. And so it should be proud ... it was the building used as the base for the *Ghostbusters*.

GHOSTBUSTERS (1984) (Movie)

Director: Ivan Reitman
Writers: Dan Ackroyd, Harold Ramis
Producer: Bernie Brillstein,
Awards: Won BAFTA (Best Original Song), nominated for 2 Oscars.
Cast: Bill Murray (Dr Peter Venkman), Dan Ackroyd (Dr Raymond Stantz), Sigourney Weaver (Dana Barrett), Harold Ramis (Dr Egon Spengler), Rick Moranis (Louise Tully), Annie Potts (Janine Melnitz), William Atheron (Walter Peck)

Notes:
It took me three goes to watch this film. I have a disposition concerning ghosts anyway, and when that library scene came on, I clichéd myself into submission by "hiding behind the sofa". But I also remember the entire school going crazy berserk at the disco when the Ray Parker Jnr single came on.

Continuing on the *Ghostbusters* tip, on the Upper West side of Manhattan just inside Central Park, we find The Tavern on the Green, a grand looking restaurant, that sits pretty among the foliage and horse and carts that scour this part of New York for tourists. In *Ghostbusters*, this is the plush eatery that Rick Moranis clings to the windows of when he's trying to escape Dana's crazed dog.

Ladies lunch here. This is where ladies lunch. I can imagine the *Sex and the City* girls here, rabbiting on about being wrinkly and single. The staff inside allow us access to the windows, and while I sit at a table, Tom goons away outside the window in a dreadful re-creation of Moranis's effort to get away from Dana's possessed woofer.

Not far up the road at West 72nd Street are the Dakota Apartments, the worth of which are given away by the security guard in coat and tails and by the fact that famous people notoriously live here. The man politely confirms – I bet for the umpteenth time already today – that just outside the entrance here was the very spot that, in 1980, John Lennon was shot by Mark Chapman. I was young. Six years old; too young really to understand the gravity of it all. But I'll never forget being downstairs while Mum got ready to take me to school, with Capital Radio on so loud that she could hear it upstairs. A news report came on saying that John Lennon had been shot dead. I didn't really know who he was, except I remembered that my mum used to talk about him quite a lot when she spoke about being young and watching concerts.

Excitedly, I ran to the bottom of the stairs and shouted in a casual way, as though I was letting her know that the kettle was boiled or the cat's been sick on the dinner table again, "Mum, John Lennon is dead."

"Oooh," she replied, followed by silence. I went back to playing with my Stretch Hulk, but I wonder now whether, at the age of twenty-six, she felt the same sort of sensation that I do now when elements of my childhood die off. That sensation of *it's over*, those days are gone now...

Never have I had a stranger, more raucous full-stomached culinary ordeal than at Katz's deli at 205 East Houston Street.

Inside Katz's, after you're hit with a wall of luncheon din, you're given a ticket and then urged to approach the various counters to ask over the echoey furore for something you'd like. Signs are everywhere in neon flash, one saying, "Send a salami to your boy in the army." I decide not to, but do manage to nervously negotiate a cheese baguette, that comes with a whole separate plate full of super-long gherkins chopped in half, from the man at the sandwich counter who's the very caricature of the brash, aggressive and loud New Yorker that the telly often tells us to expect. It's bloody terrifying; I feel totally out of order for ordering something in the first place as he barks various butter and dressing options at me through a wrinkled-up, stress-lined face.

Our table has been reserved for us by the management – we couldn't possibly sit anywhere else. No frills, just canteen style dinner tables and the naked essentials of a pepper pot and its regular friends. A sign above us with an arrow reads, "You're sitting where Harry Met Sally." Yup, Tom is Meg and I'm Billy, an arrangement that relieves me of the pressure which Tom's seat puts *him* under.

If it might help, would you like to borrow my gherkin, Tom?

WHEN HARRY MET SALLY (1989) (Movie)

Director: Rob Reiner
Writer: Nora Ephron
Producers: Rob Reiner, Andrew Scheinman
Awards: Won BAFTA (Best Screenplay)
Cast: Billy Crystal (Harry Burns), Meg Ryan (Sally Albright), Carrie Fisher (Marie), Bruno Kirby (Jess), Steven Ford (Joe), Lisa Jane Persky (Alice), Michelle Nicastro (Amanda Reece), Estelle Reiner ("I'll have what she's having")

Notes:

Behind *Back to the Future*, and ahead of *The Goonies* this is certainly my second favourite movie from the eighties. I know it's traditionally a girly film, but as I've got older, the script rings more and more bells about love and romance and the relationships between men and women. In that sense, through Billy Crystal's obnoxious but – let's face it – indicative of the species role, representing the male side of the argument, this film offers as much to the blokes as it does the girls. Is he right? Can men and women truly be friends?

Tom's moment of climax doesn't rate as highly as Meg's – how could it ever, and to be honest, thank God it doesn't, I'd hate for *Tom* to burst that bubble. He composes himself with a quick close of eyes and deep breath, probably thinking about Elisabeth Shue or Lea Thompson or, who knows, Hulk Hogan. I feed him Billy Crystal's finishing line when he argues that women never fake orgasms with him, "Well, they haven't faked it with me..." And then off he goes. But it's a red herring; he has no intention of re-creating Meg's desperately sensuous rendition.

He's not bloody stupid. Tom hardly parts his lips for a barely audible "oooh, amid the cacophony of razor-sharp New York accents and cutlery whacking against gherkin plates. What a cop out; no one asks to have what *he's* having, and I suspect most people will even steer clear of the corned beef for the rest of the day. No one even looks round; maybe they're all jealous that we had "the table" reserved for us, or maybe they're too busy living their one hundred mile and hour lives to spare us a couple of miles an hour in between crunches of insipid gherkin. Or maybe, as Tom designed, they didn't even hear him.

It's both an incredible pleasure to visit *and* escape Katz's, it's all a bit much really; probably the café I would *least* likely feel comfortable enough to have an orgasm in.

Thankfully not in need of a post-coital sleep, we remain more or less in the same area and find the pompous looking Puck Building at 295 Lafayette Street. Going further knee-deep into the folklore of Harry meeting Sally, I've discovered by talking to a sexy-voiced lady in the Puck press department that the building was used for the wedding of their best friends Marie and Jess; and also the suave bow tie-clad champagne drenched New Year's party where Sally is told a dreadful joke by a prat, before the film reaches a climax that could claim itself to be the only film that consistently makes me blub like a 1990 Gazza. It really does get to me, that scene.

We make our way up to the seventh floor, looking for the face that matches the voice, and stumble upon Jamie, who claims to be the owner of the sexy voice. Jamie is happy enough to lead us through to the function room used for the wedding. We can't help but re-enact Harry and Sally's argument at the wedding; it's where they've already slept with each other, and then he clumsily calls her a metaphoric dog and she drags him through to the kitchen and slaps him up.

We wander through the empty echoing room to the kitchen round the side. This is where Sally clumps Harry around the moosh. We've already decided that Tom can stay as Sally, seeing as he had to squeeze out that poor excuse for a climax. So he Sally-style beckons me into the kitchen, and in a instinctive, spontaneous and vividly selfish act, I swivel my role to that of Sally without notice and wallop Tom with a stinging smack on his face. I didn't plan it, honest, it just happened and immediately afterwards we look at each other confused and just as surprised as each other. Naturally, Tom takes a moment to decide he's miffed, but in a dignified manner; he walks off, avoiding what surely surely would have turned into one of our very uncouth wrestling incidents and makes sulkily for the lift. Well, *I* enjoyed myself.

Down on the ground floor, we find the ballroom used in the last scene of the film. The floor is being re-varnished and now whenever I watch the film I'm sure I'll get the sharp thrust of varnish fumes powering their way up my hooter. This is the place Harry sprints to, having realised on a lonely New Year's Eve that he *loves her*. I'm a romantic soul, and just dream of being involved in a scene like this; tears and snogging and it all *out there*, in the open. I want to be Harry in this scene. I must have subconsciously thought it might happen with Elle again; but real life doesn't really work like that. But still I find myself standing at the entrance to the ballroom, just imagining it happening to me. My Sally is someone out there who I've yet to meet; and for the first time, I get a tingle of excitement about the future. I think *I'm ready* to get back out there. Elle happened all those years ago and she stays buried in the desert along with Celine Dion's dancing water show. *I'm ready.*

A house party. They make me nervous; *so* many strangers; *don't say anything too weird, don't spill the red wine, don't say anything too weird.* I'm not good at other people's houses and one belonging to someone in New York who I don't know is even worse. I'm a kitchen dweller. At house parties, I always find that the living room is too cliquey, all the seats are always taken, people strewn on the floor and you can't just *sneak in*. If you walk into the living room, you walk into a living room *full of eyes*, all of them blinking *who the fuck is that* at you. Nope, the kitchen has a nice mixture of the fridge, other nervous kitchen dwellers, the occasional transient living room fridge visitor who you don't have to engage with properly and did I say ... the fridge: full of the beer that'll help me through it all. We do this for fun? Why go if it's such an ordeal? Well, I consider not going but Megan will be there and I would like to see her again. I start drinking early to put a protective buffer around my brittle social nerves.

As usual, I get there and find my spot in the kitchen. I can't work out whether the cool kids or the geeks are to be found in the kitchen. Maybe the *real* cool kids are on the stairs, it seems a more courageous place to be; extreme house party-going. I'm dragged briefly into the living room to stand in the middle while someone, don't know who, tells everyone who I am. I edge out almost immediately and find that someone has taken my dwelling spot in the kitchen. It's Megan. *It's OK, I've drunk enough, it's OK I've drunk enough, cool it tiger. Just go and talk to her...*

So we do the kissy cheek thing and there it is, *the scent.* She looks taller than I remember; angular, strong features and long curly hair rolling down her shoulders. She looks great. We talk and talk and talk. I'm next to the fridge, *my place*, I'm relaxed and we talk. In fact, I get to the point of drinking no return, where my guard drops and I could end up saying anything, all or nothing.

"You do know that I really fancy you," I say, biting my lip, waiting for a slap or a laugh or a walkaway or a polite *my boyfriend.* But sod it.

"I feel the same." What?

"What?" Best to say it out loud. Surely not. This doesn't happen to me. It just doesn't happen.

"Well, should we kiss then?" I say, perhaps rushing it, scared that if I don't seize the moment it'll just float away into last night's silly talk. It has to be now. There's no *my boyfriend*, he's gone. It has to be now.

We kiss.

Conspicuously, in the kitchen, as people nudge past us for the beer fridge. I close my eyes and think about being somewhere I want to be, and it's here, right now, kissing Megan. I lose myself somewhere between a bottle of Bud and Megan's eyes.

The big, ornate, French looking concrete arch heralding the entrance to Washington Square takes us back into the realm of Harry and Sally one last time. It's a big square with a massive fountain in the middle that locals jog around and boozy tramps hang around. Near the start of the film, as a pair of complete strangers, Harry and Sally share a ride to New York on their way to begin new lives in the big city. Sally drops Harry off here and they say an awkward goodbye, a handshake that slows down halfway through with a hint of *I think I know this isn't the last time I'll see you.* Even then, the audience can see a connection that neither of them have quite understood yet. The scene plays out with a wide shot of Harry wandering off through the arch with his worldly possessions in a suitcase, sending the implicit message that he's now a needle in a haystack; one of the other hordes of strangers that Sally will never bump into again.

Not quite coincidentally, because it was always going to be our last New York location as it's a great goodbye place for New York, we stand here with the car as Tom, Luke and I say goodbye to Megan, who's come out to wave us off. They all do the friendly hugs and side-cheek kisses and the boys respectfully get in the car.

"Bye then."

"Bye then."

We hug and kiss, like last night but this time eyes open, getting one last look. And just like Harry and Sally, I somehow know this won't be the last time I see Megan.

CHAPTER TWENTY-FIVE SOUNDTRACK:

Sunny
Days

Joe Raposo

Chapter Twenty-five

Back to the Future

New York to The Future

"**M**arisa, hi, how *are* you?"; "Hi, Marisa, I'm a top TV Exec, wanna chat about opportunities?"; "Marisa, darling, at last, we meet. Drink?" *or* "So, the famous Marisa Tomei says *yes* to a date with a young English gentleman..." Actually, on the boat across to Martha's Vineyard, I don't build up the guts to say *any* of those lines to Oscar-winning actress Marisa Tomei, who's sitting just across from me, looking hot and sexy and definitely snogging a big fat middle-aged bald man.

Admittedly, Jaws isn't an eighties movie, but in so many ways it *is*. Nearly everyone I know has distinctly fond (in a petrified way) memories of watching the film on TV as a kid. Maybe its TV release wasn't until the early eighties and that's why, or maybe it's such an exceptional film that it seeped across the decades like it had only just been made. Certainly no other movie made in 1975 had such an impact on my childhood.

JAWS (1975) (MOVIE)

Director: Steven Spielberg
Writers: Peter Benchley, Carl Gottlieb
Producers: Richard D. Zanuck, David Brown
Awards: Won 3 Oscars
Cast: Roy Schneider (Police Chief Martin Brody), Robert Shaw (Quint), Richard Dreyfuss (Matt Hooper), Lorraine Gary (Ellen Brody), Murray Hamilton (Mayor Larry Vaughn), Carl Gottlieb (Ben Meadows), Lee Fierro (Mrs Kintner), Jeffrey Voorhees (Alex Kintner)

> **Notes:**
> Like many films, there are rumours portrayed as facts about the casting of
> *Jaws*. Charlton Heston was considered for the role of Brody. Jeff Bridges
> was considered for Hooper and Victoria Principal for Ellen Brody.

Our one-day tribute to *Jaws* begins with a long chug along a local bus route.
It's sort of humbling to be herded onto a bus after so long being kept away
from the queuing masses in our Oldsmobile. Especially as Tomei got in a
private car directly off the boat. Now we're just tourists; just another three
guys heading for the beach. With a shark fin made out of a pizza box.

The Martha's Vineyard I expected to find would be tiny; so small that
you could walk across it in five minutes. And there would be *no* tourists –
none whatsoever – just us and Marisa Tomei and the islanders, sitting in a
tavern talking about *My Cousin Vinny* and which extra roles the locals
played in *Jaws*.

No.

It's quite a big place. The bus journey takes about twenty minutes, which
is half the distance between London and Southend. Secondly, there are
tourists by the gutful. Swarms of pram-toting families complete with grizzling
toddler and irritable parents. With all its reputation for exclusivity, there
appears to be nothing exclusive at all about Martha's Vineyard.

The bus drops us in Edgartown, which has the Main Street that features
in the *Jaws* town scenes. It's quaint enough, with its little white fishing shacks
and narrow roads. But *you* try walking along the pavement without a buggy
(disabled *or* kiddie) clipping your heels or ramming your shins. It smells nice
here though – of ice cream and sun cream and chips. It looks nice, too, all
bright and olde worlde – but there are too many people. It seems that just like
what's happened to the Amish in Lancaster County, the legend of something
untouched has been touched by *everyone* in their attempts to check if it's
untouched or not.

Down towards the harbour, we see the hardware store Chief Brody
stormed into to buy some paint and materials to make signs saying the beach
was closed. I find it a bit peculiar that the chief of police would need to go
and buy the equipment to make such signs, and I've always felt it was a notch

too far in the story-telling process to prove that Amity Island really didn't have infrastructure. Fair enough, they might not have been ready for a great, white shark, but the *chief of police* going to a hardware store to buy paint and wood for signs?

Anyhow, the "Amity Hardware Store" sign from the movie is proudly screwed to the wall (very professionally, as you'd expect) at the back of the store. Further down, we find The Wharf pub – a maritime themed bar that really could be twinned with any of the Wetherspoons chain back home. We heard from our bus driver that the manager here may have a story to tell.

Jeffrey Voorhees was twelve when Spielberg and his cameras came to the island and, just like all of his friends of the same age, he went along to be an extra. But instead of being a screaming face on the beach, Jeffrey ended up being tossed around on a lilo and killed by a shark. He played poor little Alex Kintner. As a kid, he was an awkward-looking little sod, all gangly and a little troll-like. As an adult, he's even stranger looking. Jeff has aged considerably, has a Bobby Charlton comb-over, and the vacant stare of someone who was once killed by a shark as a child and thereafter thousands of times in people's living rooms. As he speaks, his face is expressionless and his voice monotone, as he blurts out what he must have recited countless times to tourists and journalists doing *what happened to* style reports.

"I was just a little kid when they did it. Basically, we all wanted to be extras in it, we all went down and signed up to be extras. They needed a few speaking parts too. Me and my friend, we were the lucky ones. You read something in a book and they picked us. They did it up at State Beach; we were just little kids then. They wanted us to go in the water, it was like May, and the water's still cold then. They'd just say go way down in the water and you'd swim out on a little raft and they'd say *cut*. Then you have *half* of a raft and they'd say *cut*. Then they put it over a machine that's full of blood, and then it blows up. They'd say 'this is gonna blow up, and when that happens just go in the water and stay under there as long as you can'. The first time we did it my arm or leg was showing so they had to do it again. All my friends, everyone's freezing, but if you had a speaking part you could go in and get warm in a dressing room. I go in the dressing room 'cos I screwed up, but all my friends are freezing cold outside. They take hours for all the blood to clear out of the water. Then when the blood was gone they'd do it all again. After about four or five times of me messing up they got some guys in wet suits and just ... *yank* ... that's why I go up and down. It was great, you know, we got $140. Anyone who had a speaking part. All my friends that were just extras, they only got $38 a day, so that was good. But we never realised we got paid for it when it came on TV. The first time it went on TV, I was shocked. I was still young. Got a cheque for $14,500 and I still get paid anytime I die on television. That's why I love it when I die. I hope I die soon 'cos I'll get another cheque from the Screen Actors Guild. It was fun. When they did the second movie down here, we all went down again. All my friends were in it. Me? They said, 'Sorry, you're dead.' That was fine, but when you're a little kid and they say 'sorry, you're dead' you just go away all depressed, but I never knew you got royalties. And the lady who was my mother in the movie, I'd not seen her in years. She was in here a couple of years ago and there's a sandwich called the Alex Kintner Burger that the owner put on for kind of a joke for the waitresses, to get even with me about being mean. So she saw it on the menu and I went over and was like 'excuse me ladies, I've gotta ask you a very personal question. Just tell me to go away if you're offended. Do you believe in reincarnation?' She realised it was me then. She's like, yes I do. I was like 'I think I died years ago and this is my second life. I was just curious, did you have any kids that died years ago?' And she goes 'I did! I had a son that died like 30 years ago. How did you die?' and I was like 'I think I was killed by an animal' and she was like 'Was it an animal in the ocean?' and I was like 'Yes, I think it was a shark', 'You're my son!', 'Oh ma!' and she hugs me and everyone's looking at me like we're nuts. But that was fun. I just like the cheques rolling in; I'll take the free money. I get some odd letters and messages on the Internet every year. I have them all stacked up. My brother was over here and said 'you're not going to send that stuff back?' so he takes it all and starts signing *his* name on it saying he was in the film too. He said 'come on Jeff, you're not gonna sign these?' I'm like no, I'm not gonna sign that stuff, so he starts scribbling my name on it. It's kinda funny, all that stuff you get." So, all of you who have a signed Jeffrey Voorhees photo, I'm sorry to say that it's probably not a signed Jeffrey Voorhees photo. It's probably signed by Jeffrey Voorhees's brother.

I ask him if he thought Spielberg was nice.

"Everyone in it was nice except Robert Shaw [Quint]. We used to have these baseball games and everyone was there, but he was the only one who didn't want anything to do with these island kids and people."

When he finally stops talking, we stop the camera and Jeff tells us how much he hates the tourists, because they get drunk in the pub. For a manager of a *pub*, that's quite an unhealthy disposition; no wonder he looks a little savaged by the chisel of time.

At the harbour we see a scene that can't help but identify itself as the hub of chaos where all the local fishermen in *Jaws* were preparing their boats to go and find that flippin' greedy fat shark. The chief's office sits tiny like a doll's house, among a small network of piers. It was here that Richard Dreyfuss appeared amid the confusion and introduced himself to Brody. It's swarming now; little kids throwing half-hearted toy fishing lines and nets into the water, being helped by grown-ups who know they won't catch anything.

We make for town and get a bus out to between Oak Bluffs and Edgartown to find the beach and pond where all the sharking action had kicked off. *Wallop snap snap crunch, let's have it.* There's no way we're going to go all that way and *not* swim in the very places that damn shark caused such a fuss in. The pond is on the other side of the War Veteran's Memorial Bridge and it's easy to pick out the spot where the kids had been playing and where an old boy in a boat gets his leg ripped off by the toothy fish.

The old wooden bridge that Chief Brody jumped over onto the beach stretches across where long reedy grass takes over from sand and the distant shrieks of kids in cold water leap out above the crash of fizzy waves. The tougher kids swagger along the bridge holding their stomach muscles tight as the girls concentrate on bulging their busts out. Macho dives off the bridge into the pond seem to be the sport that the girls swoon over; the more risky and elaborate the leap the more chance of a quick snog under a towel.

I'm more reluctant to get in the water because of the threat of cold shrivelage, than sharks lopping my limbs off willy-nilly. I bravely shed down to my trunks and start toeing into the icy water. A bunch of teenage kids half cheer, derisively, when we let out ludicrous dolphin-esque squeaks as the water hits the midriff level and all the bits below it. This is cold and the bottom has unidentified stuff that my feet instinctively really don't want to be treading on, so I tread water instead and leave only my head above the sea like a dog with a stick.

Tom did a good job with his pizza-box shark fin. However, when we're both in the water we struggle to think what the hell we should to do with it.

Of course we do the obligatory *der der, der der, der der* Jaws music, which I've been humming involuntarily all day anyway. I thrash about in semi-mock panic but we soon realise that we have no real business being in here. On our way out of the water, we're informed by a young girl that we've been a good show and we have to explain to her what *Jaws* is, which is upsetting. Quite what else she thought we might be up to I have no idea.

Across the other side of the bridge is where all the beach scenes were shot, including Kintner's bloody demise. Poor little Alex Kintner. It's not the most attractive beach, the sea isn't strikingly clear or warm ... it's just a windy little beach which long grass is beginning to invade. It's again the case that we feel we *have* to swim in that sea, just to say we have. So I sprint in and dive and splash around like a demented eel, so Luke can film me *being killed by a shark*. We'll add the blood afterwards, using TV magic.

Meanwhile, back on the beach, Tom and Luke try to re-create that shot where Brody witnesses another attack and Spielberg brought to the world the simultaneous track-back and zoom-in to create a warped-looking pull into a subject's face. Luke works quite hard at getting Tom's reaction to my poorly acted death in the sea with that "trombone" style shot. He comes away reasonably happy that he's made a good job of it. Later I look back at the tapes and it's shit.

Tom has managed to dig around the island to find Lee Fierro. Lee is the woman who played Mrs Kintner in the film. She still lives on the island. Tom has convinced her using little else than his accent to come and meet us for a few minutes in town before we leave. The only place we can think to meet her is outside the post office. Mrs Kintner turns up and I've stupidly forgotten that thirty years have passed since she was Alex's mum. In the film, Lee was a jet-black haired lady and now, she has white locks and all the wrinkly hallmarks of older age. It's a shock. She dodders over to a wall so she can sit down and answer some questions on camera.

I ask her what she does these days.

"I run the Island Theatre Workshop, I'm the artistic director of that. I've been the Artistic Director for seven years and before that I worked there as an actor, a director, a teacher and a composer. I moved up here in 1969 from Pennsylvania."

"So what are your memories of the movie? Was it enjoyable to hit Roy Schneider?"

"No. Why would it *ever* be enjoyable to hit *anybody*? Especially as many times as I had to hit *him* in one day, which was seventeen. The poor man had to go to a chiropractor the next day. And you have to stand on your spot, and he had to stand on *his* spot, we were really very close together. Steven Spielberg was crouched down and it was very intimate and tight. But they had do a wide angle shot, a medium shot and then they had to do it with the camera looking over *his* shoulder and then *my* shoulder, and he had to stand there and behave as though it wasn't going to happen. That must have been very difficult for him.

As for me, I just did what I was told to the best of my ability. After about five or six takes, Steve stopped the camera and took me aside and said 'Lee, you're getting a bit automatic, you need to freshen it up.' It was a long time ago and I can't remember exactly what I did but apparently whatever I did was acceptable after that. One time I hit him so hard that I knocked his glasses off and I came right out of character and said, 'Oh, I'm so sorry.' And Steve came right down and said don't be sorry, it was wonderful. But they didn't use that take."

"We met the guy who played Alex Kintner yesterday; he said you'd met him a while ago."

"Yes, I think I'd found out that he was manager and I introduced myself to him as his mother. He was very sweet and welcoming. After that we saw each other several times because it was the twenty-fifth anniversary, so the movie, radio, TV companies were coming ... they were just all over the island and all over me and him. Ten or eleven interviews. Because most of the people who had feature roles had passed on by that time."

"So over the years have you been asked to hit people?"

"Young men like you."

"Do you generally hit them?"

"Oh yeah."

"Would you mind...?" asks Tom. I back off a little.

"Hitting you?"

"Yeah." She looks upwards with a sort of tired expression to suggest she's exhausted from all her admirers asking for a thrashing.

"I don't know why you want this, I really don't. Oh for heaven's sakes." She reluctantly smacks Tom. "I hit *him* harder than that."

"Oh, go on then," says Tom, begging for more.

"Honestly. *Honestly*, this is *so* silly." SMACK. "How's that?" Tom wobbles sideways a bit and a red handprint slowly emerges on his cheek. He seems quite happy about his Kintner clump.

"I feel very privileged to have been in that film. I'll tell you one thing; there was a lot of swearing in the book. I said to the casting director, I said 'I *will not* swear.' I will *not* do that. So when they called me up and asked me to do this, said, 'Is there swearing?' And she said, 'No, no, no'. But when I went down to get the script; I saw there was *a lot* of swearing. Four letter words. So the next day I sent the part back, thanked her very much and I said, 'I can't do this.' She said, 'Can't or won't?' I said, '*both*'. I won't swear. I don't honestly think the scene is well written, because the scene before it has men putting out cigarettes on the shark and swearing, and I just can't do it, thanks a lot, bye. So I got a call three days later saying 'if you don't have to swear, would you do the role?' I said yes I would. She said 'Would you mind spitting at the shark?' And I said 'No, I don't mind spitting at the shark.' The producers had taken a look at the scene and felt there might be a possibility I was right. Because it was a powerful scene, it was a turning point for the sheriff. And so they wrote another scene and they tried several people and decided on me. That was very nice."

"It was one of the most powerful scenes I've seen. I mean it's pretty amazing," licks Luke, popping up from the camera for a rare interjection.

"A couple of funny things happened with Steve. When I went down to audition with Steve in a room in a hotel, he asked me if I could improvise and I said yes. So the casting director played the part of Alex and we did the beach scene where he comes out of the water and he wanted to go back in, and I was told that I don't want him to go back in. So we started to improvise and the casting director did everything she could to get back in the water, and I wouldn't let her. Whatever argument she presented I had a better one and just said no. Finally Steve stopped us and said 'Lee, you've got to let him go back in the water or we don't have a movie.'"

"Did you see the sequels?"

"*Jaws 2* was here, and *Jaws the Revenge*. It was a terrible movie, horrible. I had a tiny part and they didn't even spell my name right in the credits. It was *not* a good movie, so don't even bother to see it. Having worked with Steven Spielberg, who is a very fine director, and he works very well with people. He worked so well in every way, at such a young age, and then to experience *Jaws the Revenge* where it was slapdash, put together with ambition and scotch tape as far as I was concerned."

The camera goes off. Long tight handshakes lead to grasping hugs and a smacker on the cheek she walloped for Tom. We thank her as sincerely as we have everyone who's made the effort to help us.

We leave Lee at the post office and jump on the ferry back to the mainland: this time without Marisa Tomei, it's over between me and her.

On our way to Boston, we've arranged to stop off for our *very last* interview.

It feels strange as we drive there, knowing that this is our last human contact with our past. Coincidence or fate, who knows, but the man we're travelling to see is actually my first ever memory of television. Way back when I was four or five, I remember being totally absorbed by him, or at least his character, and I know that having him as our last interviewee will make me a little emotional. I pop some extra tissues in my pocket.

Caroll Spinney dressed in a big yellow bird costume and he was really my only friend on television. I doubt I understood a word he said, but he did look interesting and that was all I needed. The battle for my TV affection was between Big Bird and Floella Benjamin, so he really didn't have to try too hard to be my hero.

SESAME STREET (1969–present) (TV)

Cast: Jim Henson (Ernie, Kermit, Guy Smiley), Frank Oz (Bert, Cookie Monster) , Caroll Spinney (Big Bird, Oscar the Grouch), Martin P. Robinson (Snuffleupagos), Jerry Nelson (Count Von Count, Herry Monster, Mumford)

Notes:
Sesame Street had a whole generation of kids saying *"zee" instead of "zed"*, much to our teachers' dismay, and I have incredibly vivid memories of Saturday mornings slumped in front of the box with a Tesco's toffee apple (I always secretly put the apple bit in the bin), utterly engrossed by Big Bird, Snuffleupagos, a cartoon type-writer that said *"noo nee noo neee nooo"* and a green tramp in a rubbish bin.

I've expected Caroll Spinney to somehow *look* a bit Big Birdy – not yellow and seven feet tall, but at least long and gangly with big feet. But as we drive onto his secluded woody grounds, he approaches us as a kindly looking white-haired man with the beard of either an eccentric or Getafix the Druid from the *Asterix* books.

His house looks like a perfectly kept Disney version of something Alpine, just a little too clean and plastic to look real. With older men (and Caroll is seventy odd), you never know if they're going to be a bit grumpy and cantankerous, but it looks at this point as though Caroll isn't going to be either of those.

We shake hands and immediately I detect Big Bird in his normal voice – it's that slightly high, soothing tone without the innocence of Big Bird. No sign of Oscar the Grouch though. He leads us into his workshop: a spotless garage with a full-size cut-out of Big Bird leaning against the wall, surrounded by loads of brightly coloured oil paintings Caroll's done, all of which depict Big Bird in various bizarre but realistic scenarios. One features him wind-surfing in an atrocious storm. I ask Caroll playfully whether the bird survived the storm.

"No, he was killed," he replies swiftly, grimly and with a po-face. At last, an American with a hint of dry wit.

I feel like I'm at a royal palace or something; not because the house is grand, but simply because this man is TV royalty to me. This man was at the the very beginning of my televisual eighties; the core of what this trip is about. I see him and think of the safety of those Saturday mornings.

Caroll begins a little distant and formal but soon loosens when he realises we're not weirdoes. He allows enthusiasm for his home to jut out a mile and when his wife comes over and is introduced as Deb, a lady younger than he with long hair and a motherly smile, she demands that Caroll puts us in his little golf cart type vehicle and scoots us around the grounds.

Caroll chucks the little motor all over the place and we skid by all six of his ponds and various pagodas and little granite mounds and woods: all of them named and with a story to tell. It's like a sane man's version of Michael Jackson's Neverland. He has a facade of a castle at one bit, a Celtic-style Stonehenge thing he's created and a mysterious vertical obelisk poking rudely out of one of the ponds. It's oddity with dignity: not over the top, in fact quite serene, and peaceful. Clearly created by an artistic man who constructed a little netherworld for him and his wife. It seems that seclusion was high on his list of priorities. He explains that he doesn't really talk to the neighbours because they'd only want to come and snoop around the place. He has caught them a few times wandering over the lines to catch a glimpse (including the nudists from a colony next door), and has cleared them off duly.

Back in his living room, we chat more and then, out comes Oscar the Grouch. I mean Carroll goes and gets him; Oscar doesn't just waltz down the stares unaided, that would be scary.

"This puppet would be thirty-four years old. This was originally a bath mat." With that, he gets his fist up Oscar and suddenly the thing comes alive. The voice and *everything*. I've *grown up* with this fella Oscar.

"Yeah, I hate people," says Oscar.

"No you don't," replies Carroll.

"Who asked ya?" shouts Oscar in Carroll's face.

"He never liked me," laments Carrol.

This is weird. Brilliant, but weird.

"So this is the one I'd have sat watching when I was six years old on a Saturday morning?" I would never have thought I'd get to meet the puppet twenty-six years later. I'm welling up a bit. Oscar, and the end of our journey...

"Uh huh. Right. He's been around."

"Yes, I've seen a lot. Never liked anything I saw," adds Oscar.

"He is in some ways often more difficult to operate than Big Bird, because I have to try to hide and get into awkward positions. It's rough on the back. But with Big Bird I'm almost *more* comfortable, but he's a lot heavier and bigger. My hand is almost straight up over my head and that gives him the height. I've got quite a strong right arm now. If you're *comfortable* while doing puppets, you're generally doing it wrong."

"So how did it all begin?' Tom asks.

"Jim Henson was hired by the people developing *Sesame Street*, and they decided they really should have puppets on *Sesame Street*. He said there's only one group to get and that's The Muppets. Nobody else had come up with quite a style of puppet that really worked. Jim was just a true genius. They asked him if he could come up with some puppets that live on the street. So he thought of Big Bird, and *he* was based on a dragon that Frank Oz had operated. He also came up with the idea of Oscar. There was a restaurant he liked to go to called Oscar's. That's where he invited me to when we made the deal for me to join him. So he hadn't built them yet, and had them built around me. He was pretty awful looking, the first Big Bird, looked terrible."

"Oscar started off orange didn't he? Why the change?" I ask.

"That was just a vicarious decision on Jim's part. The whole first year he was orange and the funny thing is that when he told me about the job, he said there's gonna be a grouchy *purple* character that comes up out of the trash in the gutter. At that time in New York there was a lot of trash in the gutters. It was a mess, I hated New York, literally rotting stuff in the gutter. So that's how the two characters were created."

"Were you particularly good friends with Jim Henson?"

"We became great, great friends. First ten years or so it was more businesslike, although he was never like a boss. It was never 'you do that', it was more like 'I think you should try' ... Frank Oz *was* like that, you'd be in tears with Frank when he was tough. He's famous for being harder to work with. Grover and Cookie Monster were Frank Oz characters and he lost them by not showing up. He was upset that someone else was playing them, but he would only give us one day a year. So you could only get five or six scenes taped and they paid *a lot* of money to own those characters. I mean millions. So they recast them." Hereford born Oz is, of course, not only the puppeteer who brought us the voices of Fozzie the Bear and Yoda, but in recent years he's directed films like *The Stepford Wives, Bowfinger* and *The Housesitter.*

"Are you still in touch with Frank Oz?"

"No, not really. I bump into him. He used to come up and visit, but he goes through different phases. The first few years was the angry, scary guy, then he became the sweetest guy, at weekends he come and visit. I even kept a motorcycle for him, but finally I said to my wife I think I'll sell it 'cos I don't think Frank's ever coming back. *He didn't.* Now he's very jokey, but not very close."

"How did the voice of Big Bird come about?"

"Well originally he sounded more like a certain purple dinosaur [he means that appalling Barney thing, with the scary dancing precocious children], who didn't exist then. I said to Jim, 'How do you picture him?' He said, well kinda like a goofy guy, like Mickey Mouse's friend Goofy. So when Big Bird was first on the show he acted like a big goofy guy. He was like that for the first couple months of the show. Then they started putting more character into him and I said, 'You know, I think I should play him as a kid not a goofy guy. Why do you want this eight foot goofy guy hanging round your kids?' They said how can you play him as a kid when he's so big? I was the smallest boy in my class and there was something satisfying in playing the biggest character on television. So I started lightening his voice up." He turns. 'Hi, here I am.' From a dope to Big Bird. Big Bird has just arrived. This is getting weirder and the lump in my throat is swelling. Big Bird, once my best friend, is in the same room as me. It feels like a reunion. "Doesn't sound like a six year old, but *he's a bird*, anyway. I think the success is that Big Bird is a child, but happens to look like a bird."

"Is it hard to switch between the two characters?"

"No, not bad. Only once in a while a year or two ago Big Bird spoke and Oscar's voice came out. It was just *hang on, cut, wrong voice*. I often say that after a whole day of being the bird and the last scene is the Grouch, it's almost therapeutic putting him on, getting out of the bird feet, because you can't get behind the trash can with the big feet on. It's kinda fun to do that 'cos he's an adult and it's fun to abuse people."

"How did Mr Snuffleupagos come about?"

"They were so happy with Big Bird that at the end of the second year they asked Jim to come up with another character. He always wanted to build a two-man suit, you know, like the old pantomime horse. It's a miserable job in the back of that thing. There's no air in there and it's made out of really thick thick fur. It weighs about fifty pounds on the back of the puppeteer. It's a steadicam framework, it's buckled on. The guy who does it is Audrey the Plant in *Little Shop of Horrors* on stage right now. He's a Chinese ballet dancer and has had to do it for twenty years. He's a very patient man. The pay is terrible, too."

"He's quite miserable isn't he, Mr. Snuffleupagos?"

"Not really, he's quite optimistic. He's a kid; he's supposed to be five years old. He *seems* more like a hundred."

"Do you actually consider these characters as an extension of yourself?" I wonder.

"I think of them as characters that I'm lucky enough to get to know or play and know from the inside out – pardon the cliché – but I think I do. I think of Big Bird as a kid, as *my* kid. So I don't get to feel that *I'm* Big Bird, but that I get to bring my kid to life."

"Are you careful that kids don't see you getting in and out of the costume?"

"Well, if they visit the set I can't help it, they *will* see. We've had a few kids very upset to see that it's a guy in a suit."

"Is it a real family atmosphere on the set?"

"Yes, very much so. It's all hugs and greetings."

"I grew up with Mr Hooper, who sadly passed away. Was that something that really brought the cast together?" I think most kids my age will remember the passing of the storeowner, Mr Hooper.

"Yeah. He was a lovely man. I don't know if you ever saw the scene where Big Bird discovers that he died. That scene was all done in one shot and those were real tears. He was such a good fellow. Last day I saw him, we *thought* he had cancer but he didn't *tell* us. I was sitting on the wall with the bird feet on and I put my arm around him and said in the bird's voice, 'I love you Mr Hooper.' And he said, 'I love you, Carroll.' And I never saw him again. He died four days later, that's how sick he was. It was one year later we taped the memory of him. They didn't know what to do; should we tell them that he died, or should we say he moved to Florida? I think they did the right thing. It was the first children's thing they ever did about death. Big Bird just didn't understand it."

"What do your kids or grandkids think of you being Big Bird?"

"When my grandson was very little I said to my daughter on the phone, 'Why don't you put Wyatt on the phone and I'll have Big Bird talk to him.' And he was *thrilled*, he was three or something and until he was ten, once in a while he would call up and say 'Hi Grandad, is Big Bird there?' Once in a while Big Bird wouldn't be here. So he would tell me things while I was Big Bird, 'cos he saw Big Bird as another kid. I let him know too soon, 'cos when he was ten and a half he still thought it was real. He was devastated. I think he felt betrayed. And now he's in a very bad phase ... he's a goth."

"What's it like being so famous but actually not *too* recognisable?"

"Well, it's got more positive things about it than negative. I've spent a little time with some famous people, I got to be a great buddy with Waylon Jennings, a country singer and I would sit on the stage sometimes and travel with him." Waylon Jennings, of course, was the guy who wrote and performed the theme tune to *Dukes of Hazzard*.

"Fortunately, Big Bird gets me to meet a lot of famous people. Debra and I dined with George W. before he was president. I worked with Michael Jackson when he was seventeen. He did a scene with Oscar for a Christmas special. Badly written show, there was *nothing* funny in it. So he said in his little voice 'how do you fit in that little trashcan? It's so little and you're so big'. I said well, it's cut away, why don't you come round and I'll show you. He said 'Oh no, I like fantasy. I like the fantasy that he's this little green man in there and he comes out and he's all grouchy to everyone, I like that.' I said, 'Ohhhhhkaaaaay...'"

After the interview, we stand in Caroll's kitchen, drinking Coke from paper cups and chatting like ordinary people, while he draws pictures of Big Bird on some copies of his autobiography, to give us as gifts. I've loved this.

Our final stop-off on our trek back to Toronto is in Boston. It would be immoral not to wave the trip away without going to the *Cheers* bar, which is actually just the exterior used throughout the run of the sitcom.

The night passes in the appropriate fashion, with us going back over the last three months, affectionately remembering heat-of-the-moment arguments, the people we've met and the places we've seen. We're proud of ourselves, and for the first time in a while, *I'm* proud of *my*self. Talking about the loose objectives of our journey, Tom addresses how *he* feels the trip has affected him, on camera, among the din of fellow beerpoppers at the *Cheers* bar.

"According to Spencer, the purpose of this trip was to both celebrate *and* say goodbye to the eighties. I think I've gone the other way. I'm fully expecting to buy the Goonies' house, try and get a job as Chunk's assistant and hang out with Mick from *Teen Wolf* on a regular basis. So I'm still obsessed, I haven't got over it and I'm going back to England no better than I was. But it's been fun."

I thought as much, really. But I think that's OK for Tom, he didn't feel the need to leave it behind as much as I did. And Luke? Well Luke's Luke, happy as Larry to have been a part of such a unique journey. He has a pretty pure, uncomplicated sense that he did something most others wouldn't get around to. And that's *awesome*.

And me? At times during this adventure I've revelled in the past, and at times felt a sense of loss. But all in all, I've learnt that you *have* to live for the moment. You can move on without necessarily *losing* all those things; you've just got to remember that, all the while your *present* is good, you're making things worth being nostalgic about in the future. Maybe I've wasted a bit of time in realising that; maybe there'll be a year or two gap where I didn't create nostalgia-worthy life experiences. But from now on in, however long or short that may be, I'm going to make the most of it and look back just *once in a while*; just to see what I've done and where I'm going.

Back in Toronto, Tom toys with the idea of calling Corey Haim, *again*. But we all look at each other for just a second and produce a collective "Nahhhh". Fuck him.

Sitting outside a bar on a rainy Toronto night the day before we leave for London, I sit with a beer, playing around with my phone. I find that I've got a voice-recording feature on it. I didn't notice that before. There are a few files recorded that I had no idea about, so I play the first one, and surprisingly, my own voice starts off, sounding frayed and slurry and upset.

"Do you mean never *ever*?"

"Never," replies a female voice.

Somehow, God knows how, I must have pressed a button on my phone during that awful night in pissing Las Vegas, which recorded a snippet of my conversation with Elle. A slight pain tugs at my chest and glossy, blurry images of Elle flip briefly through my brain. But they're so distant now. Really the pain is more a sadness, for myself, that I got in that state.

I delete the file, and the rest of them. Then I send a text, to Megan, just saying "Hello".

Goodbyes to the eighties and to Elle have both arrived at once and through the drizzling Toronto rain, I see a little light.

Hello future.

And really, do me a favour ... fuck off Guttenberg.

ACKNOWLEDGEMENTS

Thanks firstly to Tom Thostrup, without whose geeky passion and occasionally problematic obsession for detail we wouldn't have exhausted ourselves so thoroughly, or had some of the experiences we had. Thanks to Luke Dolan for coming along with his fancy camera and sometimes remembering to record sound. Thanks to all our interviewees, location owners, those who put us up and anyone else who embraced our lunacy by sharing their eighties with us. We'll always remember the generosity of those total strangers and old friends who helped bundle us kicking and screaming through our rites of passage. Thanks to Dad and Ian Beard for doing such a skilled job of touching up my enormous head and the rest of my heroes on the cover. Big thanks to Simon Lowe at Know the Score Books for believing people needed to hear about our story, and thanks to Melissa Weatherill and her all-knowing pencil for crossing things out that made no sense whatsoever.

Thanks, lastly, to time itself ... for tick-tocking along ... moving on, and getting me out of those goddamm leg warmers.